Balancing National and Local Responsibilities

Education Management and Finance in Four Central European Countries

Edited by

KENNETH DAVEY

Local Government
and Public Service
Reform Initiative

LOCAL GOVERNMENT AND PUBLIC SERVICE REFORM INITIATIVE
OPEN SOCIETY INSTITUTE

Address
Nádor utca 11.
H-1051 Budapest, Hungary

Mailing address
P.O. Box 519
H-1357 Budapest, Hungary

Telephone
(36-1) 327-3104

Fax
(36-1) 327-3105

E-mail
lgprog@osi.hu

Web Site
http://lgi.osi.hu/

First published in 2002
by Local Government and Public Service Reform Initiative, Open Society Institute Budapest

© OSI/LGI, 2002

ISBN: 963 7316 98 1 Ö
ISBN: 963 9419 32 X

The publication of these country reports has been funded by the British Department for International
Development and the Local Government and Public Service Reform Initiative of the Open Society Institute
in Budapest within the framework of the Local Government Policy Partnership Programme. The judgements
expressed herein do not necessarily reflect the views of the above two sponsors.

Copies of the book can be ordered by e-mail or post from LGI.
Printed in Budapest, Hungary, March 2002.
Design & Layout by Createch Ltd.

Contents

List of Tables and Figures 5

Foreword 9

1. School Management and Finance: an Overview 11
   Kenneth Davey

2. Education Management and Finance in Hungary.
   Efficiency, Equity and Quality Problems
   in the Transition Period 35
   Éva Balázs, Zoltán Hermann

3. Decentralization, Local Governments and
   Education Reform in Post-communist Poland 113
   Tony Levitas, Jan Herczyński

4. Financing and Administration of the
   Educational System in the Czech Republic 191
   *Michal Krátký, Petr Linhart,
   Lenka Dostálová, Ludmila Oswaldová*

5. Education Management and Finance
   in Slovakia 257
   *Peter Berčik, Ladislav Haas,
   Anita Lehocká, Peter Zvara*

List of Tables and Figures

TABLES

CHAPTER 2

Table 2.1: The Main Levels and Actors of Public Education in Hungary 60

Table 2A.1: The Number of Students, Teachers and Classes
in the Public Education System 100

Table 2A.2: Expenditures in Education Relative to the GDP 101

Table 2A.3: Expenditures in Education 103

Table 2A.4: Wages in the Education Sector 104

CHAPTER 3

Table 3.1: The Transfer of Primary and Secondary Schools
to Local Governments 128

Table 3.2: Preschools in Urban and Rural Areas 1990–1999 148

Table 3.3: Percent of 3 to 5 Year Olds Receiving Preschool Training 149

Table 3.4: Children per Preschool Class 150

Table 3.5: Local Government Contributions
to the Education Subvention 152

Table 3.6: Wage Payments as a Share of Gmina Education Budgets 153

Table 3.7: Education Investments as a Share
of Gmina Education Budgets 154

Table 3.8: Class Sizes in Primary Schools and Gymnasiums
by Gmina Type 155

Table 3.9: Average Annual Parental Contributions
to Public Primary Schools 156

Table 3.10: Enrollment in Lyceums
and Vocational Schools by School Type 159

Table 3.11: Further Careers of Rural
and Urban Primary Schools Graduates 161

Table 3A.1: Basic Data for Primary Schools: 1990–1999 172

Table 3A.2: Shares of the Education Subvention
by School and Pupil Type in 2000 174

Table 3A.3: Basic Data for Lyceums: 1990–1999 177

CHAPTER 4

Table 4.1: The Appointment of School Directors 210

Table 4.2: Age Compositions of Teachers 214

Table 4.3: Authority to Establish Schools 216

Table 4A.1: Expenses in the Educational Sector 1998 250

Table 4A.2: Educational Expenses 251

Table 4A.3: Average Income of Teachers 252

Table 4A.4: Number of Pupils and Teachers 253

CHAPTER 5

Table 5.1: Changes in the Age Structure of Inhabitants
in Slovakia and Women Representation 266

Table 5.2: Total Expenditures on Education in the SR
in Current and Constant Prices 313

Table 5.3: Development of Total Expenditures on Education
According to Kind of Expenditure 314

Table 5.4: State Budget Expenditures on Education 315

Table 5.5: State Budget Expenditures
on Individual Kinds of Schools and Facilities 316

Table 5.6: Revenues and Expenditures
of Municipal Budgets on Education 319

Table 5A.1: Normative Number of Pupils in a Class at Primary Schools 335

Table 5A.2: Requirements of Primary Schools 336

Table 5A.3: Kindergartens—Basic Indicators 340

Table 5A.4: Primary Schools—Basic Indicators 341

Table 5A.5: Grammar Schools—Basic Indicators 342

Table 5A.6: School-leavers, Unemployed School-leavers
(Grammar schools) and Rate of Unemployment
as of 30.9.199 343

Table 5A.7: Secondary Vocational Schools—Basic Indicators 344

Table 5A.8: Secondary Vocational Schools—School-leavers,
Unemployed School-leavers and Rate of Unemployment
as of 30.9.1999 345

Table 5A.9: Secondary Vocational Apprentice
Training Centers—Basic Indicators 346

Table 5A.10: Secondary Vocational Apprentice Training Centers
—School-leavers, Unemployed School-leavers and
Rate of Unemployment as of 30.9.1999 348

Table 5A.11: Special schools—Basic Indicators 349

Table 5A.12: Primary Schools of Arts—Basic Indicators 350

Table 5A.13: Age Structure of Teachers 351

Table 5A.14: Qualification of Teachers in the SR
by Type of School and Level of Education 352

Table 5A.15: Comparison of Salaries of Pedagogical Employees
in Budgetary Area and Average Salary in National Economy 353

Table 5A.16: Expenditures on Education in the SR
According to Kind of School Recalculated per Pupil/Student ... 354

Table 5A.17: Total Expenditures on Education According to
Kind of School—in Comparison to Total Expenditures
of State Budget and GDP 356

Table 5A.18: Primary Schools—Analysis of Current Expenditures
from State Budget in 1999 in Selected Districts 358

FIGURES

CHAPTER 2

Figure 2.1: The Proportion of Learning in Different Types
of Secondary Institutions, 1989/90–1999/00 48

Figure 2.2: Main Financial Flows
in the Hungarian Public Education System 64

Figure 2.3: Average Teacher per Class Ratio
in General and General Secondary Schools, 1990–98 76

Figure 2.4: Average Student per Teacher Ration
in General and General Secondary Schools, 1990–98 77

Figure 2.5: Average Class Size
in General and General Secondary Schools, 1990–98 77

Figure 2.6: Total Costs and Grants Received
as a Function of the Number of Students 82

Figure 2A.1: Education Levels and School Structure in Hungary 97

CHAPTER 3

Figure 3.1: Shares of Central Government Expenditure on Education 134

Figure 3.2: Shares of Local Government Expenditure on Education 135

Figure 3.3: Real per Pupil Spending on Preschool Education 150

Figure 3.4: Education as % of Total Gmina Expenditures 153

CHAPTER 4

Figure 4.1: Scheme of Financial Flow Before the Reform 234

Figure 4.2: Scheme of Financial Flow After the Reform 236

CHAPTER 5

Figure 5A.1: Structure of School Education in the Slovak Republic 331

Foreword

The chapters in this book were prepared under the "Local Government Policy Partnership" Program. This is a joint project of two donor organizations: the British Government's Department for International Development (DFID), and the Local Government and Public Service Initiative (LGI) of the Open Society Institute, Budapest, which launched this regional program. The "Local Government Policy Partnership" (LGPP) projects intend to contribute to policy development and innovations in Central and Eastern European countries.

LGPP hopes to develop expertise and to support professional cooperation among local government specialists throughout Central and Eastern Europe. Parallel to this, experiences from this region should be made available in Central and Eastern Europe, and in Central Asia. The core partner countries are the Czech Republic, Hungary, Poland and Slovakia. However, other countries have been invited to participate in these regional projects, which would help direct information exchange and comparison of policy efforts. Planned LGPP publications include policy studies and proposals discussed with government officials and experts in the countries involved.

Targeted beneficiaries of LGPP projects are national government ministries, local government associations, research and training institutions, and individual local authorities throughout the CEE region. LGI intends to publish three studies each year. In 2000–2001, (the first year of LGPP operation), the following policy areas were selected:

a)   Education financing and management;

b)   Regulation and competition of local utility services, and

c)   Public perception of local governments.

Readers of this publication will find detailed information on the management and financing of primary, secondary and vocational schools in the Czech Republic, Hungary, Poland and Slovakia. The book focuses particularly on the varied divisions of responsibility between the State, local government and school managements and the way these have evolved over the past decade. The overview chapter analyses the differences between the four countries in the allocation of responsibilities and assesses the influence these may have on the effectiveness, efficiency and equity of the educational system.

Kenneth Davey & Gábor Péteri

January, 2002

CHAPTER 1

School Management and Finance: an Overview

Kenneth Davey

Table of Contents

1.   Institutional Frameworks 15
     1.1   Introduction 15
     1.2   Governmental Responsibility 16
           1.2.1   Hungary 16
           1.2.2   Poland 17
           1.2.3   Czech Republic 17
           1.2.4   Slovakia 18
     1.3   School Management 19
           1.3.1   Hungary 19
           1.3.2   Poland 19
           1.3.3   Czech Republic 20
           1.3.4   Slovakia 20
     1.4   Finance 20
           1.4.1   Hungary 20
           1.4.2   Poland 21
           1.4.3   Czech Republic 22
           1.4.4   Slovakia 22

2.   Evaluation 23
     2.1   Introduction 23
     2.2   Effectiveness 24
           2.2.1   Change and Responsiveness 24
                   a)   Structural Change 24
                   b)   Preschool Education 24
                   c)   Secondary Schooling 24
     2.3   Funding 25
     2.4   National Regulatory Capacity 25
     2.5   Recruitment and Renumeration of Teachers 26
     2.6   Quality 27

2.7   Equity 28

  2.7.1   Funding 28

  2.7.2   Access and Differentiation 30

2.8   Efficiency 31

3. Conclusion 33

School Management and Finance: an Overview

Kenneth Davey

1. INSTITUTIONAL FRAMEWORKS

1.1 Introduction

The governance of education in central and eastern European countries has been subject to constant change and contention over the last decade. The boundaries of responsibility between the State, local self-government and the individual schools have been shifting, and are still far from clear in most countries.

Nor has the environment for reform been helpful. The school system has had to respond to significant declines in child population, to changing demands in employment opportunity for its products, and to financial stress born of fluctuating economic fortunes and a shift from public to private consumption.

The four studies in this volume examine fortunes of the school system in four diverse institutional settings. These are:

Chapter two: *Hungary* where responsibility for managing and financing pre-primary, primary and secondary education was abruptly devolved to local government in 1990,

Chapter three: *Poland* where similar responsibilities were progressively devolved over a nine year period to 1999,

Chapter four: *Czech Republic* where the State and local government have shared responsibility and where a further stage of devolution is in progress, and

Chapter five: *Slovakia* where the State has retained entire responsibility for education, although some degree of devolution is now planned.

The chapters describe these varying frameworks in detail and attempt to assess their impact on the effectiveness, equity and efficiency of the school system. The basic question in this report is whether devolution does make a difference.

It is customary to discuss school governance in terms of the relationships between national and local government. It is clear from the studies, however, that educational management is a tripartite game with the individual school as a third and active player. School directors and teaching staffs have much operational freedom, and teachers collectively exercise strong influence on both local and national decisions. School boards and parents may also play a significant part.

This Part compares the institutional frameworks of educational management, financing and staffing in the four countries. Part 2 attempts an assessment of the impact of these arrangements on the effectiveness, equity and efficiency of the school system. A brief conclusion to the chapters is given at Part 3.

1.2 Governmental Responsibility

In all four countries, private organizations including churches have the right to found and manage schools, subject to licensing, and the number of such schools has been increasing. They also qualify for financial assistance from the State or local government. However, the vast majority of pupils are still educated in publicly owned schools, which are the subject of the following country-by-country description.

1.2.1 Hungary

The 1990 Local Government Act vested responsibility for pre-primary and primary education in municipal government. This comprises over 3 140 towns and villages, varying greatly in size. Over 1 700 have populations below 1 000, including 900 below 500.

Small villages are empowered and encouraged to form associations to run schools jointly, but until recently have been reluctant to do so.

The 19 county self-governments and 21 county level cities are responsible for secondary and vocational schools, together with special institutions such as county pedagogical institutes. However, municipal governments have been able to claim ownership and management of secondary schools within their borders, so that there is no uniform or permanent location of responsibility at these levels of education; they may hand institutions over to the county at a later stage.

The Ministry of Education retains responsibility for educational content and quality. It also regulates the qualifications and employment conditions of teachers, while county public administration offices license schools and monitor the adherence of local authorities to their legal obligations. The Ministry's efforts to monitor and improve educational quality have been hampered by the absence of an inspectorate which was abolished in 1984 in a fit of socialist liberalism. It has now created a State agency, OKEV, to oversee examinations and standards. This has established regional offices which provide the germs of an inspectorate but still at a very early stage of growth. County pedagogical institutes provide a pool of staff for inspections and scrutiny of school educational plans, but in a competitive market and at the behest of school owners.

1.2.2 Poland

Poland now has a decentralized system of school ownership and management similar to Hungary, but devolution has taken place more slowly. The 1990 reform created only a single tier of self-government. This comprises 2 480 'gminas'; populations average 15 560 (as opposed to 3 240 in Hungary), only 7 falling below 2 000. Gminas were given immediate responsibility for pre-primary education, but merely an option to take over primary schools. This was to become compulsory in 1993, but the deadline was extended to 1996.

In 1993 the larger cities were given the option to take over secondary education and this became mandatory in 1996. In 1999 there was a further territorial reform creating 373 poviats and 16 voidvoidships as units of county and provincial self-government respectively. Poviats were given responsibility for secondary and vocational education, while voidvoidships took over the more specialized institutions; the large cities already running secondary schools were given dual gmina/poviat status.

The Ministry of Education has maintained professional Kuratoria at provincial level, which are responsible for licensing schools and approving their educational programs, as well as participating in the choice of school directors. They also form an inspectorate. The Ministry has retained responsibility for curricula, and for central negotiation of teachers' conditions of service.

1.2.3 Czech Republic

The Czech Republic has maintained a mixed pattern of school administration and funding, which is currently undergoing further changes.

The 1990 reforms created a single tier of self-government, which is highly fragmented. There are 6 230 municipalities with an average population of 1 650; nearly 5 000 of these have populations below 1 000, and 1 699 less than 200.

Ownership and responsibility for pre-primary and primary schools was transferred to municipalities in 1990. However, the State Budget remained directly responsible for teaching staff salaries,

17

which are paid by the Ministry of Education through School Offices maintained at district level. The School Offices also employ the teachers of those schools, which are not legal entities.

Municipalities can establish secondary schools, but this is not mandatory. Most secondary and vocational schools remained state owned until their recent transfer to the fourteen newly elected regional governments. As with primary schools, teaching staff salaries are paid by School Offices from the Ministry of Education budget.

The Ministry of Education controls curricula and the qualifications and conditions of service of teachers. A Chief Inspector of Schools is appointed by the Minister and heads an inspectorate with a network of regional branches.

District offices are scheduled for abolition under current decentralization policy, but the legislation has not yet been enacted. It is not clear how school office powers will be reallocated. However, some of the state regulatory powers in respect of schools have been delegated to heads of regional education offices which are part of the regional government apparatus; the heads are appointed by the regional government but with the approval of the Minister of Education to whom they are accountable in terms of their regulatory functions.

1.2.4   Slovakia

Public administration reforms in 1990 created a single tier of municipalities, of which there are 2 875 with an average population of 1 870. Elections to a newly created regional tier of self-government are due in December 2001.

In contrast to the other three countries no responsibility for education has hitherto been devolved to the local government, although many municipalities have made ad hoc contributions to school equipment and repair. All public schools have remained in the hands of the State. From 1990 to 1996 these were managed and funded by the Ministry of Education through district school offices. In 1996 school offices were absorbed by regional and district state administrations, which were legal entities with their own chapter within the State Budget. Regional offices took charge of secondary and vocational schools while districts managed the primary and pre-primary level. The heads of the regional and district offices are political appointees of the Government and in turn appoint the heads of school offices. The Ministry of Education thereby lost its direct administrative and financial control to a structure, which is accountable neither to the Ministry nor to the local electorate.

Under recent legislation responsibility for pre-primary and primary education will be devolved to municipal government by 2003, and that for secondary and vocational education to the new regional governments. The devolved competencies do not, however, include payment of teachers.

The Ministry of Education controls educational content and maintains a regionally based inspectorate.

1.3 School Management

Differences between the four countries are not so radical at the level of school management.

Most secondary and vocational schools in all four countries are legal entities, as are the larger primary schools. They employ all staff except the director and have some control over day-to-day expenditure. In the case of the schools which lack legal status, these tasks are performed by the 'founding body'—mainly local governments in Hungary and Poland and district offices in Slovakia. In the Czech Republic school offices currently employ teachers in schools which are not legal entities.

It is customary to have school boards representing local governments, parents, teachers and pupils. In Slovakia these were created in 1990 but were largely ignored in the mid 1990s after accusations of excessive intervention in staffing matters; their role was revived after the 1998 election. In Slovakia, also, there are district and regional level advisory boards in an attempt to compensate for the lack of local government participation in educational administration.

School boards are generally restricted to advisory powers although they normally discuss the annual pedagogical plans and have varying roles in the appointment of school directors. These are the critical processes in school management.

Powers to appoint school directors vary, although a five year, renewable term of office is general to the region. The individual arrangements are:

1.3.1   Hungary

Appointments are made by the local government council.

1.3.2   Poland

Appointments are made by an independent committee consisting of representatives of the local government, the Kuratorium, teachers, parents and unions. Under the Teachers Charter adopted in 1981 during Solidarity's first period of national influence the teachers could veto an appointment, but this was overruled by a Constitutional Court decision in 1992.

1.3.3 Czech Republic

Pre-primary and primary school directors are appointed by school offices with the approval of the municipality. Under current reforms secondary and vocational school directors will be appointed by regional governments with the approval of the Ministry of Education.

1.3.4 Slovakia

Appointments are made by regional or district offices (depending on the level of school) on the basis of nomination by the school board following public ad-vertisement. Recent legislation on devolution will shift the power of appointment of secondary and vocational directors to regional self governments and of their primary and pre-primary counterparts to municipalities; in both cases nominees would be chosen by school boards (with one State representative in an advisory capacity) after their qualifications have been verified by school offices.

In each country schools prepare an annual pedagogical plan which regulates the number of pupils and classes for the forthcoming academic year and the subjects to be taught at each level. This becomes the framework for determining the budget and staffing levels. These are normally prepared by school directors and discussed by school boards. Their financial implications require the approval of the funding body—the local governments in Hungary and Poland, the school offices in Slovakia, and a combination of municipal and school offices in Czech Republic. The educational content is approved by school offices in the Czech Republic, the *Kuratoria* in Poland, and regional and district offices in Slovakia; in Hungary approval lies with local government but only on the basis of a professional opinion by experts selected from a national register.

Staffing levels are effectively derived from national norms applied to the numbers of pupils, class sizes and curricula specified in the annual pedagogical plan. In all four countries the school director has sole rights of hiring and firing within this framework.

1.4 Finance

Funding varies substantially between the four countries, inevitably a by-product of the different governmental arrangements.

1.4.1 Hungary

All regular costs fall on county or municipal budgets including teaching salaries. Both counties and municipalities receive general grants, calculated by the Ministry of Finance by a formula which includes fixed sums per pupil in each type of school. These grant elements cover roughly two thirds of actual average costs. Local governments are not obliged to spend this grant according to its service composition. All do in practice spend more than the normative amount on education, contributing the balance from general revenues. In the case of municipalities these include the non-service related elements of the formula grant, a declining share of personal income tax, and local taxes of which a tax on business turnover is by far the most important in urban centers. County governments do not levy taxes or receive income tax shares and their discretionary resources are largely confined to the general per capita portion of their normative grant.

The Ministry of the Interior has provided grants towards school construction and there are ad hoc grants from the Ministry of Education for innovations, the procurement of professional advice and so on.

Where pupils commute to school across municipal boundaries, their home municipality is not obliged to contribute to the receiving authority's costs. Some do so, but usually only where they offer no equivalent education. The receiving municipality does, of course, receive the normative grant element which is based on pupil numbers, not school age population.

1.4.2   Poland

As responsibility for schools has been handed over progressively to the various levels of local government between 1990 and 1999, so the State budget's operating expenditure has been transferred to them by annual grant. These transfers form part of the general grants to the local governments, but there is a legal provision that the education elements must constitute at least 12% of the State Budget revenue. This provision was inserted to reassure the public at large, and teachers in particular, that financial provision for education would not suffer from devolution.

Local governments are not obliged to spend their general grants in any particular way and their education spending could, in law, fall below the education element. In practice, it exceeds the education element by an average of 25%. The balance is drawn from general revenues—a combination of tax sharing and local taxes in the case of *gmina*, and tax sharing alone in the case of the two higher tiers. This higher level of expenditure by local governments has arisen from investment costs, payment by larger cities of teachers' salaries above mandated levels, and by the reluctance of rural *gminas* to reduce employment despite low and falling pupil teacher ratios. Hopes that local governments might offset part of wage rises by retrenchment have not been fulfilled, due partly to municipal reluctance and partly to the legal impediments to firing teachers.

The education elements in the grants to individual local governments have generally been based on the cost to the State Budget at the time of transfer, increased annually by standard percentages. These incorporate historic disparities between territories in the provision and cost of schools. In 2000 allocation was converted to a normative, per pupil basis; but the redistribution was somewhat 'dampened' by a provision that no local government should receive less than 100% or more than 110% of the previous year's amount.

Local governments make their own decisions on the criteria for distributing their education budgets to individuals schools. Most use incremental methods centered around negotiations on the annual pedagogical plans.

1.4.3   Czech Republic

Teaching salaries are funded by the Ministry of Education by grants to schools channeled through school offices. These are allocated according to a formula basically comprising the number of pupils divided by a standard pupil/teacher ratio and multiplied by the average national wage for teachers of the respective level. Teachers receive a basic salary on a national scale according to their age, plus responsibility allowances and annual bonus at the director's discretion. This provides directors with considerable room for maneuver over the numbers and remuneration of staff. If a school's teachers are younger than average or class sizes above average, there is extra margin for employing more teachers (and shortening hours) or paying them more allowances or bonus. Increases in pupil numbers will be similarly rewarded.

The Ministry also provides a grant per pupil for the operating expenses of schools other than teaching salaries. However, in the case of primary and pre-primary schools these only cover roughly one sixth of the cost and the balance has to be provided from municipal budgets along with all investment costs. Municipalities meet these expenses from their general revenues which include shares of income tax and a property tax. Schools are treated as "contributory organizations" so that they may retain unspent balances at the year's end. Where pupils commute to school across municipal boundaries, their home municipality is obliged to contribute to the receiving municipality's costs.

The financial base for the educational responsibilities of the new regional governments has not been finally resolved. At present they receive targeted grants, but there is an assumption that these will be replaced by shares of state taxes.

1.4.4   Slovakia

The State Budget currently meets all operating and investment costs of schools, through the regional State Administration budgets. These are allocated to individual schools by the regional and district offices.

The Ministry of Education has been trying to convert funding from a discretionary and historic cost basis to a normative formula based on school type and pupil numbers. It has been frustrated, however, by the tightness of state budget allocations and by the reluctance of regional state administrations to follow Ministry guidance. A bill is now before Parliament to subject school funding to normative criteria, based on pupil numbers.

As a result, major disparities in per pupil funding exist between regions. Schools have accumulated substantial debts and a major backlog in repair and maintenance. The Ministry contends that the debts are largest in the regions with sparse populations and small schools.

Local governments have no financial obligations to education, but have intervened on numerous occasions to carry out emergency repairs neglected by the State Budget.

Once ownership of schools has been transferred to regional and municipal governments, they will become responsible for all non-teaching costs. These will be financed initially by targeted grants, but draft legislation envisages replacing these over time with a combination of local taxes (a surcharge on personal income tax in the case of regional governments, property, consumption and unincorporated business taxes in the case of municipalities), and shares of national taxes.

2. EVALUATION

2.1 Introduction

The following paragraphs attempt to assess the impacts of these diverse institutional arrangements on the effectiveness, equity and efficiency of the education offered by the four states since 1990, drawing upon the four country studies.

It must be recognized, however, that these institutional differences are only some of many factors which have influenced the development of education over the last decade. The economic changes which occurred so rapidly after the collapse of the Communist system destroyed much traditional industry, leading to high and unaccustomed unemployment and fiscal stress. Rates of recovery have varied between the four countries and have been associated with more permanent features such as growing social differentiation and a shift of resources from public to private consumption. These have had adverse impacts on the family environment from which many pupils are drawn and the level of resources available to support the schooling system.

Also common to all four states have been major changes in the labor market for which pupils should be prepared. The biggest decline has been in both the demand and support for the types of secondary vocational education which were tied to apprenticeship in particular manufacturing and construction industries. New market opportunities have emphasized a different balance of skills, with business management, information technology and the English language in the forefront.

2.2 Effectiveness

2.2.1 Change and Responsiveness

In all four countries school systems have had to respond both to formal structural reforms changes imposed by Government, and to the organic changes in demand emanating from demography, public expectation and the labor market.

a) Structural Change

Formal structures have changed in each country. In the Czech Republic, basic schooling was extended from eight to nine years, followed by four years in grammar or secondary vocational schools (or three in apprentice training schools). In Hungary compulsory schooling was extended in 1998 to the age of 18. A further year's compulsory schooling was also added in Slovakia. The most radical reorganization occurred in Poland in 1999 when the primary school program was reduced from eight to six years and new institutions, for example the 'gimnazjum,' were created to provide a three year preliminary to shortened courses at grammar (lycee) and vocational schools.

b) PreSchool Education

The immediate period after political change was marked by sharp declines in kindergarten popula-tions. These fell by 36% in Slovakia between 1989 and 1995, and by 19% in the Czech Republic over the whole decade. Part of this reduction was due to demography, to a smaller age cohort, but there was also a backlash favoring family rather than kindergarten care for smaller children, particularly in rural areas. Small villages gave up the effort to maintain kindergartens for very small numbers at the same time as they were endeavoring to open small grade primary schools.

More recently, the position has stabilized with a strong emphasis on provision of 'zero grade' schooling for the 5/6 year olds as a preparation for primary school. In Poland 90% of children of this age group attend kindergarten.

c) Secondary Schooling

Both social and labor market changes have promoted a radical change in demand from specific industrial skills to more general secondary education. Apprentice school enrolments have fallen by over 50% in Slovakia alone.

Municipal responsibility from 1991 onwards in Hungary has enabled a very diverse and flexible response to this market shift. The boundaries between primary and secondary schooling have been heavily breached. Grammar schools have started recruiting pupils after four grades of primary education. Some primary schools have started one or two secondary grades, and general schools have opened offering all twelve years of primary and secondary education. Comprehensive schools have opened combining grammar and vocational streams.

In both the Czech Republic and Slovakia, grammar schools have resumed the traditional practice of recruiting pupils after the fourth grade in Slovakia, and the fifth grade in the Czech Republic. Otherwise, the boundaries between primary and secondary schooling have been maintained, a reflection in the Czech Republic of the divisions of responsibility between municipalities and districts as founding bodies. But there have been major expansions of general secondary education. In Slovakia, 1 000 more classes were established between 1990 and 1995.

A general tendency has been for vocational schools to widen and change the balance of their curricula, reducing the role of manual skills, and increasing the focus on business studies, information technology and foreign language.

2.3 Funding

The clearest benefits of devolution have been in the funding of school systems. Local governments have generally shown a strong sense of responsibility for their local schools and a willingness to contribute more than they are obliged to do. In the countries where they share financial responsibility for part or all of the school system with the State, their contribution has more than compensated for relative declines in State funding.

In the Czech Republic, the local government contributions to the operation and maintenance of schools are seven times the level of the grant they receive for the purpose. When Polish local governments were responsible for primary schools alone, these were receiving more per pupil than the state funded secondary schools. Now that the latter are also in local government hands, they are receiving 18% more than the grants which are supposed to cover full costs, and local government expenditure on all forms of schooling is 25% above the grant.

By contrast, the Slovak schools, which remain totally dependent on the State Budget, show the strongest signs of financial shortage. The operating debts of schools exceeded Sk600 million in 1999 ($15 million) and the cost of outstanding repairs has been estimated at Sk4 billion ($100 million).

Differences in financial systems make exact comparisons difficult. However, general expenditure on education in Slovakia is lower at 4.2% of GDP, than in Hungary (4.8%) or Czech Republic (4.5%).

2.4 National Regulatory Capacity

Even where responsibility for managing and financing schools is devolved, the State, principally through a Ministry of Education, retains a duty to sustain consistency and quality. This may well reflect constitutional guarantees.

The four countries have shown varying degrees of difficulty in developing this capacity. There have been a number of reasons. One was the backlash against the Communist systems of supervision, which were seen as more concerned with ideology or party control than quality. Hungary actually abolished its schools inspectorate in the mid 1980s.

A second reason has been the difficulty experienced by a state bureaucracy in adjusting its behavior from administrative control to monitoring and promotion of standards. This has been reinforced by a third factor, the absence of common examination systems by which school performance may, at least to some extent, be assessed.

National ministries have generally retained responsibility for defining core curricula, the professional qualifications of teachers and the organization of pre- and in-service training.

The greatest differences have been in the areas of inspection. The Polish Kuratoria have remained in place and inspectorates with regional branches have been developed in the Czech Republic and Slovakia.

Hungary tried to avoid the reimposition of state inspection by requiring local governments to procure professional appraisals of school performance. It has also made irregular grant funds available for this purpose. However, the capacity of county pedagogical centers to provide this service has been weakened by their dependence on unpredictable commissions from schools and municipalities. The government has now reestablished a national standards agency with regional branches, also issuing a rapidly expanding corpus of regulations on all aspects of school infrastructure and management.

2.5 Recruitment and Remuneration of Teachers

Social and economic change in the last decade has created difficulty for the recruitment and retention of a skilled and motivated teaching force. Private enterprise offers better rewards for graduates in several disciplines, particularly those most in demand by schools, such as the English language, information technology and business studies. In Slovakia, for example, 34% of teachers do not possess the qualifications which regulations stipulate for their school grade and subject. All four studies report an aging in teaching staff profiles, although more at primary than secondary levels.

The degree of devolution of school management cannot make a major impact on market forces. However, there is some evidence that Czech, Hungarian and Polish local governments have used their opportunities to improve remuneration to retain or secure teachers in scarce disciplines or in cities where there is greatest competition. (Although Czech municipalities do not fund teachers' salaries they can allow their contributions to non-teaching costs to be diverted to this purpose). They have also facilitated flexible arrangements for the part time hiring of subject specialists. A specific problem in the Czech Republic is that schools are supposed to pay for the inservice training of their teachers on a commercial basis, but generally lack sufficient funds for the purpose.

Some of the problems stem, however, from the vested interests of the teaching profession itself. It has generally been strong enough in both national and local politics to resist the staffing reductions which would be justified by declines in pupil populations and which could release funds for enhanced remuneration. In Poland particularly, but to a lesser extent in other countries, there are also major legal obstacles to retrenchment.

2.6 Quality

Educational quality is notoriously difficult to measure. Even where, for example Britain, national examination systems provide some numerical bases of comparison, the interpretation of results is open to much controversy. Such data is not generally available in the four countries.

The four studies convey a mixed and muted verdict on changes in the quality of schooling over the last decade. The testing of school leavers' knowledge levels suggests some decline, though in the case of Hungary this halted after 1995. The decline pertains more to literacy than numeracy.

This has been associated with a growing differentiation in school performance. This seems to be most prevalent in the case of the upper grades of primary schools, with small rural schools lacking specialized teaching and facilities, and those losing brighter fifth grade pupils to grammar schools the most adversely affected.

The quality of small village schools is particularly contentious. They proliferated in the early 1990s, particularly as part of the backlash against the Communist policies of concentrated settlement. This was especially the case in Hungary where villages without schools had access to government grants for their construction. Both Hungarian and Polish studies report that the results of rural schools are inferior to those of urban counterparts, but the Hungarian study argues that the relative performance of village school graduates can be related to their socio-economic backgrounds rather than the quality of their schooling. The Slovak study suggests that their results are no worse than those of larger schools. There seems to be a consensus that the smallness of village schools may be costly, but is not educationally a disadvantage in the first four grades, while the presence of a school is a considerable enhancement of a village's social cohesion and cultural identity.

The Slovak case stresses the negative impacts of the deterioration in school buildings and equipment. This is not mentioned as a feature of other studies and must, as previously discussed, be attributable to the absence of municipal participation in responsibility.

Much of the past decade's development has had a positive impact on quality. All studies refer to the diversification of the curriculum, with increasing inclusion not only of information technology, business studies and English and other foreign languages, but also of ethics and environmental issues. These have been part of state sponsored changes, but the Polish study refers to the municipal provision of computers and encouragement of extra languages, after-school activities and sports.

Special needs and demands have also gained ground. Primary arts schools specializing in music, art, drama and dance have increased by 25% in Slovakia, where there are also experiments in providing intensive pre-school classes for Roma children. Everywhere there has been a growing effort to integrate handicapped children in mainstream schools.

2.7 Equity

2.7.1 Funding

Opponents of devolution argue that it will produce inequity in the funding of the school system. The resources available to schools will vary with the wealth and tax base of the local governments responsible for them.

This argument assumes that the State Budget funding which precedes devolution is equitable. This is highly questionable. The Communist system of local budget finance was supposedly normative, but the norms pertained to the input costs of a network of institutions which had grown incrementally. The overall equalization system was based on subjective judgment and political weight rather than objective formulae.

The results of a State Budget funding system based on historic costs and incremental adjustment can be most clearly seen in Slovakia, the one system out of the four financed only by the State. Financing per primary pupil varies between districts by a range of 1:1.67; i.e. some districts receive as much as two thirds more funding per pupil than others. There are no objective reasons for the differentials; the more favored areas are not, for example, more sparsely populated, colder or poorer.

Indeed, devolution may improve equity in that State Budget contributions, while remaining the dominant source of finance, are likely to be channeled through a formula driven grant. In both the totally devolved systems, Hungary and Poland, the basis of distribution is pupil numbers. In Poland the consequent redistribution has been muted by a transitional limitation on the percentage loss or gain relative to the previous year's budget, but the movement towards uniformity remains.

A funding system can only be regarded as equitable if it deals with disparities in cost as well as income. The most readily recognized difference in the costs of schooling relates to population density. Small schools cost more per pupil because of the relatively higher overheads and smaller classes. Small schools are generally a feature of rural rather than urban conditions. The alternative to maintaining village schools is the costs of transportation.

The Polish education grant system recognizes these cost differentials by the simple device of paying rural *gmina* one third more per pupil than urban counterparts. It is a simplistic solution. It is overgenerous to *gmina* which are periurban, inadequate for the extra costs incurred in the truly remote and sparsely populated areas. Some acknowledgment of the costs of the sparsest areas has been made by a special transport grant, but rural *gmina* contribute on average nearly twice as much of their own revenue to schooling as urban.

The Hungarian formula does not differentiate between rural and urban pupils *per se*, beyond providing a small supplement for pupils commuting to schools in neighboring municipalities. The non-education parts of the grant formula do, however, provide some additional funding for small villages and there is also a deficit grant for which many smaller communities qualify. Neither Hungarian nor Polish systems distinguish between the existence of smaller rural schools and the objective need for them (and degree of smallness) created by geography.

Whether responsibility for funding schools is devolved or not, State funding remains a dominant source, either through direct expenditure or intergovernmental transfers. The way in which its contribution is distributed is fundamental to equity. However, local government revenues are a significant marginal resource. Major disparities in local revenue bases are to be expected, although these may be partially equalized by the State transfer system, as in the case of Poland.

In Hungary and Poland local governments are able to influence the remuneration of teachers by the scale of their own funding. National salary scales only determine a minimum salary, and there is much scope for varying staffing levels, payment of overtime, bonuses, and so on. Although Czech municipalities do not pay salaries, their contributions to school budgets can be used for enhancing staff complements and emoluments. The wealthier towns can afford to employ more or better qualified teachers or to pay them more. Whether this creates inequity, however, is less certain. It may well be necessary to pay teachers more in cities simply to recruit and retain them, given both their employment options and the costs of city life. A higher pay packet for city teachers does not necessarily mean a higher quality education for city children. Where the latter benefit more clearly is in the access to physical facilities and equipment.

Equitable funding of municipal school owners is not the same as equitable funding of individual schools. Some Hungarian and Polish municipalities have tried to introduce normative funding of school budgets, but these are, as yet, a minority. Incremental allocation between schools coupled with negotiation are still widely practiced. In this respect the mixed funding system in the Czech Republic may have been more progressive, since the distribution of State teaching salary grants is based on normative staffing levels and national average salaries.

2.7.2 Access and Differentiation

The studies agree that the developments of the last decade have resulted in a growing differentiation in the quality of schools and the types of education and subsequent employment opportunity which they provide.

Reference has also been made to differences in some, but not all the countries in the measured performance of pupils from rural and urban primary schools. These can be attributed in part to differences in the more specialized teaching and equipment required in the upper primary grades. The Hungarian study, however, draws on research suggesting that these differences can be attributed as much (if not more) to the socio-economic background of pupils and the stimuli of the family environment. It would not be surprising if a similar conclusion applied to the other three countries.

The consequences of differentiation are more marked in the case of secondary schooling. The most significant evidence lies in the re-emergence of grammar school recruitment of Grade 4 or 5 graduates by selective examination. Hungary, where the practice antedated political reform, is now trying to regulate it, particularly with regard to the transparency of the selection process. However, vocational schools have also varied in their response to market change; the curricular range which they offer and the sensitivity of their streaming must have an increasing impact on the careers and lifestyles of their graduates.

In all four countries parents may seek to place their children in schools outside their designated catchment area. Their chances of success depend on both the capacity of the school of their choice and the ability of their children to compete in admission tests. Family background and ability to meet transport costs count significantly.

This is a report on school management and finance. It is not intended to cover educational policy and philosophy; management and finance must be judged by their success in effecting the policies of the day. How much weight should be given to differentiation in evaluating the impact of institutional changes cannot be judged here. It may be appropriate, nevertheless to draw on parallel experience in Britain.

In Britain, a number of policy initiatives have encouraged differentiation in access to quality schooling: per pupil funding, self management by school boards and directors, highly publicized comparisons of examination performances and parental choice. Critics argue that this has led to the segregation of pupils according to their own competitive ability, but heavily influenced by family location and background; there is much anecdotal evidence of correlations between school performance and real estate prices. It is also argued that examination performance does not measure the "value added" by a school to the abilities of the less gifted children, or those from deprived backgrounds. However, it is also widely argued in response that the pressures of competition have led to a general improvement so that even the worst performing schools are giving a better education. A rigorous State inspection system triggers drastic interventions to improve standards in the worst performing schools including extensive replacement of directors and staff.

Changes that enhance the education given by the better quality schools can scarcely be wrong in themselves. More fundamental to equity is the effect of competition on the absolute rather than relative quality of all schools and the degree of remedy available to those with the poorest performance. It also depends on the support for schools in dealing with disadvantaged children.

The Hungarian report refers to a process of migration stimulated by economic change over the last decade which has tended to concentrate poorer families generally, and Roma in particular, in specific catchment areas. The studies indicate some educational responses to this. The Slovak study refers to some intensively staffed 'zero grade' kindergartens designed to prepare Roma children for unsegregated primary schooling. The Hungarian grant formula has also included special provision for intensified teaching of Roma children. More generally, efforts to integrate special needs children in mainstream schooling should enhance their lifetime opportunity.

2.8 Efficiency

In all four countries, the decline in school age populations over the last decades has been matched by increases in the numbers of schools and of teacher/pupil ratios.

The clearest evidence is in pupil teacher ratios in primary schools. Over the past decade the ratio of teachers to pupils has increased by 20% in Czech Republic, 8% in Hungary, 5% in Poland and, from 1994 to 1999, by 6% in Slovakia. There have been similar growths in the case of secondary schools but these are harder to disentangle from system changes.

In Hungary and Poland, these changes are due predominantly to the fall in pupil numbers; primary teaching staffs have also decreased but not commensurately. In the Czech Republic and Slovakia there have been absolute increases in the primary teaching force—by 7% in the Czech Republic and 6% in Slovakia (although there has been some retrenchment since 1999). This suggests, interestingly, that the Czech and Slovak state budgets have been more indulgent and less resistant to teacher pressure than the Hungarian and Polish municipal budgets.

All studies refer to the proliferation of village schools after 1989. In many cases this involved reopening schools closed by Communist amalgamation programs. During the period 1990–1994 the Hungarian government actively encouraged the opening of primary schools by any settlements without such facility. The proliferation is not entirely a rural phenomenon, however. In Poland, for example, the 15% increase in the number of primary schools has occurred largely in urban areas.

These statistical changes do not necessarily prove a commensurate loss of efficiency. The increase in numbers of schools is not matched by increases in classes, with many small schools doubling up grades in single classes. Higher teacher/pupil ratios may mean not just lower productivity but more intensive teaching or the diversification of the curriculum. The Slovak study concludes that small schools are more costly, because of the incidence of overhead costs, but their quality is not necessarily lower. Evidence suggests that any deficiencies in educational provision at primary level occur mainly in the upper grades; many small schools only provide the first four grades. Moreover, the wider cultural contribution of schools to the quality of village life cannot be measured, but is greatly valued.

Equally important to efficiency is the way in which resources are used by the individual school. There is a considerable difference between countries and localities in the discretion given to schools to manage their own budgets. There is a growing tendency to give schools legal status; this generally gives schools discretion to make budgets, vire between items of expenditure and retain unspent balances at the end of the budget year. British experience suggests that this significantly increases efficiency.

Exchange of experience between Hungarian municipal finance directors suggested that those municipalities which had given schools the right to manage budgets and had allocated funding to them on a normative, per pupil basis had made most progress in rationalizing their school systems. Schools had been under direct pressure both to attract pupils and to adjust staff numbers. To some extent this is echoed by experience in the Czech Republic where teaching salary grants are now made on a normative staffing level related to pupil numbers (as already described). This has apparently halted and partially reversed the rapid increase in teacher/pupil ratios during the period from 1989 to 1994. Another contributory factor was regulations prescribing a minimum average class size for school funding. In Poland, however, national legal restrictions on the firing of teachers or even their transfer to other schools are a severe constraint on the use of per pupil funding to rationalize staffing levels and costs.

Both Hungarian and Polish ministries of education have tried to increase the productivity of teaching forces by attaching salary increases to rises in the mandatory number of teaching hours. Neither has succeeded. The result in both cases has been salary increases imposed by agreements between Government and unions, but only very partially funded by increases in the educational elements of the grant structure. This has put pressure on local governments to rationalize school systems and staffing levels, but is often hamstrung by the national employment legislation. The evidence of the studies suggests that the State is no more effective than the local government in rationalization (and possibly less). Where it funds salaries directly, as in Czech Republic and Slovakia, it does at least have to bear the financial consequences of its own concessions.

3. CONCLUSION

The Polish study argues that post-1989 policies of devolution owe more to a desire to replace local Communist apparatus than to a positive belief in local democracy. In the case of education there has been little theoretical argument about the respective roles of national and local government; this is not a sector in which there were strong pre-war traditions of local responsibility.

The four countries are still searching for the appropriate balance between national and local responsibilities in the education sector. After the initial surge of devolution, ministries of education have tended to emphasize the constitutional guarantees of education and the need for strong State supervision, if not direct funding and management of schools. They have all retained power to negotiate and set terms of employment for teachers, regardless of the financial consequences for either state or local budgets.

The need for the national government to ensure some degree of equality in access to education and some degree of uniformity in content and minimum standards can scarcely be denied. That some ministries of education have been slow in developing the capacity to fulfil this role is a separate issue.

Nevertheless, if individual schools are failing their pupils it is not only the Minister who will lose sleep. The quality of local education is a major concern for parents and for local communities as a whole. Local governments can scarcely ignore the popular pressure to "do something about" local schooling, whether it is legally their concern or not.

The evidence of the studies is that the local government is as concerned as the State over educational standards, if not more so. Its financial contributions have considerably exceeded the levels expected of them by the intergovernmental finance system and have, in some cases, compensated for the underperformance of State Budget obligations. The country where schools have suffered most from underfunding has been Slovakia where local governments have hitherto had no legal responsibilities for education.

Nor have local governments shown much propensity to interfere excessively in the professional management of schools. The Polish study argues that municipalities have been extremely reticent to get involved at this level. Their rights, for example, to scrutinize annual school plans have rarely been enforced with rigor, despite the financial implications for their own budgets.

The relationship between divisions of responsibility for schooling and its effectiveness is diverse and inconclusive. At one extreme, the early and full-blooded devolution of responsibility in Hungary can probably be associated with the degree of diversity and flexibility in the adaptation of its school system to market change. It may also be due to the fact that there is no division of responsibility for primary and secondary schools in most of the larger towns. At the other extreme, the exclusion of local government in Slovakia can be associated with the severity of the financial cut backs and its impact on buildings and plant (and possibly remuneration); the evidence of the other countries suggests that municipalities would have given priority to the needs of schools, had they been responsible for them, whatever their own financial constraints.

There is little evidence that devolution has an adverse effect on equity. On the contrary it has had its customary effect of encouraging a fairer and more transparent geographical distribution of state funding.

Much of the dynamism, however, lies in the management and responsiveness of the individual school. It is possible that municipal founders give more encouragement or present fewer bureaucratic obstacles to school initiatives than State agencies. The influence of devolution should not be overstated, however. There has also been much change in provision in Slovakia, the most State run of all the four systems.

Equally significant must be the extent to which schools are affected by market change. A key issue is the financial incentives to schools to sustain their enrolment. Systems which base teaching staff levels or even total funding on pupil numbers give the clearest encouragement to schools to maintain the relevance and quality of their education. They also provide the greatest opportunity to respond to changes in demand and the greatest spur to efficiency. However, schools grappling with the severest problems of social disadvantage need an exceptional degree of professional and financial help from state or local government—this type of positive discrimination is only beginning to develop.

Once again, the effect of financial incentives should not be overstated. The ambition and morale of the teaching force are closely associated with the attraction of motivated pupils and a sense of relevance to contemporary society. Whatever the balance of responsibility between state and local government, the key factors in school governance are the discretion and accountability of the individual school.

The challenges to government, whether national or local, are to develop the capacity for normative supervision and to combine a high degree of delegation to school management with selective intervention and support.

Education Management and Finance in Hungary. Efficiency, Equity and Quality Problems in the Transition Period

Éva Balázs

Zoltán Hermann

Table of Contents

Foreword 39

1. Education in Hungary in the 1990s 39

    1.1 Public Education of the 1990s,
         in Relation to Their Social-economic Context 39

    1.2 Changes and Reforms in Education in the 1990s 44

    1.3 Division of Responsibilities 51

    1.4 Actors and Their Responsibilities in the Education Sector 52

         1.4.1 National Level 52

         1.4.2 Regional Level 55

         1.4.3 Local Level 57

         1.4.4 Institutional Level 59

    1.5 Expenditure Assignment and the Institutional Setting
         of Financing the Public Education System 62

2. Effectiveness, Efficiency and Equity Problems in the Public Education Sector 65

    2.1 Effectiveness of the Public Education 65

         2.1.1 Students' Achievement: Trends and International Comparison 66

         2.1.2 Small Village Schools 68

         2.1.3 School Management 70

    2.2 Efficiency Problems in the Public Education Sector 72

         2.2.1 Economies of Scale and Small Village Schools 73

         2.2.2 Weak Adjustment to Demographic Change 74

         2.2.3 Factors of Competition between Schools 80

         2.2.4 Side-effects of Changes in School and Program Structure 82

    2.3 Equity Problems in Public Education 83

         2.3.1 Likely Effects of Structural Changes on Equity 84

         2.3.2 Inequalities in Students' Achievement 85

         2.3.3 Disparities in Expenditures 86

         2.3.4 Students with Special Needs 88

3.   Conclusion 90

References 93

Annex 1:   Education Levels and School Structure in Hungary 97
Annex 2:   Incentives for School Closures in a Central–local Fiscal Game 98
Annex 3:   Tables 99

FOREWORD

The study analyzes differences in the location of responsibility for the management and financing of school education and assesses their impact upon the effectiveness, equity and efficiency of the education service. The scope of the study includes pre-school, primary, secondary and vocational education services, ranging from 5 to 18 year old students. Additionally, the study touches upon the elements of the historical background where considered necessary to understand the present system and the drifting changes.

The horizon of the study refers to the 1990s, a decade in which extensive political and economical transformations took place in the country. The main focus of the study will be on the late 1990s and the present for two main reasons. Firstly, relevant changes in education, for example concerning sharing responsibilities, along with initial signs of decentralization, appeared before the transition period (however, introducing the entire process here is beyond the boundaries of this study). Secondly, changes of the last decade can be characterized by a twofold process. They show a general trend of being adapted to the new socio-economic environment and also to the Europe-wide educational proceedings (for example decentralization, deregulation, frame curricula regulation). At the same time, the waves of changes can be linked to the macro level education political movements on the basis of electoral cycles (for example decentralization and re-centralization in regionalization, direct or indirect tools for education politics). Though this view lacks a broader time perspective—the most significant changes of the period can be seen as those where education processes can be characterized by more continuity than sharp splits.

1. EDUCATION IN HUNGARY IN THE 1990S

1.1 Public Education of the 1990s, in Relation to Their Social-economic Context

In the 1990s, dramatic changes occurred in the political and economical environment of Hungarian society. Along with other public services, the educational sector had also been deeply affected by the adaptation process of transformation. The economic crisis of the late 1980s had many consequences in the conditions and functioning of both public and higher education. With the low economic performance of the bankrupted socialist economy on the one hand, and the high and gradually increasing inflation of the transformation period on the other, education had to suffer from a considerable withdrawal of state expenditure. The expenditure on public education in real terms decreased by nearly 40% by the mid 1990s [Halász–Lannert, 2000].

The first to lose out in the education sector was the lower vocational education, which had already been in crisis due to its broken industrial background—apprentice shops, maintained by the firms, were the first to close [Balázs et al., 1992].

The transformation period of education in Hungary can be characterized by elements of both discontinuity and continuity. Economic and societal transition were taking place within a new change of government which after forty years of a monolith status, became based on a pluralistic party system. Besides this common characteristic, some special features of both can be evaluated as different from those of the neighboring countries in the region. Discontinuity, the usual trend of a sharp transformation process, was a feature of education within its main fields like the ownership of schools, but not of many others. Some elements of discontinuity in education started before the political changes and they had actually anticipated the transformation. For example abolishing the teaching of the Russian language, or the re-establishment of a traditional elite eight-grade secondary grammar school model. Continuity, another feature of the Hungarian educational processes was caused partly by changes which occurred long before the transition, and partly by changes that occurred considerably later. The former can be connected to the 1985 Act on Education,[1] which gave way to some of the following elements of school autonomy:

- autonomy in the financial management of schools;
- in using school level—experimental—syllabi;
- in giving more rights to the institutional level in school governance;
- abandoning school inspectorate;
- introducing an application system for the appointment of school leaders;
- giving a wide range of rights for teachers.[2]

These proceedings can be taken as antecedents of the transformation on school level, given that the participants already were experienced in some skills needed in the new era. The latter branch of 'continuity' was caused by the delay of transformation in many fields of education. Political-ideological debates on the content of education—the main educational policy issue of the first, national-conservative government for example—hindered the introduction of a new curriculum until 1995.[3]

Along with other spheres, education was deeply affected by the cultural transformation of the period. Pluralism of values, differentiating social status and the economic situation of families claimed new approaches and methodology, not only in teaching but also in educational administration. Signs of social disintegration and incoherence (for example effects of increasing unemployment of family-members; later unemployment of the young; increasing territorial differences and segregation) were challenging for education policy debates on the extended versus restricted roles of institutional socialization. This particular branch of problems appeared in education policy discussions on equity and liberty. During the first period of transformation, there seemed to be a political consensus between parties and professionals on equity and liberty.[4] This appeared in many fields of education by declaring, for example, a free choice of schools for families and pupils; whilst students' rights appeared in the pluralism of school ownership and in a wide range of school autonomy. As far as the former, equity problems are concerned, and they have become an issue for the third education government, due to explicit inequalities and equity problems (further discussed below).

Challenges were caused also by the 'outer' determinants of social life. In the majority, these came from the economy, the collapse of which resulted in high unemployment and a problematic labor market situation. Transformation was taking place in the circumstances of extreme demographic movements, which contributed to the discontinuous elements of education. Some big cohorts, born in the mid 1970s, were followed by very diminishing ones. Concentrating its effects on education, half of the boom was in the secondary schools, whilst the other half occurred in the eight-grade general schools (in Hungary the 'general' school is primary education for students from 5–14 years, with a maximum ages limit of 16 years for those students who have to repeat years). These institutions tried to adapt to the quick changing of needs and the low turn out of pupils within a very short period. Both vertical levels of public education answered this challenge by expansion. The expansion was not directed by any national educational policy initiative at that time, while the shift in the ownership of educational institutions (discussed in detail later) resulted in the school level being very active and efficient in initiating structural changes of public education. Structural transformation tended to focus 'downwards' (i.e. on getting students in) in the secondary sector and 'upwards' in the general one (i.e. keeping students) to expend their educational provision. Many secondary schools introduced eight-grade and six-grade classes, some new institutions of which the owner had become the church, were established in these forms. In the meantime, general schools tried to substitute their pupils lost by the demographic decline and the attractiveness of the six and eight grade secondary schools. Some of them, having better human and physical infra-structural background, developed themselves to be a twelve grade school; whilst others, which accommodated pupils who were not being successful in entering any secondary school, offered schooling for the ninth and tenth grades (the latter form existed only for few years in the early 1990s). Structural changes, initiated by educational institutes, served as the main tool for saving their physical and human infrastructure by fighting for students.

The strong institutional activity was a consequence of the decentralization process of the state, the consequence of which resulted in a very wide range of power given to the local (municipal) level. In 1990, due to a unique consensus between different political parties, local authorities were established instead of the former local councils by the Act on the Local Authorities.[5] Contrary to the former local bodies, the new ones had real responsibilities, independently from the state (and the central party). The ownership of the schools shifted from the state to local authorities: local and county governments now maintain more than 90% of the schools, whilst the rest includes church, foundation and private schools. By the law, local governments have to undertake obligatory public education services, but they are free to choose their methods: for exanple by establishing new schools; maintaining the existing one; initiating joint schools and so on. Offering territorial level education services (for example maintaining secondary schools, youth hostels, professional expertise) was a free choice for local authorities but an obligatory task of the county authorities. This inconsistency—generated by the Act on Local Authorities—has had, and still has, many problems in territorial education administration. The decentralization of state administration resulted in more than 3 200 autonomous local authorities, amongst which nearly 2 500 became school owners.

This change, which was worth as much as a constitutional one, established autonomous local bodies, empowering them to decide on the local society and economy. But this process[6] was not a part of a coherent constitutional change, because many regulations did not perfectly fit into the logic of a decentralized state system.[7] That is why local tasks and competencies, prescribed by law, in reality do not fit into the state's jurisdiction and the central system of regulating tools. Latent and sometimes explicit conflicts, along with puzzling compromises have now become general. Because the act on the local authorities claims a two third majority of the parliament, the modification of it is not easy. That is why many modifications are done as smaller level regulations, allowed to be supported by a simple majority. The constitutional problem causes many inconsistencies in the local administration [Pálné Kovács I., 1999], including the administration and financing of education.

A special case of a mixture of continuity and discontinuity in the transformation occurred within the state budgetary system. In society, a personal taxation and VAT system was introduced under socialism from 1988. After the reform of fiscal incomes, fiscal expenditures were also re-considered even before the political transformation. Narrowing this debate to education, discussions on the theme were aimed at the financing of schools and at the payment system of teachers. The latter was thematized very intensively by alternative teacher unions, formed in the late 1980s, which was also supported by the last socialist educational government which—together with professionals—prepared reform policies to make the financing of education more efficient [for example see Nagy, 1996]. In the discussions between politicians, experts and teacher union leaders, completed later with people from the political opposition, the main issue was to demolish the over-centralized socialist structure. Within that, democratization and a non-radical deregulation were the focus among reform communists and the leaders of the old teachers union, while a more radical deregulation and decentralizaton were supported mainly by governmental economists and new trade unions. Except for the traditional teachers union, most of the reformists calculated with a fiscal barrier, but neither of them faced the end of full employment. Whereas one can distingvish between the underlying values of the social-democratic welfare state and of the new right liberal one (Semjén, 1991),[8] these elements in our view did not appear clearly. The per capita grant system, being approved before the political transition, did not give a strict regulation on the items of state expenditures and on the level of state spending. As far as a significant part of that, teacher salaries, the 1991 Act on Public Employment, regulating teacher employment criteria and salary ladder, a state responsibility was determined to be devoted to a minimum salary.

The per capita grant system in education seemed to be in accordance with decentralization and deregulation, providing a flexible tool for fiscal policy at the same time. In the professional and policy discussions on the introduction of the per capita system, these characteristics were taken into consideration, but there was no agreement for a while on who should actually be entitled to get the per capita amount. After the first local elections in the autumn of 1990, the settlements (local authorities, municipalities) had become the users of the grant.[9] From the point of view of schools, the per capita amount was not a subjective right for them to get. This means that any municipality—due to the act on the local authorities—has the right to use the amount, devoted to schooling by the state, to use for another purpose, which is seen to be more important for the local people.

The per capita financing system could otherwise be seen as the most appropriate method pursuing the goal of efficiency and adjusting expenditures to demographic waves, since this system is sensible to the number of the pupils. Nevertheless, given the strong trend of demographic decline, the per capita funding system simply shifted the task of adjustment to these changes to the local governments, without further support to cope with this task. On the other hand, as it will be expounded in section two, the incentive for efficiency of the financing was legitimate for the central educational government but not for the whole society. In fact, the behavior of any agents was not effective. Nevertheless in the circumstances of the problematic economic situation the central budgetary system was—or could be—more or less stable because of this regulation, but local authorities had to endure many of its consequences. They were also those which suffered from the inflation, not being handled automatically by central level since the restriction of the mid-1990s was followed by the modification of the share of the personal income tax between the state and the local governments: the share received by local governments has decreased from 100% to 20% in the past decade. Direct financial restriction in education followed a painful political stabilization program of the second (socialist-liberal coalition) government in 1995. The so-called Bokros programme (called after the name of the—socialist—minister of finance) introduced many restrictions in the central budget; their effect on the decentralized local authorities was perceptible later but harder. Before this time, municipalities and their schools had a common—not fiscal but in some respects economical and social—interest in maintaining and often more, by developing school infrastructure. Small village schools especially tended to maintain their educational institution under any circumstances, whilst bigger schools, not having a wide range of school network, also considered their schools as places of local economy and society. This interest was supported also by local people and when the effects of the growing inflation and of the fiscal restrictions forced local governments to consider any steps (school closing and fusion), inhabitants—often with the help of media—opposed it very actively. In fact, school closure has not been widespread until now. This field of educational debate was a leading theme of the mid-1990s, representing the dilemma between liberty, equity and efficiency. The third government (a right-wing coalition) preferred direct and central tools (e.g. financial resources) for supporting equity versus the previously preferred liberty.

1.2 Changes and Reforms in Education in the 1990s

After reviewing the major determinants of public education and financing education in the last decade, it is now possible to discuss the educational policy achievements in which the main educational tasks are concerned.

In the jurisdiction, very intensive work took place. Between 1990 and 1999, laws or modification of the laws on public education were brought about on five different occasions, followed by nearly 150 lower regulations. Amongst these, the 1993 reform can be seen as a concise reform, which established the main framework of the characteristics of the present system by declaring decentralization, pluralism and deregulation. Decentralization took place on the basis of the 1990s Act on Public Administration, which created a shift in the ownership of schools from the state to local authorities. Pluralism was mainly due to the 1991 law on church property, which gave the ownership of many schools back to the church, and due to the 1993 Act on Public Education, which declared the sectoral freedom of school establishment and maintenance.[10] For national and ethnic minorities it was also important to approve an act on their rights, including the rights of maintaining and supporting their schools by the state. The 1993 law described the financial frame and structure of public education, the frame of school structure and operation, determined the levels and progams, the basic rights of the agents of public education and scheduled the reshaping of the content re-regulation. It raised the compulsory education to the age of sixteen,[11] as well as approving the basic examination after fulfilling a 10 year general education. Laws on vocational and higher education were also approved in 1993, therefore the whole system of education was affected by central regulation. The 1992 act on public employees affected education by classing teachers in this category, which resulted in their central salary regulation. The jurisdiction was no less intensive in the next governmental period. The new content regulation, the National Core Curriculum (NCC) was accepted in 1995 by a governmental act. It was a dual (two-level) content regulation, which described common national frames of 10 interdisciplinary knowledge areas, expressed by standard minimum output criteria[12] in every other year, for the period of compulsory education (ten grades). On the basis of the NCC school level pedagogical programs, including school-based syllabi, were prescribed to be prepared: a three-year period was decided for this implementation. In grades 11 and 12 the content of education has become regulated by the system of a new final examination, which was approved by the government in 1997.[13] A significant modification of the 1993 act on public education was accepted by the second freely elected government in 1996. This regulation raised compulsory education up to the age of eighteen, which was to be introduced following the implementaion of the NCC in 1998. The law also established a new tool for territorial administration by prescribing counties to prepare their six-year plans for the territorial development of education. Regional development of the country has become an important issue from this period; a law on regional development was also approved in 1996 (it was in this way that the county and regional levels became separated). The 1996 modification of the act on public education introduced a new system of teacher promotion, bound to a new regulation on obligatory in-service training every seven years, and it was acknowledged by the state through extra payment for teachers, however, this was abandoned in 1999 by the next government.

After 1998, a major governmental change occurred in the educational sector by connecting the tasks of administering vocational education to the general education. From this time, the central administration of general and vocational education has been organized in one, partly new ministry, and from this period the vocational sector was divided from labour politics. The act on public education was modified again by the new education government. To assert the—increasingly involved - role of the state, the responsibilities of the minister were widened by this law, and a new de-concentrated institution was established on a regional level (OKÉV, the National Centre for Evaluation and Examination of Public Education), entitled by fulfilling several tasks of the new educational policy. Besides the main responsibility of quality management at a central level (about this, see the subchapter 1.4.1), OKÉV has become entitled to represent the minister's interest in the regional development. Concerning regional administration, the 1999 law was aimed also at improving the co-ordination between the state and the schools, as well as between the decentralized administrative bodies: i.e. the counties and local authorities. On behalf of the latter, territorial education planning was developed by introducing a plan for ordering the school network, prepared by the local authorities, in co-ordination with the county development plans. The right-wing conservative educational government added also to the content regulation of public education. The 1999 modification of the law on public education put back the three level content regulation, the unsuccessful incentive of the first government by introducing a so called frame syllabus. This syllabus was approved in 2000. To increase the effectiveness and efficiency of education, a major goal of the education policy appeared in regulations on the minimum of school infrastructure and equipment, on the teaching time and on the tasks of teachers. Equity problems were also made explicit at this time. Due to this, the government policy on secondary school enrolment and school structure was legally regulated: restrictions were introduced on the organization of school level entrance exams; a new regulation prescribed to offer also four-grade classes in the—mostly elitist—eight and six grade secondary schools. The Office of the Commissioner of Educational Rights was also established in 1999.

Due to the transition, educational administration has been widely decentralized since the political transition. Under this stable characteristic, the degree of the desirable decentralization, noticeable by the division of the roles between the state and other actors, the width of these actors, the tools for administration, its incentives and bounds were different among the three educational policies of consecutive governments. The first government had to endure a wide range of responsibilities and rights that were given for the administration of education to the newly established local governments, without having the tools for handling administrative co-ordination between the central-, local-, and—even more apparent—, the school level.[14] The government could not expound the central influence on local processes. Professional administration was to be fulfilled by municipalities, just as their legal supervision was to be supplied by de-concentrated regional offices. The education government decided to assert its central administrative rights, but the

Regional Educational Offices, established in 1993 for this very purpose, were very quickly abandoned by the next government. The education policy of the 1994–98 period tried to provide the arena by introducing mainly indirect tools and initiatives of local and school level administration and by establishing some central tools for enhancing local and territorial (county level) co-ordination in the development of education. As far as the latter is concerned, the 1996 modification of the Act on Public Education[15] introduced the institution of county development plans, which were followed by initiating county level public foundations for education development. The central government paid a moderated amount for their functioning, but the counties had the right to decide on how to use the grants. The main issue of this period, which was the modernization of education, was supported also by governmental programs.[16]

The professional administration was to be supported by building a new network of experts, accessible for both schools and school maintainers. The main field of their activity was to contribute to the preparation of the school based pedagogical program, but they could offer their services freely in a quasi-market situation. The next governmental change, also caused change in the initiatives of educational administration. The efforts of enforcing central responsibilities in educational administration resulted in many direct tools, mainly in juridical changes (see above). They extended the role of the state in the school structure, the enrolment and student flow, the content regulation and the supplement of text-books. Tendency towards centralization appeared in the widening tasks of the minister and establishing OKÉV. The office and its regional units have been set to serve as a direct administration tool for evaluation, supervision and quality assurance; among them a new kind of supervision which was initiated after a fourteen-year period.

To contribute to some major issues of the analysis, we have to describe here two concrete areas of education where significant changes took place throughout the decade, mainly issues on school structure and quality issues of education. It can be said that structural changes is an area of education in a process of continuing reform. As it was outlined before, these changes were initiated by bottom-up processes of both economy and society and schools themselves. The first structural change took place even a bit before the transition when the elitist eight-grade secondary school model (ISCED levels two and three) was allowed to be re-introduced.[17] Before the transition, the eight-grade general school (ISCED levels one and two) was the obligatory and universal type of public schooling. However, its extension up to grade ten was proposed several times. The dilemma of having the general schools up to eight or ten grades was also prolonged after the transition. At the secondary level, three main kinds of schools were offered: a three-grade apprentice school,[18] along with two kinds of the four-grade secondary school, secondary grammar ('gimnázium') school and secondary vocational school. This structure was widened by the 'four plus eight' (ISCED 1 in general school, ISCED 2 and 3 in secondary school) in 1989 and later by the six-grade secondary model. More of the twelve-grade schools also turned into a 'six plus six' structural type (6 grades in general, six in secondary school). The colors of the picture were enriched by schools and local maintainers in the circumstances of a decentralized educational scene, as previously outlined. For a temporary period in the early 1990s, pupils, who could not find lower vocational education but were not permitted to enter secondary school were taught in so called special technical schools or in general schools which maintained ninth and tenth grades.[19] The secondary school level has become more enriched by introducing bilingual secondary grammar, and later bilingual secondary vocational schools.[20] Additional grades to the institutions of secondary education appeared in the vocational sub-sector first (offered 1 or 2 grades for higher vocational training after the final exam), but in the second part of the 1990s they appeared also in the 'gimnázium' schools. They were heralds of post-secondary education, which has become an area of interest of public, higher education, as well as labour force training. Post-secondary education is not an issue we deal with in this paper, it has not been a coherent institutional system up until now in Hungary, but this kind of further training occurs also in secondary schools, making the structure even more complex.[21]

The school types, enumerated before, do not exist separately. One of the main changes of the 1990s is that within one secondary institution there are secondary grammar and vocational classes—they can be regarded as the most comprehensive schools in Hungary—there are mixed vocational schools, offering technical classes and secondary vocational ones.[22] These, along with general schools, developed themselves up to the twelfth grade in different forms of secondary schooling, and were developed on the whole quite spontaneously.[23] This very intricate school structure (see Annex 1) is a common consequence of decentralization and democratization of education on the one hand, and demographic changes in the other. Economic transformation and its handling has also played a role in its formation.

As the school supply had become even more broad amongst a declining young population, and the society expressed demand towards further schooling rather than youth unemployment, expansion in education was a natural consequence of the processes (the result of expansion of secondary education is presented in Figure 1). This issue was touched on in the previous sub-section 1.1. It is worth here to once again underline the fact that the process can be taken into account as a rather long spontaneous 'bottom-up' reform, initiated not only by institutons but by the public, and it was followed by central steps much later.

It is necessary to mention from the point of view of equity, that the expansion was accompanied by a diminishing drop-out rate. As we will see in section 2, expansion that is followed by a diminishing drop-out rate, means efficiency in its social sense, but not in its academic one. Meanwhile, efficiency in an academic sense is dubious.

Changes of the 1990s in education effected its quality in an ambiguous way. It was inevitable that direct and side effects of the transformation—for example the deteriorating supplement of schools, and inflating teachers' salary—played a role in the decreasing quality, although data is neither available nor relevant to prove it. The main change of this issue in the period investigated, is that the way of thinking about quality has been completely transformed. For the society, a shorter period was needed than for the government to accept that measuring the quality of education cannot necessarily be measured by—factually non-existing—standards,[24] but by provision that fits the social and market demands. A third possible interpretation of quality measurements: the concept of quality having the ability to fit into a contract, was proposed by the 1994–98 education policy, which considered school based pedagogical programs to be a twofold contract: one between the school and the families and, in the meantime, between the school and its maintainer. The former was to serve as a method of informing and encouraging pupils to make their own choice of school. This contract was to create a common base for offering a program by the school on the one hand, and accepting, with the promise of financing it, by the maintainer. The quality policy was reconsidered in 1998 and the education government introduced new legal regulations and tools for its new initiatives.

Figure 2.1

The Proportion of Learning in Different Types of Secondary Institutions, 1989/90–1999/00 [%]

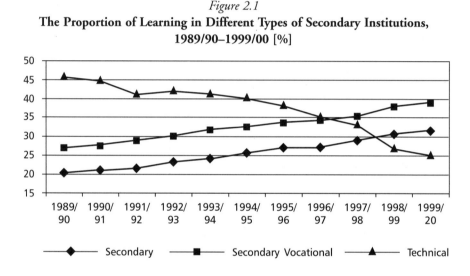

SOURCE: Jelentés a magyar közoktatásról 2000 (Report on Hungarian Public Education, 2000) OKI

The function of evaluation and quality assurance was appraised highly in the 1990s in Hungarian public education. The reason for that had been rooted mainly in the increased need of the decision-makers to have feed-backs on institutional level processes, but it can also be mentioned that there has not been any inspection of education since the 1985 Act on Education.[25] The education policies of the 1990s on the quality on education depend on the following pillars:[26]

- the growing role of the state in educational finance;

- dealing with equity problems and initiatives to support institutions in worst circumstances;

- initiating strategic and operational planning on territorial and local development;

- developing and further developing of the content regulation system; within that: the role of the state in stating the contents of education and standardization of it;

- other tools, used for quality development: for example organizational development, measuring students' achievement, and so on.

The education policies of the 1990s were concerned about different aspects of quality management, inspection, evaluation and quality assurance. Dealing with this issue was based partly on the actual education policy on quality issues but was also affected by side-effects of other policy-preferences.[27]

As far as the inspection is concerned, the old system was abandoned in 1985, and for fourteen years there was no supervision of that kind in Hungarian schools. The trial of the 1990–94 educational government was to establish an institution of state control on schools, but the Regional Educational Centres, with the intention to fulfil this, were stopped after the change of government, without solving the problem. A new approach to inspection has become a key issue for the third education government, which placed quality issue on the list of policy agenda. This policy is aiming at quality management in a complex way, dealing with supervision, evaluation and quality assurance together. To fulfil these tasks, OKÉV was established in 1999. The supervisory tasks of OKÉV are still to be finalized.

External evaluation of schools in the 1990s were and are based on experts. The 1985 act on education modified the role of County Pedagogical Institutions (CPIs), which supplied the inspection before, but after the law, they served as a resource of professional provision. After decentralization in 1990, they offered their services to school maintainers and to schools. The recruitment base for professional provision in the early 1990s grew, as other workshops and private firms also entered the market. An experts network was developed later to support and to take part in the implementation process of the NCC. A list of experts was set by the educational government[28] for two kinds of operation. Since the schools, were inexperienced in the preparation of their 'local' (school-based) pedagogical programmes (LPP), including school-based curricula, they were offered to apply for experts. On the other hand, the local maintainers had to apply for experts to have a professional report on these programs to support the local bodies' decision on their acceptance, which is the right of the representative body of the local government. Both kinds of services were operated in a co-financing system between the state and the customers; for the latter local investment and central support was also offered.[29] Though there was neither criteria of being experts (being put on the list) nor standards for regulating the experts' work, empirical research found that customers were contented with both the quality and the legality of experts.[30] In the late 1990s, the standardization of the experts' work become a key issue. This process is under preparation as a part of the central quality policy in which OKÉV has an important role.

Evaluation of the work of the school is a professional task of the school maintainer by law, but in practice the method is reliant on the maintainer. This can be done by using experts, as it was outlined before. Municipalities and other maintainers can fulfil this obligation through other means, for example they can evaluate schools by asking school councils to report about it; or

49

through self-evaluation of schools. Other indicators could also be used, for example different results of pupils' achievements; indicators or quasi-indicators of schools; the rank order of entering universities; the proportion of students having a foreign language certificate; places taken in different national competitions of subjects and so on. In reality, the professional evaluation of schools is rather weak. According to research, 27% of examinations of schools ordered by the maintainer were professional evaluation.[31] The 1999 modification of the Act on Public Education gives the right for the minister to enforce this obligation, and OKÉV takes part in this process. The evaluation of pupil and student achievements includes external and internal elements. Let us first outline some questions of external evaluation. One set of that is coming from international and national measurements, which give a diagnostic picture on student achievements.[32] The missing point in this field is that there is, at present, no external examination existing in the Hungarian system. As it was told, NCC is an output-oriented core curriculum, which presumes exams. The new examination system (consisting of two general exams: a basic examination after the tenth grade and a final examination after the secondary school; and new vocational exams of two levels) has been prepared and approved by law, but the system has yet to beintroduced.[33] The old final exam exists, but in reality it is an internal one. That is why there is no evidence on the quality of the output of schools in this respect.

Quality assurance is an issue, the importance of which is increasing in the 1990s. The three theoretical approaches to quality assurance, outlined before, are all represented in Hungarian public education.

a)   Firstly, using standards, indicators and procedures, for example accreditation in different fields of public (and higher) education, is a strong effort of the present educational policy. Processes of standardization are being advanced: Hungary supplies data for the Education at the Glance (EAG),[34] the teacher in-service training system has an accreditation system; the statistical system is in the reform process, and so on. Fitting to standards of institutional management is used in many secondary, mainly vocational schools, which apply quality assurance systems like the ISO, supported by experts.

b)   Secondly, a model of quality, measured by fitting to a contract between the customer and the 'seller' exists in the form of the Local (school based) Pedagogical Programs. This document fulfilled this aimtwofold. On the one hand it acts as a contract between the school maintainer and the school, where the school promises to offer services laid down in the LPP and the maintainer provides to finance those services. In the other, the same document is available for the public to select between schools while deciding to enter it or not.[35]

c)   The third approach to quality is the evaluation of the market, and is expressed by the contentment of local people, families and pupils/students to educational services. The free choice to enter a school entitles families to select among the different institutions.[36] This approach is being used by several ways in Hungarian education throughout the period. There is a list of the best secondary schools, based on different indicators of successfulness, used by schools and also by the public for selecting a secondary grammar school.[37] There are also other informal ways to apply ranking and judging schools. This approach does not use hard measures of quality, but rather expresses the nature of education as a public service. That is why it is relevant for quality assurance as well. More models like the TQM (Total Quality Management) are based on this theory, and they are applied in many Hungarian schools.

d) The quality assurance is an integral part of the present public educational policy. In 1999, a high amount of state expenditure was established to support school maintainers and schools in applying quality assurance methods with help of experts. A national programme, called COMENIUS,[38] was launched to contribute to the local and school level quality assurance. The COMENIUS office is operated centrally, but partly independently from the state. It prepares concrete programs and offer grants for both maintainers, schools and experts in a co-financing system. Experts are selected by an application procedure. The program has a one-year history so there is not enough feed back on its success, but the popularity is high among schools and municipalities.

1.3 Division of Responsibilities

There are some basic characteristics of the division of responsibilities for public education and within that, for management and finance, in the Hungarian system. They are as follows:

1) Public educational administration is highly decentralized and the responsibilities for education are shared between several actors;

2) Horizontally, the responsibility at the national level is shared between different ministries where the Ministry of Education is responsible for the central administration of general, secondary and vocational education (together: public education; the latter has been so from 1998). Ministry of Finance, of Interior and of Social and Family Affairs have also different responsibilities for education. The horizontal share of responsibilities at the lower levels may also be told to be typical but at the less extent.

3) Vertically, the administrative responsibility is shared between four levels, the national, the regional, the local (municipal) and the institutional levels;

4) The regional level in fact consists of two levels and two different organizational structures: the county level, which is a kind of decentralized self-government and the regional level, which is a de-concentrated governmental administrative one. (The statistical regions, established recently, are to fulfil the EU requirements). The relation between the functions and the responsibilities of the two territorial levels have not yet been satisfactorily agreed.

5) The scope of responsibilities at the local level is very broad, while the role of the regional and county level is quite weak;

6) The administration of education at the local and institutional levels is integrated into the general system of public administration so there is no organizationally separate educational administration;

7)   At the local and the county levels, public administration is based on the system of self-governments, that is under the control of politically autonomous, elected bodies. The central government cannot issue direct orders to the local governments;

8)   The number of the local authorities (local governments) is very high, while their average size is small; the local level is not homogenous.

9)   There is a big difference between the range, size, and types of school networks maintained by local bodies, therefore the legally same responsibilities are carried out through very different educational tasks, whilst the quality of educational administration is extremely varied;

10) The institutional level has got a high autonomy, but less tools to enforce their responsibilities.

1.4 Actors and Their Responsibilities in the Education Sector

The main institutions of taking responsibilities for education are shown in Table 2.1. The actors express different—political, administrative, professional or other—interests. We summarize their responsibilities briefly through the level at which they act.

1.4.1   National Level

The basic laws on education are passed by the Parliament. The political discussions on the Bills of Education are made in the Parliament Committee for Education, Scientific, Youth and Sport Affairs. The national government is responsible for issuing the regular school and pre-school curricula, the basic requirements of final examination and of in-service teacher training. The governmental responsibility for public education at the national level is shared between several ministries.

The Ministry of Education is responsible for the sectoral administration of public, vocational and higher education. Due to the amendment of the Public Education Act in 1999, within the general frame of the decentralized system, the Minister of Education has a wider range of responsibilities than before. A great proportion of these tasks are related with curricular issues and examinations. He/she issues the directives of bilingual education, pre-school and school special education and minorities' education. He/she issues the basic program and the frame curricula for colleges and basic art education. The minister gives the details of the basic and final examination requirements, and decides which textbooks and teaching aids are listed in the national textbook register. His/her duty is to evaluate the experiences on the introduction of NCC and the Frame Curricula. In institutional planning and provision, a central administrative responsibility is to lay down the general requirements for school buildings and equipment. The minister's new responsibility is to provide the education policy tasks of regional development. Concerning the assurance of quality, his/her responsibility is to ensure the conditions of quality management, and to provide for the national-level professional services. The minister takes charge of the national and the regional level professional control and evaluation of the pedagogical work carried out in the institutions. The ministry can order national and regional assessments and can ask the school maintainer to do so and give the ministry information about them. He/she can initiate an official process to halt any infringements of the law of school maintainers. Concerning the teaching personnel, the minister has got a limited regulatory competence concerning the professional promotion and in-service training of teachers. The regulations of the teachers' salaries and employment conditions fall under the general regulations on public employees.

The responsibilities of the minister for the development of education is mainly connected with the content of education (to support development projects that serve the solution of pedagogical problems and to involve innovation); with planning (to elaborate the long-term and middle-term developmental plan of public education, to provide professional support for the development of the county and local level development plans); and with quality (the elaboration, the operation and the development of the system of examinations; ensuring the conditions of educational research). To get information on education, the minister proposes the gathering of statistical data and operates professional institutes to make research into education.

The Ministry of the Interior has the overall governmental responsibility for the system of local governments, including the local and regional administration of education. The general responsibility for financing the public services and within them the financing of education lies with the Ministry of Finance. This ministry submits to the Parliament the proposal for the yearly budgetary acts, which—amongst others things—regulates the governmental support of education. There are other ministries and different national bodies that can regulate the requirements of vocational training in their own specific fields. The Ministry of Agriculture and Development of the Countryside has to be emphasized because of its main responsibility for regional development, including the development of human resources.

Concerning the national level responsibilities, the role of the Constitutional Court, dealing also with educational issues, should also be mentioned. The decisions of the Court sometimes affects public education significantly, for example a decision was made in 1993 to withdraw the teaching staff's veto right in the appointment of the prospective school director.

The main sectoral administrative institution taking responsibility for the national level evaluation, assessment and quality assurance of public education is the National Public Education and Examination Centre (the previously mentioned OKÉV). The center directs seven sub-centre offices in the statistical regions. The tasks of OKÉV include the supply of the development, the operation and direction of basic and final examinations, national competitions and to supply other tasks of public authorities of evaluation and assessment. Experts and examiners are trained and applied by OKÉV, which provides other organizing tasks concerning the National List of Experts and the National List of Examiners. This institute is responsible for operating the information system of public education and to fulfil the regional development tasks of education.

To establish the 'Office of the Commissioner of Educational Rights,' has been the duty of the Minister of Education. The office, established in 1999, deals with any kind of complaint of either educational or social organizations and individuals. The officer publishes an annual report. The professional institutes provide for the nationwide tasks of education research, development, services, and sometimes administration. These institutes are maintained by the Ministry, but they have professional autonomy, including the possibility to apply for other resources than the governmental ones; they can also compete with each for state funds, devoted to certain projects. The National Institute of Public Education (OKI) conducts research on macro and lower levels and publishes a periodical general analysis called 'Report on Hungarian Public Education,' and this also deals with the development of public education and teacher in-service training. The Hungarian Institute for Educational Research (OI) has partly the same field of interest but the activities of it include research into higher education. The National Institute of Vocational Education (NSZI) provides mainly the development for vocational education, prepares the frame curricula of different trades and conducts research in the field. The Kiss Árpád National Service Office of Public Education (KÁ OKSZI) fulfils professional, service and administrative tasks connected mainly to evaluation and assessment. The Methodology and Information Centre for In-service Teacher Training (PTMIK) organizes and prepares the tasks related to teacher in-service training program, while the professional responsibility for the quality of teacher in-service training is taken by the Body for Pedagogical In-service Training Accreditation. The COMENIUS 2000 Programme Office was established by the Minister of Education in 1999, and it provides the operation of the state development program for quality assurance.

Among the consultative bodies taking responsibilities in education at the national level, the role of the OKNT, the National Public Education Council, is the more important though it has been diminished since 1999. The OKNT involves the most important partners of the education government in issues of the content of education, textbook matters and examinations. The members of the OKNT are commissioned by the Minister of Education (among his/her personal request, delegates of the national professional organizations, teacher training higher education institutes, members of the Hungarian Academy of Science and representatives of the employee's alliances and chambers are there in the council). The roles of the OKNT include a broad set of consultation, expressing its opinion and making proposals.[39] The professional work of OKNT can be done in different committees; at present there are three: the National Pedagogical In-service Training Committee, the National Final Examination Committee and the Textbook and Teaching Aids Committee.

The body to assist the Minister of Education with preparing the education policy-decisions, phrasing opinions and making proposals is the 'Public Education Policy Council' (KT). Except for salaries and other labour issues, this council discusses all issues of public education. The eight most important actors of public education take part in the work of this council with four representatives each: the central government; the local governments; other school maintainers; the minority governments; the professional organizations of teachers; the teachers' unions; the organizations of the parents and of the students.

Interest negotiation with the social partners is extremely important in the field of vocational education. The body to provide a forum for this is called the OSZT, the 'National Vocational Training Council', where the representation—beside the employees, the employers and the central government—of the interest co-ordination bodies of the economic organizations (the economic chambers) and of the school-maintaining local governments is also ensured. The task of the OSZT is to discuss the policy issues of vocational training, and within this, to make proposals for the distribution of the Vocational Training Fund.

In the preparation of many central decision-making process different bodies and councils play roles. The National Council for Minorities—its members represent all the minorities of the country—has a wide range of rights in issues related to the education of the minorities. Its agreement has to be reached for any issue of the content of minorities' education. Rights for making proposals and expressing opinions are given to the National Council for Students' Rights in issues related to pupils' and students' rights.

The issues of labour relations and the relevant financial regulations concerning the employees of budgetary institutions (and among them the teachers working in state and local public schools) are dealt with, at the macro level, by the KIÉT, the Council for the Reconciliation of Interests in Public Institutions. The members of this council comprise of the representatives of the central government, the national trade unions of the employees of budgetary institutions, and the national federations of the local governments. The sphere of authority of this council comprises the general and overall issues of the budgetary institutions and of those employed by them, and the yearly negotiation of the minimal salaries of public employees. The KÖÉT, the 'Council for the Reconciliation of Interests in Public Education,' deals with the same issues at the sectoral level. This council also discusses the drafts of laws that concern the employees in public education and discusses the general educational proposals and conceptions in the form of three-party interest-negotiation. The roles of the teachers' unions (there are more) have to be distinguished by their status. According to the Act on Public Employees a trade union is 'representative' when their nominees obtain at least 10% of votes for the council of public employees. The biggest among them is the Teachers' Union (PSZ), organizing their members in all school types, represents teachers in also KIÉT and KÖÉT. Other teachers' unions were set up by partly political interest of the transition (e.g. PDSZ, The Teachers' Democratic Union) or by the special professional interest of teachers (e.g. musicians, dance artists). The representation of the unions in KT gives them a consultative responsibility in educational policy-making. Political lobbying previously was an important feature of teachers' unions' activities but nowadays other non-institutialized bodies are more active in this field.

1.4.2   Regional Level

There are two real levels within this one, the institutions of which take different responsibilities in public education in Hungary. County level is where there are decentralized self-governments and there is a statistical category of regions (3–4 neighbor counties per region) where there are de-concentrated governmental institutions (sometimes these institutions can be found also at county level). Professional institutes and bodies expressing their interests take also different responsibilities at that level.

The representatives of the county governments are elected by the population during the local elections. The body of political decision-making is the county general assembly, which comprises of the elected representatives. The assembly sets up committees to prepare the policy decisions,[40] and operates an office to execute the policies and to manage the administrative matters. The county level administrative responsibilities are attached to the county head notary, who is an appointed official.

The county governments enjoy competencies similar to those of the local governments. One of their special regional tasks in public education is to provide the educational services that go beyond the basic provision and to exercise the rights connected with them. The task of the county is to maintain the institutions with regional functions (besides secondary schools and vocational training institutions, student hostels, music schools and the institutions of the so-called pedagogical-educational services, dealing with speech therapy, educational counselling). The county also has to provide pedagogical-professional services. This task can be carried out by the county pedagogical institutes (MPI), which are maintained by the counties (or occassionally local governments) but private firms can also take part in the offering of services. A group of tasks of the county governments relates to the regional co-ordination and planning. The middle-term development plan has to contain the measures assuring the fulfilment of compulsory schooling, the regional planning of secondary schooling, the planning of the necessary institutional network and other conditions of education and also has to lay down the relevant responsibilities of the local governments. In order to raise the efficiency of the district-based services, it is legally ruled that the county governments have to promote and assist the co-operation between the local governments operating in the county, including the establishment of their associations. The county also has to help fulfil the tasks concerning the education of the national and ethnic minorities. The county development plans do not have a compulsory standing, but their realisation is enhanced by the public foundations, which are partly financed by the central budget (also setting the priorities on a yearly basis), partly by their own fund-raising with other sponsors. The Boards of Trustees of public foundations for the Development of Public Education are multipartite bodies of the regional interests; they prepare and decide on applications for the funds.

Regional level administration is fulfilled by different de-concentrated offices and institutes of more sectoral ministries. The most important task of the 'County Public Administration Offices,' which reports to the Minister of the Interior, is the legal control of the local governments. This activity covers all local governments on the territory of the county but it does not affect the institutions, such as the schools, directly. The administration office may only establish the fact of law infringement and may call upon the local governments to amend the illegal situation within a given deadline. This task of the county administration office is carried out by comparing the documents. The office has also to guard the legality of local decisions concerning the merger, the abolition, the foundation, or sale of institutions.

The sub-offices of OKÉV, the main institution for regional educational administration are responsible for the administration of the tasks of OKÉV concerning evaluation, assessment and examination in their regions. The professional work of the sub-offices are divided by different specified fields (e.g. quality management of pre-school education) and some of the sub-offices gives the representative of the Minister of Education in the Council for Regional Development. The county labour centers work under the Ministry of Social and Family Affairs. Their most important task is to cater for the adult unemployed, but they also take part in matters of youth unemployment and provide for some forms of vocational training. They have some public administrative tasks, register the unemployed and they operate an information network on job vacancies and on options of re-training. These centers organize re-training and further training programs, the task that can be realized through contracts with the institutions of public education as well. The county labour centers co-ordinate the processes of regional interest-negotiation in the field of vocational training. The organ of this function is the county Vocational Training Council, where besides the representatives of the employers, the employees and the central government, the representatives of the local governments and of the regional economic chambers also take part. The county centres of labour affairs make decisions on the distribution of the Vocational Training Fund by taking the recommendations of these councils and by calling for applications.

1.4.3 Local Level

At the local level the majority of decisions concerning public education is made by the representative bodies elected by the inhabitants of the settlement. The president of the representative body, the *mayor*, is elected directly by the electorate. The *notary* of the settlement is entitled by the laws to make the majority of the decisions concerning public administration and other fields of authority. It is only at the bigger municipalities that there is a separate department for public education, which, however, also usually deals with other matters (such as youth, sports, health care and social affairs). Local governments have to set up committees of education if there are at least three educational institutions maintained by them. The majority of the members of this committee have to come from the elected representatives but most of them adopt external experts as well.

The content and extent of local level responsibility in Hungary does not depend on the size of the settlement. It is the same whether we take a small settlement with a few thousand inhabitants and only one school, or towns that have a full institutional structure in public education. The only exceptions to this are the cities with county rights, which enjoy similar rights and responsibilities as the counties.

The scope of local responsibilities is very wide. Yet—to make public education more unified and to enhance equity nation-wide—there have been a number of legal regulations issued in the past few years to mark out the boundaries within which these responsibilities can be exercised.

The contents of local responsibilities according to the major administrative functions are there as follows. The local governments have to provide the inhabitants of the settlements with the services of kindergarten and basic school education. Within this general obligation the local government can decide about the foundation, the maintenance, the re-organization, the abolition of an educational institution, and about setting up an association or a co-operation agreement with another local government. Since 1999 local settlements, having at least two educational institutions have to form their middle-term plans. The educational provision for the children of the settlement and the development of the institutional network have to be included in the plans, which have to take also the county level plans into consideration.

The obligation to provide educational services does not mean that the local government actually has to maintain a school. The provision can also be fulfilled by schools of other settlements or the local body can enter into co-operation, form associations, or can make a contract with other maintainers (such as a foundation) for the provision of educational services.

The local governments can regulate the period and way of enrolment in the kindergartens and schools, and they map out the enrolment districts. The local governments generally do these tasks by issuing local decrees.

There are local tasks concerning the teaching personnel. The head of a local government-maintained institution is appointed by the local body of representatives, which acts as the head's employer. This also means that the work of the head has to be assessed and controlled by the body. Even though the employer of the teachers is the school head, the number of the teachers employed can be regulated by the local governments, which determines—within the general framework of the Public Education Act—the kinds of tasks the school has to fulfil and by determining the number of pupils in the school groups or classes. The local representative body can make a decision on different indicators from those are given by the Act in case they are able to finance the extra costs.

The most important element of administration concerning educational content is that the schools' pedagogical programs and the local curricula within them are approved by the local governments. During the adoption of the programs the local governments can assert the demands of a local educational policy. It has to be stressed that during the adoption of the schools' pedagogical programs the local governments can only examine the programs' legal and financial aspects, they are not allowed to issue an opinion on the professional-pedagogical content. This can only be carried out by the experts who are listed in the National List of Experts, and whose opinion the local governments have to ask for.

The tasks of the local body include to pass decisions in issues of educational administration and to control legally the operation of schools. The most important form of fulfilling these tasks is the adoption of the documents that are drawn up by the school staffs, regulating the internal operation of kindergartens and schools. There are some other means for the maintainers to control the schools' legality of operations. The local governments may pass decrees in which they determine what information and data the schools have to provide for them. It is the notary of the local government who may control whether the laws and regulations are abided by all the educational institutions of the settlement.

It is also the task of the local governments to assess the quality of the professional work of their schools. The form of this assessment is regulated by the Public Education Act: the assessment can be based on an expert opinion, on the report handed in by the school, or on the opinion of the school board. As a result of this evaluation process, the maintaining local government may commission the institution or its head with further tasks. Research has, however, shown that a majority of local governments neglect the task of institutional assessment.

1.4.4   Institutional Level

There is a wide range of responsibilities and decision-making competencies for the institutional actors, school heads and teaching staff, who, in a lot of cases, have to consult, or reach agreements with other actors.

The head of the educational institution is responsible for the professional and legal operation and responsible for the careful economy of the institute. He/she is the employer of the teaching and non-teaching personnel. The head decides about the issues of teacher promotion and changes in salary with the obligation to consult the opinion of the bodies of interest negotiation. The head assigns the tasks of the teachers after consulting the opinion of the school departments. Under certain conditions the school head may reduce the number of compulsory hours taught by a teacher. The evaluation of the work of individual teachers is carried out by the head. The head of the school or kindergarten is responsible for the pedagogical work of the institution and for the operation of the assessment, evaluation and quality assurance system of that.[41] He/she is responsible for the tasks related to health care and social protection of the young.

In pedagogical issues the teaching staff can make most of the decisions. The pedagogical programme (LPP), the local curricula (LC), the applied programs and methods, the selection of textbooks and teaching aids, all belong to the decision-making competencies of the teaching staff. The strong position of the teaching staffs can be highlighted by the fact that they can file in an appeal at a court if their maintainer does not approve of their pedagogical program. The yearly plan of the school's operation is prepared also by the school staff.

The organizational and operational regulations of the school and the rules of the building are drawn up by the head and adopted by the teaching staff. During the adoption or the modification of both these documents the agreement of the school board and the self-governing body of the students has to be asked for. The head is obliged to carry out consultations in every issue concerning the operation of the institution with the school staff, the school board, the self-governing body of students, and with the local council for public employees.

Table 2.1

The Main Levels and Actors of Public Education in Hungary

Actor Level	Political Level	Administrative Level	Professional Level	Bodies of Social/Other Interests, Partners Involvement
National	• Parliament • Parliament Committee for Education, Scientific, Youth and Sport Affairs	• National Government • Ministry of Education (OM) • Ministry of Interior (BM) • Ministry of Finance (PM) • Other Ministries • National Public Education and Examination Centre (OKÉV) • Office of the Commissioner of Educational Rights	• National Institute of Public Education (OKI) • Hungarian Institute for Educational Research (OI) • National Institute of Vocational Education (NSZI) • Kiss Árpád National Service Office of Public Education (KÁ OKSZI) • Methodology and Information Centre for In-service Teacher Training (PTMIK) • COMENIUS 2000 Programme Office	• National Public Education Council (OKNT) • Council of Public Education (KT) • National Council for Vocational Training (OSZT) • National Council for Minorities • Council for the Reconciliation of Interest of Public Institutions (KIÉT) • Council for the Reconciliation of Interests in Public Education (KÖÉT) • Teachers' unions (PSZ, PDSZ, other) • National Council for Students' Rights

Table 2.1 (continued)

The Main Levels and Actors of Public Education in Hungary

Actor Level	Political Level	Administrative Level	Professional Level	Bodies of Social/Other Interests, Partners Involvement
Regional (r: statistical region; c: county)	• County Governments • Committee of Education (c) • Committee of Vocational Education (c), (r in some regions)	• Educational Department of County Administration Office • County head notary • Regional Units of OKÉV • Representative of the Minister of Education in the Council for Regional Development (RFT)	• County Pedagogical Institute (MPI) • Other educational service providers (NGOs, private firms, service associations) • Public education institutes, maintained by county governments	• Vocational Training Councils • Board of Trustees of Public Foundation for the Development of Public Education (c)
Local (settlement)	• Representative Body of local representatives • Committee of Education (and Youth, Culture, Sports)	• Educational Department of local government • Town notary	• Public education institutes	• Minorities' Authority
Institution		• School director • Teaching staff		• School Board • Students' Union Board • Public Employee's Council • Teachers' unions

The school board can contribute to enhance the co-operation among the school staff, the parents, the students, the maintainer, and any other organization concerned with the operation of the institution. The school board may formulate an opinion about all the questions and issues of the school but in certain instances, such as the adoption of the school's pedagogical program, it is compulsory to consult it. It is also the school board that can decide about the usage of the school's own incomes that are generated through some economic enterprise. The Act on the Public Employees rules that at the institutional level the representative trade union has the right to set up a collective contract with the employer. A Council for Public Employees has to be formed at every institution, which has consultative rights in issues of teachers' employment and salaries.

1.5 Expenditure Assignment and the Institutional Setting of Financing the Public Education System

In the decentralized system of public education in Hungary the lower tier of government plays a dominant role. Schools are financed by the local governments that at the same time receive subsidies from the central budget. One of the most important characteristics of public education finance is the marked distinction between financial flows from the central to the local or county government level and from the latter to the school level (see Figure 2.2). Note that regarding the main financial flows, the county governments are in a similar position to local governments, i.e. county governments play no intermediary role in financial flows from the central to the local level (though county governments have intermediate level co-ordinatory functions). At the same time decentralized government funds are managed at the county level, without a direct relationship to county governments' school maintainer role.

Local governments have two kind of revenue sources: local revenues and central governmental transfers. Own revenues include local taxes (the most significant being the local business tax), rent revenues, fees, user charges, surplus of financial investment activities and revenues from selling property. The most important types of transfers are shared taxes[42] (the dominant in this category is the personal income tax), lump-sum formula grants and earmarked discretionary grants for investment projects. In general, the share of transfers in local governmental revenues has decreased in the last decade. However, one of the key characteristics of the Hungarian local governmental system is the imbalance between the exceptionally wide expenditure assignment and the restricted revenue assignment. Though the share of transfers in local governmental revenues was constantly decreasing in the last decade, the majority of municipalities (typically smaller villages) are still dependent on central governmental grants due to the poor local tax base. County governments are not allowed to levy taxes; the majority of their revenues consists of central transfers.

Local and county governments receive the central transfers from the Ministry of Interior. Since the central governmental budget is put forward by the Ministry of Finance, probably these two ministries play the most important role in deciding on the amount of grants, but others, like the Ministry of Education are also involved (especially in setting the relative shares of different grants within the category of formula grants for education). However, setting the actual amount of formula grants for education, the central government is constrained by an element of guarantee: the total sum transferred to local and county governments can not be less than the 90% of the expenditures on education of lower tiers of government two years anterior (excluding capital expenditures).

Formula grants for school maintenance are computed on a per student basis. These grants are not earmarked, i.e. local or county governments may use this amount as they wish, and not exclusively on education services. The only requirement is the continuous compliance with the standards of general legal and educational regulation. However, as the amount of these grants is regularly below the minimum costs of providing education,[43] in fact all local and county governments spend more on schools than the grant they receive for this purpose, i.e. formula grants for education have to be supplemented by school owners. Thus local and county governments allocate some of other transfers and/or own revenues to school finance. Note that while maintainers of schools are subsidised on a per student formula basis (excluding development grants), school finance at the local level usually follows a different logic: the method of allocating funds for particular schools in the annual local budget is at the discretion of the local and county governments. The allocation is most frequently the result of a bargaining process between schools and maintainers, based on budget shares of the previous year. The implementation of a local formula financing scheme is a rare exception.

It is important to note, that changes in per student formula grants are very poor measures of the fiscal burden that the maintenance of educational institutions imposes on local governments. Formula grants are only one component of central transfers and whether local governments are in a loose or stressed fiscal position can be judged only with respect to transfers as a whole, together with changes in expenditure and revenue assignment (e.g. responsibilities for additional services delegated to local governments and changes in local tax rules). Thus there is no direct relationship between changes in formula grants for education and government spending on education.

From the middle of the 1990s the system of formula grants became more and more differentiated. The central government aimed at representing the diversity of average costs in the school system in details; different amounts were assigned to years in primary and secondary school education and several additional elements were introduced (e.g. disadvantaged Roma children taking part in an ethnic programme, teaching minority languages, or for students commuting from other settlements). By the second half of the decade the necessity to reduce the complexity of the grant system became evident, and has been implemented so. However, later this shift has been reversed. While the formula grants subsidise the operation of schools, earmarked development grants are for local and county governments to finance investment projects in the physical educational infrastructure. The scope of the potentially subsidised projects and the maximum rate of cost coverage is defined by the central government (e.g. building classrooms or student dormitories). Local governmental applications for the grant are evaluated by the Ministry of Interior on a discretionary basis. After the investment projects have been carried out, local governments have to account for the usage of the grant.

Figure 2.2

Main Financial Flows in the Hungarian Public Education System

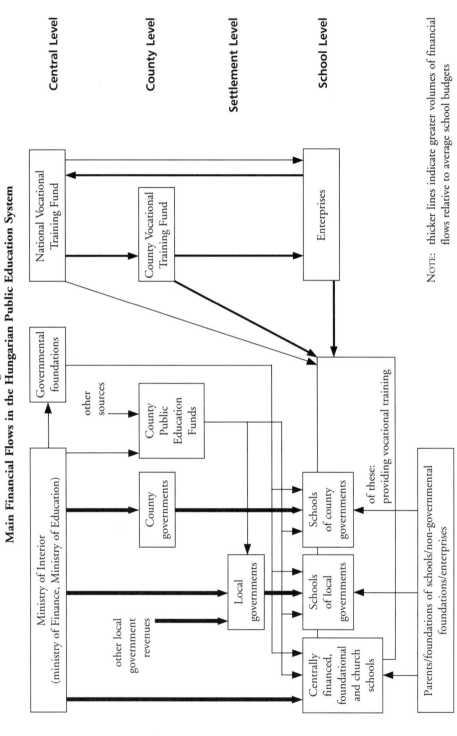

Central Level

County Level

Settlement Level

School Level

NOTE: thicker lines indicate greater volumes of financial flows relative to average school budgets

Formula grants for education are not limited to owners of schools in the government sector, but all other organizations (foundations, churches) operating primary or secondary schools are entitled to be granted. Moreover, church schools receive an additional per student transfer equal to the average per student expenditure that local and county governments spend on the schools above the formula grant.

Beside central governmental transfers, three other channels of financial flows have to be mentioned. The most important of these are the Vocational Training Fund financed by the employers in proportion to paid out wages. The Vocational Training Fund and its county level decentralized funds subsidise development projects in schools providing vocational training. Schools may apply for the grant and National and County Vocational Training Councils decide on the applications.[44] Employers may also earmark part of their charge for particular schools. Moreover, enterprises, where vocational training students are working as apprentices are also allowed to apply for transfers from the National and the County Vocational Training Funds.

Local governments and schools have access to resources from other funds in the government sector as well. Examples are central governmental foundations (e.g. the Foundation for the Modernisation of Public Education) and County Public Education Funds.

Finally, schools receive a small proportion of their revenues from outside the government sector: sources from non-governmental foundations, charges for non-curriculum courses (e.g. language teaching), rent revenues from school buildings and so on. Grants from non-governmental foundations can be substantial in the case of non-governmental schools.

2. EFFECTIVENESS, EFFICIENCY AND EQUITY PROBLEMS IN THE PUBLIC EDUCATION SECTOR

2.1 Effectiveness of the Public Education

In the last decade, the proportion of students in each cohort accomplishing secondary school, as well as those achieving a college or university degree, has been steadily growing. The expansion of secondary education, which was not accompanied by increasing dropout rates,[45] may suggest that the effectiveness of the public education system has been substantially improved. More direct measures of effectiveness (standardized test results for example), however, contradict this optimistic view. The expansion process mirrors the dissolving barriers on the supply side and the increase in the demand for education, resulting in growing differences among secondary schools.[46] In this section first the empirical evidence on student's performance is summarized, then the special problems of small village schools are mentioned, finally educational quality is analysed in the broader context of school management and quality control. Beside small village schools there is another segment in the public education system struggling with devastating problems of effectiveness: technical schools. The problems of these are discussed below in the section on equity.

2.1.1 Students' Achievement: Trends and International Comparison

Probably the most direct measures of the gross effectiveness of the school system is provided by standardized test results. In Hungary, a series of standardized test surveys have been carried out and some results of comparative international survey evidence is also available.[47]

The general conclusion is that results decrease and stagnate over time in several fields.

In reading and understanding written texts a significant[48] deterioration can be observed between 1986 and 1995 (both in the case of graduating students of general and secondary schools). The decreasing level of reading comprehension is especially alarming because this kind of competence is a basis for many other skills. In 1999 the overall results measured by standard scores were similar to that of 1995. As far as text-types are concerned, results were somewhat lower with document-type texts, and higher with the other two types and with general cognitive abilities. The favorable and unfavorable changes thus compensate each other, and on the whole reading-comprehension performance is basically identical with the results from four years ago. From 1995 to 1999 the negative trend seems to have stopped at the eighth grade[49] [Vári et. al., 2000a, Vári et. al., 2000b]. In mathematics, changes in students' results are not so sharp as in reading competencies, though the picture is far from reassuring. In the case of students at the eight grade a decreasing trend can be found in each period between 1996 and 1999 with one exception (the surveys of 1995 and 1997 provided similar results) [Vári, 1999, Vári et. al., 2000a]. Regarding students at the fourth, tenth and twelfth grades, positive changes between two waves of the survey have eventually occured, but for the longer period of 1986–1997 the negative trend seems to be prevailing [Vári, 1999]. Between 1995 and 1999 Monitor surveys make comparison in two domains, both in connection with applied mathematics: in performing algebraic-calculation and text-based tasks. In contrast to reading-comprehension results, the 1999 results in this domain fell behind the 1995 results. Although the difference is little, the trend raises concern. The standard deviation of performance grew as well.

The knowledge level of students in natural sciences (biology [the living world], physics, geology) has dropped to a smaller, yet significant degree. The decrease was larger in the case of biology and geology, which fell almost similarly, while this drop was somewhat smaller in the case of physics.

Concerning information and communication technology skills and attitudes, the 1999 survey makes 1995 data comparable in software-related and applied knowledge-areas. Both domains present a significant improvement in performance: the standard scores of 1999 are 62.8 points higher on average than the 1995 scores. This reflects the effect of regular computer use and the widespread use of certain programs and appliances. It also shows that interest in ICT has shifted to younger age groups, and that attitudes towards ICT have clearly changed in a positive way.

Civic education and attitudes have been surveyed for the first time in the 1999 Monitor samples, with 14-year-old students.[50] There were both cognitive questions on democracy and the economy and attitude questions on democracy and politics, national identity, and social cohesion and divergence. The students' economic knowledge is fairly unsteady, although analysis of the data also revealed some lingual-cultural correlation. There was an item on the non-democratic functioning of the state, which proved to be difficult, as only 43.3% of students marked the correct answer. The answers to attitude-items clearly indicated that for most young people (very similarly to the adult population) democracy denotes a welfare state, and that within civic rights they consider social rights superior to political ones.

Regarding standardized test results in international comparison, the situation is alarming, especially with respect to reading competencies. A recent international survey (SIALS) of literacy (i.e. reading competencies) of the adult population shows that Hungarians perform only slightly better than the group of four countries (out of 22) with the weakest results[51] [for the SIALS results see Vári et. al, 2001]. The analysis classified the respondents into five categories as: first (very poor skills: difficulties in the understanding of simple texts), second (poor skills: understanding simple, clearly structured texts, but difficulties with more complex ones), third (average skills, sufficient for everyday activities) and fourth-fifth (good or excellent skills). In Hungary 60–80% of the respondents has shown very poor or poor skills, while in the best-performing Scandinavian countries 60–70% has been classified into the good or excellent category.

The IEA TIMSS-survey of 1995 allows for an international comparison of student performance in mathematics and natural sciences.[52] The survey examined nine (third and fourth grade) and thirteen year old students (seventh and eighth grade), and also school-leavers who leave public education once and for all. The school-leavers category covers three groups: school-leavers of grammar and vocational schools (also called 'twelfth-graders' in Hungary), and tenth-graders of vocational training schools (who, strictly speaking, do not belong to the category of school-leavers, but for whom public education has finished in the sense that in the last year they do not usually study general subjects).

A special test, which made the study of mathematical and natural science education possible, was devised for the school-leavers. The results indicated that Hungarian students perform well below the international average. In the domain of mathematics Hungary finished fourteenth out of twenty-one, and in the case of natural sciences only eighteenth. The results of this age group are not as good as those of younger generations. The data draws attention to the assumption that the problems of student performance particularly occur in upper grades. The ranking did not change even if only the best-performing 25% of students from all countries were taken into consideration. As for the divergence of the performance of different age groups from the international average, we can distinguish between four groups of countries. In the first group the performance of school-leavers is below average, whilst that of the younger age groups is above average. In the second group, the performance of younger age groups is weaker and that of older students is stronger than the international average. In the third and fourth groups the performance is better than the international average in all age groups, but whereas school-leavers in the third group show a decreasing tendency, those in the fourth are improving. Hungary clearly belongs to the first group: for example, although students in lower grades achieve results in mathematics that are improving and which are well above international average as they progress in the system, performance in final grades is well below the international average. Results in natural sciences show a similar tendency.

The international comparison of students' knowledge in mathematics (known as TIMMS) seems to be less disturbing at the eighth grade: Hungarian students' average performance has been ranked at tenth out of the twenty-five countries surveyed. However, the Hungarian participants in these surveys emphasize that students' average performance in Hungary reaches its peak in an international comparison at the eighth grade, and relatively declines later, in part probably due to the low fraction (compared to the OECD countries) of students in general upper-secondary education as opposed to vocational secondary education and technical schools.[53]

No comprehensive empirical research evidence is available in the exploration and measurement of the causes behind the declining (or in some cases: static) trends in average student performance. It is worth to note, that in the last decade (and in the 1990s compared to the previous decades), the human capital has become more and more valuable in the labor market [see e.g. Varga, 1995]. At the same time, the proportion of students in general and especially in general vocational schools has been on the increase, whilst technical schools are losing ground. These facts suggest that the demand for public education can be expected to increase. Thus, it is plausible that the school system and educational policy is to be blamed for the unfavorable changes in students' performance.

2.1.2   Small Village Schools

Regarding the effectiveness of public education, village schools are frequently referred to as having special problems. Analyses of standardized test survey data regularly report significantly lower results in villages compared to towns and the capital [Vári et. al. 1998, Vári et. al. 2000b, see also below in the section on *Equity*]. It can be argued that the effectiveness of these schools is also weaker than the average in other dimensions like the socialization of students.[54]

Nevertheless, it should be emphasized here that small village schools vary widely with respect to their effectiveness. This variation in most part reflects differrences in the social composition of the settlements. Segregated poor villages with a high percentage of Romani people represent one extreme case, while at the other extreme, interestingly enough, one can often find villages of other ethnic minorities (for example Germans). In better-off villages, minority culture puts an extra emphasis on schools, since these have an exceptional role in preserving minority language and ethnic identity.

In the majority of small village schools the effectiveness of education is both constrained by the available teaching staff and the problems of physical school infrastructure.[55]

Regarding the upper-cycle of general schools (5–8th grades) the quality of teaching in many cases is obviously limited by the fact that schools can not employ enough teachers specialized in different subjects. This is mainly due to financial constraints: per student expenditures would increase substantially by employing teachers who can cover each of the subjects prescribed by the curricula, even if only average wages were paid, while, at the same time, sufficing the full demand for teachers in small villages would require a higher than average wage.

In many cases, the extremely low number of students forces small village schools to merge classes at different grades. Experts usually agree that this is an unfavorable (and, in fact, infrequent) practice at the upper-cycle, the quality of education in merged classes at the lower-cycle of general schools (1–4th grades) is a highly debated and more open issue. However, small-sample survey research suggests that merged classes are less popular among parents in small villages than distinct classes,[56] thus parents seem to be more inclined to send their children to bigger schools in other settlements if the local school provides teaching in merged classes.

Another aspect of quality problems in a group of village schools is related to changes in student composition due to different forms of segregation. Firstly, in the transition period, presumably new migration patterns appeared, enhancing social disparities among small settlements: lower housing and living costs motivated poor, unemployed families to move from towns and the capital to declining villages.[57] Secondly, in villages of agglomeration areas children of better-off families often commute to more prestigious schools in towns or other villages in the neighbour-hood, and thus the segregation of the poor, and often Romani children frequently goes together with declining quality. This can be explained by several factors. In theory the positive external or peer-group effects can be expected to diminish in this situation, thus resulting in worse results on average.[58] A more important factor is probably that schools with high rates of disadvantaged students are less attractive for teachers, making it difficult to employ the best teaching staff. Case studies suggest that student composition in terms of social background has a non-linear effect on the effectiveness of schools. Some kind of threshold value of disadvantaged students can be expected to exist: if the ratio of these students is below 20–40%, their presence seems to have no substantial effect on school choice of other families, while above this value it is difficult (i.e. requires exceptional efforts in the form of a uniquely attractive pedagogical program) to escape the processes leading to segregation.[59]

Nevertheless, the group of small village schools is obviously characterized by enormous variation regarding both effectiveness, educational quality and students' social background. Thus, though students' attainment is lower than in towns on average, it would be misleading to forget about the exceptions, which produce just as good results as the better schools in towns, despite of all the disadvantages.

2.1.3 School Management

Decentralization, deregulation and pluralization in education gave Hungarian school directors a broad range of autonomy in school level issues. School heads are appointed for five years after an open application procedure by the school maintainers since 1985.

Besides responsibilities in strategic and operative management, the development of human resources of the school, including the employment of school staff, has a more important role in the professional management of the school (and it has a growing relevance also for the local community).

As it was outlined before, due to the two-level content regulation in Hungary, prescribing to follow the state level frame regulation, based on the National Core Curriculum and the Frame Curriculum, the Local Pedagogical Program (LPP) and as a part of it, Local Curricula (LC) are developed by the school staff, though it is the maintainers' authority to accept or reject these. LPP and LC are the main documents of the pedagogical work of schools and school heads have an authoritative role in the preparation and implementation. LPP includes the pedagogical principles, goals, tasks, tools and methods of teaching and socialization, ways of differentiation (e.g. talent development and dealing with handicapped children), the list of school equipment and the system of evaluation, measurement and quality management of school. LC includes the description of obligatory and optional subjects by classes, their contact hours, syllabi and requirements, textbooks and teaching materials, conditions of student flow and the ways of pupils' recitation. LPP serves as a basic document for both the maintainer and the local community, informing them about the value orientation, teaching content, methods and evaluation of the school.

The changes in content regulation on the one hand and state regulation to ensure the minimal quality of school equipment on the other can cause financial problems for schools. The acceptance of the LPP and LC by the school maintainer means to accept the the tasks to be financed. However, sometimes the necessary budgetary resources are not always available for the schools. A 1999 survey shows the opinion of secondary school heads about the demands for extra sources needed for the new curricula. The likely increase is highest at the instrumental needs (4.63 point is in average at a five-grade scale; in secondary vocational schools is 4.77 and vocational schools 4.78), but operational costs are also deemed to be increasing substantially (4.42 point).

Partly independently from the introduction of the new content regulation, in 1999 a new standard for the minimal equipment of schools was introduced by law that is to be in effect from 2003. An increasing amount of resources from the central budget is devoted for this purpose (delivered via the County Public Foundations for the development of public education) but—due to experts' opinion and preliminary official estimates—it is likely that a great portion of schools cannot meet the minimal standards. It is a challenge for both the maintainer and for the school management to cope with this problem.

School heads have autonomy in the human resource management of the schools. Employment and waging of both teachers and other members of staff are at the discretion of school heads. In municipality schools all the staff members are public employees; the employment criteria prescribes to ensure the minimal wage (which is different at levels of professional qualification and working period). This requirement theoretically allows to differentiate among teachers, but in fact there is almost no room for this, due to given local budgetary constraints and the generally low level of wages. This tripartite system among the state, the maintainer and the school head in the present circumstances cannot stimulate a quality-based human resource management. To solve the financial constraints, school heads often use other ways of employment, for example by yearly contracts, part-time employment, or by offering teachers to give their lessons as enterpreneurs. The increasing local autonomy and the new challenges faced by the schools during the transition process resulted in a growing role for local initiatives in Hungarian schools in the 1990s. Approximately 20% of schools had a new curriculum and syllabi before the NCC. Preparing the new LPPs can be seen as a general innovation of schools, which resulted in 'individual' curricula in 8% of general and 15% of secondary schools,[60] while in most cases curricula developed by others elsewhere, were adapted to fit into the local goals. The procedure was supported by new kinds of teacher and manager in-service trainings.[61] Some additional indicators show other aspects of innovation and growing openness. School level foundations are nearly general characteristics of educational institutes. They give a very limited part of the school budget but serve special purposes, which is important for the families and for the professionals of schools (e.g. extra-curricular activities, outdoor programs, and so on). Participation in EU programmes since 1996 improves the perspectives of schools; it is also growing at the general level of education.

The expanding autonomy of schools, the societal transition period, the demographic decline of pupils and the reforms of education enforced some changes in attitudes of school management towards adaptation and innovation. From the late 1980s, new management skills emerged as a response to an uncertain, changing environment.[62] Local needs and conditions had to be considered by schools from the early 1990s, and it became the main dimension in the process of preparing LPPs and LCs. In these processes new elements of management cultures (e.g. managing professional debates, solving conflicts, and so on) and of management of professional promotion had to appear (even those schools where the 'own' professional development was limited). The organization culture has changed mostly in schools participating in new kinds of targeted trainings or programs. The changing role of school headteachers in not a very reassuring environment (due to fiscal pressures, demographic decline) has made the profession less attractive. It was proven by a survey in 1996/97 (with 1 200 school headteachers), that nearly half of the existing school heads do not want to apply again for the position. The newly appointed school heads, coming mainly from teaching practice, seemed to be less content with the perspectives than those who practiced a longer period as directors.[63]

2.2 Efficiency Problems in the Public Education Sector

Educational researchers still have not come up with a comprehensive empirical analysis of the efficiency of the Hungarian public education system. This is in part due to the lack of appropriate data.

School can be considered efficient[64] if the maximum level of output defined in terms of student's achievement in different fields of knowledge (or enrolment rate in the next level of education) is reached, given the amount of school inputs and student characteristics. An equivalent formulation requires a minimum amount of school inputs used to attain a given level of output, under given student characteristics. Behind this definition, a simple characterization of educational production lies: the final output of schools (defined in terms of student achievement) is a function of the intermediate output (depending on school resources and school management) and certain environmental factors (especially the students' socio-economic background), that are basically[65] beyond the discretion of schools.[66] It is crucial to take into account environmental factors in measuring efficiency, since ignoring this factor can easily lead to classifying schools with more disadvantaged students inefficient and schools working in a more favorable social environment efficient, irrespective of their actual performance. To put it in another way, efficiency should measure the 'added value' or additional contribution of schools to students' knowledge and skills. Efficiency can be analyzed empirically using different kind of models (e.g. estimating student-level production functions or analyzing cost functions at the school or a school district/local government level). In any case, school inputs, student characteristics and final outputs have to be taken into consideration directly or indirectly.[67]

Unfortunately, in Hungary, no student level sample data appropriate for estimating inefficiencies (i.e. describing students achievements, family characteristics and individual school inputs at the same time) are available. Moreover, aggregate data are problematic as well. For example, no data is available on expenditures at the school level, and since 1997, even municipality level expenditures cannot be assigned to different levels of education. Thus, only hypothetical conclusions can be drawn from existing data, without any firm empirical analysis to build on.

Looking at changes in the Hungarian public education system in the last decade three main sources of efficiency problems seem to be prevalent:

1)   extra costs related to economies of scale in the case of small village schools;

2)   a weak adjustment to demographic trends;

3)   side-effects of structural changes, mainly at the level of upper-secondary education.

The three problems may be different in terms of the magnitude of efficiency losses, but all three are more or less related to the decentralization of responsibilities in the Hungarian public education system. However, these three factors do not provide an exhaustive list of efficiency loss sources that are present in the public education system. Additional costs related to management failures are assumed to be prevalent as well,[68] but very little is known about the extent and the distribution of these efficiency losses, thus we do not discuss these in detail. The substantial increase of the share of non-teaching, physical employees in the public education sector between 1992 and 1997 [Varga, 2001] may indicate this kind of efficiency losses.

Though problems related to economies of scale are not confined to villages, it is usually formulated in this way in political and professional discourses. However, since in fact it is the most common in villages and in towns, it is closely related to, and less general than, the broader problem of the declining number of students. Therefore we will discuss economies of scale in small villages in a separate section.

2.2.1   Economies of Scale and Small Village Schools

Probably the most highlighted and debated efficiency problem in educational policy in the last decade is that of economies of scale in small village general schools.

More than half of the general schools are in settlements where only one school is at work, and a substantial share of these are small in size. Approximately half of the municipalities with less than one thousand inhabitants maintain a general school. In the 1998/99 school year 25% of the general schools had less than 100 pupils, while less than 5% of the students attended these schools.[69] Though a growing number of these small schools provide education only at the 1–4th grade, in many cases a complete general school is maintained.

In small schools class sizes, class per teacher and pupil per teacher ratios are unavoidably lower than average,[70] driving per student costs up. Empirical analysis of economies of scale shows that per student cost declines sharply with school size in the lowest range.[71] Schools may somewhat reduce average costs by operating merged classes of students at different grades. In these cases, the average costs may even be halved, but this still remains a multiple that of larger schools. This school structure is in part the consequence of the fragmented local governmental structure that came into being in 1990: many local governments established new schools in small villages, where there was no school before or re-established schools which were closed in the 1970s. The problem is not an easy one to solve: local governments and villages usually consider the local school as being the essence of local autonomy. Furthermore, the existence of a local school may have positive external effects: schools may contribute to the development of the settlement and mitigate out-migration. School closures would also incur transportation (or student dormitory) costs, and possibly other indirect costs as well (e.g. higher rate of children not finishing general school). On the other hand, it is often questioned by experts whether these small schools can provide education of an acceptable quality (see above).

Central government policies were developed to diminish efficiency losses related to economies of scale. First, financial incentives were implemented to urge co-operation among local governments in maintaining schools in the form of local governmental associations. However, most of the local governments were unwilling to co-operate or in some cases only formal co-operation was established in order to access to the additional subsidies. Secondly, local governments of small villages may receive additional subsidies for school maintenance, covering total costs on average, if only the lower cycle of primary education (1–4th grade) is provided. The latter, newer and more radical measure seems to be more effective.

However, natural limits exist in the exploitation economies of scale. In certain areas of the country, school consolidation is not a viable option due to the low density of the settlement structure and the related excessive commuting times and transportation costs.

Finally, it has to be emphasized, that, although small village schools are probably the most frequently mentioned sources of inefficiencies, it is not an easy task to find the best solution for the problem. Besides the extent of direct costs of inefficiencies (i.e. economies of scale minus the cost of other options, e.g. transportation), two other equally or even more important factors have to be taken into consideration as well. These are the social significance of and the preference for these schools in their localities and problems of educational quality and effectiveness.

2.2.2 Weak Adjustment to Demographic Change

The number of children born has been decreasing in the last decades, sometimes with smaller upward swings as echoes of former larger generations. The number of pupils entering the school system in the last decade is constantly decreasing. The decrease in general schools was around 20% between 1989 and 1999 [Sugár, 1999]. Less populous generations reached the secondary schools around the middle of the 1990s. Moreover, in the short-run, a further decrease in the number of births and school-aged children can be expected.[72]

It seems obvious that from an economic point of view, but probably not only in this respect, the primary education system has not been properly adjusted to these changes. The average number of students per class decreased by ten% from 1990 to 1998 in general schools (class size also decreased in the general secondary schools). The number of teachers has not followed the decreasing number of school-aged children. The consequences of the weak adjustment to the demographic trend can be observed at the municipality level: the smaller is the school-aged population in 1996 relative to 1990, the smaller is the pupil per teacher ratio, ceteris paribus.[73] However, since no appropriate sample data at the student level is available on students' achievements, family characteristics and individual school inputs, which would make possible the econometric analysis of the problem, considering the decreasing pupil per teacher ratio as an indicator of growing inefficiencies, remains a hypothesis. This interpretation is usually debated by referring to the point that from a pedagogical point of view, decreasing class sizes are favorable, and probably results in a higher quality of education. This counter-argument has two components (or two forms at the extremes). First, reducing class sizes and the number of lessons per teacher may be a consciously chosen instrument to enhance the effectiveness of education, thus reflecting local preferences for better educational quality. Second, better quality teaching may rise from changes in the student/teacher ratio as an unintended side-effect of sluggishness in the adjustment to demographic change. Even in the second case one should not consider the declining student/teacher ratio as an indicator of inefficiency, since rising per student costs are offset by better quality. Since the lack of data makes it impossible to measure changes in the output relative to changes in inputs of education, this reference for the possible pedagogical gains can not be directly refuted. Below we argue that better educational quality is not likely to be a major explanation behind changes in the utilization of school capacities.

Firstly, analyzing the available financial data seems to support the hypothesis of increasing efficiency problems. Comparing local governments, where the number of students decreased in a greater extent in the last decade, the pupil per teacher ratio is generally lower. The fact that indicators of the utilization of school resources correlate with the rate of demographic change suggests an inflexible adaptation of local education systems to demographic changes.

Secondly, it is contestable that schools generally can capitalize substantial gains in pedagogical quality related to decreasing class sizes (whether it is a policy instrument or the result of weak adjustment). No convincing empirical results for Hungary is available in this respect and answering the question requires not only detailed and reliable data, but a careful analysis as well. Though, from a pedagogical point of view one could expect a negative relationship between class size and students' results, in fact, probably a positive correlation could be found due to the disparities between institutions and school choice. The most prestigious schools producing the highest acceptance rates in upper levels of education usually work with the largest classes in average, due to their popularity, i.e. these schools can better utilize teaching capacities at hand. Moreover, since prestigious schools may select students with good abilities and strong motivation, these in part statistically unobservable student characteristics are difficult to control for in estimates of school inputs' effects on student achievement. It is interesting to note here that empirical data on students' knowledge in average (at the aggregate level) shows that no significant improvement in the different dimensions of standardized test results has been achieved in the last decade, especially before 1997 i.e. the period of declining student/teacher ratio in general schools.[74]

Third, since teacher wages are extremely low relative to per capita GDP compared to the OECD countries, it seems plausible that given the existing financial constraints, raising wages and with this teachers' motivation would be a more effective policy instrument than maintaining low wages and relatively low class sizes in order to enhance school quality. Low wages affect educational quality not only through the motivation of the actual teaching staff. Another important factor is that better qualified teachers with a marketable specialization (e.g. languages, information technology) tend to leave the education system expecting higher income in the business sector. At the same time, there is a relatively abundant supply of young teachers, especially with a BA degree. Thus low wages result in a change in the composition of teachers: the ratio of better-qualified teachers (as measured by the ratio of teachers with an MA degree) has decreased in the 1990s.[75] The problem of low wages and that of efficiency losses is linked in another way as well: if the utilization of the public education capacities remains at the actual low level, or even decreases further, raising teacher wages (a declared goal of the present government) would require to spend substantial additional resources for education at the macro-level.

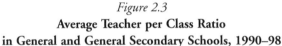

Figure 2.3
**Average Teacher per Class Ratio
in General and General Secondary Schools, 1990–98**

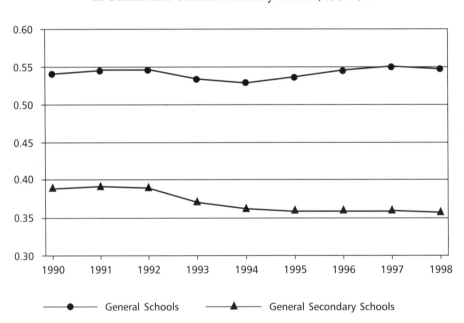

The argument above suggests that a weak adjustment to the demographic trend resulted in efficiency losses in primary education. This does not contradict the fact that per student expenditure has decreased in 1995 and 1996 (data are not available for later years). The allocation of resources has changed: both the pupil per teacher ratio and teachers' average salaries have decreased.

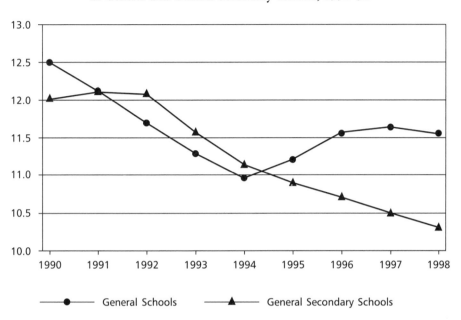

Figure 2.4
**Average Student per Teacher Ration
in General and General Secondary Schools, 1990–98**

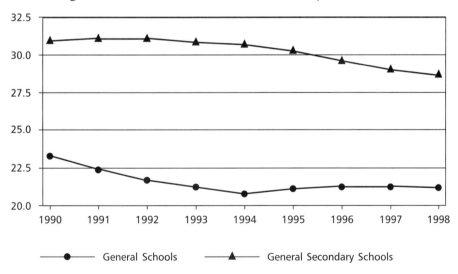

Figure 2.5
Average Class Size in General and General Secondary Schools, 1990–98

How can this weak adjustment be explained? It can be argued that the central government has missed to use certain instruments that would fit in its strategy aiming at reducing employment in education (see section The effects of central government regulation on the utilization of school capacities below). However, the main factor seems to be the risk of high political costs of cutting back educational institutions.

We argue that at the heart of the efficiency problems related to demographic change, there lies the unwillingness of both the central and local level of government to take on the political responsibility of unpopular school closures. The situation can be interpreted as some kind of 'decentralization trap', reflecting the interrelated choices of strategies of the central and local governments.

When the problem was first on the political agenda in 1995 and 1996, the central government did not come up with a direct policy, but urged local governments to take on the responsibility of cutting back the local school system. When the central government, after political conflicts with Teachers' Union raised wages in the public sector, only part of this increment was covered by central grants, the remaining sum was claimed to be financed by local governments from the savings by the reduction of teaching staff. Though, given the decentralized assignment of governmental functions, the central government has no authority to intervene into local school management, a more determined central policy could be adopted.[76] On the other side, most local governments have not decided to or not succeeded in school closures or in lay-offs, i.e. local governments typically tried to resist the central government's initiated policy in order to escape the high political costs incurred by unpopular decisions (in cases where local government leaders felt forced by fiscal stress to take unpopular decisions, they tried to transfer the political responsibility to the central level in the justification of the decisions). If the political costs altogether are greater than the potential savings, both the central and local governments can be expected to try to avoid the unpopularity of a direct school-closure policy. Even if savings exceed the political costs, it may be a reasonable local governmental strategy to wait for the central government to take the political responsibility (see also Annex 2).

Of course, the political cost that local governments face, as well as its perception by local leaders, vary substantially over municipalities. In many cases these costs may be excessively high due to the strong positions of local teachers and school directors in local governmental decision-making.[77] In these cases, local governments can be expected to resist the cut-backs until the very last moment. Regarding central governmental policies, in the period of fiscal restriction Teachers' Union guaranteed to keep potential political costs of decreasing employment in the education sector high.

In addition to the political costs, reducing efficiency losses would save resources for local governments only in the long-run and not in the actual year, when the local government should have paid more compensation for dismissed employees than it could have saved from salaries. Long-term benefits, however, can not be expected to count too much for several reasons. Firstly, in periods of severe fiscal stress, efforts are naturally focused on short-term solutions for the crisis. Secondly, local governments may hope that the central government policy urging the reduction of inefficiencies will be given up, due to economic growth and more abundant government revenues and/or to the resistance of local governments. Thirdly, long-term savings are uncertain as the central government may acquire the benefits by reducing transfers to local governments with the amount of savings.

Despite all of these difficulties, average class sizes began to increase somewhat in 1995 and 1996, but in 1998 the trend seems to turn to decreasing again (see Figures 2.3–2.5).

Altogether, the inefficiencies have not been reduced properly. Before 1994, efficiency was not an issue for the government. The number of lessons prescribed decreased in 1992 at the lower-secondary level, in order to avoid the employment problem related to demographic change, however, this change was reversed in 1996.[78]

In 1995–96, the central government did not come up with a direct policy to decrease employment in education, but tried to motivate local governments to handle the problem themselves mainly by decreasing the amount of central transfers. This way the short-run savings required by the fiscal restrictions have been realized, though not in the form of increased efficiency but in a less favorable way (i.e. keeping wages low and spending less on the physical infrastructure). Nevertheless, severe fiscal stress forced several local governments to reduce the number of teachers employed as well.

In 1997 and 1998, the government directed its attention towards reforming the content regulation of education and expected this to mitigate the employment problem as well.[79] Additional classes have been expected to absorb superfluous teaching capacities and the number of lessons has, in fact, grown.[80] Though in 1998 the new government changed the regulation to motivate local governments to increase efficiency, the existing regulatory framework seems to be ineffective.

In the case of primary education, efficiency problems related to the inappropriate adjustment to demographic change are quite clear looking at macro-level data. Municipality level empirical estimates suggest, that the efficiency losses related to the under-utilization of school capacities are more significant than inefficiencies related to economies of scale.[81] Increasing the pupil per teacher ratio by one unit would reduce educational costs by approximately 3.5–5% (note that between 1990 and 1998 the pupil per teacher ratio has in fact decreased by one). At the same time, school consolidation in the case of small village schools could hardly result in more than a 0.5–2% cost saving as an upper limit; disregarding the additional transportation costs and welfare losses incurred.

Regarding the secondary level, the picture is more complex. The expansion of secondary education (higher enrolment rate) seems to offset the decrease in the size of younger cohorts in the 1990s. At the same time significant changes can be observed within the structure of secondary education. While general secondary schools and secondary vocational schools become more popular, technical schools are losing ground (see Figure 2.1). The efficiency problems in secondary education are discussed in the context of structural changes in section 'Side-effects of changes in school and program structure' below.

2.2.3 Factors of Competition between Schools

Hungarian laws on education guarantee the right of free school choice for families: children may apply to any schools of any settlements. The only exception are those who need special education: they may choose among special schools and general schools providing special education in separate classes or in the form of an integrated programme. In practice three factors constrain school choice: transportation and accommodation costs if the school is located in another settlement, the number of places in schools and entrance criteria. With a lack of empirical evidence, it is very difficult to evaluate the actual effect of these constraints. However, the number of places in schools seems to impose an effective constraint only in the most prestigious schools and at a few settlements facing an exceptional growth of school-aged children (see below).

Regarding factors motivating competition on the supply side, financial considerations seems to be the most important. It has to be emphasized that the two levels of education finance work separately and follow a different logic. Changes in the amount of transfers from the central level modify the budget constraint faced by local and county governments and thus have a mediated effect on financial flows from the owners to the schools. However, the incentives of schools and owners are generally rather different.

Per student central grants may motivate local governments to compete for students with other local governments' schools. On the average only between half and two-thirds of expenditures per student are covered by formula grants, thus each student from other settlements imposes an extra financial burden on the community. However, the marginal cost of additional students can be lower than the per student central grant. This effect in theory has two different components. Firstly, total cost is usually assumed to have increasing returns to scale in a relevant range of school size. Economies of scale imply that the marginal cost is decreasing and is below the average cost. Thus, even if the per student grant is less than the average cost, it may exceed the marginal cost. Whether this is the case or not, is an empirical question. In the range of increasing returns to scale the owner of the school is interested in increasing the number of students in the range where the per student grant exceeds the marginal cost. However, if the per student grant is less than the minimum of the marginal cost curve, there is no financial incentive to raise the number students, independent of the size of the school.

Secondly, if the given school capacities are not fully utilized, local governments may be interested in attracting students from outside the community in order to get the additional grant revenue. However, financial incentives depend on the magnitude of school capacities relative to the number of school-aged children in the community as well. This is due to the fact that educational costs can be expected to rise non-linearly with the number of students. If class sizes can be increased, few extra students add almost nothing to the total cost (low marginal cost). The additional grant revenue can well be expected to exceed the increment in cost (on Figure 2.6 see: $G(y)-G(x)>C(y)-C(x)$). However, a bigger increase in the number of students makes it necessary to create a new class and possibly to employ additional teachers. In this case the increase in total cost is far bigger than the marginal cost multiplied by the number of additional students (on Figure 6 see: $G(z)-G(x) < C(z)-C(x)$). However, it may be impossible to identify empirically a cost function with echelons and the pivot numbers of students, the assumption of this form provides a useful illustration for our argument. In this case the goal is to fill up the schools.

Which of the two factors is the more significant? The first effect is difficult to evaluate since this would require a detailed comparison of economies of scale and per student grants. The second factor is evidently present in the case of not fully utilized school capacities. The two effects may also be difficult to decompose in real world situations but the difference is not only theoretical. If we assume that total cost is characterized by increasing returns to scale in the whole empirically relevant range of school size, the first argument predicts either an incentive to compete for students with no limit or no incentive for increasing the number of students at all. Empirical evidence from case studies[82] suggests that an excessive number of students from other communities is financially disadvantageous for local governments in towns. In villages that maintain only one school with one class at each grade, there is in practice no room to adjust school capacities downwards.[83]

Thus, the second factor seems to be the more important. In certain cases the large spillovers in secondary education motivates the local government to reduce school capacities or dispose of secondary schools;[84] this is the case for example in Veszprém [Koltay, 2001], while in other cases the local lobby of the education sector is able to hinder these efforts. At the same time, in one of the exceptional towns, Gödöllő, with non-decreasing young cohorts due to the substantial in-migration, the local government tends to restrict the number of students from other municipalities in spite of the demand in the surrounding villages, because the additional costs of expanded local school capacities would not have been covered by central grants [Rubicsek, 2001].

Financial incentives urge local governments in certain cases to attract students from other settlements. At the same time, local governments seem to be less concerned with competition among schools within the settlement, in spite of the predicted advantages in savings and quality [on the argument for quasi-market incentives see Semjén, 1999]. Although local budgetary practice is most frequently declared to be based on the number of students and the pedagogical programs of the schools, in fact elements of budgeting on the basis of the previous year seems to survive, leaving room for informal bargaining as well.[85] Formula financing of schools based on the number of students is a rare exception at the local level.

Though the financing of schools at the local level is usually not determined strictly by the number of students, schools themselves can be expected to be interested in having more students, given that school capacities are not full in the settlement. Forces of competition may be more or less compelling, depending also on the lobby power of the local education sector. However, if the number of students is low relative to local school capacities and the local government inclines to cut the number of teachers, schools with more students can be expected to have a more powerful bargaining position than less popular institutions.

81

Though schools and individual teachers may not necessarily benefit from the effectiveness of teaching in the form of higher earnings, other factors may count as well. Teaching ambitious and talented students (selected by an entrance exam) provides more experience of success and a more pleasant working environment for teachers. In the case of the most popular general secondary schools incentives of professional prestige and self-esteem maintaining competition should also be mentioned. These factors are quite important at the individual level, enabling the most prestigious and popular schools to attract teachers and thus to maintain good quality in education (since wage differentials are generally not so big).

Figure 2.6
Total Costs and Grants Received as a Function of the Number of Students

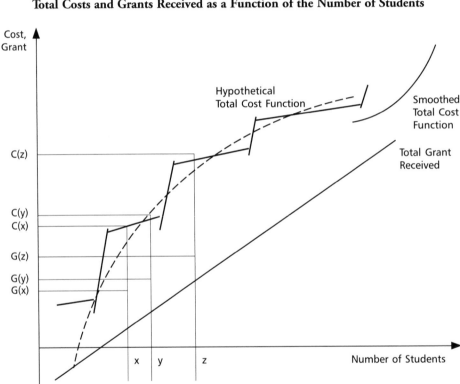

2.2.4 Side-effects of Changes in School and Program Structure

Beyond the direct effects of decreasing school-aged cohorts on the class-sizes and the class per teacher ratio, demographic change, incentives for competition between schools and the expansion of education at the upper-secondary level also contributed to the prevalent efficiency problems in a less direct and seemingly paradox way.

Since the expansion of upper-secondary education offsets decreases in the school-aged population, one would expect no under-utilization of school capacities in general and vocational secondary schools. The only program losing ground is vocational education in technical schools. However, technical schools reacted to changes in the structure of secondary education with launching secondary vocational programs, in many cases preserving their profile in specialization. Thus, the education period has been raised from three to four years in accordance with the prolonged compulsory-schooling period. Since general courses of the ninth and tenth grades in technical schools seem to be no more effective in terms of students' test results and effectiveness in a broader sense,[86] the prolongation of compulsory schooling (i.e. increasing costs) in the short-run can be interpreted as a direct decrease in efficiency.

Schools at the upper-secondary level generally purported to maintain their positions by diversifying the supply of programs. Vocational schools created classes providing a general (non-vocational) program and vice versa. Several institutions provide both general and vocational secondary education and technical school courses as well. Many schools launched six or eight grade general secondary programs: frequently parallel to each other in the same town. Duplication or multiplication of programs or specialization within the same community occurs more and more often, resulting in small programs that are possibly inefficient due to economies of scale and the lack of the appropriate number of students. Besides the incentives for competition between schools, the owner local governments in many cases are not willing to take on the conflicts of choosing from their schools when permitting to launch e.g. a six or eight grade general secondary program.[87] These factors are likely to contribute to the decreasing student per teacher ratio in general secondary schools.

Incentives for competition may have side-effects at the level of general schools as well. In order to attract more students, many schools offer special courses and launch specialized classes. However, the additional courses or teaching for smaller groups require more teachers. This can be interpreted on the one hand as a reaction of schools and local governments to the problem of employment, but on the other hand, can be regarded as a side-effect of competition between schools.[88]

2.3 Equity Problems in Public Education

There are two straightforward approaches to measure inequalities in the final outcome of the education process. On the one hand, the distribution of students' highest completed educational program is of primary interest, since this is among the most important determinants of chances on the labor market. At the same time, inequalities in students' performance are also worth to be considered, since this factor grasps the outcome of education in a more direct way. It may shed light on both disparities among schools within educational program categories and changes in the overall effectiveness of educational programs at the upper-secondary level related to the so-called extension of secondary education. The focuses of these two approaches are often labelled in the Hungarian literature as structural inequalities and inequalities in quality.[89] Unfortunately, the term 'inequalities in quality' may (and in several cases does) result in a confusion of different concepts. We use this term for inequalities in the quality of the final outcome of education measured by students' abilities and knowledge. This should not be confused with inequalities of teaching or school quality (i.e. the intermediate output provided by schools) though this factor is likely to have a strong impact on the former one.

Inequalities in the outcome of education usually imply two further questions, which are, in fact, the two sides of the same coin. Sociologists are basically interested in how strongly the observed inequalities are related to families' socio-economic status. Educational policy analysts usually ask to what extent differences in school quality contribute to inequalities (and how school resources and regulation affect school quality). For these questions there are no unanimously accepted answers based on compelling empirical evidence from the 1990s in Hungary.

In this section, first structural inequalities are discussed in the context of structural changes in the public education system and intergenerational mobility. Then, empirical evidence on inequalities in students' performance is summarized. Third, trends in financial disparities, a presumable indicator of the intermediate output of schooling, are outlined. Finally the most important problems of students with special needs is mentioned.

2.3.1   Likely Effects of Structural Changes on Equity

Changes in the school and program structure seem to strengthen structural inequalities among students. In the last decade, a polarization can be observed in completed educational levels: the number of students exiting from the education system after the general school has slightly increased, while the share of students in general and vocational secondary education is increasing, as well.[90] At the same time, the distribution of students over program categories is largely determined by parents' educational level.[91]

The appearance of 6 and 8 grade general secondary schools has also enhanced and pushed to a lower age the structural selectivity of the public education system. In the case of schools maintained by local governments, these programs are launched in order to make the schools more competitive, but these attempts are not always successful. These schools are usually among the most prestigious ones, especially those maintained by foundations, churches or the central budget. The latter group of schools is exceptionally popular among parents with a university degree.[92] Incorporating two or all the four years of the upper cycle of general schools (i.e. lower-secondary level in the ISCED terminology) introduces selection at a younger age.

At the other extreme, structural changes had a negative effect on those students left out from general or vocational secondary programs. Previously, technical schools in general provided a promise of relatively good or at least, not hopeless labor market positions. The greater share of these schools ensured a more heterogeneous group of students, who had better results in general schools compared to students attending technical schools now. However, the vocational school degree has lost much of its value on the labor market and the fewer and fewer students, not accepted for the expanding secondary vocational courses, in average arrives with weaker knowledge and less motivation than before. The prolongation of compulsory schooling forces the students to wait longer for almost nothing. Schools and teachers either strive to make up for what the students have missed in the general school and create a chance to continue learning towards the final exam of the upper-secondary level or admit their failure and just maintain these courses without any further ambitions.[93] However, raising the standards in vocational programs without properly attenuated pedagogical programs implies the risk of unacceptable drop-out rates and enhancing the frustration of students, thus reinforcing failures.[94]

However, the differentiation of education supply should not be over-estimated. To some extent, formerly officially ignored but well-known differences in quality among formally identical schools has become explicit.[95] At the same time, in many cases school specialities are introduced and working as mere signals of quality in response to incentives of competition.[96] Thorough decisions on school choice would require information usually not available for parents. Moreover, when the first specified classes, with advanced sport or music education, appeared in the Hungarian educational system, they were used by schools as an opportunity for selection among students (often not or not only with respect to the special skills required) and for creating elite classes.[97] Thus, specialized classes have been identified with better educational quality in the 1970s and 1980s. This may also contribute to the signalling effect at work nowadays. In sum, popularity and quality do not always go hand in hand.

2.3.2   Inequalities in Student Achievement

Analyses of the MONITOR surveys usually discuss inequalities in student test results in the context of disparities among settlement-categories and the impact of family characteristics on the student's performance.

Regarding settlement size as a dimension to describe inequalities, markedly growing disparities among villages, towns, county towns and the capital can be observed in the last decade, both in reading competencies and mathematics.[98]

Unfortunately, the published results do not allow for estimating changes in time in the impact of parents' socio-economic status (measured by educational level). However, in a cross-section analysis Vári et al. (2000b) demonstrates that disparities among settlement categories in a large extent can be attributed to differences in the social composition of the population. That is excluding the impact of parents' educational level, the effect of settlement-size on students' performance is much weaker than the raw effect, especially in the case of parents with university or college degree. Vári et al. [2000b] interpret this finding as higher status families are more successful in escaping the disadvantages of presumably weaker school quality. An ad hoc path analysis of the relationships between family characteristics, settlement size, school resources and student performance [Bánfi, 1999, see also in Vári, 1999, ch. 1.] suggests a more complex picture. First, it reinforces the hypothesis that settlement size has a negative effect on school equipment (an indicator of school resources) and through this, a negative effect on students' performance in mathematics, while the impact of parents' educational level is controlled for. Second, it is worth to note, that settlement size has a negative correlation with direct indicators of families' cultural capital (one of these indicators is the number of books owned by the family), *even if*, again, the impact of parents' educational level is excluded. This result suggests that settlement categories may correlate with unobservable (i.e. other than educational level and family income) factors of families' cultural capital. However, explaining weaker performance in village schools requires a more thorough investigation than the actually available analyses. Just to mention one possible additional factor of explanation, the lower average socio-economic status of families in villages may also contribute to the weaker performance in addition to the individual impact of family background through peer-group effects (i.e. producing a less motivating environment for the individual students).

In an international comparison inequalities among students in Hungary seems to be substantial. Regarding eighth grade students' knowledge in mathematics, the dispersion of standardized test results (measured by the difference between the 5th and 95th percentile values) has been found to be close to the greatest value out of the 25 participant countries when the groups of girls and boys are analyzed separately.[99] In fact, gender differences seem to be negligible relative to other countries, while inequalities caused by other factors are significant. Regarding adult literacy, in the SIALS project factors of inequalities can be compared only in indirect ways (unfortunately direct estimates of inequality measures are not published in the Hungarian report).[100] First, average performance is compared by the level of respondents' educational attainment. The differences with respect to educational level seem to be around the average of the participant countries (it is worth to note, that schools at the upper-secondary level form an especially hetero-geneous group with respect to quality). Second, the correlation between respondents reading competencies and their parents' educational level has been estimated for each country. The effect of parents' educational level has been found to be the greatest in Hungary. However, this result is not easy to interpret, since it comprises two effects: first, the effect of parents' educational level on children's educational level (i.e. educational mobility) and second, the effect of children's education on their reading competencies in adult age.

2.3.3 Disparities in Expenditures

Increasing disparities in the fiscal situation of local governments result in growing inequalities in per student expenditures. Financial disparities stem from differences in the local tax base. Local taxes are far from the most important components in local governmental revenues, though having an increasing share. The dominant local tax source is the local business tax which has a much more unequal distribution than personal income or wealth. Beside local taxes general revenue sharing (i.e. sharing the personal income tax) in part also reflects financial disparities among municipalities. Though financial disparities are strong between regions and with respect to settlement size, these dimensions represent only two aspects: settlements of the same size in the same region may well face very different conditions. The location of a single large industrial plant or an extended service infrastructure (hospitals, secondary schools, social institutions suppplying many surrounding municipalities) may lead to an extremely adventageous situation or severe fiscal stress.

The empirical analysis of disparities in per capita expenditures found that financing general schools is moving off from fiscal neutrality. Between 1991 and 1996 the elasticity of per student expenditures with respect to per student personal income tax (as a proxy of income) has increased from 0.037 to 0.088 and decreased to 0.071 in 1997 [Varga, 2000]. That is, a one percent difference in per capita income between settlements implies 0.07–0.09% difference in per student expenditures. In international comparison this value can be considered relatively small.[101] However, fiscal disparities measured by the income elasticity tells only part of the story since only the distribution of personal income is considered, while the distribution of the local business tax base is much more unequal among municipalities. Unfortunately, reliable data on the local business tax base are not available.

Nevertheless, fiscal disparities can not be considered as exact indicators of inequalities in educational quality. First, the higher utilization of school capacities in more prestigious schools may in part disguise differences of quality in financial data. Though forces urging schools to compete are not strong and sometimes ambiguous, free school choice enhanced disparities among schools. Prestigious schools (especially at the secondary level, with high rate of students going to university and college) are more popular among families, resulting in higher average class size in these institutions. Thus, though from a pedagogical point of view one could expect a negative relationship between class size and students' results, in fact probably a positive correlation could be found due to the disparities between institutions and school choice. But can we assume that schools with better results also provide higher quality of education? Regarding the first question, since students' achievement is mainly determined by family characteristics, the quality of education can not be measured by student results directly. Moreover, results like enrolment rate in higher education are much easier to observe by families than the quality of education. Thus it is conceivable that families demand school with respect to other students' social status rather than the quality of education. However, prestigious and popular schools can be assumed to provide higher quality, as well, since better teachers can be expected to move towards these institutions. Differences in teachers' wages among schools are probably not really significant, but professional success and less class room difficulties can be assumed to attract teachers into prestigious schools.

Secondly, better-off local governments can be expected to tolerate higher efficiency losses in schools. In this case higher per student expenditures may reflect less efficient rather than better quality in schoolwork. This can result in over-estimating inequalities in quality indicated by financial measures.

Thirdly, cost differences between local governments should have been taken into consideration as well when concluding from disparities in expenditures to inequalities in quality. Communities with more disadvantaged students have to spend more per students to attain the same student results as schools with an average student background.

Within the present system of local governmental transfers, in the last decade the central government applied two methods to curb fiscal disparities: to increase the share of general (i.e. not service-specific) redistribution among municipalities (since 1994) and to increase per capita grants (after 1997). Looking at the past years, these policies seem to be less effective than expected. General redistribution may achieve equalization at a large price in education since it is not targeted, while further limiting local governmental autonomy. Increasing per capita grants is an inefficient method, since it subsidises better-off municipalities as well as poor ones.

2.3.4 Students with Special Needs

Regarding the equity problems related to the education of particular groups of students, two groups have to be mentioned: students with disabilities and Romani children.

The education of students with disabilities is separated from the main stream of public education. In 1986 national and county level committees were established to assess physical and mental handicaps, sensory or speech impediments. National boards of experts deal with the examination of visual, hearing and speech abilities. Examining and supervising professional boards are operated at the county level and in Budapest, applying special teachers, psychologists and medical specialists. The committees' opinions regarding the examined handicapped child serve as a base for recommending possibilities for his/her positioning in school or nursery school. Educational Counselling Services in each district of the capital and in every major town explore and diagnose problems in the behavior, education and learning process of children between 3 and 18 year-olds. Professional services for speech therapy function in divisions according to districts in the capital and to regions in the country where those with speech impediments may receive individual or group therapy. Boards of special teachers might decide not only on sending children to special classes but also on transferring children from special classes into mainstream ones. On the other hand, according to the provisions of the 1998 Act on Equal Opportunities, parents of handicapped children do have the right to decide which of the offered institutions shall educate their children.

Due to legal regulation, parents are entitled to choose the educational institution on the basis of an expert opinion given by the Expertise and Rehabilitation Committee for the examination of learning abilities. However, the parents' freedom of choice is somewhat restricted since the law declares that handicapped students may only enrol in educational institutions that have the necessary staff and funds for this special form of education.

The educational system for the handicapped consists of pre-school, general and lower vocational institutions. The special nursery and primary schools deal with 'teachable' children with special needs aged 3–16. Additionally, certain 'mainstream' nursery and primary schools also have groups, classes or divisions for the education of special needs. Some of the nursery or primary schools may pursue their studies fully or in a partially integrated manner with other children but this form of teaching is currently less typical. In the 1998/99 school year more than 44 000 pupils were taught in 200 special education institutions and 481 primary school divisions. 0.5% of nursery school children, 3.35% of pupils in primary schools attend special institutions. These figures are among the highest ones in the group of the OECD countries and have grown in the last decade substantially.

Mainstream and special forms of education converge in several respects. While designing their pedagogical programs, the schools participating in special education are obliged to take into consideration the principles issued with reference to the education of children with deficiencies. As it was outlined before, education is performed along a largely common curriculum regulated by the National Core Curriculum. (The core curriculum of special schools is being prepared nowadays.) Each school or other educational institution for handicapped children has the right to decide which methods they regard most sufficient to use in the process of education and care. Education in school classes with a small number of students appears typical, however; individual (speech therapeutic) or individual and small group corrective activities are also widely practised. Handicapped students usually receive a final school-leaving certificate identical with that of able students.

Most of the students with special needs attend special schools for handicapped children or special classes within general schools; integrated education occurs only as an exception. While separated education is probably beneficial from a narrow pedagogical point of view, some experts argue that these benefits may be offset by the difficulties of students in finding a job and establishing social connections after the school years.[102]

The share of children in special education at the primary level has been growing in the last decade, probably in part due to financial incentives. The hypothesis below is formulated by Radó [2000b]. The per student grant for special education has been exceeding the 'non-special' grant in the whole period providing an incentive for local governments to increase the volume of special education. At the same time, for general schools facing the declining number of students establishing new classes providing special education is one of the means in the competition for students. This hypothesis is in accordance with the fact that the increment of students in special education mostly appears in special classes in general schools, not in the special schools [Radó, 2000b].

The high share of students in special education, classified as mentally handicapped, relative to the total of students at the primary level[103] is striking in an international comparison. This in part can be attributed to the exceptionally high rate of Romani children in special schools [Radó, 2000a]. This way a substantial share of Romani children become segregated within the school system due to the lack of sufficient conditions and teaching competencies to deal properly with these pupils, at the same losing the chance of an educational career towards an advantageous labor market position.

The share of Romani children in special schools is only one aspect, though probably the most astonishing one, of the failure of the public education system in providing effective education for the Roma minority. The empirical analysis of the proportion of Romani children entering and completing general, secondary and technical schools has shown that the odds ratio of Roma relative to non-minority children to complete general school had increased in the 1980s, but the odds ratio regarding the secondary level was still decreasing in this period.[104] Finally, the tendencies of segregation seem to strengthen in the past years.[105] First, the territorial segregation of the Romani population is increasing. Second, where the share of Romani children is significant (reaches 20–40%), non-Roma parents tend to move their children into other schools. Third, within schools frequently explicit or implicit[106] 'Roma classes' are established.

3. CONCLUSION

Educational policy now and in the next few years faces several still unsolved problems. These problems can be summarized under four headings: (1) employment, efficiency and teacher wages, (2) declining trends in student achievement, (3) growing disparities between schools, regarding both financial resources and school quality and (4) equity and quality problems related to special groups.

First, wages in the education sector are still extremely low. Financing the maintenance and reconsruction of school buildings seems to be insufficient as well, nevertheless, the problem of low wages seems to be more demanding. In the long run, this reduces the attractiveness of the profession and possibly the quality of new entrants. In order to cure the problem either efficiency losses should be substantially reduced to release resources within the education sector, or public expenditures on education should be increased (or a combination of these measures can be applied). Regarding the second option, it is an open question whether economic growth will enable the government to follow this strategy without substantially increasing the share of educational spending relative to the GDP. Without increasing the share of educational expenditures, however, even if real wages can be increased, wages would remain at the same low level in international comparison (i.e. average teacher wages relative to the GDP per capita). The other way, financing higher wages from reducing efficiency losses is not an easy one to follow from a political point of view. In the period of restrictions on government spending fiscal stress urged central and local decision-makers to seek solutions for the prevailing efficiency problems, but the threat of high political costs and increasing costs in the short run (e.g. compensation for teachers) effectively banned local school reform policies. Thus fiscal incentives in the simplest form without other central policy initiatives proved to be unsatisfactory to achieve efficiency goals. In the period of economic growth it would be even more difficult for the political parties in government to come up with a policy of adjusting general school capacities to demographic changes. Regarding secondary education, the process of expansion and structural changes may provide an opportunity to treat efficiency problems at the same time without additional conflicts (or expansion may provide a chance to ignore efficiency problems, covered by the process of highlighted structural changes as well).

Another efficiency problem is posed by the fragmented local governmental and school structure and the spillovers in the provision of secondary education. Both problems would require co-operation among local governments: joint school maintenance could contribute to the exploitation of economies of scale, while co-ordinated planning of secondary school structure in a county or regional level might result in a broader supply of educational programs also in accordance with labor market conditions. Again, fiscal incentives (additional grant for joint school maintenance) had poor results until now. However, the forced amalgamation of schools is inconceivable regarding local autonomy.

Altogether, active central level policies aiming at enhancing efficiency seems to be inescapable, though the choice of measures to be applied are far from unambiguous.

Secondly, declining and stagnating trends in student achievements measured by standardized test results are alarming, even taking into consideration that the interpretation of standardized tests results as general indicators of the effectiveness of the public education system can be debated. In an international comparison, Hungarian students perform poorly regarding reading competences and somewhat better, but worse than before, in mathematics. Since educational attainment is an apparent determinant of labor market success urging students to compete for places in the best secondary schools, declining school quality seems to be the most plausible explanation for the unfavourable trends. However, the available empirical analyses do not answer the question whether these trends are mostly due to growing inequalities (i.e. quality falls only on the lower end of the distribution) or it is a general phenomenon in the public education system.

It has to be noted that in international comparison, Hungary's position is not reassuring but equally, it is neither disasterous. The astonishing results of the SIALS literacy survey reflect the adult population's reading and understanding skills, which mostly shows the effectiveness of the past school system (in the case of older cohorts) and, at the same time, the development of skills after leaving formal education.

Nevertheless, the actual focus of educational policy on school quality themes can hardly be objected. However, it is an open question whether fashionable business-like quality assuarance programs are the most appropriate means for improving student achievement. It has to be noted, that the declared goal of the quality assuarance campaign is not improving student achievement directly, nevertheless, this can hardly be missing from the final purposes. Occasional campaigns and additional financial resources can rarely offset structural effects like the unfavorable changes in teacher composition. Due to low relative wages in the education sector, many better qualified teachers leave the profession, while in the long run low wages, few job for the entrants and the expansion of tertiary education (i.e. other increasing opportunities) deter students with high or middle level results from the teaching profession when choosing college or university.

Third, growing disparities among local governments with respect to general fiscal conditions and per student educational spending can be expected to pose a serious problem for educational policy. In the last years, redistribution among local governments was based mainly on indicators of general fiscal conditions. To curb rising inequalities with this method required increasing equalization in the second half of the last decade, building new constraints for local fiscal autonomy. From a theoretical point of view it seems preferable to use service-specific equalising transfers (e.g. a matching grants with matching rate depending on the wealth of the municipality) instead, but the institutional rigidity of the regulation of the local government sector makes it unlikely to adopt this kind of 'new' measures on the short run. The policies of the present government suggest that the centralization of financial resources will continue (this is in accord with the current plans to introduce a unified wage scheme for teachers). This way the fiscal disparities can be tackled but the price is giving up a growing part of local fiscal autonomy. This may be disadvantageous regarding local political accountability, thus also curtailing the incentives for improving efficiency. It has to be noted that disparities between schools within large municipalities may increase independent of central local fiscal relations.

Fourth, the educational opportunities of certain special groups in the public education system are a serious problem to be solved.

With the expansion of secondary education technical school programs cannot provide attractive career opportunities any more. These programs are for the less able students, the losers in the educational system; however, the national core curricula do not properly take into account the needs of this group of students. The prolongation of compulsory education has not yet initiated substantial positive changes in technical school programmes. The quality of education and the function of general education in the ninth and tenth grades is a serious challenge for education policy.

Children in special schools, especially their extremely high proportion in international comparison, pose a serious problem. Central educational policy urges the integrated education of these children, but local educational policy makers can hardly be expected to cope with the problem without stronger central programs, though the trend of demographic change presents an incentive for expanding integrated education (i.e. this way the declining number of students in part can be offset in non special school). Possibly the system of qualification of children requiring special education or not needs to be revised.

Providing better educational opportunities and a more effective education for Romani children is one of the most serious debts of educational policy in the transition period. Unfortunately, the efforts of current educational policy are not focused on this issue; a firm determination to improve the situation can not be seen.

It is difficult to judge which is the most serious of the four sets of problem. Nevertheless, while in the case of the prevailing low efficiency—low wages circle and the problems related to special groups the harmful effects are evidently already present, declining or stagnating trends in student achievement and increasing disparities are rather warning signs for the future.

REFERENCES

A Comenius 2000: *Közoktatási minőségfejlesztési program,* Minőségfejlesztési Kézikönyv, Oktatási Minisztérium, Budapest, 1999.

A Nemzeti Alaptanterv bevezetése, az iskolák helyi tanterve 1998 őszén (Introducing the National Core Curriculum and local curricula on the fall of 1998). Szocio-Reflex Kft.–Országos Közoktatási Intézet Kutatási Központ. Budapest, 1999. www.om.hu (in Hungarian language).

Andor M.–Liskó I. (2000): *Iskolaválasztás és mobilitás* (School choice and mobility), Iskolakultúra, Budapest, 2000.

Balázs, Éva (ed.): *Iskolavezetők a 90-es években* (School headteachers in the 1990s). OKKER, Budapest, 1998.

Balázs Éva: *Önfejlesztő iskolák* (Self-developing schools), in.: Vágó (ed.): Tartalmi változások a közoktatásban a 90-es években (Content changes in public education in the 1990s). OKKER, 1999.

Balázs É.–Lannert J.–Surányi B.: *Demográfiai hullám, iskola, ifjúsági munkanélküliség* (Demographic wave, school, youth unemployment), Akadémiai Kiadó, Budapest, 1992.

Balázs É.–Halász G.–Imre A.–Moldován J.–Nagy M.: *Inter-governmental roles in the delivery of eucational services (Hungary),* Study for the World Bank, National Institute of Public Education, Budapest, 1999. Manuscript.

Balogh M. (1997): *A demográfiai változások hatása a közoktatásra* (The effect of demographic changes on public education), in: Új Pedagógiai Szemle, 1997/2.

Bánfi I. (1999): *Az iskolai teljesítményt befolyásoló háttértényezők* (Determinants of student performance), in: Új Pedagógiai Szemle, 1999/6.

Borbola I. (1998): *A közoktatás jövőjének megtervezése és a közoktatás* (Public education and planning the future of public education), in: Új Pedagógiai Szemle, 1998/2.

Bradford, D.R.–R.A. Malt–W.E. Oates (1969): *The rising cost of local public services: some evidence and reflections,* in: National Tax Journal, 22., pp. 186–202.

Deák Zs. (1998): *A pedagógusok munkája* (Teachers' work), in: Nagy M. (ed.): Tanári pálya és életkörülmények (Teacher career and living standard), Okker Kiadó, Budapest, 1998.

Duncombe, W. D.–J. M. Yinger (1999*): Performance standards and educational cost indexes: you can't have one without the other,* in: H. F. Ladd–R. Chalk–J. S. Hansen (eds.): Equity and adequacy in education finance, National Academy Press, Washington, 1999.

Enyedi György–Pálné Kovács Ilona*: A kormány és az önkormányzatok* (The govenment and local governments), in.: Gombár Cs.–Hankiss E.–Lengyel Gy.–Várnai (szerk.): Kormány a mérlegen 1990–1994 (Government on the balance 1990–1994), Korridor, Budapest, 1994.

Értékelés és minőségbiztosítás a magyar közoktatásban: Jelentés. (Evaluation and quality management in Hungarian public education. A Report). Magyar Gallup Intézet, Budapest, 1999.

Feldstein, M.S. (1975): *Wealth neutrality and local choice in public education,* in: American Economic Review, 65., pp. 75–89.

Forray R. K. (1998): *A falusi kisiskolák helyzete* (Conditions of small schools in villages), Educatio Füzetek 220, Oktatáskutató Intézet, Budapest, 1998.

Hajdú E. (2000): *A Nemzeti Alaptanterv bevezetésének hatása a tantárgy- és tanórarendszer alakulására* (The effect of introducing the National Core Curriculum on the structure of subjects and lessons), in: Új Pedagógiai Szemle, 2000/3.

Halász G. (2000): *Az oktatás minősége és eredményessége* (Education quality and effectiveness), in: Halász G.–Lannert J. (eds.) (2000), pp. 303–326.

Halász G.–Lannert J. (eds.) (2000): *Jelentés a magyar közoktatásról 2000* (Report on public education in Hungary), Országos Közoktatási Intézet, Budapest, 2000.

Halász G.–Garami E.–Havas P.–Vágó I. : *Az oktatás fejlődése Magyarországon: Nemzeti jelentés* (The development of education in Hungary: A national report). Manuscript. OKI, 2000.

Harsányi E.–Radó P. (1997*): Cigány tanulók a magyar iskolában* (Roma students in Hungarian schools), in: Educatio, 1997/1. pp. 48–59.

Henderson, V.–P. Mieszkowski–Y. Sauvageau (1978): *Peer group effects and educational production functions*, in: Journal of Public Economics, 10., pp. 97–106.

Hermann Z. (1999): Economies of Scale in Hungarian Local Public Education, in: Hermann Z.–Horváth M. T.–Péteri G.–Ungvári G. (1999): *Allocation of Local Functions: Criteria and Conditions 3 Analysis and Policy Proposals for Hungary,* Washington, DC: The Fiscal Decentralization Initiative for Central and Eastern Europe, 1999, pp. 83–132.

Hermann Z. (2000): *Local governmental policy networks in middle-size Hungarian towns,* manuscript.

Hermann Z. (2001): *Hatékonysági problémák a közoktatásban: A demográfiai változások hatása az iskolai kapacitások kihasználtságára, méretgazdaságosság* (Efficiency problems in the public education: the effects of demographic changes on the utilisation of school capacities, economies of scale), unpublished paper, Országos Közoktatási Intézet, Budapest.

Homolya D. (2001): *Helyi oktatáspolitika és iskolafinanszírozás Kazincbarcikán* (Local education policy and school finance on Kazincbarcika), unpublished case study, Országos Közoktatási Intézet, Budapest, 2001.

Horváth Zs. (2000): *9. évfolyamos tanulók tanulási problémái a szakképző iskolákban* (Learning problems of 9th grade students in vocational schools), in: Új Pedagógiai Szemle, 2000/9.

Imre A. (1997): *Kistelepülési iskolák* (Small school villages), in: Educatio, 1997/3, pp. 24–31.

Kertesi G. (1995): *Cigány gyerekek az iskolában, cigány felnőttek a munkaerőpiacon* (Roma children in the school, Roma adults in the labor market), in: Közgazdasági Szemle, XLII., pp. 30–65.

Koltay G. (2001): *Oktatáspolitika és iskolafinanszírozás Veszprémben* (Education policy and school finance in Veszprém), unpublished case study, Országos Közoktatási Intézet, Budapest.

Ladányi J.–Szelényi I. (1997): *Szuburbanizáció és gettósodás* (Suburbanization and slums), in: Kritika, 1997/7.

Lannert J. (2000): *Továbbhaladás a magyar iskolarendszerben* (Educational paths in the Hungarian public education system), in: Kolosi T.–Tóth I. Gy.–Vukovich Gy. (eds.) (2000): Társadalmi Riport (Social report), TÁRKI, Budapest, pp. 205–222.

Lazear (1999): *Educational production,* NBER Working Paper No. 7349.

Liskó I. (1998): *Bokros-csomag a közoktatásban* (The Bokros-pack in the public education), in: Educatio, 1998/1, pp. 67–89.

Liskó I. (1999): *Az oktatás minősége és az iskola presztizse* (Education quality and the prestige of schools), in: Educatio, 1999/3., pp. 609–624.

Mártonfi Gy. (2000): *Az iskolarendszerű szakképzés struktúrájának átalakulása és a 9–10. osztály* (Changes in the structure of vocational education in schools and the 9–10th grades), unpublished, Országos Közoktatási Intézet, Budapest, 2000.

Nagy M. (1996): *A tanárok közalkalmazotti státusa Magyarországon* (The public employee status of teachers in Hungary), In.: Hatékonyság és közszolgáltatás II. (Efficiency and public service II.) Budapest Közgazdaságtudományi Egyetem, Budapest, 1996

Nagy M. (2000): *A hat- és nyolc évfolyamos gimnáziumi képzés a kilencvenes évek oktatási rendszerében* (Six- and eight grade general secondary education in the public education system in the 1990s), unpublished, Országos Közoktatási Intézet, Budapest, 2000.

Pálné Kovács Ilona: *A területi közigazgatás szervezete és a dekoncentrált szervek* (The structure of territorial administration and the deconcentrated governmnet agencies), in.: Agg Z.–Pálné Kovács I. (eds.): A rendszerváltás és a megyék (Transition and county governments). COMITATUS, Veszprém, 1994.

Pálné Kovács Ilona: *A területfejlesztés intézményrendszerének kialakulása, szabályozásának és működésének értékelése* (Assesment of the formation, regulation and operation of institutions of regional development), MTA Regionális Kutatóközpont, Pécs, 1999. Manuscript.

Radó P. (2000a): *Speciális igények az oktatásban* (Special needs in education), in: Halász G.–Lannert J. (eds.) (2000), pp. 327–342.

Radó P. (2000b): *Egyenlőtlenségek és méltányosság a közoktatásban* (Inequalities and equity in public education), in: Halász G.–Lannert J. (eds.) (2000), pp. 343–361.

Rubicsek Á. (2001): *Gödöllő város oktatáspolitikája és oktatásfinanszírozási gyakorlata* (Education policy and school finance in Gödöllő), unpublished case study, Országos Közoktatási Intézet, Budapest, 2001.

Semjén A. (1999): *Hatékonyság az oktatásban* (Efficiency in education), in: Educatio, 1999/3., pp. 575–597.

Semjén András: *Bérek, alku és hatékonyság a tanárok munkaerőpiacán* (Wages, bargaining and efficiency in the teacher labor market), PM–GTI, Manuscript. Budapest, 1991.

Sóstói A. (2001): *Oktatáspolitika és iskolafinanszírozás Sárospatakon* (Education policy and school finance in Sárospatak), unpublished case study, Országos Közoktatási Intézet, Budapest, 2001.

SArensen, R. J. (1997): *Local government school priorities: teaching input and class size in Norway, 1980–1992*, in: Education Economics, Vol. 5/1, pp. 63–89.

Study for the OECD–BIE. National Institute of Public Education, manuscript, Budapest, 2001.

Sugár A. (1999): *A közoktatási rendszer szerkezeti változásai, jellegzetes trendek az oktatási statisztika tükrében* (Structural changes and trends in the public education system revealed by education statistics), unpublished, Országos Közoktatási Intézet, Budapest, 1999.

Vágó I. (2000): *Továbbhaladás az iskolarendszerben* (Educational paths), unpublished, Országos Közoktatási Intézet, Budapest, 2000.

Varga J. (1995): *Az oktatás megtérülési rátái Magyarországon* (Rates of return of education in Hungary), in: Közgazdasági Szemle, XLII, pp. 595–605.

Varga J. (2000): *A közoktatás-finanszírozási rendszer hatása az egyenlőségre* (The effect of education finance on equality), 1990–1997, in: *Közgazdasági Szemle*, XLVII, pp. 531–548.

Varga J. (2001): *A közoktatásban foglalkoztatottak összetételének és keresetének változása* (Changes in the composition and wages of public education employees), 1992–1999, unpublished, Országos Közoktatási Intézet, Budapest. 2001.

Vári Péter (ed.) (1997): *MONITOR '95: A tanulók tudásának felmérése* (MONITOR 1995: Surveying students' knowledge), Országos Közoktatási Intézet, Budapest, 1997.

Vári P. (ed.) (1999): MONITOR '97. *A tanulók tudásának változása* (MONITOR 1997: Changes in students' knowledge), Országos Közoktatási Intézet, Budapest, 1999.

Vári P.–Andor Cs.–Bánfi I.–Bérces J.–Krolopp J.–Rózsa Cs. (1998): *Jelentés a Monitor '97 felmérésről* (Report on the MONITOR 1997 survey), in: Új Pedagógiai Szemle, 1998/1.

Vári P.–Bánfi I.–Felvégi E.–Krolopp J.–Rózsa Cs.–Szalay B. (2000a): *A tanulók tudásának változása I. rész, A Monitor '99 felmérés előzetes eredményei* (Changes in students' knowledge, preliminary results of the MONITOR 1999 survey, part 1), in: Új Pedagógiai Szemle, 2000/6.

Vári P.–Bánfi I.–Felvégi E.–Krolopp J.–Rózsa Cs.–Szalay B. (2000b): *A tanulók tudásának változása II. rész, A Monitor '99 felmérés előzetes eredményei* (Changes in students' knowledge, preliminary results of the MONITOR 1999 survey, part 2), in: Új Pedagógiai Szemle, 2000/7–8.

Vári P.–Andor Cs.–Bánfi I.–Felvégi E.–Horváth Zs.–Krolopp J.–Rózsa Cs.–Szalay B. (2001): *Felnőtt írásbeliség vizsgálat: egy nemzetközi felmérés tapasztalatai* (Adult literacy: the results of an international survey), unpublished, Országos Közoktatási Intézet, Budapest, 2001.

Vári P.–Krolopp J. (1997): *Egy nemzetközi felmérés főbb eredményei* (TIMMS) (Main results of an international survey: TIMMS), in: Új Pedagógiai Szemle, 1997/4.

Várnagy T. (2001): *Hatékonysági problémák a közoktatásban és helyi oktatáspolitika* (Efficiency problems in the public education and local education policy), unpublished, Országos Közoktatási Intézet, Budapest, 2001.

Weber, W. L. (1991): *Fiscal neutrality and local choice in public education*, in: Economics of Education Review, Vol. 10., No. 1., pp. 37–44.

ANNEX 1

Education Levels and School Structure in Hungary

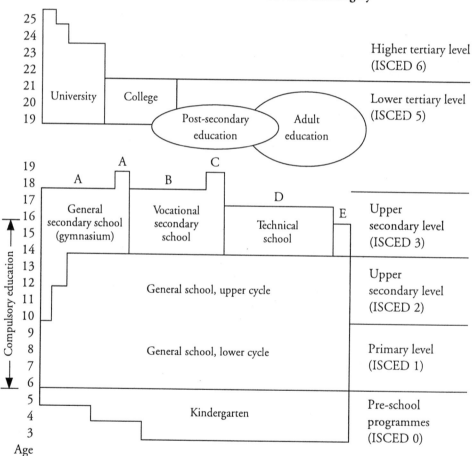

Figure 2A.1
Education Levels and School Structure in Hungary

A: secondary school leaving certificate
B: secondary school leaving certificate and vocational qualification
C: technician qualification
D: skilled worker qualification
E: lower-level trade school qualification

ANNEX 2

Incentives for School Closures in a Central—Local Fiscal Game

To sketch the argument concerning the logic of the incentives for school closures as a non-co-operative strategic game in its simplest form, let us assume, that:

1. both of the actors in the game, central government and a representative local government has two options with respect to decreasing school capacities;

2. if either of them takes the pro-school-closure strategy (sharp policy measures and non-resistance respectively), school capacities are decreased;

3. actor's gains are measured in two dimensions: savings (S_{CG} and S_{LG}) and political costs (P);

4. if both actors takes the pro-closure strategy, total political costs are shared (0<a<1);

5. the distribution of savings is independent of who takes the pro-closure strategy;

6. total political costs are higher than either actor's savings, i.e. it is not worth to take the political responsibility alone.

As it can be seen from the pay-off matrix of the game, 'against-closure' is a dominant strategy for both actors (i.e. both actors ends up better-off *independent of* the other actor's choice).

		central government			
		sharp measures (pro-cl.)		soft measures (against-cl.)	
local	not resist (pro-cl.)	$S_{LG}-(1-a) * P$	$S_{CG}-a * P$	$S_{LG}-P$	S_{CG}
government	Resist (against-cl.)	S_{LG}	$S_{CG}-P$	0	0

Under the above assumptions the game results in the maintenance of the inefficiencies, *even if* savings are high enough to offset *shared* political costs for each actor. If savings would compensate shared political cost ($S_{CG}-a * P > 0$, $S_{LG}-(1-a) * P > 0$) the game follows the logic of the prisoner's dilemma.

In the opposite case (shared political costs exceed savings) the situation becomes trivial: none of the actors is interested in enhancing efficiency.

There is an interesting third case. If the Assumption 6 is reversed, i.e. savings are bigger than *total* political costs, it is still not certain that school closures will occur. The game has two Nash equilibria both resulting in school closures ('against'–'pro' and 'pro'–'against' outcomes). However, especially in a repeated game context, even in this case it may be reasonable to gamble: to wait for the other actor to take on the political costs alone.

ANNEX 3

Table 2A.1

The Number of Students, Teachers and Classes in the Public Education System

Indicator	1990	1991	1992	1993	1994	1995	1996	1997	1998
Pupils at Kindergartens–ISCED 0	391 129	394 091	394 420	397 153	396 184	399 339	394 327	383 486	37 486
Pupils at Primary Schools–ISCED 1+2	1 130 656	1 081 213	1 044 164	1 009 416	985 291	974 806	965 998	963 997	964 248
Students at Secondary Schools–ISCED 3	517 358	535 213	539 645	535 184	528 838	527 265	525 165	517 816	509 249
• Out of this students of General Education Stream	123 427	130 378	136 729	138 198	140 352	140 884	140 867	141 402	142 196
• Out of this students of Vocational Ed. Stream	393 931	404 835	402 916	396 986	388 486	386 381	384 298	376 414	367 053
Pupils and Students at Special Schools	36 742	36 400	35 475	35 503	36 150	37 262	37 738	38 292	39 919
Teachers at Kindergartens–ISCED 0	33 635	33 159	33 140	32 957	33 007	32 320	31 891	31 848	31 986
Teachers at Primary Schools–ISCED 1+2	90 511	89 276	88 917	89 655	89 939	86 891	83 658	82 904	83 404
Teachers at Secondary Schools–ISCED 3	35 808	36 939	38 039	39 691	40 612	40 522	40 179	40 095	40 592
Teachers at Special Schools	6 036	6 017	6 117	6 238	6 413	6 428	6 027	6 268	6 569
Classes at Kindergartens–ISCED 0	16 055	15 982	16 009	15 952	16 072	15 813	15 701	15 641	15 630
Classes at Primary Schools–ISCED 1+2	48 729	48 497	48 330	47 676	47 578	46 425	45 521	45 495	45 589
Classes at Secondary Schools–ISCED 3	17 279	18 002	18 496	18 499	18 605	18 681	18 623	18 630	18 371
Classes at Special Schools	3 406	3 375	3 617	3 344	3 248	3 268	3 461	3 385	3 572

SOURCE: HCSO and Ministry of Education
NOTES: *teachers* are full-time employees instead of the full-time-equivalent data the number of *pupils/students* and *classes refers* to data of full-time students only

Table 2A.2
Expenditures in Education Relative to the GDP

Indicator	1990	1991	1992	1993	1994	1995	1996	1997	1998	1999 est
GDP volume index (1995=1)	1.128	0.994	0.963	0.957	0.985	1.000	1.013	1.060	1.112	1.160
GDP per capita, current prices [USD]	2 070	3 228	3 608	3 745	4 046	4 376	4 433	4 504	4 651	4 787
GDP per capita, current prices [HUF]	201 577	241 476	285 040	344 707	425 365	548 836	676 315	841 039	997 415	1 135 980
GDP per capita in PPP [USD]****	7723,3	7 407.2	7 683.0	7979.3	8 307.9	9 056.7	9 315.6	9 825.2	10 466.1	11 137.1
Total government education expenditure,* current prices [bill. HUF]	110.4	143.3	195.9	231.5	278.3	306.5	340.6	425.6	493.2	427.6
Total government education expenditure,* current prices [mill. USD]	1 133.5	1 915.9	2 479.0	2 515.4	2 647.3	2 444.0	2 232.2	2 279.2	2 300.0	1 801.8
Total government education expenditure,* [%] of GDP	5.28	5.79	6.67	6.54	6.38	5.46	4.94	4.98	4.89	3.74
Direct public expenditures on education,** [%] of GDP	5.0			5.9	5.7	4.9		4.5		
Total expenditure from public and private sources on education,** [%] of GDP	5.3			6.6	6.4	5.5		5.2		

Table 2A.2 (continued)
Expenditures in Education Relative to the GDP

Indicator	1990	1991	1992	1993	1994	1995	1996	1997	1998	1999 est
Share of education expenditure in GDP'''		5.1	5.2	5.2	5.1	4.2	4	3.9		
Total education expenditure in [%] of GDP	5.89	6.34	6.8	6.54	6.4	5.46	4.98	4.98	4.83	
Central government education expenditure, [%] of total education expenditure		48.0	45.5	45.1	35.6	33.1	42.4	43.4	43.3	
ISCED 0–2 education expenditure in [%] of GDP	3.12	3.36	3.53	3.49	3.44	2.9	2.65			
ISCED 3 general education expenditure in [%] of GDP										
ISCED 3 vocational education expenditure in [%] of GDP										
ISCED 3	1.47	1.57	1.73	1.66	1.54	1.31	1.20			
ISCED 0–3 education expenditure in [%] of GDP	4.59	4.93	5.26	5.15	4.98	4.21	3.85	3.76	3.67	3.67
ISCED 4 education expenditure in [%] of GDP										
ISCED 5–7 education expenditure in [%] of GDP	0.81	0.88	1.06	1.07	1.08	0.96	0.86	0.94	0.90	0.96
Other education	0.28	0.32	0.28	0.32	0.34	0.29	0.27	0.28	0.29	

     SOURCE OF DATA: HCSO
     SOURCE OF DATA: OECD Education at a Glance (1996, 1997, 1998, 2000)
     SOURCE OF DATA: 1991–97: OECD Economic Surveys, Hungary, 1999
     SOURCE OF PPP INDICES: http://www.oecd.org/std/ppp/pps.htm

SOURCE OF OTHER DATA: Ministry of Education and Ministry of Education, quoted in Halász
     G.–Lannert J. (eds.): Jelentés a magyar közoktatásról 2000 [Report
     on Public Education in Hungary]

NOTES: From 1997 financial data are not collected separately for the primary, lower-secondary and general upper-secondary levels of education.

Even before 1997 total expenditures for different branches of (upper-)secondary education are not published separately: expenditures on student hostels and food are available only together.

Table 2A.3
Expenditures in Education

Expenditures, 1998	Total	ISCED 0	ISCED 1–2				
Current expenditures–Total	92.3%	97.4%	92.6%				
Staff income (wages, salaries, etc.)	44.6%	51.6%	51.4%				
Capital expenditures–Total	7.7%	2.6%	7.4%				
Total expenditures	493 240	62 229	236 108				
Expenditures, 1996	Total	ISCED 0	ISCED 1–2*	ISCED 3	ISCED 3	ISCED General*	ISCED 3 Voca- tional*
Current expenditures–Total	88.8%	97.1%	86.7%	82.4%	78.7%	1.0%	64.8%
Staff income (wages, salaries, etc.)	45.1%	48.8%	48.9%	53.4%	44.3%	49.9%	45.0%
Capital expenditures–Total	11.2%	2.9%	13.3%	17.6%	21.3%	99.0%	35.2%
Total expenditures	340 562	49 325	131 679	99 956	82 395	17 743	49 868

SOURCE: Ministry of Education

Notes: *: education of full-time students only, excluding social expenditures (student hostels, food, day-care of students)

Expenditures of special education is included in expenditures of primary education

Expenditures of other education are excluded because it mainly refers to post-graduate or post-secondary forms of education, out of the public education system

Table 2A.4
Wages in the Education Sector

	1992	1993	1994	1995	1996	1997	1998	1999
AVERAGE GROSS WAGE IN EDUCATION [HUF]								
Education (including higher education)	21 928	24 495	30 912	34 866	38 996	49 460	59 822	72 869
Teachers in public education	24 376					56 375		77 619
Teachers, school leaders and other teachers* in public education	23 854					58 477		80 551
Public education**	21 033					49 016		67 218
AVERAGE GROSS WAGE IN EDUCATION RELATIVE TO THE AVERAGE IN THE TOTAL ECONOMY [%]								
Education (including higher education)	98.4	90.1	92.8	89.6	83.3	86.4	88.3	94.4
Teachers in public education	109.3					98.4		100.6
Teachers, school leaders and other teachers* in public education	107.0					102.1		104.4
Public education**	94.3					85.6		87.1
AVERAGE GROSS WAGE IN EDUCATION RELATIVE TO THE GDP PER CAPITA [%]								
Education (including higher education)	92.3	85.3	87.2	76.2	69.2	70.6	72.0	77.0
Teachers in public education	102.6					80.4		82.0
Teachers, school leaders and other teachers§ in public education	100.4					83.4		85.1
Public education**	88.5					69.9		71.0

SOURCE OF DATA: wages in the education sector: Varga, 2001
wages in the economy, GDP per capita: HCSO

NOTES: * other teachers include non-qualified teachers (i.e. teachers without the required degree), teaching assistants etc.
   ** Public education total also includes physical workers and administration staff

NOTES

[1] I. Act of 1985.

[2] For example a very strong, veto right was given by the enforcement regulation of the 1985 act to teachers for the appointment of the school director. This was abandoned in 1992, due to a Constitutional Jury declaration, initiated by the fist, conservative government.

[3] The previous, obligatory central curriculum was introduced in 1978 and its regulative role was melting by the late 1980s which caused a deep gap in content processes in schools.

[4] However, it must be noted here that later, it came to light that opposing the socialist monolithic structure did not necessarily result in united opinions amongst the different parties.

[5] Because the Act on the Local Authorities was a law, claiming a two third majority of the Parliament, its approval claimed the support of opposition parties. The winner of the first general election were conservative parties but the local election gave majority to opposition parties in many municipalities. This is the political root of confrontations between central and local level, accompanying many problems throughout the decade.

[6] In fact, the present Hungarian Constitution originated in 1949, though since then it has had hundreds of modifications.

[7] For example the centrally set personal tax system or the incoherent mixture of decentralized and de-concentrated institutions of territorial administration.

[8] Semjén (1991) argues that most of the reform proposals intended to restrict the operation of the market through administration. However, monetary restrictions were not supported by the same arguments by the different actors. Those proposed by economists of neo-liberal paradigms and the ones supported by members of the political opposition, having already a culture of democratization, supposing circumstances of a welfare state had a common characteristic of deregulation but not more.

[9] A more centralized system would have not been accepted by the opposition, a more liberal regulation, eg. a voucher system, sent directly to the families, was not supported by most experts.

[10] In the first period of the transition, the state per capita grant for other than authority-maintained schools was bound to an individual contract between the school and the municipality. Later the law entitled church schools to get the grant automatically. The third government applied positive discrimination in financing church schooling and—from 2001—in recruiting pupils to these institutions.

[11] The age was the same as previously, but by this law the whole compulsory period should be devoted to general education and not vocational training.

[12] The requirements of the 10th grade gave the basIS for the content of basic examination.

13　The new final exam was planned to be introduced from 2004, with the first cohorts of learning by the NCC (it was initiated to be introduced at two grades, 1 and 7). In reality the following government postponed the introduction of the new final exam.

14　The first government interpreted its responsibility towards the individual schools. In reality, it did not have the required experience or tools for reaching this aim.

15　LXII. Act of 1996.

16　The most successful one was the so-called SULINET (School-Net) program, which provided schools (in its first phase just secondary ones) with computers with internet connections, and the state increased the circle of labelled central financial grants, serving modernization in schools.

17　Between the two world wars this was the exclusive type of secondary grammar school.

18　There were two even lower types of this school, having grades 9–10, one for the mentally handicapped pupils, finishing special general school and another for pupils to be trained to be some non-physical semi-skilled administrative work.

19　Special teaching programs were developed for this type of schools (see the previous footnote), supported by the government.

20　More of them were institutions of the so called World Bank schools, developed by a World Bank credit. In a bilingual school, one year is given for learning a foreign language, and then a four year education process takes place, in the majority of cases in the foreign language.

21　The post-secondary system is to be held by accreditation processes. This is a tool for quality management, having its regulations and institutions and applying independent professional bodies. Accreditation in higher education works, in post-secondary training is under introduction.

22　It is hard, at present, to qualify what exactly secondary grammar schools 'mean'—or are 'worth.' Theoretically, the two-level final examination solves this problem as it shows which schools direct and promote their children to university, and which ones to the labour market. But the system does not exist, and since the higher education is independent from public education, there is no guarantee to enter the university without another entrance exam.

23　We have not mentioned some insignificant changes, for example a general school of less than eight grades (e.g. four or six). Except for the schools of small villages, several general schools have underdeveloped themselves, trying to be fit either to an imagined school structure or to the double push of the demographic decline and—not independently from that—the extractor effect of the eight and six grade secondary schools.

24　This concept has been prefered by the 1998 government, which aims intensively at developing standards in education.

25　I. Act of 1985.

[26]   Halász–Garami–Havas–Vágó, 2001.

[27]   For example, the introduction of the NCC supposed that the new final examination system was also to be introduced soon. In fact, there is still a delay in its introduction. That is why a great effort should be taken for external evaluation.

[28]   Individuals working in different institutions or firms of pedagogical services or working in schools, having competencies in this kind of expertise, were got onto the list with two supporters, being also on the list. The training of the experts was organized but being put onto the list was without clear recruitment criteria or examination. The professional preparation and application of experts, devoted to a broader range of tasks, were developed by the third educational government and is being done by OKÉV.

[29]   In fact the application of experts for more goals than the obligatory ones depends much on the financial condition of the local municipality. That is why it is regular in bigger cities and wealthymunicipalities of well-being.

[30]   A nemzeti alaptanterv..., Szocioreflex-OKI KK, 1999.

[31]   Értékelés és minőségbiztosítás..., Hungarian Gallup Institute, 1999.

[32]   IEA, TIMMS, SIALS are the main international measurements whilst in the national context the so called MONITOR survey is used, see below in section 2.1.

[33]   The basic examination system is ready. Its introduction is connected to the new vocational training system, which claims to have a basic exam before starting professional training after the 10th grade. The final exam was intended to be introduced in an upgrading system after the introduction of NCC. In the plans the new system was to be applied from 2004 but the third educational government decided to modify the content regulation (a three level regulation was introduced in 2000) and therefore the new examinations will exist after 2010.

[34]   The ' EAG' is a yearly booklet of OECD Indicators, issued by the Centre for Educational Research and Innovation. Indicators of Education Systems. OECD, Paris.

[35]   This logic was used by the educational government of the period when NCC and LPP were introduced.

[36]   Certainly, this kind of freedom is greater in settlements which have a broad network of schools. The barriers of free entering can be limited by schools of specialist programs (e.g. sport, or musicdepartments); they can organize entrance exams or skill-measuring.

[37]   The following indicators are used for ranking schools: the proportion of pupils, having successful university entrance; that of in foreign language certificates; that of the 1–20 places in national subject competetitions. The indicators have a nearly 10-year period so regrouping can also be detected.

[38]   The COMENIUS programme works in the form of an earmarked central grant, used by an application system. There are other central tools for quality development; the teacher in-service training is co-financed by the state budget yearly in a form of per-capita grants

(it is obligatory to carry out this goal); there is central support for the internal quality management.

[39] The previously given veto right in NCC matters was withdrawn in 1999. Concerning the frame curricula, OKNT has the right to make proposals.

[40] Generally there are committees of public and of vocational education. These times the forming of regional comittees has been started in some regions.

[41] The local (school-based) pedagogical progam should contain this system since September, 2001.

[42] The shared PIT consists of two parts: one part is in proportion of tax-payment from the settlement and the other part is redistributed among municipalities. The share of the latter has increased above 50% since 1994.

[43] Formula grants (without special formula grants) are estimated to cover 40–70% of per student costs [Halász G.–Lannert J. (eds.), 2000]. In exceptional cases the grant coverage may approach or even exceed 100%, this can be assumed in the case of special education Local governments in fact do not save this money, since they spend much more on non-special primary and secondary schools.

[44] Representatives of employers, employees, central government, school maintainers (mainly local governments) and economic chambers constitute the councils.

[45] Halász–Lannert, 2000.

[46] As for the admission rate, large and growing discrepancies seem to exist between different groups of secondary schools. While an average of 44.7% of students leaving general secondary schools were admitted into higher education between 1991 and 1998, the rate was 24.6% with mixed secondary schools (schools of both general and vocational education), and 16.3% with secondary vocational schools [Halász–Lannert, 2000]. The highest admission rate can be observed in six-grade general secondary schools and the lowest in four-grade schools.

[47] Results of representative surveys are available retrospectively for more than a decade, therefore it is possible to analyze the change in students' performance. Previously, surveys using standardized tests primarily focused on the degree to which students had mastered the body of knowledge in certain subjects. Recent investigations, however, put the emphasis on general competence, the so-called instrumental knowledge instead of factual. Such series of surveys, called Monitor, have been conveyed on a regular two-year basis since 1986. On the Hungarian standardized test surveys (the MONITOR surveys) see: Vári, 1997, Vári et al., 1998, Bánfi, 1999, Vári, 1999, Vári et al., 2000a, Vári et al., 2000b. On comparative international surveys see e.g. Vári–Krolopp, 1997, Vári et al., 2001.

[48] The decrease in reading competencies is estimated to be around 20% in the case of students in the twelfth grade [Vári, 1997].

[49] In 1999 only students at the eighth grade were surveyed.

[50] The survey was based on a questionnaire devised in the Civic Education project, organised by the IEA, an international body dealing with the success of learning. The project involved 24 countries.

[51] The list of participant countries: Australia, Belgium (the Flemish region), Canada, Chile, the Czech Republic, Denmark, Finland, Germany, Ireland, Hungary, the Netherlands, New Zealand, Norway, Poland, Portugal, Slovenia, Sweden, Switzerland, the United Kingdom, the United States. In the analysis the German-, French- and Italian-speaking regions are considered separately. The four countries with the weakest performance are Chile, Poland, Portugal and Slovenia.

[52] For the TIMMS survey paragraph see Vári–Krolopp, 1997.

[53] On the basis of MONITOR survey results Vári et. al (1998) concluded that students' knowledge in mathematics does not grow even in absolute terms between the eighth and tenth grades. The authors interpret this finding by referring to technical schools, where only minor importance is given to mathematics.

[54] Imre, 1997.

[55] For some empirical evidence on the latter see: Bánfi, 1999.

[56] Forray, 1998.

[57] Ladányi–Szelényi, 1997.

[58] On peer-group effects see e.g. Henderson et. al., 1978, on externalities within the classroom see e.g. Lazear, 1999.

[59] Vágó, 2000, Sóstói, 2001, Rubicsek, 2001.

[60] Vágó, 1999.

[61] Halász–Lannert, 2000.

[62] Balázs, 1998.

[63] Balázs, 1998.

[64] Note that *school efficiency* defined above is a much narrower concept than the concept of efficiency may appear in the economics of education literature. Models of investment in human capital analyze the efficiency of investment decisions from the individual and social point of view. The analysis of school efficiency focuses on the costs of the provision of school services, and defines the output as students' achievement at the end of the school years. Estimates of the rate of return of education also incorporate individual expenses and foregone income on the cost side and define the benefits on a longer run in terms of earnings, sometimes taking into account external social benefits of education as well.

[65] School decisions may affect the composition of students if schools are allowed to select among the applicants. However, in the case of primary education, student characterisitcs can be considered as given at the settlement level.

[66] See the seminal paper of Bradford et. al., 1969.

[67] Duncombe–Yinger, 1999.

[68] See, for example, Várnagy, 2001.

[69] Sugár, 1999.

[70] In 1998/99 the average class size is 12.5 in schools with less than 100 students and more than 22 in schools with more than 300 students [Sugár, 1999].

[71] Hermann, 1999.

[72] Sugár, 1999.

[73] Hermann, 2001.

[74] Halász, 2000.

[75] Varga, 2001.

[76] It is very difficult to implement a central policy aiming at reducing local capacities in education provision successfully, since the concrete decisions (i.e. which institution to close) can not be made at the central level and local governments can be expected to resist.

[77] Local governmental employees in the education sector are frequently present among local representatives and in the group of the local political elite. A small survey research of 11 middle-size (10 000–40 000 inhabitants) Hungarian towns shows that approximately 19% of the municipality leaders were employed in the education and culture sector [Hermann, 2000].

[78] Deák, 1998.

[79] Borbola, 1998.

[80] Hajdú, 2000.

[81] Hermann, 2001.

[82] Koltay, 2001, Sóstói, 2001, Homolya, 2001.

[83] Balogh, 1997.

[84] Local governments are allowed to transfer secondary schools to county governments. Case studies suggest that towns are less inclined to transfer general secondary schools (especially in the case of small towns these schools contribute to the settlements identity of township) than vocational schools or student dormitories. However, in the last two years central grants for vocational education have been relatively raised, and vocational schools and student dormitories have access to other revenues as well (grants from vocational education funds and revenues for providing accommodation in the summer). Thus, general secondary schools are the most expensive for local governments but usually these are also the most important, in several cases resulting in no transfer of schools for the county government [e.g. Sóstói, 2001].

85   Homolya, 2001, Koltay, 2001, Sóstói, 2001, Rubicsek, 2001.

86   Horváth, 2000, Mártonfi, 2000.

87   Nagy, 2000.

88   See, for example, Liskó, 1998.

89   See, for example, Lannert, 2000, Radó, 2000b.

90   Radó, 2000b.

91   Radó, 2000b.

92   Nagy, 2000.

93   Mártonfi, 2000.

94   Horváth, 2000.

95   Andor–Liskó, 2000.

96   Liskó, 1998, Liskó, 1999, Andor–Liskó, 2000.

97   Andor–Liskó, 2000.

98   Vári et al., 2000b.

99   Disregarding the differences with respect to gender, inequalities in students' performance are below the average of the countries, due to the fact that in Hungary boys' and girls' performances are quite similar [Vári–Krolopp, 1997]. That is, the variation in performance in many countries, as opposed to Hungary, is in part caused by gender differences.

100   Vári et al., 2001.

101   In comparison, estimates for different states of the US generally vary between 0.22 and 0.48, but a 0.82 value has also been found [see Feldstein, 1975, Weber, 1991 or Sarensen, 1997].

102   Radó, 2000a.

103   In 1996 this share was 3,56% [Radó, 2000a].

104   Kertesi, 1995.

105   Harsányi–Radó, 1997, Radó, 2000a.

106   In these cases either students are sorted with respect to their school performance in order to enhance the effectiveness of teaching or programs to handle the problems of socially disadvantaged children are introduced.

Decentralization, Local Governments and Education Reform in Post-communist Poland

Tony Levitas
Jan Herczyński

Table of Contents

Introduction 117

1. The Legacies of the Old Order 118

2. The Politics of Decentralization: The Reforms of 1990 120

3. The Emerging Legal Framework for Education Reform 122

4. The Transfer of Schools to Local Governments 127

5. The Financing of Education: 1990–1999 133
    5.1   The Financing of Primary Education 136
    5.2   The Financing of Secondary Education 139
    5.3   The Reform of the Teachers Charter and the Crisis of 2000 145

6. The Management of Schools: 1990–1991 147
    6.1   The Management of Preschool Education 147
    6.2   The Management of Primary Schools and the Creation of 'Gimnazjum' 151
    6.3   The Management of Secondary Schools 158

7. Conclusions 162

Bibliography 165

Laws of Sejm Discussed in the Text 170

Annex 1:   Basic Data for Primary Schools: 1990–1999 172
Annex 2:   Shares of the Education Subvention by School and Pupil Type in 2000 174
Annex 3:   Basic Data for Lyceums: 1990–1999 177

Notes 179

INTRODUCTION[1]

Between the fall of Communism in 1989 and the year 2000, Poland transferred responsibility for the management of some 35 000 preschools, primary schools and secondary schools to democratically elected local governments. At the same time, the national government significantly changed the structure and content of primary and secondary education, and reformed the way it regulates and finances the sector. These profound changes have come rapidly and, not surprisingly, remain incomplete.

In the following, we examine the devolution of educational responsibilities to local governments. We focus on this element of educational reform for three reasons. Firstly, because both lay and expert observers have devoted remarkably little attention to local governments when discussing education reform in Poland, despite the fact that over the last ten years local governments have been made responsible for the ownership and management of all primary and secondary schools. Secondly, because from here on in, all further efforts to improve Polish education will be mediated by local governments and will have to account for their interests, powers, and behaviors. And thirdly, because we believe that the assignment of managerial and financial responsibilities to local governments remains confused. It is unclear who is responsible for setting and financing teachers' wages, the national government or local governments, and who is responsible for hiring and firing them, local governments or school directors. And it is unclear who is responsible for monitoring school performance and intervening when they fail.

The lack of clearly defined roles with respect to both teachers' pay and employment and the monitoring of school performance, has reduced the willingness and ability of local governments to squarely address many of the challenges that face their school systems. It has also made it difficult to determine how the national government should help them meet these challenges. Because we believe that continued reform of the sector is critical to Poland's socio-economic success, the following attempts both to explain how and why these confusions arose, and to assess their implications for the future. As a result, the paper shifts back and forth between an historical narrative and more analytical or policy driven observations.

We begin with a brief overview of the Polish education system under Communism, an overview that is necessary to understand both the motives behind the devolution of education responsibilities to local governments, and some of major structural problems they have encountered since. This prelude is followed by a closer examination of the politics behind the transfer of education responsibilities to local governments, and the tensions which shaped the basic, if still unclear, character of their responsibilities. We then track the complicated process through which schools were actually handed over to local governments before examining in somewhat greater detail the evolution of Poland's education finance system. Finally, we analyze what local governments have—and have not—done with their school systems and conclude with some policy recommendations.

1. THE LEGACIES OF THE OLD ORDER

Between 1947 and 1990, education policy in Poland was subordinated to the attempts of the Polish United Workers' Party (PZPR) to centrally plan the entire economy. In the 1950s, the PZPR rapidly increased the percentage of children attending primary schools and successfully eliminated illiteracy.[2] It also tried to increase the number of working class and peasant children who attended general education high schools (lyceums) and universities to reduce its dependency on the existing 'bourgeoisie.'[3] Most importantly, it built large numbers of specialized vocational schools to produce the workers needed by the Plan. At the peak of Stalinism, more than 15 different sectoral ministries and a ministerial level coordinating agency[4] ran vocational schools. Meanwhile, the Ministry of Education controlled universities and, through a network of provincial Education Offices (Kuratoria Oświaty i Wychowania), primary schools and lyceums. The Kuratoria set school budgets, hired and fired school directors, and imposed strict programmatic and political control on teachers and pupils.[5]

By the 1960s, the Party began to restrict university enrolment because it felt that the country did not need to educate the masses for a few positions at the 'commanding heights' of the economy. Similarly, as the economy stagnated and the Party's revolutionary zeal waned, it made less and less effort to improve the educational chances of disadvantaged groups. Thus, by the time the regime collapsed, only 10% of rural children attended lyceums, and less than 5% received university degrees.[6]

Despite the PZPR's instrumental attitude towards education, competitive entrance exams and the persistence of pre-war teaching traditions along with Poland's relative openness to the West preserved the quality of the country's elite institutions.[7] Nonetheless, pedagogical techniques were based on rote learning and the mastery of specialized bodies of knowledge deemed necessary for industry. Needless to say, Party propaganda deformed learning (especially of history and literature) while the central determination of teaching curricula and school budgets left little room for variation or innovation at the school or classroom level.[8]

The central financing of education and the use of competitive entrance exams for secondary schools made legally binding school districts unnecessary. For primary schools, the local or district school had to accept pupils living in the area, but parents were free to send their children elsewhere if they chose. For secondary schools, there were no districts at all and parents were free to send their children to any school that accepted them. Moreover, because most secondary schools were built in cities, there was considerable commutation between rural and urban areas.

Initially, the Party devoted large shares of GDP to education. As elsewhere in the Communist world, however, expenditures on public services (including education) fell with declining growth and the accompanying attempts to jump-start the economy with new industrial investment drives.[9] Indeed, the investment and expenditure targets for education set in the Party's five-year plans were met only once.[10] Moreover, and more generally, as coercion and commitment waned, subordinate actors within the polity began to more aggressively game the plan, ultimately turning the planning process into a free-for-all punctuated by periodic attempts to rewrite the rules.[11] By the late 1970s, education policy, like virtually everything else within the body of the single-party state, had lost its coherence.[12]

As in industry, the funding of particular types of schools was generally based on historical expenditures with school directors, provincial Kuratoria, and national ministries all fighting for additional resources at the margins. Every once in a while however, a new reform initiative, or the changing fortunes of particular players would generate a more radical shift in the allocation of resources. As a result, per pupil expenditures came to vary dramatically across schools of different types and schools of the same type in different areas of the country.

With the dramatic emergence of the Solidarity Trade Union in 1980, the opposition movement demanded an overhaul of the country's educational system. On both sides of the political divide, people called for the consolidation and streamlining of school administration, the modernization of teaching methods and curricula, a reduction in the role of vocational education, and not surprisingly, increased public spending.[13] Moreover, both groups argued that low wages had led to negative selection within the teaching profession.

Solidarity however, stressed that both this negative selection,[14] and the more general problems of the sector were being generated by the subordination of education to ideology. Thus, while within the Party a handful of reformers talked about the 'socializing' of school management (*uspołecznienie szkół*) through the creation of oversight councils composed of teachers, parents, and outside experts, Solidarity demanded the right to create 'self-governing' schools (*samorządne szkoły*), in which directors would be elected by Teachers Councils (*rada pedagogiczna*).[15] These demands paralleled the union's efforts to take enterprises out of the hands of central planners by strengthening the powers of factory managers while at the same time subordinating them to newly formed Employee Councils (*rada pracownicza*).[16] Indeed, Solidarity's attitudes towards education reform in the 1980s were part of a broader strategy in which the union attempted to take control over spheres of social life without directly challenging the principle of single-party rule.[17] Not surprisingly, the union also demanded an end to the state-enforced atheism of the school system and fought heated, if rarely successful, battles to liberalize school curricula.[18]

In December 1981, the PZPR declared Martial Law and delegalized Solidarity, bringing to an end a chaotic eighteen months of national awakening. One month later, the government passed the Law on the Teachers' Charter.[19] Like a number of other pieces of legislation enacted immediately after the declaration of Martial Law, the Charter tried to co-opt opposition by acceding to some of Solidarity's demands.[20] The law increased the powers and job rights of both teachers' councils and school directors. It also reduced teacher work loads from twenty-one teaching hours a week to eighteen (the so-called 'pensum').

119

Throughout the 1980s, however, neither Solidarity nor the regime connected education reform with local governments. On the one hand, even during the interwar period, Poland had no tradition of local government involvement in schools. On the other hand, the idea that local governments were critical to the establishment of a future democratic order had yet to become widespread. In fact, until the regime collapsed, linking education reform with local government reform was probably unthinkable.

With this said, we now turn to the unlikely story of how this linkage became policy in post-Communist Poland. Here, we will argue that local governments were assigned responsibility for schools not because they were seen as important players in educational reform, but because Solidarity saw 'decentralization' as the fastest way to dismantle the Communist state. Indeed, we will show how education reform has been shaped by two contradictory desires. On the one hand reformers sought to give local governments ownership and financial control over schools in order to break up the power of the old apparatus. On the other hand, they sought to maintain central control over education so that the newly sovereign Polish state could rebuild a national identity deformed by forty years of communism.

2. THE POLITICS OF DECENTRALIZATION: THE REFORMS OF 1990

Over the first six months of 1989, the PZPR and representatives of the Solidarity Trade Union movement engaged each other in the so-called Round Table Negotiations. These negotiations were designed to find a peaceful way to extricate the country from its self-evident political and economic impasse and covered virtually all spheres of social and political life.

At the Sub-Committee on Education, Solidarity succeeded in getting the Party to agree in principle to the ideological neutrality of schools and to loosen state control over the education system. Teachers were given greater authority in the selection of textbooks, the subject 'science of society' was removed from the lyceum exam system, and parents and teachers were granted the right to set up 'community schools' (*szkoły społeczne*). In a compromise between the union's demand for the election of school directors by teachers, and the Party's desire to preserve their appointment by Kuratoria, the government agreed to set up independent selection committees. The government also promised to radically increase education spending from about 4 to 7% of GDP, a promise that was never kept.[21] Neither side, however discussed the role of local governments, and no linkage was made during the negotiations between the work of the subcommittees on Education and Local Government.

More importantly, the negotiations did produce an historical agreement to hold partially free parliamentary elections in June of 1989 as well as a more general understanding that whatever its results, the opposition would not try to criminalize the Party for forty years of communism.[22]

Solidarity-backed candidates swept these elections and in August the PZPR's satellite parties abandoned it. In September, Solidarity forces formed Poland's first non-Communist government since World War II.

This government faced a daunting array of political and economic challenges. Most immediately, it had to reassert control over an economy on the brink of hyperinflation. More strategically, it sought to create the foundations of a market economy and a multi-party democracy as rapidly as possible. Education reform *per se* was far from its most pressing priority. Instead, the Ministry of Finance hastily prepared a radical program of economic stabilization and market liberalization.

On 1 January 1990, the government freed most prices, opened the economy to foreign goods and new private firms, and slashed state spending. Foreign competition and fiscal austerity produced a steep drop in industrial production. Not surprisingly, the dramatic contraction of the economy created serious tensions between the government and the trade union that remained its sole institutional base.[23]

Despite declining popular support and huge day-to-day problems of mastering the government itself, reformers decided to push forward with the creation of democratically elected local governments. This decision was dictated by two visceral fears. Firstly, reformers felt they could not trust the administrative apparatus they had inherited from the past. Indeed, they felt that the longer the Party's bureaucrats were left in place, the greater the chances that their efforts would be 'sandbagged.' And secondly, reformers were painfully aware that they had no political parties capable of competing with the PZPR's heir, the newly transmogrified Democratic Left Party (SLD). Worse still, the forces that had coalesced into Solidarity were clearly splintering. In short, and whatever the other merits of the case, reformers came to see the rapid creation of democratically elected local governments as the best way to dismantle a bureaucracy they couldn't trust and to create the political space to build the political parties that they didn't have.[24]

Thus, over the spring of 1990, the government rushed to pass the legislation necessary to elect councils for 1600 rural and 800 urban communes (gminas) in May. This legislation defined local government election rules and their governance structure. It also assigned them the responsibility for essential public services such as water, sewage, solid waste, local roads, district heating, public transport, land use planning, and municipal housing and gave them ownership of a good deal of local real estate as well as the assets associated with these services. Finally, and perhaps most importantly, gminas were guaranteed independent budgets and statutorily defined revenues from shared taxes, grants, and own taxes.[25] In short, the legislation passed in the heady year of 1990 set in motion local electoral politics, stripped significant functions away from the national government, and equipped gminas with the rights, assets, and revenues necessary to become independent economic and political actors.

3. THE EMERGING LEGAL FRAMEWORK FOR EDUCATION REFORM

Within the Solidarity camp, there was a hot, if not also hasty debate over assigning gminas responsibility for schools between reformers whose principal concern was using the creation of strong local governments to weaken the old regime, and those that entered the Ministry of National Education (MEN).

The former insisted that gminas immediately be made responsible for preschool and primary education. For them, the most important issue was to take control over schools out of the hands of state bureaucrats once and for all. Thus, they insisted that the law define preschool and primary education as the local government's 'own' functions and not as functions delegated to them by the national government, and that the ownership of all preschool and primary school facilities be immediately transferred to gminas. Indeed, they argued that in the near future, new poviat or county level governments should be created and assigned responsibility for secondary schools on a similar basis.

Meanwhile, reformers within MEN, and education specialists outside of it, were far from enthusiastic about involving local governments in education at all. To be sure, giving citizens more control over their schools sounded like a good idea, as a useful step towards rebuilding the 'civil society' that the Communist state had destroyed. At the same time, however, it was difficult to think through what local government control over schools really meant in a country where the national government had always run the education system. Moreover, Communism had not only inhaled civil society, but the sovereignty of the Polish state. Indeed, for many, it was clearly the state's political and moral responsibility to use the education system to restore a weakened national identity. Similarly, the country's immediate and pressing socio-economic challenges seemed to call for rapid and concerted state action to reform the country's schools.

Not surprisingly then, MEN saw curriculum reform as the most important and pressing challenge of the day. Indeed, to the degree that the Ministry thought about the administration of schools, it tended to think in terms of restoring prewar institutional traditions.[26] And when it thought about education finance, it thought not about how local governments were supposed to finance schools, but about defending the size of national government's education budget, a budget that was shrinking under the pressures of fiscal austerity.

In fact, the Ministry, as well as the teachers' section of Solidarity and the larger SLD-affiliated Union of Polish Teachers (ZNP), were afraid that making gminas 'responsible' for schools would weaken the government's commitment to financing the sector. Thus, they argued that gminas' assumption of responsibility for schools should be voluntary, and not obligatory. They also insisted on legal guarantees that the national government would fully fund the operation and maintenance costs of schools, and that the 1982 Teachers' Charter would remain on the books.

In the end, the struggle between advocates of strong local governments and education reformers produced a confusing set of legal compromises.[27] The laws on local government made preschool and primary education the gmina's 'own' functions. As its 'own' functions, gminas were to be transferred ownership rights to school facilities and given control over school finances. The transfer of ownership and financial responsibility for preschools was immediate. But in a concession to education reformers and the unions, their legal obligation to take over primary schools was postponed until 1993. In the interim, however, gminas were free to take over not only some or all of their primary schools, but some or all of their secondary schools as well.

By giving gminas ownership of school facilities, reformers had clearly made local governments responsible for financing capital improvements out of their general revenues. How reformers expected gminas to finance the operation and maintenance costs of schools, however, was less clear. The Law on Gmina Income guaranteed gminas transfers to support the operational costs of primary and secondary schools. But no such guarantee was made for preschools. Instead, gminas were expected to finance not only preschool education, but also school transport out of their general revenues and without specific support from the national government.

Reformers justified the different treatment of preschool and primary education by arguing that while primary school attendance is obligatory, parents do not have to send their children to preschool.[28] In fact, however, local governments were legally obliged to provide preschool training for all six year olds whose parents chose to send them to a preparatory 'zero' class. Moreover, more than 90% of all 6 year olds do in fact attend 'zero' classes, and unlike other levels of 'preschool' education, local governments are not allowed to charge parents fees for zero classes.

Thus, despite the (de facto) obligatory nature of at least the 'zero' component of preschool education, reformers created two very different systems for financing the educational responsibilities of local governments. Nevertheless, they insisted on considering both preschool and primary education as gmina 'own' functions. Indeed, they argued that because the transfers the government envisioned for primary and secondary education were to come through a freely disposable general subsidy,[29] they should be considered 'own revenues' going to support 'own functions.'[30]

Even more importantly, reformers maintained very significant constraints on the managerial powers of gminas with respect to their schools, despite having declared preschool and primary education local government "own functions." In line with the Ministry's prewar role, the new Law on the Education System of 1991 strengthened MEN's control over the kuratoria by taking them out of the hands of the regional voivods.[31] It also reaffirmed the powers of kuratoria to inspect school conditions, analyze teaching effectiveness, and issue directives to school directors. Indeed, kuratoria were empowered to issue directives not only to school directors but to local governments if they felt that local government schools were not operating in accordance with the law or were failing to provide adequate schooling.[32]

At the same time, the law bestowed extremely little authority on local governments. They were empowered to create schools and liquidate them, but only subject to kuratorial approval. Similarly, they were given the right to request formal explanations from school directors about educational policy, and to pay for additional educational services such as foreign language or computer programs if they so desired. But gminas were expressly forbidden from directly involving themselves in the pedagogical decisions of school directors. Moreover, they were not given the right to hire, or even unilaterally fire, school directors.

Instead, in line with the Round Table Talks, the Law mandated the creation of independent committees to select school directors for five-year terms. Local governments, kuratoria, teachers' councils, and parents were each given the right to name two members of these committees, and the two teachers' unions, one apiece.[33] As a result, school directors are formally employed, and paid, by local governments, but not hired by them. Indeed, local governments can only fire directors for gross financial mismanagement. Similarly, the law defines school directors as the chief executive officers of "workplaces" (zakłady pracy), giving them the sole right to make employment decisions within schools.[34]

Meanwhile amendments to the Teachers' Charter made in 1990 simply transposed the national government's wage and benefit obligations to teachers onto local governments.[35] These obligations are incredibly detailed, creating a large number of narrow pay grades and an archaic system of statutory benefits and bonuses. For example, local governments must provide teachers employed in rural areas with apartments, heating fuel, garden plots, and a ten percent pay supplement. Indeed, the only significant right given to local governments with respect to teacher employment was the right to provide teachers with motivational bonuses beyond those mandated by the law.

The amended Charter also maintained the 18 hour 'pensum' from 1982. This is low by European standards and, as we shall see later, has contributed to the relatively high share of wages in total education expenditures. Meanwhile, other ministerial ordinances specify the number and types of program hours for each class at a given grade level. But the Charter does not specify employment standards for teachers in terms of pupil/teacher ratios or class sizes. Instead, these kinds of norms are contained in a variety of other ordinances and are expressed as pedagogical *minimums*, not employment standards. This means that while it is possible to determine the minimum number of teachers needed to teach any given grade level, there is no easy way to determine a maximum number of teachers that should be employed in any given school or for that matter in any given jurisdiction. The lack of these standards has proved problematic for at least two reasons.

The first reason is because the Charter limits the right of local governments to reduce teacher employment to situations in which there is no work available in the jurisdiction as a whole. Without clear normative standards for the maximum number of teachers a jurisdiction should employ, there is no easy way to determine whether a local government has the right to fire teachers. Thus, in practice, local governments have only been able to reduce employment by closing schools and even here they are constrained by high severance payments and the obligation to try to employ redundant teachers in other schools.

The second reason is that the laws on Gmina Income and on the Education System both guarantee that the national government will provide local governments with the "financial resources necessary to realize their education responsibilities, including teachers' pay and the maintenance of schools."[36] Without the specification of employment norms, this legal guarantee becomes an unconditional promise by the national government to fully fund the hiring practices of school directors and local governments. This has created profound conflicts, less because local governments have consciously set out to pad their employment rolls, but rather because of the steep demographic decline of the last ten years and the difficulties gminas face in letting teachers go, which have left many of them, particularly rural ones with small schools, employing significantly more teachers than they actually need. Not surprisingly, however, the national government has proved unwilling to fund these "excess labor costs," despite the fact that the existing laws suggest it should, and local governments have been given little power to effect the situation on their own.

Indeed, the most significant power accorded to local governments by the Law on the Education System, the right to set school budgets and control school finances, has rarely been used by gminas to change staffing patterns. Every year, school directors are required to prepare so-called 'organizational forms' (arkusz organizacyjny) for their schools. These forms specify the number of teachers employed, the number and types of pupils served, the number and size of classes, and the allocation of teachers to all school tasks, such as teaching, tutoring, and various supervisory functions. The forms also include yearly financial plans whose wage components are the result of the proposed staffing plan.

Directors send these forms first to the Kuratoria for pedagogical approval, and then to local governments for acceptance. In theory, local governments can require directors to revise these forms if they consider their financial consequences excessive. In practice, however, the statutory obligations imposed on local governments by the Teachers Charter's, kuratorial approval of the pedagogical standards, and the lack of clear employment norms have all inclined local governments to routinely accept the staffing component of the forms and to instead focus only on the those aspects of the plan which concern building maintenance. Thus, the regulatory framework created by the Teachers Charter and the Law on the Education System have, as we shall see in greater detail later, essentially restricted the role of local governments in the sector to facility maintenance, capital improvement, and payroll functions.

Curiously, the Law on the Education System also made possible, but did not mandate, the creation of community oversight councils at the school, district, regional, and even national levels. If created, these councils have the right to inspect and review both the pedagogical and financial performance of schools, and to make policy recommendations to school directors, local governments, and the Kuratoria. In practice, however, almost none were established, and throughout the early

1990s, education reformers within and outside of MEN debated whether they should be made mandatory. In short, even when education reformers did think about subjecting schools to community oversight, they did not think in terms of local governments.[37]

Indeed, through at least the middle of the decade, and before most gminas had taken over primary schools, the Ministry's energies were focused on curriculum reform, and not the administrative or financial implications of the regulatory system it had created. Under the Law on the Education System, the Ministry continued to define basic educational programs (*podstawy programowe*) and general teaching plans (including subject- and grade-specific teaching hours), and officially certified curricula and textbooks. But in an important departure from the past, the Ministry began to certify a number of different curricula and teaching materials for each basic program. Moreover, the law clearly gave teachers the right to choose which certified curricula and texts they wanted to use. This immediately opened up Polish education to a wide variety of new currents, and stimulated the development of a thriving new textbook industry.[38]

The development and certification of new teaching materials proved a complicated and contentious process. Reformers rejected the orthodox atheism of the old regime and, after a lengthy battle, reintroduced religious instruction into schools. Unlike in interwar Poland, however, there were no morning prayers, and optional ethics classes were made possible for non-believers. There was also a prolonged struggle over the Ministry's efforts to introduce a unit on sex education into the core program, a struggle that the Ministry ultimately won. Similarly, there were bitter conflicts over how the country's post-war history ought to be taught, and more particularly what should be said about the nature of *Polish* Communism and Communists. Finally, and perhaps most importantly, the Ministry had a hard time determining what schools should teach in order to prepare pupils for a world that had changed overnight.

The Ministry also devoted a fair amount of energy to making possible the establishment of non-public schools. Under the Law on the Education System, individuals, firms and teacher-parent associations were allowed to set up private and community schools.[39] Moreover, the law guaranteed these schools a measure of national government funding so long as they employed certified teachers and followed the Ministry's programmatic standards. This funding, however, was—at least initially—relatively modest. It was also poorly defined. As a result, the Ministry found itself in continual conflicts with both local governments and the private and community schools it was trying to support.[40]

In sum, it is fair to say that the reformer's vision of the division of labor within the education sector during the early 1990s ran something like this: The national government would determine curricula, set pedagogical standards, and provide local governments with the funding necessary to pay for the operating costs of primary and secondary schools, but not preschools. Kuratoria would insure that these standards were met, and directors would actually run schools. Local governments, in turn, would provide investment funds to the sector, and play the role of beneficent uncles with respect to teachers pay. But they would not be involved in determining educational policy, or in monitoring the quality of education which 'their' resources bought.

In the next sections we will examine how schools were actually transferred to local governments and what they have done with them. We will argue that this division of labor worked reasonably well during the first half of the decade because national government transfers to local governments for education were, in general, in line with the basic operating costs of schools, and because local governments were in fact primarily concerned with improving school infrastructure.

With time however, this division of labor has become increasingly problematic for three reasons. Firstly, and most importantly, the demographic decline of the last ten years has radically increased the per pupil costs of small rural schools, costs that the national government has been unwilling to fully finance. Secondly, the national government has increased teachers' wages, without increasing commensurably the transfers it provides to local governments. And thirdly, popular pressure on local governments to improve and restructure their school systems has not only forced them, like falling state transfers, to contribute increasingly significant shares of their general revenues to the sector, but also to become concerned with what their resources are actually buying in terms of educational quality. In short, these forces have not only increased the financial burden being placed on local governments, but are pushing them towards an involvement in educational policy that reformers neither anticipated nor wanted.

4. THE TRANSFER OF SCHOOLS TO LOCAL GOVERNMENTS

Table 3.1 shows the pace at which primary and secondary schools were transferred from the national government to local governments during the 1990s. As can be seen from the table, this transfer has taken place in a piecemeal fashion. Nonetheless, by the end of the decade, local governments had taken over the vast majority of all schools and almost no schools remained in the hands of the national government. In this section, we describe how this process unfolded and the politics behind it.

In 1991, all gminas assumed responsibility for the ownership and management of preschools. Moreover, they had to finance preschool education entirely out of their general revenues and without specific financial support from the national government. This put considerable stress on their budgets, budgets which they had never administered before and which they were trying to master in new and unstable circumstances. As we shall see in greater detail later on, many gminas, particularly rural ones, responded to this stress by closing preschools.

These closures enhanced the fears of reformers who were skeptical about making local governments responsible for primary and secondary education. They also dampened the willingness of newly elected gmina officials to take over primary (and secondary) schools on a voluntary basis. As a result, by the end of 1992, only about 240 gminas (10%) had elected to take over their primary school systems, systems that accounted for about 16% of the country's 16 621 primary schools and about the same percent of total primary school enrollment.[41]

Table 3.1

The Transfer of Primary and Secondary Schools to Local Governments

	1990	1991	1992	1993	1994	1995	1996	1997	1998	1999
Primary schools	17 554	17 653	16 841	16 621	16 589	16 464	16 363	16 251	16 177	15 475
Of which run by gminas	995	2 302	2 253	2 745	5 283	5 735	16 042	15 890	15 796	15 093
As % of total	5.7	13.0	13.4	16.5	31.8	34.8	98.0	97.8	97.6	97.5
Lyceums	1 091	1 331	1 511	1 561	1 625	1 688	1 734	1 824	1 980	2 132
Of which run by gminas	0	12	17	18	227	183	506	595	626	1 686
As % of total	0.0	0.9	1.1	1.2	14.0	10.8	29.2	32.6	31.6	79.1
Vocational schools	7 745	7 603	7 542	7 749	7 860	8 083	8 026	8 138	8 272	8 659
Of which run by gminas	0	0	0	19	725	523	1 478	1 571	1 548	7 815
As % of total	0.0	0.0	0.0	0.2	9.2	6.5	18.4	19.3	18.7	90.3

SOURCE: GUS Statistical Yearbooks. The 20 percent of lyceums not run by local governments in 1999 were run by private institutions. These however accounted for only 5 percent of total lyceum enrollment.

The reluctance of gminas to take over schools was used by the Peasant Party within the government, and the ZNP and the SLD outside of it to argue against the compulsory assumption of responsibility for primary education in 1993. As a result, government extended the deadline to 1996. Nonetheless, larger urban gminas, often controlled by Solidarity-backed forces, increasingly decided to take over their primary schools. Thus, by the beginning of 1994, about 25% of gminas (626) had taken over 5 238 primary schools, representing almost 45% of all enrollment.[42]

Gminas were provided funding for education through the so-called education component of the general subvention. In the early 1990s, the education component was calculated separately for each gmina that had decided to take over its schools. The 49 voivodship-level (regional local government) Kuratoria summed the historical budgets of the schools located in a particular jurisdiction and used this sum, adjusted for inflation, as the baseline for a local government's education subvention.[43] The value of this subvention, however, was typically negotiated, in part because the government wanted to encouraged gminas to take over schools, and in part because gminas frequently objected to the government's initial calculations.

A particularly contentious issue concerned the debts that many schools had run up with suppliers, most frequently with utilities, over the previous years. Usually, the government agreed to pay off these debts. But gminas argued that at least some portion of them should be factored into their grants as recurrent fixed costs. They also demanded that the Kuratoria provide additional funds to repair particularly neglected infrastructure and/or to complete unfinished investment projects begun by the national government. Sometimes these demands were met, and sometimes not. But in general, gminas that took the plunge early do not seem to have suffered a dramatic worsening of their financial condition.

In 1993, in anticipation of the obligatory assumption of all primary schools by gminas, the government introduced substantial changes in the Law on Gmina Finances.[44] These changes were designed to create a systemic mechanism for allocating national funds to local governments. The Law guaranteed that 6.6% of national budget revenues were earmarked for the education component of the general subsidy and had to be allocated, unlike in the past, in accordance with a universal and transparent algorithm. By legally pegging the value of the education subvention to a fixed percentage of national budget revenues, reformers insured gminas a reasonably stable level of funding for primary education. Indeed, given the revival of economic growth in 1993, the Law allowed the national government to basically fulfill its promise to fully fund the operational costs of gmina-run primary schools through most of the decade.

After the passage of the law, but before all gminas actually took over their primary schools, the Ministry began experimenting with algorithms for allocating the subvention to local governments. The formulas used in 1994 and 1995 however, all contained components based on the inflation adjusted costs of the schools in a given jurisdiction and were still heavily negotiated. This combined with the fact that half of all schools were still receiving funding directly from the Kuratoria, meant that the mechanism for allocating national government transfers to gminas was still far from universal, and largely if not exclusively, based on historical expenditures.[45]

Despite the reluctance of most rural gminas to take over primary schools, and the Ministry of Education's continued uncertainty about how the education subvention should be allocated, advocates of strong local governments continued to push forward decentralization. These reformers, as we have indicated earlier, hoped to use the rapid establishment of county level (*poviat*) self governments to further dismantle the communist state. Indeed, by 1992 they had formulated an ambitious plan to create poviats by 1994, and to make them responsible for secondary education and general hospitals. Resistance from the PSL and the SLD, however, once again forced reformers to postpone their plans. Nonetheless, in 1993 they initiated the so-called pilot poviat program to keep the decentralization process moving.

Under this program, Poland's 46 largest cities could negotiate with the national government the voluntary assumption, on a delegated basis, of some or all of the service responsibilities that reformers eventually hoped to assign to poviats. Ultimately, 34 cities participated in the program, with all of them assuming responsibility for at least some of their secondary schools. As the negotiations were taking place, however, the government lost a no-confidence vote, forcing new parliamentary elections in the fall of 1993. The political parties associated with the Solidarity movement lost these elections, ushering in a new coalition government composed of the SLD and the PSL. Not surprisingly, this government did not push forward the previous government's plans to create poviats. At the same time, however, and despite fears to the contrary, the new government made no attempt to roll back the reforms. Indeed, it not only continued the pilot program, but ultimately expanded it in 1996.

In 1994 and 1995, the 34 cities participating in the program received earmarked grants from the national government for the operation and maintenance of the particular services they had agreed to take over. As with primary schools, these grants were based on the inflation adjusted historical expenditures of the institutions each city had decided to run. And as with primary schools, disputes arose over who should be responsible for the debts of these institutions, for the cost of repairing particularly devastated infrastructure, and for completing unfinished investment projects. Indeed, these disputes became so heated that a few cities decided to fully or partially withdraw from the program in 1995. As a result, the national government was forced to take back responsibility for some of the schools and other institutions that the cities had taken over in 1994.[46]

In an attempt both to stabilize the situation and placate the opposition's demand to continue the decentralization process, the government passed the Law on Large Cities.[47] The Law made Poland's 46 largest gminas responsible for secondary schools, general health care hospitals and a variety of other public services as 'own functions' (*zadanie własne*). The Law went into effect at the same time that all gminas had to finally assume control of their primary schools. As a result by 1 January 1996, gminas had become responsible for more than 16 000 primary schools, 312 000 teachers, and 4.9 million pupils,[48] as well as 29% of all lyceums and 18% of all vocational and professional schools (see Table 3.1 earlier). As with primary schools, gminas were to be provided the funding for these new responsibilities through increased transfers from the national government. But unlike with primary education, the transfers to large cities for secondary education were not to come through the education component of the general subsidy.

Instead, each city was given an additional increment of shared taxes (the so-called "U" co-efficient) whose yield was equal to the inflation-adjusted sum of the historical budgets of the institutions the cities took over. From the point of view of the cities, the additional increment of shared taxes was preferable to earmarked grants because the money was freely disposable, and because they could expect the additional increment of shared taxes to yield greater revenues with the economy's overall growth. It also allowed reformers to argue that these new service responsibilities were being fully decentralized because cities were going to support "own functions" from freely disposable "own revenues".[49]

This system for funding the poviat functions of large cities was problematic for a number of reasons. Firstly, it effectively gave the big cities substantial portions of the national budgets for health and secondary education on the basis of past historical expenditures, and not on objective measures of need. Secondly, it effectively took these resources out of the national health and education budgets, thus making it extremely difficult for future governments to shift the allocation of health and education funding in line with changing workloads. And then thirdly, it made the overall intergovernmental finance system extremely complicated because cities were now receiving different percentages of shared taxes not only from other gminas, but also from each other.

In the fall of 1997, a coalition of post-Solidarity parties defeated the ruling SLD-PSL coalition in parliamentary elections. The new government set out to make-up for what it felt was lost time by aggressively pushing forward four extremely ambitious and interrelated reform programs for public administration, education, health, and social security. The public administration reforms were understood as a continuation and completion of the decentralization process that had begun with the creation of gminas. And as before, one of the central features of the reform was the transfer of secondary schools to poviats.[50]

Now, however, the government sought not only to establish poviats, but to reorganize the existing voivodship administrations of the national government. Here, the plan was to radically reduce the number of voivodships and to introduce alongside them (i.e. in cohabitation) new regional self-governments. The primary function of these new regional governments would not be, as with gminas and powiats, the delivery of public services. Instead, they were to design and implement regional development plans, plans which the government saw as crucial for the country's ability to absorb European Union support after accession. With these planning functions, self governing voivodships were assigned responsibility for the allocation of the vast majority of budgetary funds earmarked for special programs and investment grants, including those for education. As a result, and at least in theory, regional self governments, and not the Ministry of Education, will be responsible for determining the use and allocation of all special funds intended to help poviats and gminas restructure the school systems.[51]

Initially, reformers hoped to create about 200 poviats and to consolidate the existing 49 voivodships into about 12 new ones. Resistance to the redrawing of jurisdictional boundaries however, set in motion a bargaining process and reformers were forced to increase the number voivodships from 12 to 16 and the number of powiats from 200 to 384. Moreover, 64 poviats were in fact urban gminas that had been were granted poviat rights. The proliferation of poviats, and the creation of gminas with poviat rights had serious, and badly thought through implications for the educational system.

Historically, the vast majority of Poland's secondary schools have been located in cities or towns. As a result, rural pupils have traditionally commuted to urban secondary schools. By creating so many poviats, and by giving certain gminas poviat rights, reformers placed large numbers of schools that served rural pupils in jurisdictions other than those in which they lived. Indeed, in many cities as much 50% of the secondary school population comes from surrounding rural poviats. This has created a classic free rider problem in which the residents of one community are effectively forced to carry some or all of the costs of serving the residents of another community.

The government had also hoped to use the creation of poviats and self-governing regions as an occasion to rewrite the foundations of the intergovernmental finance system. But an effort to introduce true local income taxes failed because of parliamentary resistance to decentralizing tax powers and the Ministry of Finance's inability to determine the tax base of each local government. As a result, reformers had to settle for a simpler "extension" of the basic structure of the Law on Gmina Finances to poviats and self-governing voivodships.[52] This extension entailed, among other things, the elimination of the "U" coefficient for large cities discussed above, and the placement of all local government education responsibilities within the mechanism of the education component of the general subsidy.

But whereas gminas had been given a healthy piece of the fiscal pie in the early 1990s through a combination of significant shares of shared taxes and some limited but still important tax powers, the extension of the Law on Gmina Finances gave poviats and self-governing regions almost no revenue generating capacity, and very modest shares of PIT and CIT. In practice, this meant that both poviats and self-governing regions, unlike gminas, were going to have much less general revenue with which to contribute to education should the education component of the general subsidy fall short.

On 1 January 1999, virtually all remaining educational institutions were transferred to the new poviats and self-governing regions.[53] The vast majority of secondary schools and almost all primary schools for students with disabilities were taken over by poviats. Poviats were also made responsible for most of the non-school educational institutions that had previously been administered by the Kuratoria, including boarding houses (110 000 places),[54] Special Education Centers (32 000 places),[55] various cultural institutions, sport facilities, and youth hostels, and most importantly, psychological and pedagogical advisory centers.[56] Meanwhile, the self governing voivodships were assigned responsibility for 272 medical high schools for nurses (26 000 pupils) and about 100 teacher colleges and in-service vocational training centers (16 000 users).[57]

This massive transfer of educational responsibilities to local governments was accompanied by the start of an ambitious set of reforms designed to change the structure and content of Polish schooling. These reforms were motivated by a desire to reduce the percentage of children attending basic vocational schools and increase the percentage who received general secondary education.[58] The reforms had two central components. First the creation of new tier of three year, lower secondary schools (henceforth left in the Polish terminology 'gimnazjum,' referring to Polish middle schools for grades 6–8), designed to prepare more children for lyceum type schooling later on. And second, the shortening of all secondary schooling by one grade combined with the transformation of the vast majority of professional schools, vocational schools and lyceums into new lyceums with a professional profile (Profiled Lyceums). As a result, a system in which eight-year primary schools were followed by four-year lyceums, five year professional schools or three year vocational schools, was replaced by system in which six-year primary schools, are followed by three-year gimnazjums, and then three-year Profiled Lyceums or two year vocational schools.[59]

To implement the reforms the Ministry of Education required gminas to reorganize their school systems with the beginning of the 1999/2000 school year. This entailed converting some of their of existing 1–primary schools into new 7–9 gymnasiums. Indeed, in an effort to ensure that the gimnazjums fulfilled their anticipated function, the Ministry insisted that they be located in separate facilities designed for no less than 150 pupils and that they be equipped with computer laboratories and sports facilities. The government, however, did not provide gminas with any additional funding for the associated investments and the entire cost of the reform had to be carried by local governments. Not surprisingly, and as we shall see later, this produced protests which have forced the Ministry to accept less rigorous standards for the new facilities.[60]

Meanwhile, poviats will have to reduce the size of their secondary schools by one year with the school year 2001/2002 to accommodate the first class of ninth graders in gimnazjums. In theory, this shift of responsibility for a grade level between poviats and gminas should result in a re-deployment of teachers across the two levels of government. In practice, however, this redeployment has been hampered by the demographic decline of the last ten years. This has encouraged gminas to hire 'their own' currently underutilized teachers, instead of looking to the presumably better qualified staff that will become available with the shortening of secondary schooling. Similarly, it is unclear how poviats are going to finance the refurbishing of secondary schools that should accompany the creation of new lyceums.

5. THE FINANCING OF EDUCATION: 1990–1999

We now turn to a closer examination of the evolution of the education finance system in Poland during the 1990s. We begin with a macro economic overview, before discussing in greater detail the financing of primary and secondary education, and the crisis precipitated by the reform of the Teachers' Charter in 2000. The graphs below expresses the shares of public expenditure on preschool, primary and secondary education in terms of percentages of the GDP. Figure 3.1 shows the expenditures of the central government, Figure 3.2 shows that of the local governments. They show that total public spending on education has remained reasonably stable during the 1990s, at about 4.25% of the GDP.

133

There has, however, been a radical change in the division of public expenditures on education between the national and local governments. Direct state expenditures on education have virtually disappeared,[61] while local government expenditures have risen to take their place. Or put in another way, the national government, while still in the business of allocating educational resources to local governments, is now no longer in the business of allocating education resources to schools. This is now the exclusive domain of gminas, poviats and voivodships.

Equally importantly, local governments now finance almost 25% (1.1% of the GDP) of all public expenditures on education from revenues other than those coming to them through the education component of the general subsidy or from earmarked grants. In fact, it is the increase in spending on education that local governments are making out of their general revenues that has allowed total public expenditure to remain stable in the face of declining expenditures of the national budget (from 3.5% of the GDP in 1991 to 3.15% in 1999).

Figure 3.1
Shares of Central Government Expenditure on Education [as a % of GDP]

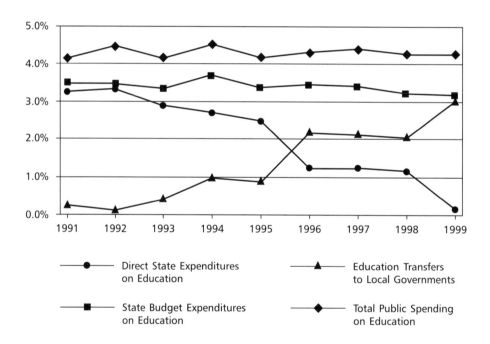

Own calculations: Based on GUS Data and MEN annual reports to parliament

Figure 3.2

Shares of Local Government Expenditure on Education [as a % of GDP]

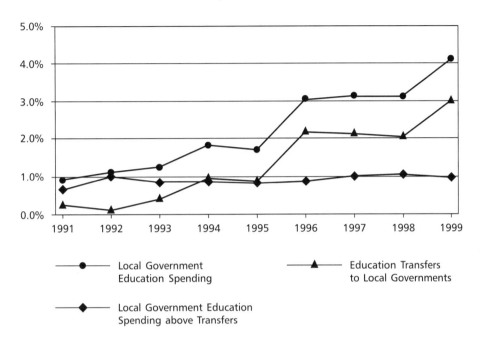

Own calculations: Based on GUS Data and MEN annual reports to parliament

Also of interest is the composition of the 1.1% of GDP that local governments pay for education above the transfers form the state budget. Here, the most significant change has come in the form of local government contributions to the operating and maintenance costs of primary and secondary schools, costs that at least in theory the national government is supposed to fully fund through the education subvention.

These contributions have risen from 0.22% of the GDP in 1994 to 0.38% of the GDP in 1999, or by roughly the same amount that total state budget expenditures on education have declined (0.32% of the GDP) since 1991. Thus, it is fair to say that while the local government's 'own' spending has not increased total public expenditures on education, it has defended an existing level from further erosion. This is no small feat in era of fiscal austerity.

Nonetheless, from the point of view of local governments, this increasing obligation for the operating and maintenance of schools appears as an unfunded mandate. With this said, we now turn to an examination of the evolution of the mechanism for allocating the education component

135

of the general subsidy to local governments, and the complex of political and technical questions that this 'unfunded mandate' raises.

5.1 The Financing of Primary Education

As we have noted, the passage of the Law on Gmina Finance in 1993 required MEN to develop an algorithm to allocate the education subvention to local governments. And as soon as the Ministry began to think about how to construct this algorithm, it was forced to confront a painful legacy of the old regime. Even a casual review of education finance data revealed profound differences in per pupil education expenditures across jurisdictions of different types. In particular, the per pupil costs of rural schools were on average one third higher than those of urban schools. Worse, in many rural jurisdictions, per pupil costs were three or four times those of their urban counterparts.[62]

In part, these additional expenditures were driven by the fixed costs of smaller rural schools. More importantly, however, it was clear that they were being driven by significantly smaller class sizes and lower pupil/teacher ratios. These differences raised profound political questions. The most important question was simply to what degree the additional costs of rural primary schools were socially desirable or justifiable. Here there was no easy answer.

On the one hand, rural population densities clearly made it harder to create larger schools and to obtain the pupil/teacher ratios of urban jurisdictions. On the other hand, Poland—with a few notable exceptions—is not a particularly sparsely populated country and both the pupil/teacher ratios of all its schools and of its rural schools in particular, are substantially higher than those of more developed nations with similar settlement patterns.[63] Moreover, and equally importantly, the relatively poor performance of rural children at the secondary and tertiary levels suggested that whatever else might be said, the small size of rural classes was not doing much to equalize the educational chances of rural children.[64] Worse still, it was clear that the steep demographic decline of the decade was exacerbating the problem.

In short, the Ministry sensed that these differences were unacceptably high and though it didn't know by how much, it did believe that over time the per pupil funding levels that local governments received through the education subsidy would have to be brought closer together. But bringing these levels closer together raised other problems. While allocating money to gminas on the basis of the existing costs of their schools seemed both unjust and unwise, changing this allocation pattern necessarily entailed squeezing some jurisdictions by providing them with education subventions less than they needed to maintain historical spending patterns.[65]

And this, in turn, raised questions about what the national government's promise to gminas to fully fund the wage and maintenance costs of schools really meant. In fact, it raised many of the same questions that reformers stumbled over when they began the decentralization process.

Here, it will be remembered that to push through the legislation that made possible the devolution of education responsibilities, reformers not only had to promise to fully fund the operational and wage costs of gmina run schools, but they avoided articulating clear normative class sizes or teacher/pupil ratios that might have suggested to the unions or gminas that decentralization was going to entail laying off teachers, or for that matter closing rural schools.

In this sense, the Ministry was poised to start using the algorithm to effect a policy whose clear expression in law had been, and seemed to remain, politically unacceptable.

Indeed, by the mid 1990s, the Ministry found itself in a legal box. On the one hand, it felt compelled to squeeze some jurisdictions in order encourage the rationalization of the sector. On the other hand, it knew that the squeezing would push the government to the edge of its legal promises.[66] Worse, MEN was technically unsure about how to go about squeezing gminas without immediately sending large numbers of them into adjustment shock.[67]

Not surprisingly then, MEN's tried to make the algorithm mimic the existing allocation of resources so that it produced pressure only at the margins. In the run-up to the drafting of the Law on Gmina Finances in 1993 it toyed with using a combination of the number of teachers, weighted more or less in accordance with existing class sizes, and a multiplier based on the wage structures of individual gminas.[68] This was attractive because it seemed to promise that the Ministry could squeeze first on the fixed costs of schools, and only afterwards put pressure on employment— obviously the most sensitive political issue. Indeed, the idea of allocating money in accordance with the number of teachers would periodically return over the course of the decade.

But here there was a major technical problem. The Polish government in fact had very limited data on teachers' wages and employment at the local level. On the one hand, the financial reports submitted by schools to the Main Statistical Office (GUS) grouped the wages of all school personnel together. On the other hand, and more importantly, GUS did not require schools to report part-time teachers in terms of full-time equivalent positions. Taken together, this meant that it was impossible for the Ministry to calculate how many (FTE) teachers were employed in any given jurisdiction and what their wage bill was.[69]

These technical difficulties enhanced the more general feeling that the number of pupils enrolled in a given jurisdiction,[70] and not the number of teachers employed by it, was a better measure of a jurisdiction's need for education funding. Nonetheless, all versions of the algorithm that MEN used to allocate the education subvention between 1994 and 1999 contained factors for teachers, pupils and historical costs that essentially worked together to keep the *status quo* from changing too much from year to year.[71]

The basic feature of these algorithms was a system of per pupil weights or multipliers designed to shift resources to those jurisdictions that had low pupil/teacher ratios. Initially, these multipliers were tied to the average class sizes of primary schools. A multiplier of 1.86 was used for all pupils in rural gminas whose class sizes were less than 15; 1.44 for rural classes of between 15 and 18 pupils; 1.33 for rural class sizes greater than 18 and 1.2 for urban pupils in classes less than 24. In other words, the per pupil multipliers were really designed to reflect existing staffing patterns, and not the relative workloads associated with different categories of pupils, such as pupils with disabilities.[72]

These multipliers were progressively lowered, and by 1996 decoupled from average class sizes.[73] As a result, in 1996 there was a single multiplier of 1.33 for all pupils attending schools in rural areas, and another of 1.18 for pupils attending schools in towns with less than 5,000 inhabitants. The rural multiplier reflected the fact that on average the class sizes of rural gminas were one third smaller than those of urban ones (18 to 24). The small town multiplier, however had no such justification, as class sizes in small towns were the same as in cities.[74]

The weighted number of pupils was then divided by a normative class size (26) and multiplied by a normative number of class hours per week (27). The result was then divided by the pensum (18) to yield what looked like a normative number of teachers for every jurisdiction based on a normative class size of 26. In fact, however, this was extremely misleading because the normative class actually reflected weighted pupils and not actual pupils. Nonetheless it represented the Ministry's only public indication that the national government would not fund employment above a certain level and that in fact many rural gminas classes were too small. Finally, the number of teachers that this calculation produced for each gmina was then multiplied by a weighted average of teacher salaries based on the number of teachers employed by the gmina belonging to each of first three, and then five centrally determined pay categories.

The justification for this part of the algorithm was twofold. Firstly, the Ministry wanted to ensure that the allocation of resources in some way reflected the different composition of teaching staffs across local governments so that neither gminas nor the unions could argue that the subvention failed to account for differences in teacher qualifications, and hence pay, in different gminas. And secondly, the Ministry wanted to encourage local governments to hire better-qualified teachers.[75] Whether this part of the algorithm ever fulfilled either one of these functions is hard to say. What can be said, is that statistical analysis of the algorithm in 1999 showed that the component for teacher qualifications did not account for any statistically significant variation in local governments' education subventions.

Most importantly, the component of the algorithm that had the greatest effect on the actual distribution of funds over time was almost invisible. This was because it appeared not in the formula itself, but in the text of the Ordinance that laid out the formula every year. This text stated that no gmina's subvention could be less than 100%, or more than a 110% of the inflation adjusted subvention it received the previous year.[76] These 'hold harmless'[77] provisions meant that the education subventions of a large number of gminas were not determined by the weighted per pupil or salary components of the algorithm, but by their previous year's subvention, a subvention which in most cases regressed quite smoothly to the sum of the inflation adjusted historical budgets of a jurisdiction's schools. In short, and despite appearances, the algorithm was not in fact allocating money on per pupil basis, but on the basis of historical costs.

Even these 'hold harmless' clauses, however did not guarantee that the education subventions of all gminas were sufficient to cover their teacher wage bills. There are a variety of reasons for this but the most important one is that over the course of the decade, the Ministry was slowly raising teachers' real wages. Indeed, the percentage of state budget revenues earmarked by the Law on Gmina Finances was raised twice to take into account these wage increases. Increasing the global funds available for the subvention in line with the anticipated global costs of the wage increase however, did not ensure that the subventions of individual gminas actually increased in line with their new wage bills. So long as the algorithm allocated money on the basis of pupils or historical expenditures, gminas that had more teachers per pupil than average, got less of the additional wage funds than they needed to fund their existing employment rolls.

Indeed, analyses of the types of gminas that contribute most to the operational costs of schools out of their general revenues yield a very clear picture of two distinct populations. On the one hand, there are rural gminas with small class sizes, fragmented school networks and often very low per capita incomes. And on the other hand, there are large urban jurisdictions with higher than average per capita incomes, and larger than average class sizes. The implication of this picture is that poor rural gminas are paying into the subvention because they have to, while richer ones are paying in because they 'want to' or because if they don't teachers will make use of the other employment opportunities available in the city and leave the sector.[78] It is these two forces which account for the increasing contribution of local governments to the operating costs of schools that we observed when examining the shifts in shares of public expenditure on education over the last decade. Indeed, these forces were at work even though the Ministry had yet to adopt a true per pupil funding mechanism at the primary school level.

5.2 The Financing of Secondary Education

The transfer of secondary schools and non-school educational institutions to poviats and self-governing regions in 1999, extended and intensified the problems the Ministry was having with the allocation of funds to local governments for education. Indeed, in many ways the Ministry faced even more complex philosophical, political and technical problems than those we have described earlier with respect to primary education.

In the chaotic spring of 1998 however, most of the Ministry's energies were focused simply on making inventories[79] and evaluating the costs of schools and non-school educational institutions that previously had been in the hands of other ministries and the Kuratoria, and which now had to be transferred to poviats, gminas with poviat rights, and self-governing voivodships. As we have noted, the per pupil costs of secondary schools, particularly those of vocational and professional schools controlled by different ministries varied radically both across schools of different types and schools of the same type in different parts of the country.[80] Moreover, not only was the distribution of non-school educational institutions extremely uneven across the new jurisdictions but in many cases it was impossible to determine how many people these institutions were serving, and hence what their unit costs actually were.

The Ministry's first reaction to these problems was similar to its reaction to the problem presented by the unequal per pupil costs of primary education at the gmina level. In short, the Ministry attempted to find some compromise between funding powiats and self-governing voivodships on the basis of pupil enrollment while ensuring that they were given enough money to cover the inflation adjusted historical costs of the particular group of institutions that were being transferred to them. To this end MEN first summed the historical budgets of all secondary schools and non-school educational institutions in a given jurisdiction to get a baseline against which to judge the consequences of any shift in resources that might result from using enrollment as the basis for allocating fund.

MEN then grouped all secondary schools into 27 different types and calculated the nation-wide average per pupil costs for each type.[81] Finally, a nominal education subvention for each poviat was then calculated by multiplying the number of pupils enrolled in each type of secondary school by their average per pupil costs, and adding to this sum the historical costs of the non-school educational institutions located in the jurisdiction. The sum of these normalized school costs, and historical non-school costs for each jurisdiction was then compared to its initial historical budget, with each jurisdiction actually receiving no more than 110%, and no less than 95% of the latter. As result, the 1999 allocation of the education subvention to poviats and self-governing regions remained a peculiar form of mixed per pupil funding for schools and historical funding for non-school institutions, in order to guarantee that overall there was little shift in past allocation pattern.

The Ministry, however, was aware that this was an extremely ad hoc solution to its allocational problems. Indeed, the Ministry felt ever increasing pressure to move towards a clearer per pupil funding mechanism not only for secondary education but for primary education as well. These pressures and problems require a somewhat extended discussion.[82]

The first problem was quite simply that the Ministry knew that it made little sense to allocate money for secondary education on the basis of the historical per pupil costs of different types of schools. As we have indicated, one of the major legacies of the old regime, a legacy that the Ministry was painfully aware of, was that not only were too many children attending vocational and pro-fessional schools (80% of schools, 66% of enrolment)[83] but the highest cost schools were often the most archaic and doing the least to improve the life chances of their students. Most glaringly, vocational schools tied to smoke-stack industries like mining and steel had per pupil costs three to five times those of lyceums and vocational schools associated with the much underdeveloped service sector. As such, allocating money to poviats on the basis of enrollment in the existing array of secondary schools provided no incentive to restructure them. In fact, it created perverse incentives to preserve high cost, industrial vocational schools at the expense of improving lyceums and more desirable vocational schools.

The second problem was related to the allocation of money for non-school educational institutions like in-service teacher training facilities, apprentice training facilities for pupils and adults, and psychological counseling agencies. On the one hand, the distribution of these facilities was extremely uneven across jurisdictions. On the other hand, twenty years of administrative decomposition under Communism and ten years of profound labor market change had left the Ministry with extremely limited knowledge about what services these institutions were actually providing. It thus seemed irrational and unjust to provide funding to those jurisdictions who had more than their share of these institutions on the basis of their historical costs, while under funding others.

Indeed, in many ways MEN was confronting a more extreme version of the dilemma it faced with respect to primary schools. Here, however, not only was it unsure of what the normative costs of secondary schools and non-school educational institution should be, but it really had no idea which types of these institutions should be supported at all. In fact, the Ministry began to realize that in transferring these responsibilities to local governments, it was really asking them to make decisions about how to restructure the sector, decisions it lacked the information in Warsaw to make on its own. Nonetheless, the existing legal framework still defined local governments role in education as the payments agents, auditors, and the 'beneficent uncles' of schools.

The third problem pushing the Ministry towards the development of a per pupil funding mechanism was related to a shift in the relative shares of public spending on primary and secondary education that had occurred over the course of the decade. This shift was the product of a combination of the politics of decentralization and demographic trends. As we have seen, reformers set the global value of the education subvention for primary schools equal to a percentage of state budget revenues. The value of this share increased with the expanding economy. Moreover, gminas proved politically powerful enough to force the government to increase it two times over the course of the decade. As a result the real value of the subvention was rising at the same time that primary school enrollment was falling.

At the secondary school level, however, the opposite trend was at work. Here enrollment was increasing as the children of the post-war baby boomers entered adolescence while budgetary responsibility for the sector was fragmented across a variety of ministries and lacked a clear political champion. Thus, public expenditures on secondary education at best kept pace with inflation as enrollment rose. Taken together, per pupil expenditures on primary education had become about ten percent higher than those on secondary education by 1999.

This disproportion disturbed MEN for two reasons. First, the Ministry knew that in most OECD countries per pupil expenditures on secondary education typically ran fifteen to twenty percent higher than those on primary education. And second, as we have noted earlier, MEN understood that the new Law on Local Government Revenues of 1998 had given poviats and self-governing regions much less general revenue from shared and own taxes than it gave gminas. As a result, education spending in these new levels of government was going to be significantly more dependent on the education component of the general subsidy than it was in gminas, and it was unlikely that they would be able to correct this disproportion on their own.

In short, MEN wanted to begin to correct this imbalance, but was unsure how to go about it. The new law now required that 12.4% of national budget revenues be set aside for the education component of the general subsidy for all local governments. Theoretically, it was possible for MEN to divide these funds into two distinct pools, earmarking a larger share for secondary education. This however would have required openly admitting that the Ministry intended to take funds away from gminas, something which it was loath to try politically. Equally importantly, the creation of gimnazjums was shifting the percentage of students enrolled in gmina and poviat run schools, a shift that seemed to once again necessitate a move to per pupil financing, and which made dividing the education budget into two pools undesirable over the short term.

Finally, in one of the stranger episodes of the entire decentralization process, the Ministry was being pushed towards developing a per pupil funding mechanism by political demands for the introduction of school vouchers. A number of post-Solidarity political parties had used "school vouchers" as a campaign slogan in the 1998 parliamentary elections and their representatives were now leaning on MEN to introduce them.[84] The problem was that nobody was quite sure what policy goals vouchers were supposed to achieve or how they should operate. Indeed, even among their advocates, there seemed to be little awareness that school choice was already an established element of the Polish school system and that the national government was already providing voucher-type funding to private schools.[85]

For most, the attraction was purely political because the idea of giving everybody an equal amount of money to spend on their children's educations was clearly popular. For others, vouchers held out a promise for higher levels of public support for private and community schools.[86] Finally, officials in the Ministry of Finance were concerned that employment in the sector was declining slower than enrolment. Moreover, they were reforming the health and pension systems by separating the financing of these services from their provision and saw no reason why the same sort of privatization shouldn't be pushed forward in education as well. Indeed, representatives of the Ministry often talked as if they thought schools were firms that if subjected to the market discipline of pure per pupil funding—to a hard budget constraint—would be forced to produce value, or go under.[87]

The apparent simplicity of giving people the "same amount of money to spend on their children's educations" however, became horribly complicated when it ran up against the dramatic differences in the per pupil costs of Polish schools. Actually financing schools on the basis of a single per pupil value or standard, say average costs of all schools, would push an unacceptably large number of them into either receivership or bankruptcy. Conversely, developing vouchers with multiple values reflecting, say, the different per pupil costs of different types of schools seemed to defeat the purpose of the exercise. On the one hand, the system got complicated because someone in the government would have to figure out how many vouchers of each type should be created, and who should get them. On the other hand, creating vouchers of different values presumed that someone in the government knew, *ex ante*, not just what different types of schools cost, but what their real value was. Since this was precisely what nobody knew, and indeed exactly what a free market was supposed to reveal, creating vouchers with multiple prices would segment the market before it was born.

Indeed, the debate over vouchers, like MEN's difficulties with determining the normative costs of secondary schools, was forcing the Ministry to reconsider what decentralization really meant. On the one hand, thinking through the implications of vouchers had convinced the Ministry that the problems associated with restructuring schools were too profound to leave to the market.[88] On the other hand, its own difficulties in figuring out how much money should be allocated to particular types of secondary schools and non-school educational institutions had pushed it towards the realization that it lacked the necessary information to restructure the sector from Warsaw. In sum, by 1999, the Ministry saw the development of a mechanism to allocate funds to local governments on a per pupil basis as its best defense against vouchers, as the most promising way to redress the imbalance in funding between primary and secondary education, and as the only way to facilitate the restructuring of the sector by local governments.

As a result, by the fiscal year 2000, and after a year of concerted analysis and simulation, the Ministry moved to put the allocation of the education subvention on a true per pupil basis. This involved introducing significant changes in the algorithm. First, and perhaps most importantly, the baseline for the buffers or hold harmless clauses for both primary and secondary education were changed from a percent of the previous year's total education subvention to a percent of the previous year's *per pupil* education subvention. This meant that no longer would the allocation mechanism be insensitive to changes in enrollment across jurisdictions or levels of education. It also meant that for the first time, a jurisdiction's education subvention could be less in absolute terms than it was before, even if in per pupil terms it stayed the same or actually increased.

Secondly, the Ministry set the multipliers for urban primary schools and urban lyceums at parity (1)[89] to begin to correct for the imbalance in per pupil spending between primary and secondary education. The Ministry, in other words made a conscious—if not particularly transparent—decision to shift funds away from gminas towards poviats, firstly, because secondary education had been shorted during the 1990s, and secondly, because the Ministry knew that poviats had virtually no general revenues with which to supplement their education subventions.

Thirdly, MEN replaced the twenty-seven different per pupil standards for different types of secondary schools with a single multiplier for all lyceums (1) and a single multiplier for all vocational and professional schools (1.15). Simulations showed that the use of this multiplier provided most powiats with levels of funding similar to that of the previous year. More importantly, by eliminating the 27 standards, the Ministry removed from the funding formula any financial incentive for powiats to game the system, or any suggestion from the Ministry about which types of secondary schools should cost more than others. The Ministry, in other words, was clearly placing the responsibility for making decisions about the allocation of resources across secondary schools on the shoulders of poviats, effectively acknowledging that poviats were in a better position to make decisions about restructuring the sector than MEN itself.

Fourthly, MEN calculated the average per user or per student costs of all non-school educational institutions and then expressed these average costs within the funding formula as distinct per user or per pupil multipliers. In practice, this meant that MEN was financially squeezing those jurisdictions that 'overprovided' these services on behalf of those who underprovided them. In theory, it meant that MEN was leaving it up to poviats to make decisions about the level and quality of these services, hoping that they would pay where they had to, or where they thought it made sense.

Finally, MEN left in place the multipliers for rural and small town primary schools. But it introduced a new multiplier for rural gminas who transported children to school. This was an implicit acknowledgement that MEN understood and accepted the fact that its funding formula was putting financial pressure on rural gminas that had particularly low pupil/teacher ratios and small class sizes. But instead of accepting these small classes as a necessary cost that had to be funded, it was providing local governments with help in rationalizing their school networks.

Taken together, these changes allowed the Ministry to create a mathematically coherent algorithm for allocating 12.4% of the national government's revenues to all local governments solely on the basis of the number and types of pupils enrolled in their schools (see Annex 2 for a list of all weights and their share of the education subvention). By dividing the national government's resources for the education subvention by the sum of all weighted pupils, the algorithm yielded a nominal financial standard for a 'physical pupil'—in fact the financial standard for urban primary school and lyceum students. This financial standard the Ministry called an "indicative school voucher," in a more or less successful effort to finesse the demands of the voucher movement: a clear per pupil standard was used to allocate money to local governments and not, as with vouchers, directly to schools or parents.[90]

By its very nature, the new algorithm clearly shifted resources away from their historical allocation, an allocation that above all reflected the past distribution of teachers across schools. As such it implied a weakening of the government's promise that the education subvention would be sufficient to cover the wage and operating costs of all schools in a given local jurisdiction. Or put another way, MEN was using the algorithm to create *de facto* financial standards that it was too weak to establish *de jure*.

5.3 The Reform of the Teachers Charter and the Crisis of 2000

At the same time that MEN was placing the education subvention on a per pupil basis it was also pushing forward a reform of the Teachers Charter. Serious negotiations with the unions, particularly with the stronger SLD-affiliated ZNP, began over the summer of 1999 and continued virtually non-stop until the passage of the new legislation in February 2000. These negotiations took place without the participation of Poland's local government associations who preferred to pretend that the determination of teachers wages or working conditions was none of their business. Worse still, the Ministry itself encouraged this fiction despite the fact that at least some of its officials were aware that changes in the algorithm would further decouple the allocation of the subvention from local government wage bills.

MEN's primary objective in these negotiations was to increase the number of hours that Polish teachers spend in the classroom and to streamline and incentivize the rules governing teacher wages and advancement. The 18 hour pensum defined by the Teachers' Charter had long been considered too low by both the Ministry and the World Bank, while the existing wage system—based entirely on seniority and formal qualifications—was clearly too rigid. MEN thus entered the negotiations ready to trade an expansion of the pensum and changes in the wage system for pay increases.[91] Not surprisingly, the ZNP opposed changing the pensum and the wage system and focused its energies on winning unconditional wage increases.

In the end, the reformed legislation[92] demonstrated the ZNP's strength and the Ministry's weakness, a weakness compounded by its desire to 'successfully' conclude the negotiations before the presidential elections of the late fall. MEN failed to win an across the board increase in the pensum. Instead, the pensum could be adjusted upward only if schools (not local governments) and their teachers agreed to the change. The legislation also created a new, four-level system of professional advancement that was to be phased in over 4 years. These levels (apprentice, contract, nominated and with diploma) permit much wider salary steps than before and were to allow salary determination to be based not just on formal qualifications and seniority, but on performance.[93]

To make possible the implementation of the new performance-based aspects of the system, it was necessary to create an elaborate and costly set of procedures for the independent evaluation of teachers.[94] Under these procedures, independent committees composed of education specialists will pass judgment on the movement of teachers from one pay grade to another. This means that neither MEN nor local governments will control promotions, and with them teachers' wages. This is particularly important with respect to the movement between the third and fourth pay grades (nominated and with diploma) because the statutory pay increase here is very large. Moreover, 80% of all employed teachers were automatically placed in the third pay grade with the passage of the legislation. As a result, the future financial consequences of the reformed Teachers' Charter are hard to anticipate. Nonetheless, they are undoubted significantly higher than MEN's extremely conservative projections.

Indeed, shortly after the law was passed, the Ministry appealed to both teachers and local governments not to abuse the promotion rules of the new system. Local governments, however, were puzzled by this appeal because no role in the process had been assigned to them. In short, MEN's blurred vision of the role of local governments in the sector, and local governments willingness to let the national government 'take care' of teachers' pay, created serious financial liabilities for both.

The new Charter also introduced major changes in the way base pay was calculated, streamlined a long list of pay supplements and made some of them non-obligatory. The Ministry, however, lacked reliable data on many of these supplements and in a fatal error stated that base pay had to be 75% of total pay. As result, when local governments increased base pay to meet the new statutory norms, they were legally required to raise supplemental pay in ways unanticipated by the national government. Not surprisingly, they argued that that the national government had very significantly underestimated the costs of the legislation.[95]

At the same time, however, while the Charter clearly stated in numerical terms a base wage rate for each of the four pay grades of the new system, it only obligated local governments to pay these base wages *on average* for all the teachers of given qualification that they employed. This meant that it was impossible for individual teachers to easily determine what their wages under the new system should be.[96] Worse still, when combined with the lack of good data on supplementary pay, this provision made it possible for local governments to simultaneously demand more than they actually needed from the national government to meet the provisions of the law, while also paying teachers less than they were actually entitled to.[97]

Finally, the Charter contained provisions that required the Ministry to issue an ordinance defining normative employment standards for all schools. Indeed, the Charter clearly stated that the national government would only be responsible for the wages of teachers employed within these standards. These provisions constituted MEN's first attempt to close the government's open-ended liability for teachers' wages and to resolve a problem that, as we have seen, has haunted the reform from the start. In the rush to reach agreement with the ZNP, however, MEN rather remarkably failed to issue this ordinance, in effect making the government liable for funding the wages of all currently employed teachers.

MEN's failure to issue these standards combined with its miscalculation of the relationship of base pay to total pay immediately produced a profound crisis. Local governments claimed that MEN had underestimated the costs of the Charter by more than 2 billion zlotys, or about 10% of the entire education subvention.[98] In July, the Minister of Education resigned, and shortly thereafter a number of other high officials lost their jobs. Intense negotiations between the national government and local governments ultimately produced a fragile compromise on how much the government owed local governments for the unanticipated costs of the Charter in 2000. The Ministry also succeeded getting the Sejm to approve a change in the relationship of base pay to total pay, thus reducing the national government's liabilities for fiscal year 2001.

MEN, however, remained incapable of issuing the ordinance defining employment standards that the Charter in fact requires. Indeed, the Ministry is still paralyzed by the political issue that has clouded its financing of the sector from the start. If it sets employment standards in line with current employment patterns, the Ministry will have accomplished nothing with respect to the rationalization of the sector or the reduction of the now significantly higher wage costs for which it remains liable. If, however, standards are set to reflect more reasonable employment levels, or to what the national budget can afford, then teachers will have to be fired and/or local governments will have to make up the shortfall.

Either way, the still not fully foreseeable changes in the costs of providing education created by the new Charter will undoubtedly put more of the burden for financing teachers' wages and determining teachers' employment on the backs of local government. Nonetheless, neither the national government, nor local governments, seem to have the political will to think through what this might entail with respect to either the intergovernmental finance system or the managerial prerogatives of local governments.

6. THE MANAGEMENT OF SCHOOLS: 1990–1991

In the early 1990s, the architects of Poland's local government and education reforms envisioned a division of labor within the sector that left control over the pedagogical process almost entirely in the hands of kuratoria while restricting the role of local governments to improving the management of school facilities and providing additional funding for new investments and supplementary teachers pay. In this section we look more closely at what local governments have done with their schools over the course of the decade and try to trace from the bottom up the fault lines of a regulatory framework that we have already suggested is breaking down.

6.1 The Management of Preschool Education

In 1991, gminas were made responsible for the ownership, maintenance and operational costs of preschool education. Because preschool is not obligatory in Poland, they were left free to choose the level of preschool services they wanted to provide for children ages 3 to 5. They were however obliged to provide preschool training for all six-year olds whose parents wanted to send them to preparatory 'zero' classes and has to do so with certified teachers paid at the rates set by the Teachers' Charter.

The non-compulsory character of preschool education combined with a more general sense that the communist state had invaded the family, led reformers to place the entire burden for financing preschool education on the general revenues of gminas, and to leave preschool education out of the education subvention. Nonetheless, and despite the non-compulsory character of preschool education, about 90% of Polish six year olds attend 'zero' classes (see Table 3.3).

Gminas were thus forced to shoulder a very serious financial burden for education at the very start of the decentralization process. Between 1991 and 1993, when the vast majority of gmina education spending was only on preschools and funded entirely out of gminas' own revenues, between 18 and 25% of all gminas expenditure went on education,[99] spending which was equal to approximately 0.5% of the GDP (see Figure 3.1 earlier). Table 3.2 shows that since 1990, gminas have responded to this burden by closing almost 30% of all preschool establishments.[100] These closures disturbed many observers and generated a stream of accusations that local governments, particularly rural ones, did not appreciate the importance of early childhood education. These accusations contributed to the postponement of the obligatory assumption of primary schools by gminas from 1993 until 1996 and continue to fuel many of the more general reservations that education specialists have about involving local governments in educational policy.

Table 3.2
Preschools in Urban and Rural Areas 1990–1999

	1990	1995	1999	[%] Decline
Number of Preschools	12 308	9 350	8 733	29
Urban	7 009	5 625	5 453	22
Rural	5 299	3 725	3 280	38
Preschool Enrolment	856 600	823 200	719 600	16
Urban	665 800	661 800	574 700	14
Rural	190 800	161 400	144 900	24

SOURCE: 2000 Statistical Annual, GUS p. 248.

The charge that local governments have mismanaged preschools is, however, largely unjustified. Table 3.3 shows that the percentage of preschool age children receiving preschool education actually rose over the course of the decade despite preschool closures, and after taking into account the steep demographic decline of the decade. This is particularly true in urban jurisdictions where the percentage of children in both 'zero' classes and in preschools for 3–5 year olds rose significantly after falling in the early 1990s. In short, urban gminas have both streamlined the delivery of preschool education and responded to the increased demand for preschool services from urban workforces.[101]

Table 3.3

Percentage of 3 to 5 Year Olds Receiving Preschool Training

	1990	1993	1995	1997	1999
% Of 6 year olds in zero classes	95.3	94.9	97.3	97.1	96.7
Urban	98.3	98.0	102.2	103.2	103.5
Rural	90.8	89.4	90.8	89.7	88.5
% Of 3–5 year olds in preschools	31.0	25.5	28.7	31.3	34.0
Urban	40.5	34.7	40.1	44.9	49.3
Rural	17.8	13.6	14.1	15.2	15.7
% Of 3–6 year olds in preschool	48.2	43.6	45.3	49.0	50.8
Urban	56.3	51.6	56.5	60.6	63.9
Rural	36.6	33.1	33.4	35.0	35.2

SOURCE: MEN Materials for Sejm, 1996, 1997, 1998, 1999, and 2000.

The situation in rural areas, however, is less encouraging. As in urban gminas, the percentage of children receiving preschool training declined immediately after the service was devolved to local governments. And as in urban gminas, the percent of children receiving preschool training increased after 1995. But the increase for rural gminas has been less pronounced and the share of rural children enrolled in both 'zero' classes and preschools for 3–5 year olds remains below 1990 levels. Worse still, the percentage of rural 3–5 year olds receiving preschool education is extremely low (15.7%) by European standards and the percentage of rural six year olds attending 'zero' classes remains more than ten points below that of urban six year olds.

Rural gminas, however, should not be pilloried for bad management. In fact, all things considered, they have not done badly. The persistence of traditional family structures and agrarian work patterns continues to limit the demand for early childhood care (education) in the Polish countryside. At the same time, the cost of maintaining separate schools for 3–5 year olds is high in rural areas. As a result, rural gminas closed or consolidated separate preschools, and brought most 'zero' classes into primary schools. This has allowed them to maintain enrollment in 'zero' classes at about the same level as before. Moreover, they have brought the average class size of rural preschools in line with those of urban jurisdictions as can be seen by Table 3.4.

Table 3.4
Children per Preschool Class

	1991	1999
Rural	7.8	20.8
Urban	18.6	23.6

SOURCE: MEN Materials for Sejm, 1992, 2000

This is remarkable because, as we have seen, rural Poland is typified by lots of very small primary schools with very small class sizes (see Annex 1). Finally, rural gminas have managed to increase per pupil spending on preschool education at rates similar to those of urban jurisdictions despite significantly weaker per capita incomes. This can be seen in Figure 3.3 below.

Figure 3.3
Real per Pupil Spending on Preschool Education

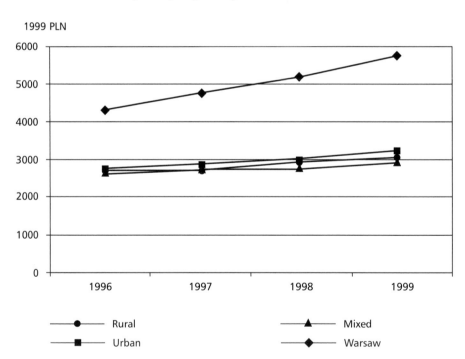

SOURCE: Own calculations on the basis of GUS enrollment and spending data.

Despite the reasonably rational management of preschool education by rural gminas, however, there is little doubt that there remains a crying need to improve early childhood education in the countryside. At present, 38% of the Polish population lives off the land. More than half of the next generation of rural Poles will probably have to find new livelihoods as the liberalization of food markets eliminates marginal or subsistence agricultural undertakings. The present generation of rural children is already at risk because of the relative, and sometimes still brutal, poverty of the Polish countryside, and because their parents are much less educated than those of its urban counterparts.

In short, rural schools will be forced to play a difficult game of catch-up, if rural children are going to be given fair life chances. This game will require a concerted national effort and significant energy, innovation and perseverance at the local level. Given the importance of early childhood education in determining life chances, it is also clear that the game will entail getting farmers to send more of their children to school at earlier ages and to rapidly improve the quality of preschool *education.*

6.2 The Management of Primary Schools and the Creation of Gimnazjums[102]

As with preschools, there has been a significant difference between what the devolution of education responsibilities has meant in practice for rural and urban gminas.[103] On the one hand, rural and urban jurisdictions have faced different structural challenges over the last ten years. On the other hand, they have brought to these challenges very different financial and human resources. In the following, we therefore focus on describing the differences in the way urban and rural jurisdictions have coped with the challenges of decentralization.

Table 3.5 shows for 1998, how much gminas of different types contributed to the subvention from their general revenues for the operating and maintenance costs, without investment, to their schools. On average, all gminas contributed 160 PLN ($40) or about 8% of all school operating costs. There were, however, significant differences in these own contributions across types of gminas. Rural gminas contributed 64 PLN ($17), or about 3% of school costs, while urban ones contributed about 200 PLN ($50) or about 11% of their school costs. Remarkably, Warsaw contributed out of its general revenues almost 40% of the school costs (65% of the subvention).

If these own contributions simply reflected unfunded mandates imposed on gminas by the national government's funding formulas, it would be fair to say that the additional funding preferences for rural jurisdictions through the 0.33 multiplier (thanks to which the average per student subvention was equal to 2 400 PLN in rural gminas as opposed to 1 676 PLN in urban gminas) are at least partially unjustified. This, however is not the case, and as we stated earlier there is a bipolar division in the population of gminas that pay into the subvention most: urban jurisdictions with high per capita incomes and rural gminas with low per capita incomes and/or very low pupil/teacher ratios. The reasons for this become clearer if we look more closely at the shares of gmina budgets devoted to education, and to the composition of education gmina education spending.

Table 3.5
Local Government Contributions to the Education Subvention

		[mln PLN]	[%]	Per Pupil [PLN]
Total	Current Expenditures	10 220	100	2 125
	Education subvention	9 450	92	1 965
	Local government contribution	770	8	160
Rural	Current Expenditures	3 476	100	2 465
	Education subvention	3 385	97	2 400
	Local government contribution	91	3	64
Mixed	Current Expenditures	2 379	100	2 092
	Education subvention	2 273	96	1 999
	Local government contribution	106	4	93
Urban	Current Expenditures	3 964	100	1 874
	Education subvention	3 546	89	1 676
	Local government contribution	418	11	198
Warsaw	Current Expenditures	401	100	2 722
	Education subvention	246	61	1 670
	Local government contribution	155	39	1 052

SOURCE: Herbst (2001)

As can be seen from Figure 3.4, the share of local government budgets devoted to primary education differs significantly across different types of local governments, though for all education constitutes the single largest expenditure category. Rural and mixed gminas respectively devote 45 and 40% of their budgets to preschool and primary education. Urban gminas, however, spend only 33% of their budgets on education, a share that includes the substantial spending on secondary education made by "cities with poviat rights." Because urban local governments have more public responsibilities than rural ones, the lower share of their total expenditures on education is not a reliable measure of the relative fiscal burden which education places on different types of gminas. Nonetheless, it does suggest that there are differences in the pressure that education is placing on different local governments.

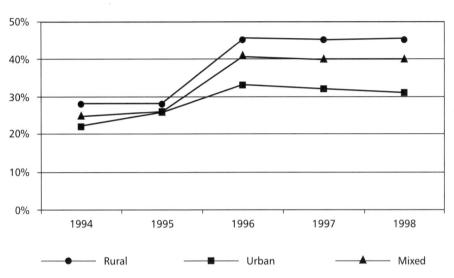

Figure 3.4
Education as % of Total Gmina Expenditures

The nature of this pressure becomes clearer if we look at the composition of education spending by gmina type. As can be seen from Table 3.6 rural gminas spend 3.2% more of their education budgets on wages than do urban ones. Wages constitute about 80% of school expenditures in Poland as a whole, and about 85% in rural gminas.[104] This is very high by international standards, and education experts generally agree that wages should not account for more than 65–75% of the operational costs of schools. The difference between rural and urban gminas with respect to the share of both education and school budgets going to wages reflects the lower pupil/teacher ratios of rural schools.

Table 3.6
Wage Payments as a Share of Gmina Education Budgets [%]

	1994	1995	1996	1997	1998	1999
Warsaw	47.8	46.6	51.1	49.3	51.2	54.9
Urban	49.3	48.6	63.6	63.8	63.6	68.7
Mixed	45.0	47.2	65.8	65.6	66.8	69.2
Rural	48.6	51.1	68.1	68.0	69.5	71.9

More surprisingly, rural gminas spend significantly larger shares of their education budgets on investments than do urban ones, as can be seen in Table 3.7. Some of this is because a slightly higher share of the national government's (ever shrinking) budget for investment grants quite rightly flows to rural gminas. These grants however constituted less than 10% of all rural gmina investment spending in 1999 (down from a high of about 28% in 1997) and do not account for the difference in the investment efforts between rural and urban jurisdictions.[105]

Table 3.7
Education Investments as a Share of Gmina Education Budgets [%]

	1994	1995	1996	1997	1998	1999
Warsaw	9.2	5.3	8.0	10.4	9.2	5.4
Urban	5.7	6.0	5.2	6.1	6.2	5.0
Mixed	11.2	13.2	9.1	11.1	10.4	9.6
Rural	18.3	19.5	13.6	14.8	13.8	12.6

Taken together, the higher shares of rural gmina education budgets that are devoted to wages and investments mean that less than 15% of the education expenditures of rural gminas go to teaching materials and other educational costs as opposed to 25% in urban jurisdictions. Equally importantly, the higher share of investment spending by rural gminas suggests that their school systems are in greater need of restructuring than those of their urban counterparts.

The reasons why this is true become clear if we review the changes in primary school enrollment, employment, class size and facility-use that have occurred since the beginning of the 1990s in gminas of different types (See Anex 1). Nationwide there has been a 13% decline in primary school enrollment, 14% in urban areas but only 8% in rural ones (this decline will continue until about 2003). There has been a corresponding, but slower, overall decline in full-time (not FTE) teacher employment of 9%. But in cities, where enrollment declined particularly sharply (14%), employment declined moderately at 8%, while in rural areas enrollment declined moderately (8%) and employment by a sharper 11%.

Because of the faster decline in teacher employment in rural areas, pupil/teacher ratios (and class sizes) have actually gone up slightly from 13.34 to 13.87. Meanwhile, in urban areas the faster decline in enrollment has led to a drop in pupil/teacher ratios from 18.68 to 16.90. Put another way, rural gminas have had to retire more teachers to keep an already very low pupil/teacher ratio from going off the map, while urban gminas have not only had to exert less effort on the employment front but have received a demographic bonus in terms of teacher workloads and class sizes.

Similarly, demographic decline has also had very different impacts on facility use in rural and urban gminas. In urban gminas, the decline has been experienced as an easing of the pressure on existing facilities, and both school sizes and pupils per classroom have dropped by a remarkable 18–20%. In rural gminas, however, it has led to school closures. Indeed, the fact that rural gminas have kept average school sizes from dropping[106] over the course of the decade, like their faster labor force reductions, demonstrates how much harder they have had to run just to stay in the same place. In fact, the painful irony of the situation is that school closures are driving the higher share of investment spending in the education budgets of rural gminas, while urban gminas are investing in new schools and classrooms because they can afford to reduce facility use beyond that which they received as a demographic bonus.

Rural gminas have also had more trouble creating gimnazjums that urban ones. Dispersed pupil populations combined with dispersed and small schools have made it difficult for them to establish separate gimnazjums of the size and scope required by the Ministry. Indeed, it has typically required them to make considerable investments in new plant and transport systems. Moreover, as we have indicated, protests from rural gminas forced MEN to suspend these requirements and many of them have yet to establish separate gimnazjums with the requisite number of pupils (150).[107] These difficulties stand in stark contrast with the situation in urban jurisdictions where the creation of gimnazjums has been possible simply by selecting some primary schools for conversion. Nonetheless, rural gminas have used the creation of gimnazjums as an occasion to rationalize average class size and pupil/teacher ratios, as can be seen from Table 3.8.

Table 3.8
Class Sizes in Primary Schools and Gimnazjums by Gmina Type

	Primary schools			Gimnazjums		
	Urban	Rural	Total	Urban	Rural	Total
Schools	4 924	12 018	16 942	2 726	2 686	5 412
Class size	24.44	17.70	21.23	25.39	23.01	24.60
Student/teacher	16.44	12.99	14.87	20.09	31.07	22.57
Students/classroom	25.47	15.46	20.27	24.78	21.67	23.73
Students/schools	477.99	128.55	230.11	151.83	69.40	110.92

In sum, it seems fairly clear that, in urban schools, teaching loads and facility conditions have improved substantially over the decade, in part because of the willingness of urban gminas to make investments, and in large measure because of the demographic bonus we have mentioned earlier. It is also clear that many rural gminas have responded to cost pressures by closing schools and ratio-nalizing the school networks, and that they have been forced to invest in consolidated schools.

Nonetheless, many rural gminas have found it extremely difficult to close schools because of resistance from parents, and because of the financial and political costs of reducing teachers' employment. In these jurisdictions, the high per pupil costs of small schools make it impossible to provide children with educations comparable to those available elsewhere, despite the fact that the gmina is receiving (and spending) one third more funding from the national government for its pupils. This can be illustrated by looking at the allocation policies of a stylized mixed gmina.[108]

This hypothetical gmina has 16 schools, three in the city and 13 in the countryside. The urban schools have at least 350 students and function comfortably with funding equal to 75 to 90% of the financial standard for urban primary schools (c. 2 000 PLN). Nonetheless, the gmina allocates to these schools the full amount that it receives from national government through the subvention, allowing directors to use the additional funds as they see fit. Most often this results in spending across three or four areas, such as extra language and computer training, expanded after-school programs and improved sports programs.

But the average cost of the 13 rural schools is 3 000 PLN per pupil, about 15% more than per pupil subsidy for pupils attending rurals schools (c. 2 700 PLN). Two of these rural schools are large and have real per pupil costs in line with those of their urban counterparts. Nonetheless, the gmina provides them with only 90% of the *urban* per pupil standard in order to reduce the contribution it has to make up from its own budget to cover the shortfall between the *rural* per pupil standard and the exceedingly high costs of the remaining 11 rural schools. In other words, the gmina beggars even those rural schools that are large enough to provide a higher quality education within existing funding norms in order to preserve schools so small that only minimum quality educations can be provided despite spending more than a third more per pupil.

Worse still, as exemplified in the following Table 3.9 based on nationwide data, urban school directors generally have greater access to parental contributions than their rural counterparts, further increasing the difference in the quality of urban and rural schools.[109]

Table 3.9

Average Annual Parental Contributions to Public Primary Schools [PLN]

Primary Schools	Rural	Mixed	Urban	Warsaw	Total
Students	1 361 267	1 068 631	1 908 791	123 770	4 462 459
Parental contribution per student	15.01	14.08	18.89	55.70	17.57
% of national average	85.41	80.11	107.47	316.92	100.00

SOURCE: GUS, S-02

This example also illustrates a more general pattern of behavior on the part of gminas with respect to their primary schools. In short, most gminas do not yet see their schools as parts of a system whose overall quality is their responsibility. Instead, they see themselves as the owners of school properties, some of which cost more than others and all of which have to be maintained within the funding constraints of the subvention, but whose educational performance is the responsibility of individual school directors. This attitude has been encouraged by a legal framework that gives them little control over school directors, and which places responsibility for monitoring the quality of schools in the hands of the Kuratoria. In practice, this has meant that gminas have concerned themselves primarily with improving the school facilities, while leaving what goes on within them up to directors. Moreover, and at least initially, most gminas set school budgets on the basis of their inflation-adjusted historical costs.

With time, however, more and more gminas are becoming conscious of differences in the per pupil costs of their schools and many of them have earmarked their investment funds for those capital improvements that will reduce these differences, such as new heating or thermal systems. Nonetheless, it remains relatively rare that gminas examine these differences from the perspective of educational quality, additional program offerings or lower workloads for teachers. In fact, over the years, many directors have been able to either protect inefficiency or 'sneak' into their organizational forms additional services that are really responsible for their higher per pupil costs.

Some gminas, however, have begun to actively use their allocation and investment policies to facilitate larger changes in the pedagogical process. The most interesting examples of this are drawn from a handful of gminas that took to heart the idea of school vouchers. Indeed, these cases are profoundly paradoxical, because despite their claims to the contrary, these gminas did not in fact allocate money to their schools on the basis of an identical per pupil sum or 'voucher'.[110] They did however, calculate the per pupil expenditures of individual schools and progressively push directors towards the average per pupil cost of all schools. In other words, under the political slogan of vouchers these gminas began to move away from historical budgeting towards more base-line measures.

More importantly, in the most dynamic of these gminas, the town of Kwidzyn, the attempt to standardize school costs was accompanied by other policies of more direct pedagogical consequence. First, the gmina decided not to make major investments in individual schools but to build a new central sports facility and computer lab to serve the pupils of all its schools. Indeed, this strategy of externalizing school investment has become increasingly visible in other jurisdictions over the past few years and is no doubt primarily the result of reasoned judgments about the benefits of economies of scale. At the same time however, the strategy may also be a response to the fact that the existing regulatory framework leaves gminas with relatively little influence on what takes place inside of schools.

This gmina also hired outside consultants to examine the educational performance of all its schools.[111] These assessments have revealed that there are significant differences in pupil test scores across the gminas schools.[112] The gmina provided this information to school directors and teachers. But it did not make this information available to parents, nor did it use the information in making decisions about how to allocate its education budget. This suggests that even gminas that are clearly interested in the quality of their schools, have not fully connected their pedagogical concerns with their role as the owner and manager of school facilities.

This lack of association is disturbing for at least two reasons. First, it suggests that the existing legal framework is encouraging many gminas to see cost rationalization as the long and the short of their role in the sector. And second, and more importantly, the reality of school choice in Poland is likely to lead, as it has led elsewhere, to the concentration of better situated and easier to educate pupils in particular schools. Indeed, in select schools in large cities, the percentage of enrolled pupils living outside of the schools' (nominal) district already exceeds 20–25%. This suggests that the 'creaming off' associated with school choice has already begun. Moreover, there is strong anecdotal evidence suggesting that primary schools that are considered particularly good, collect more voluntary parental contributions than others. As a result, gminas may not only find themselves having to deal with increasing numbers of 'problem schools' but they may have to begin to allocate money schools on an *unequal* basis, if they want to ensure that all their pupils have more or less *equal* educational opportunities.

6.3 The Management of Secondary Schools

Before the assumption of secondary education by all local governments (gminas with powiat rights, poviats, and self-governing regions) on 1 January 1999, a sizable share of secondary and post secondary schools had already been transferred to large urban jurisdictions under the Law on Large Cities of 1995. Indeed, by 1996, large urban gminas controlled schools which taught 42% of all lyceum students, 23% of all vocational school students and 9% of all post lyceum students. The table below shows the increase in students attending local government run secondary schools after that Law, and after the creation of poviats.

Because poviats are so new, most of what can be said about the management of secondary schools at local government level must focus on the Large Cities. Unfortunately, the financial data on Large City secondary schools is poor because between 1996 and 1999 central government transfers to large cities for secondary education were calculated as part of an additional increment of shared personal taxes (the so-called "U" coefficient).[113] In many cases it is unclear what this educational part of the additional increment really represented. Moreover, the real value of that part changed differently for each city because of variations in their annual PIT yields, and was obviously insensitive to changes in enrollment.

Table 3.10

Enrolment in Lyceums and Vocational Schools by School Type

	Lyceums		Vocational		Post Lyceum	
	1998/99	1999/00	1998/99	1999/00	1998/99	1999/00
Central government [thousand]	422.5	0.7	1 162.2	23.5	87.3	2.9
Local governments [thousand]	346.9	821.1	370.3	1 493.4	18.3	97.3
Non public [thousand]	40.3	39.3	35.8	20.9	97.2	105.3
Total [thousand]	809.8	861.1	1 568.3	1 537.8	202.8	205.5
% central government	52.19	0.08	74.11	1.53	43.05	1.41
% local government	42.84	95.35	23.61	97.11	9.02	47.35
% non public	4.98	4.56	2.28	1.36	47.93	51.24

SOURCE: Own calculations GUS Yearbook 2000

Rough estimates, however, suggest that in 1997 Large Cities spent 18% more than they received from the national government on the operating costs of secondary schools.[114] This figure is high. It also masks a huge amount of variation across the cities, with 10 of them contributing more than 30% to the transfer, and a number of them substantially under-spending it. How much these figures reflect the haphazard construction of the U coefficient and how much bad data, however, is unclear. In any case, more reliable data on gminas with powiat rights show that in 1999 this group of local governments spent 10% more on secondary schools than they received through the education subvention, of which 3.5% was spent on investment and only 6.5% on current operating costs.[115]

In 1999, the Foundation for Local Democracy conducted case studies of the managerial practices of five big cities.[116] The report found striking similarities across the cities, and indeed with what we know about the managerial practices of gminas with respect to primary schools. City officials were largely satisfied with school directors and in the vast majority of cases made no efforts to block their re-nomination by independent selection committees. None of the cities had conducted analyses of their school networks and most did not use data on per pupil expenditures to inform their budgeting decisions. Indeed, they rarely sought to impose cost cuts on schools.[117]

Instead, they generally accepted the 'organizational forms' submitted to them by directors without question. Moreover, they explained their attitude by saying that since these forms had been previously approved by the Kuratoria, there was no real reason to worry about them. Here, however, it must be stressed that the Kuratoria examine the forms to make sure that schools are meeting the minimum programmatic standards required by the government, and rarely comment on above standard programmatic offerings. As a result, city officials were clearly accepting budget propositions that contained more than these minimums, despite their financial consequences. Only one city requested that a director reduce his budget, and this was because the city thought he was padding-out his support staff unnecessarily. Otherwise, cities did not interfere in the employment or curricula decisions of directors and to the degree that they worried about employment at all, it was to express fears about laying off teachers. Not surprisingly, school directors enthusiastically supported the transfer of responsibility for secondary education to big cities and of all stakeholders questioned were the most positive about the reform.

Many of the cities quickly declared that their goals in the sector were to increase enrollment in lyceums, improve teaching quality and adapt vocational schools to the local labor market. But these 'strategic' declarations were rarely accompanied by the formulation of specific policy measures. City officials did however, immediately set out to inventory the assets and liabilities of schools, to pay down their debts, and to establish investment priorities. They also sought to engage directors in the formulation of the city's educational policies and most invited their directors to form an informal advisory committee.[118] In some places these committees succeeded in establishing a priority order in which to conduct major repairs of individual schools. And in one city, directors agreed to locate a major new investment in a computer lab in a particular school.

Nonetheless, the results of these efforts in cooperative deliberation were usually more modest and generally directors were unable to agree on specific policies to restructure secondary schools in the city. In particular, the directors could not agree among themselves about which vocational schools should be eliminated, and which transformed into lyceums in order to meet the clear demand for new places in general education high schools coming from parents.[119] Instead, school directors were generally left to make programmatic changes on the basis of their individual understandings of the labor market and parental expectations.[120] As a result, there is some evidence that many vocational schools were rushing to develop similar new specializations such as accounting or computers skills. The cities however, did not intervene even when they sensed a stampede because they assumed directors knew better.[121]

This is in some ways undoubtedly true, and it was clear that in all the cities studied, competition for pupils had forced school directors, particularly those of vocational schools, to introduce substantial curriculum changes despite the absence of clear ministerial or city-level guidelines. More importantly, a combination of school level adjustment and local government support has made it possible to substantially increase the number of places in lyceums. As a result, there has also been a very marked decline in the number of pupils attending vocational schools, and an increase in the numbers attending degree granting lyceums and professional schools, as can be seen from Table 3.11 (see also Annex 3).

Nonetheless, and over the long term, it seems that the restructuring of the sector will require a more visible hand if the number and profile of vocational schools is in fact going to mesh with local labor market needs.[122] Indeed, recently, some cities have begun to fire school directors for not introducing programmatic changes. This is in violation of existing law which restricts the right of local governments to fire directors to cases of financial mismanagement. Nonetheless, in most cases the Kuratoria have not objected to these actions, while the courts have responded by forcing local governments to pay special severance penalties, but not to reinstate directors.[123]

Table 3.11
Further Careers of Rural and Urban Primary Schools Graduates [%]

	1996/1997		1999/2000		Change	
	Urban	Rural	Urban	Rural	Urban	Rural
Lyceum	38.14	18.99	45.11	24.84	6.97	5.85
Professional	30.28	33.18	31.17	38.77	0.89	5.60
Basic Vocational	27.57	46.10	20.17	35.21	−7.40	−10.89
Not continuing	4.00	1.74	3.55	1.17	−0.45	−0.56

SOURCE: GUS Statistical Yearbooks for Education.

Finally, while cities knew that many of the students enrolled in their secondary schools came from other jurisdictions and were keenly aware that they were paying more for schools than they received from the national government, only one was aware that this meant they were subsidizing the educations of other taxpayers' children. Meanwhile, another city attempted to restrict access to its lyceums to pupils residing in the jurisdiction. Here, however, the policy was motivated not so much by financial concerns as by ethnic politics. Moreover, the policy was quickly blocked by the local Kuratoria. Nonetheless, it remains unclear what will happen around this issue when more cities begin to understand the financial implications of inter-jurisdictional commutating.

As for poviats, there is relatively little information on their managerial policies towards secondary schools, because they are only two years old. Moreover, the only financial data available is for 1999, their first year of operation.[124] In this year, total poviat spending on education equaled 100.5% of the education subvention. There were, however, significant variations across poviats and 128 spent less on education than they received through the subvention, 173 spent between 100% and 110% of their subventions, 7 poviats spent more than 110% of the subvention. While these figures suggest that the education subvention generally reflected the historical spending of the national government on secondary schools, they should not be interpreted to mean that the education subvention was sufficient for poviats to meet their challenges in the sector.

Instead, under spending reflects the fact that some poviats actually received slightly more than the national government had previously spent, and were unable to use it for necessary investments because they had no time. Meanwhile those that spent more than they received through the subvention were generally making up for shortfalls in the operating costs of their schools. Indeed, the most important fact to remember about poviats is that, unlike gminas with poviat rights, they have very little disposable income to contribute to the subvention because they derive almost no revenues from own and shared taxes.

As discussed earlier, the education subvention for 1999 was calculated on the basis of the average per pupil costs for 27 different types of secondary schools. Despite the fact that the money received through the subvention is freely disposable, most poviats used the Ministry's standards to allocate resources to individual schools. Indeed, in 2000, when a single per pupil multiplier for all professional and vocational schools was introduced, many poviat education officials complained that they had lost a convenient tool to define school budgets. This complaint suggests how far poviats are from taking an active managerial role in the sector.

Indeed, a report on the education policies of a few poviats[125] suggests that they are faring even worse than Large Cities or gminas with poviat rights. Unlike the former, 'normal' poviats not only have less disposable income, but considerably smaller school systems characterized by a larger share of vocational and professional schools. In other words, more of their schools are in need of profound restructuring, and there are less of them across which to adjust budgeting strategies. Worse still, because the number of schools in each jurisdiction is small and students have extremely limited choices, school directors are under little competitive pressure to introduce programmatic changes on their own.

Most of the poviats studied had yet to make even declarative statements of policy goals, or to prioritize investment needs. There was little evidence of cooperation between the education departments of powiats and their labor departments, which were also decentralized in 1999, and receive central government grants for both the payment of unemployment benefits and for the creation of active labor market policies. This despite the fact that as much as 70% of the graduating classes of some vocational schools immediately enter the unemployment system. Indeed, as in the big cities, whatever contact there was between schools and the labor offices was almost exclusively bilateral. Similarly, none of the poviats studied made any attempt to bring employers and school directors into contact with each other despite the fact that local employers routinely complain that school graduates lack fundamental work skills, like the ability to follow instructions, keep to schedules, and understand foreign languages. In short, powiats seem a long way from being able to meet the daunting structural challenges facing them in secondary education.

7. CONCLUSIONS

Local governments are now responsible for the management of virtually all the institutions involved in delivering preschool, primary and secondary education in Poland. They are also financing at least 25% of the costs of these institutions out of their own general revenues. In short, the national government has clearly decentralized much of the responsibility for education in Poland to local governments over the last decade. Equally important is the reality of school choice, and the provision of public monies for non-public schools, which means that the decentralization of education in Poland has been accompanied by its marketization.

In general, we think that both decentralization and marketization have been good for Polish education.[126] Local governments have at a minimum been able to maintain public spending on education in a period of fiscal austerity, and have clearly made efforts to improve and rationalize their school systems. There has also been a substantial decline in the number of pupils attending vocational schools, and a substantial increase in the numbers attending degree granting lyceums and professional schools. Most importantly, programmatic reform, curricula liberalization, parental pressure, and competition for pupils have led to adjustment, innovation and increasing variation at both the school and local government levels.

Not all of this variation, however, has been or will be positive, and it is clear that the quality of educational services in Poland will increasingly differ across schools and local governments. Moreover, it will become increasingly difficult to determine what is driving these differences. They will be based on complex interactions between wealth, preference, and objective obstacles at the local government, school, and parental levels. In short, it seems clear to us, that the major challenge facing the national government in the immediate future is to preserve and enhance the scope of this variation, while simultaneously ensuring that disadvantaged jurisdictions and socio-economic groups are not left behind. To meet this challenge we think the national government must revisit and substantially reform the regulatory framework that it established at the beginning of the decade.

As we have tried to make clear, this regulatory framework was built on two assumptions that have become increasingly untenable. The first assumption was that the national government could fully fund teachers' wages without defining employment standards. This assumption, guaranteed in law, effectively made the national budget liable for the employment policies of local governments and school directors. Through most of the decade the national government was generally able to fulfill this guarantee by not substantially raising teachers wages, and by allocating the education subvention more or less in line with historical expenditure patterns. Over time however, the guarantee was eroded with demographic shifts and the ever decreasing pupil populations of rural gminas.

The guarantee collapsed in 2000 when, in response to a variety of compelling forces, the government placed the education subvention on a per pupil basis and *at the same time* introduced ill-considered changes in the Teachers' Charter. Until normative employment standards are introduced, there will be no way to reconcile per pupil funding with this guarantee. Worse still, until some control is established over teachers' advancement from the third to fourth pay grades and/or the wage implications of this advancement, the budgets of the national government and those of local governments will be exposed to large and unpredictable financial liabilities. It is thus clear to us that, at a minimum, the government must move rapidly to introduce employment standards and controls on teacher advancement if the system is to regain some stability.

163

The second assumption that informed the construction of the regulatory regime at the beginning of the decade was that local governments should not be responsible for the pedagogical quality of schools. As result, they were given extremely limited control over what goes on inside of them. This, combined with the assumption that the national government would fully fund teachers' wages, has made local governments relatively indifferent to how directors spend their operating budgets or to the quality of services that schools provide. Not surprisingly, local governments have instead focused their energies on improving the physical infrastructure of their educational facilities, and supplementing teachers' pay.

This indifference to both cost and quality, however is breaking down. In part, it is breaking down because the national government is having increasing problems in meeting its promise to fully fund teachers' wages. And in part it is breaking down because social and electoral demands to improve school quality are pushing local government officials to think about more than the physical condition of their schools. Nonetheless, this thinking remains in its infancy. Worse still, school choice and the profound challenges involved in restructuring secondary education in general and vocational schools in particular will make it imperative that local governments develop more substantial educational policies in the immediate future. At a minimum, restructuring secondary schools will require coordination, consultation and planning, while school choice, and the phenomena of 'creaming-off'[127] that comes with it, will require robust and sustained efforts to monitor school performance.

For local governments to take these policy responsibilities more seriously, and for them to actually be able to implement them, it is clear that their managerial powers with respect to hiring, firing and redeploying teachers must be increased. Indeed, it seems clear to us that the provisions of the Teachers' Charter that make it virtually impossible for local governments to fire or redeploy teachers short of closing schools, should either be scrapped or relaxed. It is also desirable to increase the local government control over the hiring and firing of school directors. Finally, it would be desirable to introduce into the legislative framework provisions that require local governments to establish mechanisms to monitor school performance.

Most importantly, the national government must become both more aware and more concerned with variation in the quality of Poland's educational system. In particular, it should be concerned with reducing the obstacles to improve the quality of schools in poor rural jurisdictions at both the primary and secondary school levels, as well as helping to ensure that rural pupils have equal access to quality secondary schools located in the cities. At a minimum, this will require action on three fronts.

Firstly, the national government will have to make a substantial effort to improve Poland's educational statistics, because the existing statistics do not allow for the tracking of crucial indications of difference in educational performance such as teachers' wages, attendance rates, drop out rates, or the fates of different pupil cohorts. It will require the continued development of standardized tests.

Secondly, the national government will have to pay increasing attention to both the different fiscal capacities of local governments and the different costs they face in providing similar educational services. Here, it seems obvious to us that over the coming years substantial investment grants and other programmatic fund—notably for teacher retraining—will have to be made available to poor rural gminas and poviats if they are to consolidate their school networks, restructure their vocational schools and provide educational services of reasonably similar quality within the constraints of the education subvention. This will require both an increase in public spending on education, and the clarification of the relationship between the national government and the new regional self-governments. On the one hand, the national government must make sure that additional funds are in fact provided to regional self-governments for those types of programs that it considers most important. On the other hand, regional governments must be obligated to develop clear priorities and transparent rules for the allocation of these special funds.

Finally, but in a similar vein, the existing subvention formula should be reformed to ensure that resources flow to local governments on the basis of their objective need for funds. As we have indicated, because the rural multiplier is based on an administrative distinction, it now directs substantial funds to suburban jurisdictions with school networks and per capita incomes that are no different from urban ones. It thus seems desirable to replace this multiplier with one based on a more objective characterization of a jurisdiction's need, such as its per capita income, or, better still, the number of pupils from poor households enrolled in its schools. At the same time, a multiplier should be introduced for that small number of rural jurisdictions that must maintain small isolated schools because of geographical realities. It may also be desirable to introduce a multiplier for those urban jurisdictions which, because of objective labor market conditions, must pay substantially higher wages than other local governments just to keep teachers in their system. Similarly, the national government should consider providing those gminas with poviat rights that spend significantly more on secondary education than they receive, grants to equalize the part of their additional spending that is in fact going to support children commuting from other jurisdictions.

BIBLIOGRAPHY

The word *processed* describes informally reproduced works that may not be commonly available through libraries.

Barański, A.: *Zadania gmin w zakresie oświaty*, (*The Education Responsibilities of Gminas*) Biuro Studiów i Analiz Kancelarii Sejmu, Warsaw, 1996.

Barro, S.: *Money, Students and Teachers*, Assistance to the Polish Ministry of Education, USAID/ RTI Warsaw, 2000.

Białecki, I.: *Alfabetyzm funkcjonalny*, (Functional Illiteracy) Res Publica Nowa, 6 (93), Warsaw, 1996.

Białecki, I.: *Governmental Roles in the Delivery of Educational Service in Poland,* Warsaw, 1999, processed.

Bochwic, T.: *Narodziny i działalność Solidarności Oświaty i Wychowania 1980–1989,* (The Origins and Activities of the Teachers' Section of the Solidarity Trade Union), Warsaw, 2000.

CBOS (Centrum Badań Opinii Spolecznej): *Reforma edukacji–pierwsze doświadczenie, nadzieje i obawy,*(Education Reform–Experience, Hope and Fears), Warsaw, 2000.

Chaber, A.: *Bon edukacyjny: kontrowersje i realia,* (Education Vouchers: Debates and Realities) Master's Thesis, Uniwersytet Warszawski, Warsaw, 2000.

Connelly, J.: *The Captive University,* Chapel Hill North Carolina, 2000.

Czarnobaj, L.: *Finansowanie placówek oświatowych w Kwidzynie,* (Financing Educational Institutions in Kwdzyn, University of Warsaw, Warsaw, 1998, processed.

Dec, A., and T. Matusz.: *Finansowanie oświaty samorządowej,* (Financing of Local Government Education), Biuro Studiów i Analiz Kancelarii Sejmu, Warsaw, 1996.

Dera, A.: Biuletyn Kancelarii Sejmu, Nr. 598/II kad. Komisja Edukacji, Nauki i Postępu Technicznego (No. 28), Warsaw, 1994.

Dolata, R., B. Murwaska, E. Putkiewicz, E., and M. Żytko. 1998. *Diagnoza poziomu osiągnięć szkolnych absolwentów edukacji podstawowej w Kwidzynie w roku szkolnym 1996/1997,* (Diagnosing the educational attainments of primary school graduates in Kwidzyn in 1996/1997), Kwidzyn, 1998, processed.

Dolata, R., B. Murwaska, and E. Putkiewicz.: *Diagnoza poziomu osiągnięć szkolnych uczniów klas drugich szkoły podstawowej w 1998–1999,* (Diagnosing the educational attainments of second graders in 1998/1999, Kwidzyn, 1999, processed.

Dolata, R., B. Murwaska, and E. Putkiewicz.: *Diagnoza poziomu osiągnięć szkolnych uczniów klas trzecich szkoły podstawowej,* (Diagnosing the educational attainments of third graders), Kwidzyn, 2000, processed.

Doświadczenie i Przyszłość.: *Polska pięć lat po sierpniu, (Poland five years after August),* Libella, Paris, 1985.

Gęsicki, J.: *Po co gminom szkoły,* (Why give gminas schools), Instytut Badań Edukacyjnych, Warsaw, 1994.

Golinowska, S.: *Rola Centrum w kształtowaniu struktury spożycia,* (The Role of the National Government in Shaping Consumption), PWE, Warsaw, 1990.

Golinowska, S., and J. Herczyński.: *Wykształcenie i przygotowanie zawodowe Polaków,* (Education and the Professional Preparedness of Poles), Raport CASE–Doradcy, Warsaw, 2000, processed.

Golinowska, S., and E. Rumińska–Zimny (eds): *Access to Education. Report on Social Development in Poland,* UNDP/CASE, Warsaw, 1998.

Grzegorzewski, P.: *Szkoły podstawowe w gminach wiejskich: analiza statystyczna*, (Primary Schoold in Rural Gminas: Statisctical Analysis) Warsaw, 1999, processed.

GUS: *Budżety Gmin w Latach 1992–1994*, (Gmina Budgets 1992–1994) ,Wydawnictwo GUS, Warsaw, 1995.

Herbst, M.: *Mechanizmy finansowania oświaty w Polsce–algorytm oświatowy a dopłaty samorzadów do otrzymanej subwencji*, (The Mechanism for Financing Education in Poland—the algorithm for allocating the education subvention to local governments, and their own contributions.) Studia Regionalne i Lokalne, 3 (3), 2000.

Herbst, M.: *Realizacja zadań oświatowych przez powiaty*, in Gorzelak, G. (ed.) *Monitorowanie skutków reformy terytorialnej organizacji Kraju*, (The Realization of Education Responsibilities by Poviats) Warsaw EUROREG, 2001.

Herczyński, J.: *Komentarz do Rozporządzenia Ministra Edukacji Narodowej z dnia 16 grudnia 1999 w sprawie zasad podziału części oświatowej subwencji ogólnej dla jednostek samorządu terytorialnego*, (Commentary to the Ordinance of the Ministry of National Education of December 16, 1999 on the principles governing the allocation of the education subvention for local governments), MEN web site, Warsaw, 2000.

Hibner, E.: *Ustrojowe aspekty wprowadzenia nowego systemu finansowania oœwiaty*, in, *Finansowanie szkół średnich przez powiaty—doświadczenia wielkich miast*, (The Systemic Aspects of the New Mechanism for Financing Education) Wyższa Szkola Biznesu w Tarnowie, Tarnów, 1999.

Jeżowski, A.: *Raport cząstkowy na temat kosztów uczniów w szkołach resortowych w roku 1997*, (Partial Report on the per pupil costs of ministerial schools in 1997),Warsaw, 1999, processed.

Komitet Ekspertów do Spraw Edukacji Narodowej.: *Raport o stanie i kierunkach rozwoju edukacji narodowej w Polskiej Rzeczpospolitej Ludowej*, (Report on the state and developmental direction of national education in the Peoples Republic of Poland), PWN, Krakow, 1989.

Konarzewski, K.: *Infrastruktura oświatowa w pierwszym roku reformy systemu oświaty*, (Educational infrastructure in the first year of systemic reform) Wydawnictwo ISP, Warsaw, 2000.

Kornai, J.: *The Socialist System: The Political Economy of Socialism*, Princeton University Press, Princeton, New Jersey, 1992.

Kosiński, K.: *O nową mentalność (życie codzienne w szkołach 1945–1956)*, (About the new mentality (everyday life in schools 1945–56),TRIO, Warsaw, 2000.

Kowalik, J. (ed.): *Samorządy a szkoły ponadpodstawowe: Doświadczenia wielkich miast 1996–1998*, (Local Governments and secondary schools: the experience of large cities 1996–1998), Wydawnictwo Samorzadowe FRDL, Warsaw, 1999.

Kowalska, I., M. Olszewski, A. Reca, and M. Zahorska: *Analiza wykorzystania środków na oświate na poziomie samorządu lokalnego i na poziomie szkoły*, (Analysis of the use of educational resources by local governments and schools), Wydawnictwo ISP, Warsaw, 2000.

Kowalska, I.1999a.: *Dobre szkoły wiejskie* (Good Rural Schools) Raport z badań prowadzonych przez Zespół ds. Koordynacji Badań nad Reformą Oświaty, MEN Warsaw, 1999.

Kowalska, I. 1999b.: *Procedura rozdziału środków na inwestycje oświatowe z budżetu państwa,* (Procedures for allocating investment funds for education from the state budget) Raport z badań prowadzonych przez Zespół ds. Koordynacji Badań nad Reformą Oświaty, MEN Warsaw, 1999.

Kupisiewicz, Cz.: *Zarys koncepcji przebudowy systemu szkolnego w Polsce,* (Outline of a conception for the reconstruction of the Polish school system), PWN, Krakow, 1989.

Lavoie, D.: *Rivalry and Central Planning: The Socialist Calculation Debate Reconsidered,* Cambridge University Press, Cambridge, 1985.

Levitas, A.: *The Political Economy of Fiscal Decentralization in Poland: 1989–1999,* East European Regional Housing Sector Assistance Project, Project 180-00034, Urban Institute, Washington, July 1999.

Levitas, A. and M. Federowicz: *Polish Works Councils under Communism and Neoliberalism: 1944-1991,* in Rogers, J., Streek, W. (eds.), *Contemporary Works Councils,* University of Chicago Press, Chicago, 1995.

Levitas, A. and J. Herczyński: *Select Policy Issues of the Financing of Education in Poland,* Democratic Governance and Public Administration Project/DAI, USAID Contract No. DHR-C-95-000026-00, Warsaw, 1999.

Levitas, A., J. Herczyński, and M. Herbst, *Reforming the Algorithm for the Education Subvention,* Presentation to MEN, June 16. 1999, processed.

Levitas, A., J. Herczyński, and M. Herbst. *Jak poprawić algorytm,* (How to correct the Algorithm), Wspólnota 39, Warsaw, 2000.

Levitas, A., and R. Rafuse: *Methodological Issues in Calculating and Financing a Second Tier of Local Self-Government in Poland,* Democratic Governance and Public Administration Project/ DAI, USAID Contract No. DHR-C-95-000026-00, Warsaw, 1998.

Levitas, A., R. Rafuse, C. Marks, and J. Swiecicki: *Issues Related to the Calculation of a Financial Standard for Secondary Education and the Introduction of School Vouchers* Democratic Governance and Public Administration Project/DAI, USAID Contract No. DHR-C-95-000026-00, Warsaw, 1998.

Leszczyński, A., and K. Gołąb: *Bon oświatowy,* (Vouchers), Reports 1, 2 and 3, PHARE SMART Program for Financing Education Responsibilities, subcomponent SCO2, Warsaw, 1998, processed.

Marcinkiewicz, K. 1992. *Szkoły w nowej rzeczywistości* (Schools in a new reality), Gazeta Wyborcza, Warsaw, July 7. 1992.

Marcinkiewicz, K.: *Nareszcie bon edukacyjny,* (Finally Vouchers) Rzeczpospolita, Warsaw. May 11. 1999.

MEN (Ministerstwo Edukacji Narodowej): *Informacja o realizacji podstawowych zadań oraz budżetu w 1992 w zakresie oświaty i wychowania oraz szkolnictwa wyższego* (Information on the the realization of basic educational responsibilities and expenditures), Material dla Sejmowej Komisji, Warsaw,* 1993.

MEN 1999a. *Ministerstwo Edukacji Narodowej o zasadach finansowania oświaty w 1999 roku,* (The Ministry of Education on the Principles of Education Finances, Biblioteczka Reformy 6, Warsaw, 1999.

MEN 1999b: *Ministerstwo Edukacji Narodowej o reformie programowej–gimnazjum,* (The Ministry of Education on programmatic reform–gymnasiums), Biblioteczka Reformy 9, Warsaw, 1999.

MEN 2000: *Ministerstwo Edukacji Narodowej o nowelizacji Karty Nauczyciela,* (The Ministry of Education on reform of the Teachers Charter), Biblioteczka Reformy 23, Warsaw, 2000.

MEN 2001: *Uwagi w sprawie ustalania przez jednostki samorządu terytorialnego regulaminów w świetle art. 30, ust. 6 ustawy—Karta Nauczyciela,* (Comments on local government determination of regulations in light of article 30, paragraph 6 of the Law on the Teachers Charter, Warsaw, 2001.

Miller, J.: Presentation at Conference *"Finansowanie szkół średnich przez powiat –doświadczenie wielkich miast"* (The Financing of Secondary Schools by Poviats). Tarnów, Wyższa Szkola Biznesu w Tarnowie, 1998.

Nowakowska, E.: *Podwyżki przez obniżki,* (Pay hikes through pay cuts) Polityka No. 41, Warsaw, October 7. 2000.

Ost, D.: *Solidarity and the Politics of Anti-Politics,* Ithaca, Cornell University Press, New York, 1990.

Piwowarski, R.: *Szkoły na wsi–edukacyjne wyzwanie,* (Rural Schools—an educational challenge), Instytut Badań Edukacyjnych, Warsaw, 1999.

Radziwiłł, A.: *O szkole, wychowaniu i polityce,* (About schools, education and politics), WSiP, Warsaw, 1992.

Sławiński, S.: *Reforma szkolna w III Rzeczypospolitej,* (School reform in the 3rd Republic), WSiP, Warsaw, 1996.

Staniszkis, J.: *Poland's The Self-Limiting Revolution,* Princeton University Press, Princeton, New Jersey, 1984.

Starczewska, K.: *Bony oświatowe,* (Education Vouchers), KOS 15 (165), Warsaw, 1989.

Szczepański, J. (ed.): *Raport o stanie oświaty,* (Report on the state of education) WSiP, Warsaw, 1973.

---

* This is an annual report submitted to Sejm by MEN every year. We used these reports for all years from 1992 to 1999, and refer to them in the text as MEN materials for Sejm.

Tabor, M.: *Finansowe skutki wdrożenia zmian w Karcie Nauczyciela na przykładzie kilku wybranych miast,* (The financial consequences of changes in the Teachers Charter on the basis of a few selected cities), Vulcan, Wrocław, 2000.

Winiecki, J.: *The Distorted World of Soviet Type Economies,* University of Pittsburgh Press, Pittsburgh, PA, 1987.

Zespół d.s.: *Oceny Skutków Karty Nauczyciela,* (Assessment of the consequences of the Teachers Charter), Protocol of July 25. 2000, processed.

ZNP (Związek Nauczycielstwa Polskiego): *Informator Zarządu Głównego* (Information from the Board) ZNP 14 (325), Warsaw, 1999.

Związek Gmin Śląska Opolskiego: *Wydatki na funkcjonowanie oświaty publicznej,* Expenditures on the functioning of Public education, Opole, 1998, processed.

Żurek, J.: *Wybór źródeł do historii Solidarności Oświaty i Wychowania 1980–1989,* (Selected Sources on the History of the Teachers' Section of the Solidarity Trade Union 1980–1989),TYSOL, Warsaw, 2000.

LAWS OF SEJM DISCUSSED IN THE TEXT

Ustawa z dnia 25 września 1981 r. o samorzadzie zalogi przedsiebiorstwa państwowego. Dz. U. 1981 nr. 24 poz. 123 (Law on Employee Councils of September 25, 1981)

Ustawa z dnia 26 stycznia 1982 r.—Karta Nauczyciela. Dz. U. 1982 nr. 3 poz. 19 (Law on the Teachers' Charter of January 26, 1982)

Ustawa z dnia 4 maja 1982 r. o szkolnictwie wyższym. Dz. U. 1982 nr. 14 poz. 113 (Law on Universities of May 4, 1982)

Ustawa z dnia 8 marca 1990 r. o samorzadzie gminnym, Dz. U. 1990, nr. 16, poz. 95 (Law on Gminas of March 8, 1990)

Ustawa z dnia 17 maja 1990 r. o podziale zadań i kompetencji określonych w ustawach szczególnych pomiędzy organy gminy a organy administracji rzadowej oraz o zmianie niektórych ustaw, Dz. U. 1990 nr 34 poz.198 (Law on the Division of Responsibilities between the National Government and Local Governments of May, 17 1990)

Ustawa z dnia 17 maja 1990 r. o zmianie ustawy o rozwoju systemu oświaty i wychowania oraz ustawy—Karta Nauczyciela. Dz. U. 1990 nr 34 poz. 197 (Law changing the Laws on the Development of Education System and Teachers' Charter of May 17, 1990)

Ustawa z dnia 14 grudnia 1990 r. o dochodach gmin i zasadach ich subwencjonowania w 1991 r. oraz o zmianie ustawy o samorzadzie terytorialnym. Dz. U. 1990 nr. 89 poz. 519 (Law on Gmina Income of December 14, 1990)

Ustawa z dnia 7 września 1991 r. o systemie oświaty. Dz. U. 1991 nr. 95 poz. 425 (Law on Education System of September 7, 1991)

Ustawa z dnia 10 grudnia 1993 o finansowaniu gmin. Dz. U. 1993 nr. 129 poz. 600 (Law on Gmina Finances of December 10, 1993)

Ustawa z dnia 24 listopada 1995 r. o zmianie zakresu dzialania niektórych miast oraz o miejskich strefach uslug publicznych Dz. U. 1995 nr. 141 poz. 692 (Law on the Scope of Activities of Some Cities of November 24, 1995)

Ustawa z dnia 26 listopada 1998 r. o dochodach jednostek samorzadu terytorialnego w latach 1999 i 2000. Dz. U. 1998 nr. 150 poz. 983 (Law on Local Government Revenues in Years 1999 and 2000 of November 26, 1998)

Ustawa z dnia 18 lutego 2000 r. o zmianie ustawy—Karta Nauczyciela oraz o zmianie niektórych innych ustaw. Dz. U. 2000 nr. 19 poz. 239 (Law Changing the Teachers' Charter of February 18, 2000)

Ustawa z dnia 12 maja 2000 r. o zasadach wspierania rozwoju regionalnego, Dz. U. 2000 nr. 48 poz. 550 (Law on Regional Development of May 12, 2000)

Ustawa z dnia 21 grudnia 2000 r. o zmianie ustawy o systemie oświaty. Dz. U. 2000 nr. 122 poz. 1320 (Law Changing the law on the Education System of December 21, 2000)

ANNEX 1

Basic Data for Primary Schools: 1990–1999

Table 3A.1
Basic Data for Primary Schools: 1990–1999

		1990/1991	1995/1996	1999/2000	1991–1995	1991–1999
Shares of rural	Cities	63.64%	62.75%	61.52%		
and urban pupils	Rural	36.36%	37.25%	38.48%	Dynamics	
	Total	100.00%	100.00%	100.00%		
Pupils	Cities	3 295.6	3 147.1	2 767.5	95.49%	83.98%
	Rural	1 882.6	1 868.1	1 731.3	99.23%	91.96%
	Total	5 178.2	5 015.2	4 498.8	96.85%	86.88%
Classes	Cities	122.3	123.1	112.6	100.65%	92.07%
	Rural	104.4	100.9	95.4	96.65%	91.38%
	Total	226.7	224.0	208.0	98.81%	91.75%
Teachers	Cities	176.4	174.2	163.8	98.75%	92.86%
	Rural	141.1	135.8	124.9	96.24%	88.52%
	Total	317.5	310.0	288.7	97.64%	90.93%
Classrooms	Cities	89.8	103.7	109.1	115.48%	121.49%
	Rural	102.6	110.0	108.5	107.21%	105.75%
	Total	192.4	213.7	217.6	111.07%	113.10%
Schools*	Cities	4 638	5 029	7 650	108.43%	164.94%
	Rural	14 808	13 916	14 704	93.98%	99.30%
	Total	19 446	18 945	22 354	97.42%	114.95%
Class size	Cities	26.95	25.57	24.58	94.87%	91.21%
	Rural	18.03	18.51	18.15	102.67%	100.64%
	Total	22.84	22.39	21.63	98.02%	94.69%
Pupils per teacher	Cities	18.68	18.07	16.90	96.70%	90.44%
	Rural	13.34	13.76	13.86	103.10%	103.89%
	Total	16.31	16.18	15.58	99.20%	95.55%

Table 3A.1 (continued)
Basic Data for Primary Schools: 1990–1999

		1990/1991	1995/1996	1999/2000	1991–1995	1991–1999
Pupils per classroom	Cities	36.70	30.35	25.37	82.69%	69.12%
	Rural	18.35	16.98	15.96	92.55%	86.96%
	Total	26.91	23.47	20.67	87.20%	76.82%
School size	Cities	710.56	625.79	361.76	88.07%	50.91%
	Rural	127.13	134.24	117.74	105.59%	92.61%
	Total	266.29	264.72	201.25	99.41%	75.58%
Teachers per class	Cities	1.44	1.42	1.45	98.11%	100.86%
	Rural	1.35	1.35	1.31	99.58%	96.87%
	Total	1.40	1.38	1.39	98.81%	99.10%
Classes per school	Cities	26.37	24.48	14.72	92.83%	55.82
	Rural	7.05	7.25	6.49	102.84%	92.03%
	Total	11.66	11.82	9.30	101.42%	79.82%
Classrooms per school	Cities	19.36	20.62	14.26	106.50%	73.66%
	Rural	6.93	7.90	7.38	114.08%	106.50%
	Total	9.89	11.28	9.73	114.01%	98.38%

Own calculations: GUS Data

. In 1999, because of the introduction of gimnazjum some of the trends discussed in the text become less pronounced. Nonetheless the net effect of introducing gimnazjum on the structural characteristics of the Polish education system is only that the number of school increased, and accordingly the average size of the schools went down. All other trends were maintained such as the increase in pupil/teacher ratios in rural schools and their decrease in urban ones.

ANNEX 2

Shares of the Education Subvention by School and Pupil Type in 2000

Table 3A.2

Shares of the Education Subvention by School and Pupil Type in 2000

Student Category	Number of Students	Weight	Weighted Students Number	Amount per Student	Total Amount [thousands PLN]	% of the Total Subvention
PRIMARY SCHOOLS AND GIMNAZJUM						
Students	4 453 683	1.00	4 453 683	1 932.97	8 608 827	47.50
Students of rural schools	1 728 957	0.33	570 556	637.88	1 102 866	6.09
Students of schools in small cities	183 536	0.18	33 036	347.93	63 858	0.35
Special classes in regular schools	5 269	0.50	2 635	966.48	5 092	0.03
Integrated classes in regular schools	5 368	3.00	16 104	5 798.90	31 129	0.17
National minorities students	34 818	0.20	6 964	386.59	13 460	0.07
Students bussed to school	611 212	0.30	183 364	579.89	354 436	1.96
Sport classes and school	20 627	0.20	4 125	386.59	7 974	0.04
Sport mastery schools	556	1.00	556	1 932.97	1 075	0.01
Non-public school in rural areas	755	0.80	602	1 542.51	1 165	0.01
Non-public school in small cities	120	0.71	85	1 368.54	164	0.00
Non-public schools in cities	35 505	0.60	21 303	1 159.78	41 178	0.23
Adult students in rural areas	220	0.93	205	1 799.59	396	0.00

Table 3A.2 (continued)

Shares of the Education Subvention by School and Pupil Type in 2000

Student Category	Number of Students	Weight	Weighted Students Number	Amount per Student	Total Amount [thousands PLN]	% of the Total Subvention
Adult students in small cities	71	0.83	59	1 596.63	113	0.00
Adult students in cities	5 931	0.70	4 152	1 353.08	8 025	0.04
Handicapped children in general classes	13 950	0.25	3 488	483.24	6 741	0.04
Revalidation for serious disabilities	4 050	0.50	2 025	966.48	3 914	0.02
POST GIMNAZJUM						
Number of students	2 483 132	1.00	2 483 132	1 932.97	4 799 815	26.49
Adult students in lyceums	70 369	0.70	49 258	1 353.08	95 215	0.53
Adult students in professional schools	174 607	0.81	140 559	1 556.04	271 695	1.50
Special schools non-vocational	78 350	2.40	188 040	4 639.12	363 475	2.01
Vocational special schools	32 727	1,00	32 727	1 932.7	63 260	0,35
Vocational schools	1 509 090	0.15	226 364	289.95	437 553	2.41
National minorities	2 240	0.20	448	386.59	866	0.00
Non-public lyceums for youth	41 965	0.60	25 179	1 159.78	48 670	0.27
Non-public vocational schools for youth	38 078	0.69	26 274	1 333.75	50 786	0.28
Non-public lyceums for adults	43 065	0.35	15 073	676.54	29 135	0.16
Non-public vocational schools for adults	121 548	0.40	48 923	778.02	94 567	0.52
Medical schools	26 903	1.00	26 903	1 932.97	52 003	0.29

175

Table 3A.2 (continued)

Shares of the Education Subvention by School and Pupil Type in 2000

Student Category	Number of Students	Weight	Weighted Students Number	Amount per Student	Total Amount [thousands PLN]	% of the Total Subvention
Special sailors' classes	1 569	1.00	1 569	1 932.97	3 033	0.02
Teacher colleges	15 619	1.00	15 619	1 932.97	30 191	0.17
Non-public teacher colleges	1 843	1.20	2 212	2 319.56	4 275	0.02
Students of schools in rural areas	174 677	0.33	57 643	637.88	111 423	0.61
Students of schools in small cities	74 809	0.18	13 466	347.93	26 029	0.14
NON SCHOOL TASKS						
Boarding houses	118 833	1.77000	210 334	3 421.35	406 570	2.24
Special preschools	3 056	4.50000	13 752	8 698.36	26 582	0.15
SOSW	32 990	7.37000	243 136	14 245.97	469 975	2.59
Extramural education activities	7 470 892	0.01000	74 709	19.33	144 410	0.80
Pedagogical advisory centers	10 080 490	0.01100	110 885	21.26	214 338	1.18
Holiday centers for children	29 558	0.22100	6 532	427.19	12 627	0.07
Methodological help for teachers	7 470 892	0.00800	59 767	15.46	115 528	0.64
Total			9 375 445		18 122 435	100.00

ANNEX 3

Basic Data for Lyceums: 1990–1999

Table 3A.3

Basic Data for Lyceums: 1990–1999

		1995	1996	1997	1998	Dynamic
Schools	Total	1 704	1 754	1 844	1 988	116.67%
	Loc. Gov.	183	506	596	625	341.53%
	MEN	1 216	931	890	947	77.88%
	non public	305	317	358	416	136.39%
Classrooms	Total	25 486	26 163	26 938	28 640	112.38%
	Loc. Gov.	3 056	8 961	10 405	10 947	358.21%
	MEN	19 585	14 255	13 278	13 901	70.98%
	non public	2 845	2 947	3 255	3 792	133.29%
Classes	Total	23 539	24 387	25 556	26 960	114.53%
	Loc. Gov.	2 870	8 822	10 394	10 959	381.85%
	MEN	18 784	13 616	12 993	13 563	72.21%
	non public	1 885	1 949	2 169	2 438	129.34%
Teachers	Total	33 845	35 439	38 182	40 105	118.50%
	Loc. Gov.	4 410	13 843	16 623	17 821	404.10%
	MEN	27 490	19 557	19 279	19 672	71.56%
	non public	1 945	2 039	2 280	2 612	134,.29%
Pupils	Total	682 637	714 445	756 497	803 569	117.72%
	Loc. Gov.	88 660	273 363	325 297	345 985	390.24%
	MEN	563 588	409 290	395 346	416 666	73.93%
	non public	30 389	31 792	35 854	40 918	134.65%
Share of Enrolment	Loc. Gov.	12.99%	38.26%	43.00%	43.06%	331.51%
	MEN	82.56%	57.29%	52.26%	51.85%	62.80%
	non public	4.45%	4.45%	4.74%	5.09%	114.38%

Table 3A.3 (continued)
Basic Data for Lyceums: 1990–1999

		1995	1996	1997	1998	Dynamic
Pupils per Teacher	Total	20.17	20.16	19.81	20.04	99.34%
	Loc. Gov.	20.10	19.75	19.57	19.41	96.57%
	MEN	20.50	20.93	20.51	21.18	103.31%
	non public	15.62	15.59	15.73	15.67	100.26%
Pupils per Class	Total	29.00	29.30	29.60	29.81	102.78%
	Loc. Gov.	30.89	30.99	31.30	31.57	102.20%
	MEN	30.00	30.06	30.43	30.72	102.39%
	non public	16.12	16.31	16.53	16.78	104.11%
Teachers per Class	Total	1.44	1.45	1.49	1.49	103.46%
	Loc. Gov.	1.54	1.57	1.60	1.63	105.83%
	MEN	1.46	1.44	1.48	1.45	99.11%
	non public	1.03	1.05	1.05	1.07	103.83%
School Size	Total	400.61	407.32	410.25	404.21	100.90%
	Loc. Gov.	484.48	540.24	545.80	553.58	114.26%
	MEN	463.48	439.62	444.21	439.99	94.93%
	non public	99.64	100.29	100.15	98.36	98.72%

NOTES

[1]   This paper would not have been possible without the past and present analytical work of Mikolaj Herbst. We also thank Eugeniusz Buśko, Irena Dzierzgowska, Anna Radziwiłł, Stanisław Róg, and Anna Urbanowicz for discussing with us the politics of education reform at both the national and local levels, and Ken Davey and Luis Crouch for comments on an earlier draft. Janusz Twardowski of the Ministry of Education's Statistical Center has provided us invaluable help. For almost two years we had the honor of working closely with Andrzej Karwacki, former Vice-Minister of Education. We owe him a great deal. All errors of fact and interpretation are entirely our own.

[2]   Functional illiteracy however remains high. An international study conducted by the OECD in 1995 showed that Poles of all ages understand considerably less from written texts than most of their European counterparts. See Bialecki (1996).

[3]   Polish Communists did not, however, make use of the class quota systems frequently employed by their counterparts elsewhere. Instead, they provided generous stipends to working class and rural students to attend lyceums and gave them additional points on university entrance exams.

[4]   Centralny Urzad Szkolenia Zawodowego (Central Office for Vocational Training). After 1956, the Ministry of Education took over some vocational schools, and verified the curricula of all of them, including schools run by line ministries and those owned by large industrial enterprises.

[5]   For an account of Party's ideological control of the schools and universities under Stalinism, see Kosiński (2000), and Connelly (2000).

[6]   See Golinowska, and Rumińska–Ziemny (1998). Approximately 38% of the Polish population still lives in rural areas.

[7]   Connelly (2000).

[8]   By the 1960s the Party had by and large abandoned its hope of turning young Poles into Communists. Nonetheless, pupils were still forced to participate in the Party's political rituals organized in schools, receiving in the process a reasonably effective lesson in social conformity and obedience.

[9]   See Kornai (1992), and Winiecki (1987) for good treatments of this dynamic.

[10]   The exception was the 1966–1970 plan. See Golinowska (1990).

[11]   For the best theoretical treatment of why attempts to internalize all social and economic transactions within the structure of a single agent degenerate into bargaining regimes punctuated by shake-ups see Lavoie (1985).

[12]   In the early 1970s, the PZPR made its last serious attempt to reform Poland's education system. A preparatory 'zero' class was introduced for six year olds and efforts were made to

consolidate small rural schools, as well as to introduce, on the Russian model, obligatory 10 year universal schools as opposed to eight year primary schools. These reforms were abandoned in 1980 under pressure from Solidarity. See Szczepański (1973) and Golinowska (1990).

[13]   For a summary of the PZPR's ideas about school reform in the late 1980s, see Komitet Ekspertów do Spraw Edukacji Narodowej (1989), and Kupisiewicz (1989). For the opposition's ideas see the chapter on education in collection of reports assembled by the group Doświadczenie i Przyszłość (1985). For a discussion of the basic similarities between the ideas of the opposition and Party reformers see, Radziwiłł (1992).

[14]   It is worth noting that, after the army and the police, teaching was the profession with lowest share of Solidarity members.

[15]   This was Solidarity's position during the negotiations with the Ministry in April 1981, see Bochwic (2000).

[16]   Levitas, and Federowicz (1995).

[17]   For a good discussions of the opposition's general strategy in these years see, Staniszkis (1984), and Ost (1990).

[18]   For example, it obtained the introduction of history classes in the curriculum of basic vocational schools. For an account of Solidarity's position on education and a selection of documents, see Bochwic (2000), and Żurek (2000).

[19]   Law on Teachers' Charter of January 26, 1982.

[20]   Most notably the Law on Employee Councils of September 25, 1981, and the Law on Universities of May 4, 1982.

[21]   See Bochwic (2000) and Żurek (2000).

[22]   Differences within Solidarity over how former Communists should be treated helped precipitate the movement's perhaps inevitable fragmentation. Indeed, they continue to hamper the creation of a stable block of center right parties. The struggles within the Solidarity camp have also hampered the ability of the Solidarity backed coalition governments to articulate and execute coherent policies in many areas, including education.

[23]   In the spring of 1989, Citizens Parliamentary Committees grew up around the union to support the electoral efforts of Solidarity-backed candidates. Like the union, these also splintered, in part because of the government's economic policies, in part because of the government's forgiving attitude towards former Communists.

[24]   For more discussion of these issues see Levitas (1999).

[25]   It is worth noting that the Law on Gmina Income was only passed in December 1990, after the election of gmina officials and after the assignment of their service responsibilities.

[26]   Interviews with Anna Radziwiłł and Eugeniusz Bućeko. During the interwar period, the Ministry of Education ran schools through regionally based Kuratoria. The jurisdictions

of these Kuratoria were independent from those of both local governments and the central government's regional gubernators. Moreover, school directors, though subordinated to the Kuratoria, had considerable operational autonomy. As a result, many education reformers in the early 1990s considered the strengthening of the Ministry, its Kuratoria, and school directors as the precondition, if not necessarily the essence, of education reform. In short, their political project was very different from the one motivating the advocates of strong local governments.

[27] Law on Gminas of March 8, 1990, Law on the Division of Responsibilities between the National Government and Local Governments of May, 17 1990, Law changing the Laws on the Development of the Education System and Teachers' Charter of May 17, 1990, and Law on Gmina Income of December 14, 1990.

[28] Most education specialists strongly opposed making gminas responsible for financing preschool education out of their own revenues because they feared local governments would not appreciate the importance of early childhood education. Their concerns however, were overruled because, as we have stressed, the driving force behind the devolution of education responsibilities to local governments came not from the education community but from reformers primarily concerned with dismantling the Communist state. There was also considerable feeling that communism, with its high labor market participation rates for women, had undermined the family. Permitting. or even encouraging, the reduction of publicly provided early child care was thus seen as a way to correct for the presumed excess of the past.

[29] The various components of the general subsidy have changed substantially over the decade. It now includes an education component and equalizing element, an element for roads, and an element to compensate local governments for income lost to them because of changes in the tax code. Despite the distinct calculation of each of these components all funds received through the general subsidy are freely disposable. See Levitas (2000).

[30] From the point of view of the American literature on fiscal federalism, this argument was confused along at least two dimensions. On the one hand, Americans tend to define own revenues as only those revenues coming from locally generated taxes and fees. On the other hand, they tend to define own functions as only those that are supported primarily by own revenues. The word primarily here, however, allows for some blurring of the distinction in practice. Indeed, recent State Supreme Court decisions have forced state governments in America to provide significant additional financial support to local governments with weak tax bases in order to ensure that all pupils receive reasonably equal educations.

The European literature on local government finance, however, tends to use more permissive definitions of both own functions and own revenues. Here, own functions are often defined simply as those functions over which local governments exercise significant control, and somewhat less frequently, own revenues as all revenues that local governments can reasonably anticipate and spend as they see fit. These more permissive definitions are justified essentially on pragmatic grounds. Because in practice it is very difficult to assign local governments the tax powers that would be necessary for them to fully fund services for which they can be given significant levels of control, it is better to use more permissive definitions.

Behind this pragmatism, however lurks an often unstated normative assumption that even if sufficient tax powers could be assigned to local governments so that they could independently finance their own functions, this would be undesirable because fiscal inequality between jurisdictions would lead to unjustifiable differences in the quality of essential public services. Indeed, it is precisely this normative judgment that has led State Supreme Courts to blur in practice the meaning of education as an own function in America. Nonetheless, the more pragmatic and permissive European definition of an own function does not sit entirely comfortably with the normative assumption that in fact often motivates it: If local governments derive significant general revenue from (differential) local tax bases and at the same time can spend these revenues on 'own' functions for which they are also receiving central government transfers, than the issue of fiscal inequality and reasonably equal services once again raises its head.

In short, the restrictive, American definition of an own function has been undermined in practice by the normative problems it in some ways creates, while the European and more permissive definition does not resolve the normative questions it attempts to assume away. This is obviously not the place to resolve, or transform this terminological dispute. But it is our suspicion that in Poland the use of the European definitions allowed reformers to avoid directly addressing the problem of fiscal inequality for education per-se, while the use of the American definitions would not have resolved these problems, but might have forced reformers to think about them up front.

[31]   Law on Education System of September 7, 1991. Under the banner of decentralization, control over the kuratoria was given back to the voivods later in the decade. This has made it difficult for the Ministry to target investment and operating grants.

[32]   In practice, kuratoria do not monitor the quality of schools, but rather their compliance with legal norms. In the mid 1990s, the Ministry began to develop standardized, nationwide tests in order to get more objective measures of school performance.

[33]   In practice, a shrewd sitting school director can influence the choice of six members of the committee (teachers and parents) and thus assure his reelection in spite of the local government's wishes. ZNP was generally against these committees (for instance, in July 1992 it appealed for the suspension of this mechanism).

[34]   This represented a significant strengthening of directors' powers with respect to the kuratoria but once again left local governments out of the picture. See Barański (1996).

[35]   Unlike in some Central and Eastern European countries, teachers are not members of a distinct class of civil servants.

[36]   Article 5a point 3. The Laws on Gmina Income and later, on Gmina Finances also contain similar guarantees.

[37] This reluctance to assign pedagogical oversight roles to gminas persisted well into the decade. See Gęsicki (1994) and Białecki (1999).

[38] It has also generated some problems with quality control and a few cases of publishers paying teachers to use their textbooks.

[39] In fact the Law strengthened and clarified a right that had been granted in 1989. The law was first used to create 'community schools' (*szkoły społeczne*) organized by parents and non profit education establishments. Later there appeared confessional schools (mostly Catholic), and commercial private schools.

[40] Local governments were required to provide publicly accredited private and community schools with 50% of their average per pupil expenditures of public schools of the same type in their jurisdiction. Meanwhile, the national government provided local governments with 50% of the per pupil subvention that it provided for public school pupils, for each private school pupil enrolled in the jurisdiction. As result, local governments that spent more per pupil than they received from the national government for their public school pupils also had to provide private schools with more than they received through the subvention. Despite the provision of public monies to private and denominational schools, private education remains relatively limited. 3.7% of all pupils attend non-public schools but this varies greatly by the school type. For primary schools, the percentage is under 0.8%, for lyceums it is 5.0%, and for professional and vocational schools it is only 2.1%. However for schools for adults it is 24.4%, and for post lyceum schools is 47.9%. Thus the greatest impact of private education has been in the commercially attractive area of continuing and professional education.

[41] MEN 1992. (the yearly reports of MEN to Sejm are henceforth referred to as MEN materials for Sejm, and year).

[42] Report of Vice Minister Dera (1994).

[43] Gminas that assumed control over secondary schools received a similarly calculated sum as a categorical grant for a delegated function. In 1993, only 18 lyceum and 19 vocational schools were run by gminas. In 1994, this number increased to 227 and 725 respectively. See Table 1 on page 15.

[44] Law on Gmina Finances of December 10, 1993.

[45] Dera (1994)

[46] See Kowalik (1999).

[47] Law on the Scope of Activities of Some Cities of November 24, 1995

[48] MEN Materials for Sejm, 1997. The national government remained in control of special primary schools (80 000 pupils, 784 schools), artistic schools (8000 pupils in 35 schools, and 39 000 part time pupils in 302 schools), a few primary schools for adults, and a few schools located in correctional facilities, With the exception of the latter all of these schools were eventually transferred to poviats in 1999–2000.

[49] Throughout the decentralization debates, reformers have frequently considered "shared taxes" as "own revenues" or even "own taxes." This expresses a more general tendency to equate the devolution of managerial responsibility with the decentralization of fiscal responsibility. See Levitas (19999).

[50] Poviats, however were not, as initially expected, made responsible for financing primary health care. Instead, the government established sixteen regional Health Care Funds (Kasa Chorych). The jurisdictions of these funds are identical to those of the new regional governments. The management boards of the funds are named by the regional self-governments, and the regional self-governments are, at least theoretically, their lenders of last resort. The funds, however, get their monies directly from a nationally set percentage of the personal income taxes collected in their jurisdictions. They are free to contract for the provision of health cares services from both private or public providers. Powiats were, however, assigned ownership of public hospitals.

[51] In 2000, the Parliament passed the Law on Regional Development. This Law calls for the regional self-governments to draw up comprehensive regional plans in line with the government's national development strategy. On the basis of these plans, the national government is supposed to enter into so-called regional contracts with the self-governing voivodships. These contracts will define the total funding that the national government will provide to each region, as well as the breakdown of this funding by major programmatic categories. The regional governments, however, will determine how funds are used and allocated under these broad programmatic categories. Despite the passage of the law, however, the system remains in its infancy and as such it is still largely unclear who is responsible for programming and allocating special purpose funds and grants to local governments. Indeed, responsibility for allocating funds earmarked for education is now dispersed across the Ministries of Agriculture, Education, and Labor, the regional self-governments, and a variety of special purpose ministerial agencies.

[52] See Law on Local Government Revenues for Years 1999 and 2000 of November 26, 1998, and Levitas and others (1998).

[53] Ministries still control the following schools: Ministry of Interior Administration–3 schools for firefighters; Defense–2 military lyceums; Justice–34 primary schools for youth, 30 vocational schools for youth, 24 schools for adults. In 2000, a year after the creation of poviats, the Ministry of Culture transferred 161 secondary artistic schools with over 19 000 pupils to local governments.

[54] They were usually but not exclusively associated with particular schools and are most often used by rural pupils commuting to urban areas for secondary education.

[55] These are for students with severe disabilities and usually contain boarding, medical, and rehabilitation facilities.

[56] These provide help to schools and pupils in diagnosing and treating psychological problems and learning disorders. They also provide other services, such as career advice for students.

[57] They also operate 28 primary schools located in hospitals and 14 secondary schools for social workers. One Special Education Center and a few boarding houses for primary schools were assigned to gminas.

[58] See MEN (1999b).

[59] The creation of this lower tier of secondary education or upper tier of primary education brought the Polish system more in line with those of other developed countries.

[60] The ZNP also opposed the reform, arguing that it was extremely costly, ill prepared, and served little purpose.

[61] These figures do not include the Ministry of Education's spending on its own operations, including those of the Kuratoria, or those administrative expenditures incurred by local governments in running schools (i.e. the costs of their own education departments.) See Barro (2000).

[62] See Grzegorzewski (1999) and Piwowarski (1999).

[63] See Levitas, Herczyński (1999).

[64] See Kowalska (1999a).

[65] See Dec, and Matusz (1996).

[66] Throughout the decade, rural and urban gminas brought a number of individual suits against the government for failing to provide them with adequate funds for the maintenance and operating costs of primary schools. Until 1999, the courts refused to hear the cases. Recently however, they have begun to accept them and there are a number of rulings pending that could have a profound impact on the Ministry's behavior.

[67] Many of these confusions and tensions are expressed in the reports of the European Union supported program for the Financing of Education Responsibilities, Leszczyński, and Gołąb (1998).

[68] Draft version of the Law on Gmina Finances, processed, Ministry of Finance, 1993.

[69] See Barro (2000).

[70] The legal right to attend school in another jurisdiction precluded a funding formula based on the number of school age children residing in a given jurisdiction. It also however, created the potential free rider problems that we mentioned earlier when discussing "gminas with poviat rights." The scale of inter-jurisdictional commutating for primary schools is, however much smaller than for secondary schools. Demographic decline has also made school directors happy to receive pupils from other jurisdictions, masking a problem that might nonetheless provoke conflicts in the future.

[71] Until the late 1990s, the mathematical basis of the formula used by MEN was not internally coherent or transparent: some weights were used multiplicatively, some additively, and the derivation of the subvention amount per weighted student was not explained.

[72]   The algorithm also had multipliers for pupils with disabilities, ethnic minorities who require instruction in a language other than Polish, and for athletically or artistically gifted pupils in special schools or classes.

[73]   This was a significant improvement because class size can easily be affected by local government behavior, effectively making it possible for gminas to game the system by splitting classes.

[74]   See Levitas, Herczynski, and Herbst (1999). The rural and small city weights explained 96% of education subvention variation between the gminas in 1999 (before applying the thresholds).

[75]   It is worth adding that so long as the national government did not increase the global sum of the education subvention to reflect the increase in teacher *qualifications* that it was trying to promote—which it did not—gminas were essentially being invited to participate in a race towards a zero-sum outcome.

[76]   Upper and lower bounds evolved over time, and by 1999, the upper bound had been eliminated. While some buffering provisions are necessary, they should be based not on a jurisdiction's previous *total* subvention but for instance on its previous *per pupil* subvention.

[77]   A 'hold harmless cause' is a legal provision that ensures that changes being introduced by legislation do not negatively or immediately effect the financial resources of a public agency.

[78]   See Herbst (2000).

[79]   Obtaining a complete inventory turned out to be a difficult task. For instance, it turned out that some schools, even well known Warsaw schools, had for years neglected filing their required GUS reports and thus could hardly be included in the devising and calculation of education subvention for their prospective owners. For non school tasks the situation was even worse.

[80]   See Jeżowski (1999).

[81]   MEN (1999a).

[82]   In July of 1999, the authors of this report began working within the Ministry under a USAID funded program designed to improve the allocation of the education subvention to local governments. This section of the paper draws heavily from our research work conducted for MEN during the subsequent 14 months. The direction of education finance reform was set by Vice-Minister Andrzej Karwacki for whom we worked.

[83]   Before 1999, ten different Ministries controlled vocational schools: Agriculture, Labor and Social Welfare, Transport, Environment, Culture, Health, Justice, Defense, Interior, and MEN.

[84]   See the comments of Ministers Marcinkiewicz (1999) and Hibner (1999).

[85]   This discussion is described in Chaber (2000), see also Levitas, Herczyński (1999) and Levitas, Rafuse, (1998).

[86] In fact, the early demands for the introduction of school vouchers were formulated by people involved in non-public education, see Starczewska (1989). The state support for non-public schools is described in footnote 39. In December 2000, the Law on Education System was changed and now local governments must provide the full per pupil financial standard to private schools, instead of half of their average expenditures.

[87] Comments of Vice Minister of Finance Miller (1998).

[88] In this battle, for once, it was supported by ZNP, see ZNP (1995).

[89] By the end of the decade, the national government was specding 10–15% more on primary school pupils than on secondary ones, by making equal the weight or multiplier for urban primary school pupils and urban secondary school pupils the government was effectively redirecting resources from primary to secondary education.

[90] The main shortcomings of the 2000 algorithm were the continued use of the administrative category of rural students, using the number of students actually bussed rather than those legally eligible for free transport for the transport multiplier (which probably should have been a categorical grant anyway), and unclear weights for pupils with disabilities. See Herczyński (2000).

[91] MEN (2000).

[92] Law Changing the Teachers' Charter of February 18, 2000.

[93] MEN (2001).

[94] A crucial element of this system was the introduction of individual professional development plans for teachers. In some ways the system tries to introduce teacher accountability without measures of class performance. Teachers, for their part, are already complaining about the large amount of paper work involved in producing their own development plans.

[95] See protocols of joint MEN-local governments commission to determine the effects of the amended Teachers' Charter, Zespół d/s Oceny Skutków Karty Nauczyciela (2000).

[96] See Nowakowska (2000).

[97] See Tabor (2000) and Levitas, Herczyński, and Herbst (2000).

[98] This figure was almost certainly exaggerated, but the nature of the loopholes in the law made it impossible to accurately calculate the actual shortfall. In the end, MEN agreed to cover the estimated shortfall of 1 290 million PLN, which has to be considered very high.

[99] GUS (1995).

[100] It should be noted that firms and state farms ran between 5 and 10% of all preschools in 1990. Some of these were closed by firms and state farms, and some were communalized. Of the latter many were then closed.

[101] Some of the 100%-plus figures for 6 year olds in urban preschools comes from children residing in rural (suburban) districts but going to urban preschools. Some is the result of the enrollment of 5 and 7 year olds. Meanwhile, some of the growth of preschool enrollment

[102]   in rural areas probably comes from suburban communities that are legally characterized as rural gminas but in fact resemble urban ones in per capita income.

[102]   As stated before, 'gimnazjum' refers here specifically to middle schools for grades 6–8.

[103]   It is important to note that the term 'rural' here defines an administrative and legal category. With urbanization there are an increasing number of suburban gminas. These suburban gminas are often among the richest jurisdictions in Poland. They also generally have consolidated school networks and brought pupil/teacher ratios in line with urban jurisdictions. There is thus no objective reason for them to get the additional rural multiplier. Statistical analysis of the allocation of that part of the education subvention (c. 6% of the total subvention) that flowed to rural gminas as a result of this multiplier, showed that approximately one third of it (2%) flowed to 'rural' gminas that had per capita incomes and/or pupil/teacher ratios similar to urban jurisdictions schools (See Annex 2).

[104]   See Związek Gmin Śląska Opolskiego (1998).

[105]   Own calculations. See also Kowalska (1999b).

[106]   In fact it was growing until 1998, before the primary schools were split into new, 6 year long primary school and 3 year long gimnazjums.

[107]   There is also a problem with so called *virtual schools*, that is parts of a 'single' gimnazjum located in more than one rural primary school. See Konarzewski (2000).

[108]   A composite illustration based on our experience with four rural and mixed gminas

[109]   A survey of 10 schools revealed that parent contributions (off budget) represent 1–3% of school budgets with higher percentages for urban schools. Kowalska and others (2000).

[110]   See Czarnobaj (1998) and Chaber (2000).

[111]   In recent years, schools and to a lesser extent gminas have been making increasing use of methodologies designed to measure the satisfaction of stakeholders within their schools. Indeed, a number of foundations have been established that provide funding for this type of self-assessment. What is exceptional about this gmina is that it paid for a much more sophisticated and costly set of procedures based on repeating a similar standardized test across schools and over time.

[112]   See Dolata and others (1998), Dolata, Murwaska, and Putkiewicz (1999, 2000).

[113]   See page 16.

[114]   See Levitas, Herczyński (1999).

[115]   As gminas with poviat rights include both the 46 cities that had been covered by the Law on Large Cities and 18 substantially smaller towns with significantly less disposable income, this figure may underestimate the contribution of the largest cities to the subvention. The differences in the per pupil hold harmless measures for primary and secondary education also make it difficult to determine the amount of the subvention going to primary and secondary education in gminas with poviat rights.

[116] See Kowalik (2000). The cities were: Bialystok, Kielce, Kraków, Opole, and Rzeszów.

[117] One city considered introducing financial standards for its secondary schools, but failed to define them and abandoned the proposal.

[118] It is worth noting that in Kraków, there was an initial emphasis on increasing the social involvement of parents in the running of schools through the creation of School Councils. This, however was later largely abandoned in favor of a more managerial approach.

[119] This was a painful process involving the closure of schools, or the elimination of certain vocational training programs simply because parents refused to enroll their children in these schools or programs.

[120] Cities had to approve the creation of a lyceum in the existing units composed of a few vocational schools or to upgrade a school (from a vocational to a technical school). Such requests were of course always granted, irrespective of the level of teacher qualifications. Approval by the Kuratoria also had to be secured, but that was a formality.

[121] They consulted the local Labor Offices on their own initiative and often cooperated in this area.

[122] An analysis of country-wide fit of professions taught with projected demand of the labor market show that even under optimistic assumptions more than 50 percent of students of vocational schools will find it hard to find jobs for which they are trained. See Golinowska, Herczyński (2000).

[123] Interview with Irena Dzierzgowska, former Vice-Minister of Education. This is another indication of the breakdown in the existing regulator framework.

[124] Because of the timing of poviat elections, the national government actually set the initial budgets of poviats before local officials took office. They were however free to amend these budgets over the course of the year.

[125] See Herbst (2001).

[126] Surveys on attitudes toward education reform in general and local government reform in particular reveal general, if not unambiguous, support for the changes that have occurred over the last ten years. On the one hand, most respondents support the goals of the reform and take an agnostic position on whether they have been achieved. On the other hand, many express concerns about the ability of all local governments to provide reasonable education services of similar quality and perceive relatively few gains from decentralization at their own schools. See CBOS (2000).

[127] This phenomenon is common when there is school choice because better schools attract the better students, leaving worse schools with harder to educate, often poorer students. This, in turn, also often (but not always) affects the quantity and quality of teachers attracted to the school.

CHAPTER 4

Financing and Administration of the Educational System in the Czech Republic

Michal Krátký

Petr Linhart

Lenka Dostálová

Ludmila Oswaldová

Table of Contents

Introduction 195

1. Education and Organization of the Educational Process 196
   1.1 Basic Principles of Education 196
   1.2 Organization of the Educational Process 196

2. Institutions Responsible for the Educational Process 198
   2.1 Ministry of Education, Youth, and Sports 199
   2.2 School Offices 200
   2.3 Municipality 202
   2.4 Czech School Inspection 203
   2.5 The School Board 203
   2.6 Public Administration Reform in the Czech Republic 204
       2.6.1 Regions and Regional Authorities in the Area of Education 205
       2.6.2 Change of the Ministry's Competencies 207
       2.6.3 Change of the Municipality's Competencies 207
   2.7 Legal Position of Schools 207

3. Assignment of Responsibilities 209
   3.1 Directors of Schools 209
   3.2 Teaching Staff 211
   3.3 Remuneration of Directors and Teaching Staff 212
   3.4 School Planning and Development 215
       3.4.1 Establishment or Abolition of Schools 215
       3.4.2 Curriculum and Development 217
       3.4.3 Enrolment Process 218
   3.5 Infrastructure 219
       3.5.1 Ownership of School Buildings and Other Property 219
       3.5.2 Employment and Salaries
             of Technical–economical School Employees (TEE) 221

      3.5.3   Construction, Repairs, and Maintenance of the Buildings 221

      3.5.4   Provision, Maintenance, and Replacement of Teaching Equipment ... 222

      3.5.5   Supply of Power and Other Utilities 225

  3.6   Professional Supervision 224

      3.6.1   License and Registration of Schools 224

      3.6.2   Education of Teachers 225

      3.6.3   Inspection and Monitoring 226

  3.7   Financing of Schools 229

      3.7.1   Direct Educational Expenses: Teachers' Salaries 230

      3.7.2   The Role of Municipal Budgets in the Financing of Education 232

      3.7.3   The Role of School Revenues 234

4.   Effectiveness, Fairness, and Efficiency of Education 237

  4.1   Possible Impact of the New System of School Administration 238

  4.2   The Decrease in Population and the Impact on Schools 239

  4.3   Integration of Handicapped Children and Ethnic Minorities 240

  4.4   Basic schools in Villages 241

  4.5   Private Schools 243

  4.6   Apprenticeship Schools 246

Annex 1:   Basic Comparative Data from Czech School Office (1990 and 1995) 249

Annex 2:   State Expenses for Kindergartens, Basic and Secondary Schools 250

Annex 3:   Educational Expenses 251

Annex 4:   Average Income of Teachers 252

Annex 5:   Number of Pupils and Teachers 253

Annex 6:   List of Basic Laws 255

Note 256

INTRODUCTION

This National Report was written as supporting material for a study analyzing the differences regarding responsibility sharing in the area of management and financing of education in the Czech Republic, Hungary, Poland, Bulgaria and Slovakia.

The purpose of this study is to compare the effectiveness, fairness, and efficiency of education in the above mentioned countries based on the system of management and financing of schools and to specify problems resulting from the existing system of administration and financing.

The first part of the National Report gives a detailed overview of the responsibility sharing among public institutions in the area of financing and management of schools in the Czech Republic. The second part of the report discusses the effectiveness, fairness, and efficiency of the educational system and objective problems of the current situation.

In 2000, a reform of the public administration of the educational system was launched in connection with the establishment of regions, which are referred to as "higher self-governing units." Upon the coming into force of the approved legislation, the newly established regions or regional bodies with transferred competencies (state administration) will take on many competencies in the area of school management and financing, which will be transferred both from the abolished centrally administered regional (district) components of the state administration—school offices— and from the central body of the state administration—the Ministry of Education, Youth, and Sports of the Czech Republic. The first part of the National Report includes a separate section on the reform of public administration and compares the current situation with the new system to be introduced. However, relevant experience is available only with respect to the existing system. Only some aspects resulting from the new methods of school financing and administration can be expected to cause problems and which are currently not being solved satisfactorily as part of the reform.

Responsibility sharing in the area of financing and education of schools is based on the valid laws and concrete experiences of school employees and employees of public administration and self-administration bodies in the educational system. Information on effectiveness, fairness, and efficiency is a compilation of experiences of these employees. Problems of a general and objective nature occurring in the areas in question have been emphasized. An overview of school legislation is included in the National Report as an appendix. The statistical section and supporting material used in the National Report are based on data from the 1999/2000 school year and 1999 and 2000 calendar years. Sources of the Czech Statistical Office and the Institute of Educational Information have been used for this report.

1. EDUCATION AND ORGANIZATION OF THE EDUCATIONAL PROCESS

1.1 Basic Principles of Education

Pursuant to Article 3, Law No. 1/1993 Coll., Constitution of the Czech Republic, as amended, the Charter of Fundamental Rights and Freedoms is part of the constitutional order of the Czech Republic. Constitutional Law No. 23/1991 Coll., as amended, stipulates that the Charter of Fundamental Rights and Freedoms is constitutional law. Pursuant to Article 1 of this law, constitutional laws, other laws, other legal regulations, and the interpretation and use thereof must be in accordance with the Charter of Fundamental Rights and Freedoms. Pursuant to Article 2, fundamental rights and freedoms specified in the Charter of Fundamental Rights and Freedoms enjoy protection of the Constitutional Court.

Pursuant to Article 33, everyone has the right to education. School attendance is mandatory for a period of time determined by law. The citizens have the right to a free-of-charge education in the basic and secondary schools. As far as universities are concerned, the free-of-charge education depends on the capabilities of the citizen and the possibilities of the society. The establishment of schools other than state schools and the teaching at such schools is only allowed under conditions determined by law. The law shall determine under which conditions the citizens have the right to be supported by the government during their studies.

The constitutional laws guarantee free-of-charge education up to the secondary school level and limited government support for education at universities. All citizens regardless of age, sex, religious or other faith, race, nationality and citizenship, have access to education in the Czech Republic.

The citizen has the opportunity to choose any school on the territory of the Czech Republic up to the basic school level. At the same time, the government guarantees free-of-charge school education in a basic school, which is located in the area of his permanent residence. Free-of-charge education and open choice are also guaranteed with respect to secondary schools. However, the citizen must meet the performance criteria for acceptance required by the school.

1.2 Organization of the Educational Process

The educational process in the Czech Republic can be divided into several levels according to the age groups of the population. *Nurseries*, i.e. healthcare facilities, which are usually established by the city, are for children under the age of 3 years. At the moment, the number of these facilities is decreasing, which has several reasons, including longer maternity leave and the considerable financial burden of families with small children.

Children from the age of three (in exceptional cases from the age of two) to the age of six (in exceptional cases older children, whose school attendance has been postponed) can attend the *kindergarten*—a pre-primary facility. The municipality establishes such facilities and they are part of school facilities. Attendance is not mandatory; however, the attendance of children aged over five is high. Handicapped children are also accepted to kindergartens. These children can be integrated among healthy children or attend special or specialized classes. In 1998/99, the number of kindergartens decreased by 19% compared to 1989/90.

School enrolment takes place at the age of six. At that time, an assessment is made as to whether or not the child is psychosomatically mature for school attendance. Based on this, the child is either enrolled in a class or the school attendance is postponed if requested by parents or recommended by a pedagogical-psychological consultant. School attendance is usually postponed by a year. Most children complete their mandatory school attendance at the *basic school. Special schools* are established for handicapped children. In addition to basic and special schools, children can complete a part of their compulsory education in the lower classes of multi-year *grammar schools* or the lower classes of dance conservatoires.

There is a compulsory education of nine years in the Czech Republic, upon the completion of which the child obtains his/her basic education. Children attending a basic or special school can, without any limitations, apply to all theoretical and vocational courses of study at secondary schools. Auxiliary schools are established for severely handicapped children. The completion of these schools takes ten years. The entire educational system is interconnected with courses for the completion of education at the individual types of schools: auxiliary, special and basic. If a pupil cannot attend school because of his/her health problems, the school office can provide another form of education enabling the pupil to receive the same education as it would be the case during school attendance. The director of the school office can excuse heavily handicapped children from the mandatory school attendance for a certain period of time A different organizational form of basic education—home education—is currently being tested.

The number of basic schools has been increasing between 1989 and 1994, followed by two years of stagnation and continuing decrease in the number of basic schools. The share of non-state schools at the basic education level is low. In the 1997/98 school year, non-state schools (private and patrimonial) accounted for 1.2% of basic schools. The relatively rapid decrease in the total number of pupils at the basic schools reflects the demographic development. The growing interest in studies at multi-year grammar schools is also a key factor of the decrease of pupils at the secondary level of basic education.

Currently, there are three educational programs for basic schools: basic school, common school, and national school, which have comparable results at the end of the primary level. Some basic schools use alternative educational systems, for example the Waldorf or Montessori schools.

Upon the completion of the compulsory school attendance, the child can continue his/her education at *secondary schools*. The attendance of such schools is no longer mandatory and the completion usually takes three years at apprenticeship schools and four years at grammar schools or vocational schools.

Upon the completion of the secondary school education there is an opportunity of further education at *higher vocational schools* and *universities*. The cost of the studies at state schools is covered by the government.

Other facilities and institutions of the educational system include the following:

- *Basic art schools*: provide the basics of music, arts, dancing, literature, and theater education. The activities at such schools are not designed as elitist education since they are attended even by children who do not plan on becoming professional artists or studying at conservatoires or art schools;

- *Day-care centers* are established at basic and special schools. They provide extracurricular care for children, predominantly at the primary level, develop the children's knowledge and skills and provide assistance to employed parents;

- *School clubs*: are established at basic and special schools. They provide extracurricular care for children, predominantly at the secondary level in the form of hobby activities;

- *Leisure centers for children and youth and hobby centers*: the programs of these facilities target all age groups of children and those interested;

- *State language schools*: provide education for the entire population and at all language levels. The studies can be completed by a state language exam;

- *School cafeterias*: provide catering;

- *Youth homes* provide housing;

- *Facilities for institutional education, protection education, and preventative educational care, special educational facilities, diagnostic institutions*: provide replacement family education, protection education or preventative educational care. Parents of pupils who attend such facilities cover part of the expenses.

2. INSTITUTIONS RESPONSIBLE FOR THE EDUCATIONAL PROCESS

The responsibility of institutions for the management of state schools and apprenticeship schools and the financing of all schools and school facilities is described in Law. 564/1990 Coll. on Public Administration and Self-administration in the Educational Sphere, as amended.

1. *Ministry of Education, Youth, and Sports of the Czech Republic* is the central body of the state administration responsible for the financing and management of schools.

2. *School offices* with regional competencies, which are established directly by the Ministry of Education, Youth, and Sports of the Czech are the regional components of the state administration responsible for the financing and management of schools.

3. *Municipalities* are responsible for the self-administration in the educational sphere with respect to kindergartens and basic schools.

4. The *Czech School Inspection* was established for state monitoring of education.

5. The parents are represented at schools in the form of *school boards.*

The responsibility of the above mentioned institutions will be described in the following sections only as it relates to the topic of the National Report. In fact, the activities of the institutions involved in the Czech educational system are much more comprehensive. It means that the description of the responsibility of institutions focuses on the financing and management of kindergartens, basic and secondary schools, as well as apprenticeship schools. The capacities in some school facilities, basic art schools, universities, higher vocational schools, and so on, are not described in the National Report.

2.1 Ministry of Education, Youth, and Sports

In particular, the Ministry has the following functions in the area of management and financing of education in the Czech Republic:

a) *Management*

- Manages the state administration in the area of education and creates prerequisites for achieving educational goals;

- Manages pre-primary facilities and schools with respect to education;

- Establishes and abolishes secondary schools, apprenticeship schools, conservatoires, special schools, state language schools, short-hand institutions, school institutions specializing in art production, pre-primary institutions, schools and school institution where the language of instruction is other than Czech, school facilities for institutional education and protection education, as well as facilities for continuing education of teaching staff;

- Appoints and dismisses the directors of pre-primary facilities, schools, and school facilities that it establishes, the directors of school offices, the central school inspector and, on his proposal, school inspectors;

- Determines types of certificates and other school documents and the requirements they have to meet, as well as the methods of their processing and filing.

b) *Financing*

- Determines norms such as yearly non-investment expenses and funds for wages per child or pupil in a pre-primary facility, school or other school facility;

- Provides school offices with an analysis of all funds earmarked from the state budget for pre-primary facilities, schools, and school facilities of all establishing entities, excluding those that are funded from other sources, according to the number or children;

- Provides school offices with an analysis of funds earmarked from the state budget for their activities.

It issues a decree determining the following:

- Seat and geographical reach of school offices;

- Details of the establishment, abolition, and organization of pre-primary facilities, schools, and school facilities and their educational activities;

- Completion of the compulsory school education, as well as education in schools outside the territory of the Czech Republic, which is to be agreed upon with the Minister of Foreign Affairs of the Czech Republic;

- rules for the evaluation and grading of pupils, methods of disciplinary measures and the use thereof;

- Details of equivalence of certificates issued by foreign schools and the conditions of their validation;

- Conditions and organization of the acceptance of pupils at vocational schools;

- Fees to be paid for care provided to children and youth at school facilities or for the institutional education or the protection education;

- Methods of integration of handicapped children into pre-primary facilities, schools, and secondary schools.

2.2 School Offices

School offices are established as administration offices in the area of education, the territorial scope of which is the district. They are budgetary organizations managed directly by the Ministry. The Ministry issued a decree determining the seats and territorial scope of 86 school offices in the Czech Republic.

The head of the school office is the director who is appointed and dismissed by the Ministry.

The role of the school office is in the areas of:

a) *The Management of State Schools*

- establishes special basic schools at healthcare facilities, auxiliary and special schools, pre-primary facilities at healthcare facilities, and facilities for continuing the education of teaching staff;

- appoints and dismisses the directors of schools and school facilities that it establishes and, upon the approval of the establishing entity, it appoints and dismisses the directors of schools and school facilities established by the municipality;

- plays the role of employer in case of all schools that are not a legal person;

- depending on local needs, it guarantees classes in languages other than Czech at pre-primary facilities, schools and school facilities;

- based on the results of school inspections, it takes appropriate measures at pre-primary facilities, schools and school facilities;

- plays the role of an appellate body with respect to the decision making at schools and municipalities in public proceedings (acceptance proceedings, placement of children in kindergartens);

- decides about the validation of certificates issued by foreign schools;

- decides about the release of pupils from the duty to attend schools and the release of pupils from the mandatory school attendance;

- approves exceptions regarding acceptance of pupils at secondary schools;

- approves mergers of schools;

- approves abolition of schools by municipalities that were established by municipalities;

- at a school's or school employees' request, it provides methodological assistance and consultations regarding labor-law relations and wage issues concerning the school sector employees.

b) *The Financing of Schools*

- to earmark funds for pre-primary facilities, schools, and school facilities established and administered by municipalities, which are to be used for wages and wage compensations, salaries or salary compensations, wage deductions, other personal expenses and other expenses resulting from labor-law relations, expenses for textbooks and other school supplies, if provided to pupils free-of-charge, and it monitors the use thereof;

- to provide full economic assistance to schools and school facilities that it established or that were established by the Ministry, to monitor the effectiveness of their management of the funds and carries out financial settlement with them;

- to provide full economic assistance to pre-primary facilities, schools, and school facilities established by churches or religious communities, to monitor the effectiveness of their management and to carry out financial settlement with them;

- to earmark financial subsidies to pre-primary facilities, schools, and school facilities, the extent and conditions of which are determined by legal regulations; as well as monitoring the effectiveness of management of the earmarked subsidies and to carry out the financial settlement.

2.3 Municipality

One of the basic duties of the municipality in the area of education is to create prerequisites for the fulfillment of the mandatory school attendance. The municipality creates appropriate material-technical conditions at basic schools that it has established in order to place all children from the surrounding area that are capable of mandatory school attendance. The territory of the municipality is the catchment area of the basic school. The municipality issues an order determining the surrounding area of two or more basic schools, taking into account their alternative educational programs. The municipality can reach an agreement with a neighboring municipality or surrounding municipalities to establish a common catchment area of a basic school. If such an agreement has not been reached and the fulfillment of mandatory school attendance of pupils is jeopardized, the responsible district authorities in agreement with the responsible school office will decide about the common catchment area of the basic school.

The role of the municipality in the areas of:

a) *The Management of State Basic Schools and Kindergartens*

- to establish and, upon the approval of the responsible school office, to abolish basic schools, kindergartens and school facilities serving them;

- to decide about the acceptance of children into/in kindergartens, if the number of applying children exceeds the number of children that can be accepted;

- to play the role of an appellate body with respect to the acceptance proceedings in kindergartens, excluding non-acceptance because of a small capacity of the kindergarten;

- upon the approval of the Ministry, it can establish schools that are otherwise established by the school office or the Ministry, if it receives a proof of meeting prerequisites for educational activities (especially funds for material and personal security, that will not be provided by the school office). In such a case, the municipality appoints and dismisses the director upon the approval of the school office;

- to inform the school office about the approval of the appointment and dismissal of the directors of schools that it establishes.

b) *The Financing of Basic Schools and Kindergartens that the Municipality Establishes*

- to secure investment expenses and non-investment costs excluding wages, textbooks, school supplies, and necessities paid by the state.

The municipality defends its interests, the interests of parents or other legal representatives of children, pupils (hereinafter: 'legal representatives') and teaching staff with respect to the development of education in relation to kindergartens and basic schools in the municipality.

The municipality discusses the following with the directors of kindergartens and basic schools that it establishes:

a)   plans for the development of the school;

b)   budget and material prerequisites for given activities;

c)   personal and social conditions of employees;

d)   the municipality's requests to increase the quality of care provided by the kindergarten, educational activities of kindergartens and basic schools and methods of covering the resulting increase in costs;

e)   reports on the results of the educational activities of kindergartens and basic schools.

Similarly, the municipality discusses the above mentioned topics with directors of schools that it did not establish but that are located within its territorial scope of power.

2.4 Czech School Inspection

The Czech School Inspection (hereinafter: 'ČSI') is a public administration body established directly by the Ministry, which is administered as a budgetary organization. The head is the central school inspector who is appointed and dismissed by the Ministry. The central school inspector proposes the appointment and dismissal of school inspectors to the Ministry.

The ČSI monitors the results of education and the educational process in schools of all levels according to valid educational plans and educational guidelines, personal and material-technical prerequisites for the given educational activities, the effectiveness of use of the funds earmarked from the state budget and the compliance with generally binding legal regulations.

2.5 The School Board

The school board can be established at a school. The school board is a school body enabling the legal representatives of minor pupils, major pupils, school employees, residents of the municipality, and other persons to participate in the school administration. The school board is established by the establishing entity of the school based on a request of adult pupils or the legal representatives of pupils or based on a request of the absolute majority of the teaching staff of the school or based on their decision. Major pupils or the legal representatives of minor pupils, teaching staff, and the representatives of the establishing entity are represented in the school board.

The school board approves the following:

- the annual report of the school;

- the budgetary proposal of the school;

- the report on management of the school.

Furthermore, the school board expresses its opinion on theoretical and apprenticeship courses of study, the conceptual plans for the development of the school, appointment and dismissal of the director of the school. It can make a proposal to dismiss the school director and can ask the ČSI to conduct an inspection or the school to carry out a check of management.

2.6 Public Administration Reform in the Czech Republic

The establishment of higher self-governing units, aimed at the decentralization of the public administration in the Czech Republic, is part of the constitutional order in the Czech Republic. The state education and the financing of education in the Czech Republic are one of the areas on which the reform will have a considerable effect. This holds true not only for the area of self-administration (competencies of establishing entities) but also in the area of state administration of education. Elections for the councils of regions were held on 12 and 19 November 2000.

The reform of the public administration in the area of education, in the connection with the establishment of higher self-governing units, can be divided into two phases:

- Phase 1—i.e. years 2001 and 2002 as a transition period of the transformation process, during which the transfer of the secondary school education to regions and the abolition of school offices will be completed. The district authorities will fulfill the tasks of the school offices during this transition period;

- Phase 2—which is the basis of the entire reform of public administration—i.e. after 2002. The district authorities will be abolished and their competencies in the area of education will be transferred to regional authorities (municipal authorities).

The following paragraphs will include a description of the transfer of competencies between institutions, according to the approved and valid legislation. However, there are public discussions in the Czech Republic on the future responsibility of the public institutions for the educational process. As to the regional school system, the focus of the discussions is particularly the distribution of funds from the state budget, appointment of teaching staff, appointment and dismissal of directors of kindergartens, basic schools, and school facilities established by municipalities. Two opposite opinions exist as to whether or not the above mentioned competencies should be fulfilled by regional authorities as a transferred competency (regional body=public administration), which is a principle embodied in the approved legislation, or whether they should be transferred to municipalities (local authorities).

In the new system of public administration, there are another two institutions that have not been mentioned in the previous sections. As discussed above, at stake are the temporary competencies of the existing district authorities until 2002. In 2001, they will take on the following competencies currently fulfilled by school offices, which will be abolished:

- the district authorities will earmark funds for pre-primary facilities, schools, and school facilities that were established and are managed by municipalities to be used for wages, wage compensations, salaries and salary compensations, wage deductions, other personal expenses and expenses resulting from labor-law relations, as well as expenses of school tools, text books and other school supplies, if they are provided to pupils free-of-charge;

- temporarily, the district authorities will play the role of employer in case of schools that are not a legal entity and were established by municipalities.

2.6.1   Regions and Regional Authorities in the Area of Education

The responsibilities of regions in the educational sector of the Czech Republic can be divided into the following two parts: the responsibility of regions as higher self-governing units independently fulfilling the functions of establishing entities in the area of state education, which will be transferred to them from the Ministry as part of the decentralization of the management of the school system in the Czech Republic; and the responsibility of regional authorities fulfilling transferred competencies (public administration), which will be transferred to them from the school offices which are to be abolished.

a)   *Regional Authorities with Transferred Competencies*

The competencies will be transferred from *86* abolished district school offices to *13 regional authorities* and the *Municipal Authorities of the Capital City of Prague.*

The regional board (an organ of the Regional Government) appoints and dismisses the head of the division of the regional authorities that is responsible for the state administration in the area of education, youth and sports, upon the approval of the Ministry.

The management of state schools (competencies from the abolished school offices):

- upon the approval of the establishing entity, to appoint and dismiss the director of schools and school facilities established by the municipality;

- to play the role of employer in the case of all state schools that have not been legal entities since the school offices were abolished;

- based on the results of the school inspection, to take appropriate measures in pre-primary facilities, schools and school facilities;

- to play the role of an appellate body with respect to the decision-making at schools and municipalities in public proceedings (acceptance proceedings, placement of children in kindergartens);

- to decide about the validation of certificates issued by foreign schools;

- to decide about the release of pupils from the duty to attend a school and the release of pupils from the mandatory school attendance;

- to approve exceptions regarding the acceptance of pupils at secondary schools;

- to approve the mergers of schools.

The financing of schools (competencies from the abolished school offices):

- it earmarks funds for pre-primary facilities, schools, school facilities established and managed by municipalities to be used for wages and wage compensations or salaries and salary compensations, wage deductions, other personal expenses and other expenses resulting from labor-law relations, expenses for textbooks and other school supplies, if provided to pupils free-of-charge, and it monitors their uses;

- it provides full financial assistance to pre-primary facilities, schools, and school facilities established by churches or religious communities, monitors the effectiveness of their management and conducts financial settlement with them;

- earmarks financial subsidies to pre-primary facilities, schools, and school facilities, the extent and conditions of which are determined by legal regulations, it monitors the effectiveness of their management of the earmarked subsidy and conducts the financial settlement.

b) *Region with Independent Competencies*

The following highlighted functions in the area of the management of the state school system, will be transferred from the Ministry to the regions fulfilling independent competencies:

- the establishment and abolition of secondary schools, apprenticeship schools, conservatoires, special schools, language schools, school institutes specializing in art production, and short-hand institute (a transfer of competencies from the Ministry);

- to establish special basic schools and healthcare facilities, auxiliary and special schools, as well as pre-primary facilities at healthcare facilities and facilities for continuing education of teaching staff;

- depending on the local needs, to guarantee classes in languages other then Czech at pre-primary facilities, schools and school facilities;

- to appoint and dismiss the directors of schools that it establishes, upon the approval of the Ministry.

The regions with independent capacities in the area of financing of schools that are established, have roles, including:

- to secure investment expenses and non-investment costs, excluding wages, textbooks, school supplies, and necessities paid by the state;

- are able to contribute funds for non-investment costs for wages, textbooks, school supplies, and necessities paid by the government in case of schools that it establishes.

2.6.2 Change of the Ministry's Competencies

The change of the Ministry's competencies are particularly emphasized in the areas of:

a) *School Management*

- to approve the appointment and dismissal of directors of schools established by the region with independent capacities;
- in cases where special approach is necessary, it can also establish the following schools that are otherwise established by regions fulfilling independent capacities: secondary schools, apprenticeship schools, higher vocational schools, and special schools.

b) *The Financing of Schools*

- to distribute funds from the state budget to schools that it establishes (former competency of school offices);
- to distribute funds earmarked from the state budget to schools established by other establishing entities if their expenses are not covered from other sources.

2.6.3 Change of the Municipality's Competencies

The change of the Municipality's competencies are particularly emphasized in the areas of:

a) *School Management*

- in addition to basic schools and kindergartens, it establishes basic art school and leisure centers for children and youth.

b) *The Financing of Schools*

- it can contribute funds to schools that it establishes for wages, text books, school supplies, and necessities paid by the state.

2.7 Legal Position of Schools

In order to describe precisely the responsibility of institutions for the management and financing of schools, and the resulting consequences for the effectiveness, fairness, and efficiency of the school system in the Czech Republic, it is necessary to describe the legal position of schools first, because the responsibility for concrete areas greatly varies according to the legal position of state schools.

State schools (including common schools) can be divided into two major groups according to their legal position:

- schools that are a legal entity;

- schools that are not a legal entity.

Secondary schools, most basic schools, and some kindergartens are managed as economic-legal entities. Beginning in 2001, all state (common) schools that are a legal entity will be managed as contributory organizations.

On 1 January 2000, two types of contributory organizations were introduced: those established by the state and those established by self-governing bodies (municipalities and regions). It is not necessary to explain the difference between both types since schools on which the National Report focuses will be managed as contributory organizations are established by self-governing bodies. Only during the transition period, when the district authorities will play the role of establishing entities of those schools that will be transferred to regions within a year (secondary schools, apprenticeship schools, etc.), will the management method of state contributory organizations be applied.

The basic principles of contributory organizations (CO) established by the self-governing bodies (starting on 7 January 2001, the absolute majority of governmental schools, excluding schools established by the Ministry)—hereinafter the CO, are as follows:

- in addition to contributions from the establishing entity, state subsidies and subsidies from public budgets, the CO uses the financial means from its own funds that are not subject to annual accounting/settlement and are transferred to the following business year. The funds particularly serve as an incentive tool for the CO with respect to the economic results since better results are distributed to the funds in accordance with criteria determined by law;

- the CO does not have to be limited by the establishing entity with respect to the funds for operation (excluding wages) depending on the individual types of expenses (power, repairs, material, etc.). The establishing entity cannot change the relationship to the CO within a year (especially the contribution amount);

- the CO can also accept donations and, upon the approval of the establishing entity, loans, non-repayable financial aid from the establishing entity and, upon approval of the establishing entity it can buy on installments;

- the CO cannot buy shares or securities and provide donations to other entities;

- the CO reproduces property that has been earmarked for its activities through an investment fund;

- in addition to the main activities, the CO can also conduct complementary activities (for example to rent out available rooms, sell products and services, which must not be to the detriment of the CO's main activities).

State schools that are not a legal entity are managed as organizational parts of the facility of their establishing entity. The budget of the organizational part is included in the budget of the establishing entity. Organizational components can only have financial means at their disposal that are provided as operational advance payments that relate to their regular activities, which must have an operational character. In case of an absolute majority of school organizations managed as organizational components of their establishing entity, district authorities play the role of employer and after the completion of the transformation process, the regional authorities fulfilling transferred competencies will play this role.

3. ASSIGNMENT OF RESPONSIBILITIES

3.1 Directors of Schools

The appointment and dismissal of school directors depends on the establishing entity of the given school. The following table specifies the body that appoints and dismisses the director and the body that gives approval of the appointment or dismissal of the director in the existing and the new system of the public administration of the school system.

The directors of state schools are appointed on the basis of a public tender. Applicants who want to participate in the tender must meet the prerequisites required for this tender.

The most frequent prerequisites are:
- appropriate qualification;
- prescribed number of years of practical experience;
- integrity.

During the tender, the pedagogical expertise is tested and it is determined if the applicants meet other prerequisites required for the leading position. Based on a recommendation of the tender commission, the decision about the appointment is usually made by the establishing entity. As in the basic schools, the school office makes the decision (after the reform the regional authorities with transferred capacities), upon an approval of the establishing entity.

The work of the director is evaluated periodically (every 4 years) by the ČSI, the establishing entity, the school board, and so on. If the evaluation is positive, the proposal is made to reconfirm the director in his position for the next period of office. If the evaluation is not positive or if the establishing entity (in case of basic schools the school office—after the reform regional authorities fulfilling transferred capacities, in cooperation with the establishing entity) decides so, a tender can be announced. The current director can participate in this tender. He can be appointed as director for the next period of office if he is successful in the tender.

Table 4.1
The Appointment of School Directors

Type of School	Current Situation		Situation After the Reform	
	Appointed and Dismissed by	Approval with the Appointment Given by	Appointed and Dismissed by	Approval of the Appointment Given by
Kindergartens State (common) schools	School office	Municipality as establishing entity	Regional body with transferred capacities	Municipality as establishing entity
Basic schools State (common) schools	School office	Municipality as establishing entity	Regional body with transferred capacities	Municipality as establishing entity
Secondary schools State schools	Ministry	n.a.	Region with independent capacities	Ministry
Private schools	Private establishing entity	n.a.	Private establishing entity	n.a.
Patrimonial Schools	Church or religious community	n.a.	Church or religious community	n.a.

The director of the school appoints a deputy. The number of deputies depends on the size and type of the school. The director decides about the division of competencies within the framework of the school management. If there are more deputies at a school which is a legal entity, the director determines the statutory deputy who will represent the director in his/her absence within the full scope of his/her capacities. The director of the school also dismisses his/her deputy.

The director can transfer some capacities to other school employees. However, he/she will remain liable for activities transferred to his/her deputies or authorized employees.

3.2 Teaching Staff

At schools that are a legal entity, the director of the school is responsible for the employment and the activities of the teaching staff. Legal entity (in case of state schools the contributory organization) is the employer of teaching staff and the director of the school plays the role of a statutory body. The situation is different in case of schools that are not a legal entity where directors and teaching staff are employees of the institution responsible for public management in the area of education. As mentioned before, this holds true for the majority of kindergartens and some basic schools. In this case, the director of the school only proposes the hiring or release of a teaching staff. However, the state institution is responsible for the conditions of the labor-law relationship. The director proposes the employment category and remuneration of his teaching staff. Currently, the school offices play the role of the employer. However, during the transitional period, it will be the district authorities, and upon the completion of the transformation process the regional authorities with transferred capacities.

'The Work Rules for the Employees of Schools and Other School Facilities' issued by the Ministry of Education, Youth and Sports are binding for the teaching staff. In accordance with the legal regulations of the Labor Code and other legal regulations, these work rules specify and govern some aspects of the labor-law relations based on the special conditions in the educational sector. The work rules include the following areas:

- duties of employees of schools relating to starting and terminating the employment;
- duties, activities, and scheduling of working hours;
- special duties of teaching staff and employees holding leading positions;
- safety, health protection, and protection of property;
- supervision of pupils.

Teaching staff have the same work duties—the same working hours as all other employees. These working hours are divided into:

- direct pedagogical duties—teaching;
- indirect pedagogical duties—supervision of pupils;
- preparation for teaching and work relating to teaching and the functioning of the school.

Among the duties of the teacher are the replacement of an absent colleague within the full scope of his activities. The director determines if this replacement is still within the scope of the working hours or if it is overtime. The increase of the direct pedagogical activities is also considered as overtime. The teaching staff at the primary and secondary level and the teaching staff at several-year grammar schools corresponding with this age group have a direct teaching duty of 22 teaching hours. The teaching staff in secondary schools and apprenticeship schools have a direct teaching duty of 21 hours. Teaching beyond this limit is considered over-time work.

211

The teacher can be commissioned to work as an educational consultant. Depending on the size of the school and the number of pupils, his direct pedagogical duty is reduced.

Activities of a class teacher are remunerated and this work is a stable component of the wage. Based on the difficulty of the work, the remuneration paid can be in the upper range.

Teaching hours—direct pedagogical duties of directors and deputies are lower. The teaching hours of deputies of the director are about a half. The teaching hours of the director are about a third. The exact number of hours depends on the number of classes. As to the directors of basic schools, the number of day-care centers and school clubs also plays an important role. The director and the deputy also receive remuneration for holding their offices.

With regards to a very low number of employees with certain specializations, for example technical-economical employees and a lack of auxiliary teaching staff, teachers must complete all activities related to teaching. Among these activities are the preparation of tools, material necessary for teaching, the administration of specialized laboratories, correction and evaluation of pupils' assignments, inventories, the administration of teacher offices, and so on. They also have to file all pedagogical and non-pedagogical documents related to teaching and their position. Internal rules of the organization specify the work rules valid for individual schools in greater detail. They specify the previous legal regulations, taking into account the specific conditions of the school. Among the duties of an employee in a leading position is to issue these rules and to monitor compliance with them.

The scheduling of working hours mainly depends on the direct pedagogical duties and the indirect pedagogical duties. It is possible that one day the number of working hours is lower and another day higher. However, it is not allowed to shorten the work week to fewer days in the case of full-time employees. Employees do not have to conduct certain types of work on site (for example the correction of the pupils' assignments, preparation for classes, and so on).

3.3 Remuneration of Directors and Teaching Staff

The funds for the remuneration of directors and other school employees are earmarked by the Ministry. The payment category classification is done by directors at schools that are legal entities. At schools that are not legal entities the responsible school office (regional authorities with transferred capacities) plays the role of employer, which is also responsible for the payment category classification of all other school employees.

The salary of directors of state schools is determined by the responsible school office (regional body with transferred capacities) in case of schools established by the school office or the municipality, Ministry in case of schools established by the Ministry, and the establishing entity in case of other schools.

The wage of school directors consists of a basic tariff component, extra pay for management and personal extra pay.

Extra pay for management and personal extra pay is usually recognized for a year, normally from 1 November of the current year to 31 October of the next year. The school offices have been making proposals regarding extra pay so far. Binding rules only exist for the determination of extra pay for directors of schools and school facilities established by the Ministry.

Extra pay for management is determined based on the number of pupils in a school, the type of school, school parts and other criteria, on which the person making the proposal has no influence. The exact amount paid for the individual activities is determined by the Ministry. Thus, a director who is not very active receives the same remuneration as a colleague of his who is more active, if they work at facilities of a comparable size. On the other hand, this mechanism has an advantage, which is the limitation of the state employees' influence on the calculation of extra pay. There is a maximum limit determined for extra pay for management, which cannot be exceeded even if the total amount calculated is higher at large schools. This is a disadvantage for directors of large school complexes.

Personal extra pay for directors of schools and school facilities is provided on the basis of very good results of the evaluation of quality of educational activities, the quality of teaching staff, and the excellent fulfillment of a large amount of tasks. The proposed personal extra pay amount can be up to 50% of the basic tariff wage of the director.

The methods and the system of remuneration is well-thought out and the remuneration is transparent. However, opportunities to remunerate very good directors with high-quality performance are too limited.

The director is entitled to *extraordinary extra pay* twice a year, the maximum amount of which (per year) is determined. Sometimes a paradox situation occurs—directors of kindergartens receive higher remuneration than directors of secondary schools, who fulfill the function of state administration and are managers of their schools. The Ministry does not approve remuneration for a director that would be higher than the maximum limit. However, in basic schools and kindergartens, the remuneration is recognized by the school office. The remaining funds for wages are used for the remuneration of directors. The remuneration amount depends on the school office's management of the available finances. Therefore, remuneration recognized by the school office is sometimes higher than remuneration recognized by the Ministry. The situation might be corrected as a result of the establishment of regional authorities, which will be able to distribute the funds within the financial package for wages in the educational sector based on the needs and remunerate the work of the best directors.

Remuneration of teaching staff and other school employees depends on the establishing entity.

In state—(i.e. common) schools, tables determined by law are used for the calculation or the remuneration. Employees are divided into payment categories according to the character of their work and payment grades according to the prescribed education and recognized years of practical work.

Only in the lowest qualification classes (1–3), the employer can determine the classification of the employees within the entire range of payment levels by issuing his own rules. This holds true for the remuneration of manual workers. The table only determines the basic salaries. Extra pay for management and replacement, an extraordinary extra pay (extra pay for class teachers and work under difficult conditions) are part of the regular component of the wage.

Table 4.2
Age Compositions of Teachers

Age	State Basic Schools 1998		State Basic Schools 1999	
	Total Number	[%]	Total Number	[%]
Older than 70	102	0.22	88	0.19
60–70	1 888	4.12	1 868	4.13
50–60	13 256	28.96	12 235	27.06
40–50	11 171	24.41	11 251	24.88
30–40	12 326	26.93	12 292	27.18
20–30	6 850	14.97	7 306	16.16
Younger than 20	177	0.39	179	0.40
Average age	42.99		42.53	
Age	State Secondary Schools 1998		State Secondary Schools 1999	
	Total Number	[%]	Total Number	[%]
Older than 70	91	0.59	96	0.66
60–70	767	4.99	741	5.06
50–60	3 915	25.49	3 696	25.24
40–50	4 584	29.85	4 410	30.12
30–40	4 343	28.28	3 984	27.21
20–30	1 649	10.74	1 701	11.62
Younger than 20	8	0.05	14	0.10
Average age	43.72		43.65	

Personal extra pay, which is an irregular component of the wage, can be recognized to school employees. However, this extra pay cannot exceed 50% of the basic wage of the highest payment level of the given payment class. Furthermore, an extraordinary extra pay for extraordinary work can be recognized to employees.

The amount of extra pay that is an irregular component of the wage corresponds with the age structure of the school. The older teaching staff, the lower the irregular component of the wage. The average irregular component is calculated based on the 'average' payment level, which has 19 years of experience in the field. Even distribution of employees of the individual age groups is ideal: i.e. one third of young employees, one third of middle-aged employees, and one third of older employees. The employment of retirees, especially old retirees, has negative impact. Sometimes, the management of the school recognized high irregular components of the wage to these employees instead of using the funds for the stabilization of young teachers.

Table 4.2 shows the age distribution of teaching staff in basic and secondary school in 1998 and 1999 and illustrates the previously made point. Secondary schools include grammar schools and vocational schools. Art schools, apprenticeship schools and special schools have not been included. The relatively high average age of teaching staff in basic and secondary schools with regard to the remuneration system has a negative impact on the effectiveness of the system of remuneration of school employees and the system of normative allocation of funds for wages. The higher the average age of teachers at a school, the lower funds for wages that the director of the school can use for irregular components of the wage.

3.4 School Planning and Development

3.4.1 Establishment or Abolition of Schools

As for the establishment and abolition of schools, schools can be divided into two different groups of establishing entities that are responsible for the establishment and abolition of schools in the Czech Republic. On the one hand there are the public administration bodies in the case of state or common schools, and private establishing entities and churches or religious communities on the other. The establishing functions in case of state schools of public institution are described in Section 2 of the National Report. However, in addition to state school, there are also patrimonial and private schools in the Czech Republic. Patrimonial schools are, regardless of the educational level, schools established by a church or a religious community. Private schools are established by non-state domestic legal entities or physical entities, which are not municipalities, churches or religious communities, regardless of the educational level of education they provide. The following table shows institutions responsible for the establishment or abolition of schools, according to their establishing entities.

Table 4.3
Authority to Establish Schools

Type of School	Current Situation		Situation After the Reform	
	Established and Abolished by	Abolition Subject to Approval of	Established and Abolished by	Abolition Subject to Approval of
Kindergartens State (common) schools	Municipality	School office	Municipality	Regional authorities with transferred competencies
Basic schools State (common) schools	Municipality	School office	Municipality	Regional authorities with transferred competencies
Secondary schools State schools	Ministry	n.a.	Region with independent capacities	n.a.
Private Schools	Private establishing entity	n.a.	Private establishing	n.a.
Patrimonial schools	Church or religious community	n.a.	Church or religious community	n.a.

The number of schools of all establishing entities is regulated through a network of schools, pre-primary facilities and school facilities registered by the Ministry. The following sections discuss in greater detail the registration in the network of schools as a necessary prerequisite for receiving state subsidies and the registration of the school in the educational system of the Czech Republic. The director discusses the development of the school with the establishing entity and the school board.

The capacity of the school mainly depends on the space limitations of the school building. The school building is considered a special building in the Czech Republic. Approval for use is necessary, which determines the capacity of the building with regard to the safety of pupils, valid hygiene regulations that specify the number of restrooms and so on, for the given number of students, the size of corridors and stairways in the building, the space capacity, the illumination of classrooms, the size of cloakrooms, etc. If it is necessary to enlarge the school's capacity as a result of an increase in the demand of pupils, the establishing entity provides a technical solution. It can also transfer this capacity to the school. If the number of pupils increases, the director of the school mainly guarantees the material and personal conditions of the school from funds provided by the establishing entity and the state budget or other sources. A similar approach is used if there is a need to reduce the capacity of the school, e.g. as a result of a decrease in demand.

The capacity of the classrooms must correspond with the technical conditions in a manner discussed above. The technical prerequisites are the same for all schools of all establishing entities (private, patrimonial, and state schools). Another limiting factor for state basic schools and kindergartens is the minimum capacity of classrooms that is determined by the school law for basic schools and by a decree for kindergartens. Pursuant to the school law, at a basic school consisting of one or two classes, the average number of pupils per class at the primary level must be at least 13 pupils. This is only possible if the basic school is the only one in the municipality. In case of other state (common) schools, there is a rule that the minimum average number of pupils per class must be 17. The Ministry can decide about exceptions where a special approach is needed after discussing the situation with the school office (regional body with transferred capacity). The decree on basic schools determines that classes usually have up to 30 pupils. However, the director can decide that the number of pupils in a class will be higher than 30. He/she must take the hygiene, pedagogical and space conditions into account. Similar rules are also valid for kindergartens.

3.4.2 Curriculum and Development

There are three fundamental documents—educational programs—valid for basic schools:

- basic school;
- common school;
- national school.

All programs are based on existing standards. The content of the curricula does not differ considerably. The school as well as teacher's approach to these documents is important. Every teacher develops his or her own personal plan. Curriculum determined by valid guidelines can be changed as far as the time sequence of its parts is concerned. The content can be changed up to 30%. The management of the school must coordinate and approve such steps. The director of the school is responsible for the compliance with and the changes of the educational plans. He/she is also liable to the inspection. The director can establish a curriculum commission—a consulting methodological body providing him/her with expert support. However, the director will still remain liable. He/she has the same responsibility with respect to the choice of the educational program.

The educational program including the teaching guidelines is a binding legal document. It is not allowed to be changed by other documents, for example methodological manuals. È I also monitors the compliance with this document and can impose sanctions on the director who is liable for the compliance. If the director of the school discovers that the teaching staff does not comply with the educational plan, he/she imposes sanctions on his employees. The director is responsible for changes made by the teaching staff (he approves them). He is responsible for the continuity of education within the school, for the compliance with the curricula, and the correctness and appropriateness of the changes to the curricula made by teaching staff.

If the school decides to develop its own document, this educational program must be evaluated by the Ministry of Education Youth and Sports, which will decide about the accreditation. Currently, it is possible to adjust these documents to the needs of the school. This holds true for educational programs, both the teaching plan and the teaching guidelines.

3.4.3 Enrolment Process

There are no general criteria for the acceptance into kindergartens. There is only an age limit of three years. Other criteria for acceptance are determined by the municipalities that usually consider the social conditions in the family, the employment of the parents and so on.

There are two aspects taken into account during the acceptance process at basic schools. The first aspect is the psychosomatic maturity of the child. The second aspect is the permanent residence of the child. As mentioned before, the municipality has to guarantee school attendance for children. The municipalities issue generally binding decrees, in which the catchment area of basic schools is defined, as discussed in the previous sections. Every basic school must give preference to children from its catchment area, i.e. children whose permanent residence is in the catchment area. The capacity of the basic school can be also used by pupils who do not live in the catchment area.

Upon the completion of the basic school, the pupil can apply to two secondary schools. The prerequisite is the completion of all grades of the basic school. The school listed first will invite the pupil to take acceptance exams. If the pupil does not pass these exams, he/she can take acceptance exams at the second school.

The director of the school determines conditions for the acceptance of pupils to the first year. He/she can determine other criteria, as well (for example grades at the basic school). In this case, the acceptance exams do not take place. These criteria must be known at least on the day of the acceptance exams. The criteria are valid for all applying pupils. The school director decides how many places he/she will keep open for the appellate processes of those pupils who were not accepted. The school office decides during this appellate process.

If talent is key at a certain school (art schools), the pupils must take talent exams before the acceptance exams. The successful completion of talent exams is a prerequisite for the participation in further acceptance proceedings.

The pupil can apply to multi-year grammar schools after the completion of a certain grade (the fifth grade in case of eight-year grammar schools, the seventh grade in case of six-year grammar schools). The school office decides about exceptions. The pupil can submit only one application to this type of school.

Acceptance exams at state schools are taken on the same day.

The number of accepted pupils must correspond with the number of pupils approved for the school. Thus, appropriate financing of the classes is guaranteed. The number of pupils is specified when the school is registered in the school network.

The number of study places has recently increased due to the decrease in population and the small increase in the number of first classes (thanks to private schools). In some fields, schools must compete for pupils.

3.5 Infrastructure

3.5.1 Ownership of School Buildings and Other Property

The establishing entity of the school is responsible for providing room necessary for teaching. The principle of 'public ownership' from the time before 1989 is still valid for school buildings in the Czech Republic. During the transformation process, many buildings were returned to the original owners. Thus, not only institutions responsible for the educational process in the Czech Republic but also private physical and legal entities are owners of buildings where state or common schools are located.

Within the framework of the transformation of the school sector in the Czech Republic after 1989, buildings where basic schools, kindergartens, and school facilities were located, were transferred from the state to municipalities free-of-charge. Property claimed by original owners was not transferred to the municipalities, however. Currently, some claims of original owners have not been solved in the case of the buildings where schools are located. In such cases, the property is administered by commissioned firms and the establishing entity is responsible for obligations resulting from the rental agreement. The laws on restitution in the Czech Republic determined a protection period of ten years in case of property where schools and school facilities were located. The owner could not force the school or the school facility to move out on the basis of generally valid regulations and had to accept minimal income from the rent.

The protection period will end in 2001. Some establishing entities will have to reach an acceptable agreement with the private owners regarding the rent to be paid. The self-governing and state institutions try to situate schools and school facilities that they establish in buildings they own. In the recent years, this resulted in an increase in investment expenses for the construction. Buildings necessary for the operation of schools have been built, rebuilt, renovated, and repaired. Only the proprietary rights of the establishing entity to the building are a guarantee of the existence of the school and a prerequisite of the realization of a long-term plan for the development of the school.

The methods of management of property are embodied in the establishing documents and statutes of school organizations. The scope of rights and obligation with respect to the property, which is determined in the aforementioned documents, differs according to the owner of the property.

Based on the methods of the use of the property, schools can be divided into three groups:

- *The State—the Ministry—as owner*

    The methods of use of the state property are determined by law. Until 2000 the "right of management of state property" will remain valid. In addition to general legal norms in the economic area, the state administration bodies will specify the methods of the use of the state property. The earnings from the state property will be discussed in greater detail in the section relating to the income of schools. In 2001, a new law on the management of state property will be introduced.

- *Property of the municipality*

    Only generally valid guidelines are valid for municipalities as they determine rules for the management of their property regarding organizations they establish. These guidelines enable municipalities as establishing entities to transfer more capacities to organizations they establish in the area of property management than it is the case with respect to schools established by the state. Therefore, the relationship of schools established by municipalities to the property greatly varies. Some schools have all rights and obligations of owners regarding the buildings. Other school rights to the property are more limited than it is the case with respect to state property. The situation can be even more different if the property of the municipality is used by a school that was not established by the municipality. The approach depends on the priorities of the local authorities and on the importance they attach to the development of education and culture in the municipality. Some municipalities provide their property to schools of other establishing entities free-of-charge. Others classify schools as lessees using the room for commercial activities.

- *Private ownership of school buildings*

    As to the private ownership, the particular owner and his/her approach to the school is crucial. The main characteristic of the use of the private property by schools is the commercial approach of the owners of the property and the pressure to gain maximum profits. This is usually not acceptable for state schools or their establishing entities because of their financial limitations, especially if the building is situated in attractive locations where high rents can be demanded.

3.5.2 Employment and Salaries of Technical-Economical School Employees (TEE)

The responsibility for the employment and the remuneration of TEEs is shared in a similar manner as in the case of teaching staff. Once again, it is necessary to differentiate the responsibility of the school employees in leading positions based on the legal position of the school.

Problems with employment of TEEs occur at common schools since the municipality is responsible for the operation of school building, financial management, and the property of the school but does not have any influence on the employment of technical or economic employees. For example, the school is heated by a gas boiler, which was provided by the municipality. Now, the municipality, which is the owner, is also the operator of the gas boiler. Nowadays, it is common that the school is the user of the boiler and the municipality is the operator, without having any influence on the employees operating it. A similar situation exists with respect to the relationship of the municipality to all economical-operational and technical employees of the school. The question as to who should be responsible for the employment of TEEs has been discussed several times on different levels. However, no changes have been made so far and the responsibility sharing remains the same as described above.

3.5.3 Construction, Repairs, and Maintenance of the Buildings

Funds for the construction of the school buildings are an investment expense item in the state budget and the budgets of the local self-administration. The state invests in the construction of schools that it establishes. It also participates in the construction of school buildings of private schools and schools established by municipalities within the framework of governmental support programs in the area of education.

The investment in construction of school buildings is given high priority in local budgets. Municipalities are responsible for investment expenses of schools that they establish.

It means that mainly the establishing entity is responsible for sufficient sources of investment in the state school buildings. Individual schools can contribute funds from the earnings from the rent of available commercial rooms. However, these funds are a negligible part of the total investment in the property.

As far as construction financed by schools is concerned, there are differences depending on the way schools can use the property and depending on what capacities the establishing entity transferred to them. State institutions use the subsidy principle when it comes to investment construction. Schools propose a plan to the Ministry and upon the approval thereof they are promised funds. The school ensures the development of the architectural documents and chooses a firm to carry out the construction in a public tender. The state will provide funds for the individual phases of the construction based on a signed contract.

There are differences in financing of school buildings from the budgets of the local self-administration. Some municipalities provide funds to the school in the form of a subsidy and only supervise and monitor its appropriate use. Other municipalities carry out the investment construction of school buildings by themselves in cooperation with the school.

As to the renovation of school buildings, the time factor is problematic. If it is not possible to find replacement rooms for classes, the renovation must be carried out during the two-months main summer break. Therefore, the renovation of school buildings is considered one of the most difficult projects as far as the time factor is concerned.

3.5.4   Provision, Maintenance, and Replacement of Teaching Equipment

Expenses for teaching tools are part of direct educational expenses, which are covered by funds from the state budget provided by regional school offices (regional authorities—districts). The funds provided to individual schools are determined on the basis of determined units—number of pupils. The teaching tools were delivered centrally until 1989. The basic teaching tools were delivered free-of-charge, the rest based on an order.

After 1990, the central delivery firm Komenium ceased to exist. Many firms distributing school tools were established. Until approximately the mid-1990s, the deliveries of school tools could not be complete since there were not enough producers. After 1995, distributors started buying teaching tools from abroad. Czech firms developed new high-quality tools. At the moment, there is no firm delivering the full range of tools. However, there are many distribution firms that meet the common needs of schools regarding teaching tools. Prices of teaching tools have risen considerably.

The same holds true for textbooks, which did not meet the new needs after 1989 with respect to their ideology, content, and methodology. Many firms publish textbooks. Their appropriateness is guaranteed by the approval clause of the Ministry of Education, Youth, and Sports. The schools can choose from a wide range of textbooks. New textbooks are being brought to the market.

However, schools are facing financial problems. The budget of the educational sector has not changed for many years. Salaries have been increasing only moderately. This increase has been covered from the funds for teaching tools and textbooks to a great extent. The schools do not have enough funds to buy new textbooks or new modern teaching tools. Unfortunately, pupils cannot buy the textbooks themselves because they are supposed to received them free-of-charge according to the valid legal regulations.

The lack of funds for textbooks and tools is critical because schools have been facing this situation for many years. The replacement of textbooks is very slow.

In addition, a new medium is coming that is very important but also expensive—computers. Currently, the Ministry of Education, Youth, and Sports is preparing a project aimed at problems related to the use of computers and the Internet.

However, this will not solve the problems related to textbooks and other tools. At some schools, it will be very difficult to use the provided computers since they will not have qualified employees. The availability of computers and having access to the Internet does not solve the computer-illiteracy of pupils. Only a well-equipped classroom and qualified teaching staff using well-defined teaching methods would be the right step in the right direction.

3.5.5   Supply of Power and Other Utilities

Heating and the supply of material necessary for heating, power, and water is part of other expenses of schools. Against this background, it will be useful to provide a description of different categories of school expenses.

1.   As mentioned in the previous sections, direct educational expenses covered by the state include: the cost of teaching staff and the operation of the school; -expenses for textbooks, teaching tools, and school supplies.

2.   Other expenses include the following:

*   the cost of investment construction and renovation, repairs;
*   *the maintenance of the buildings*, power, heating, water, and other utilities;
*   services;
*   school equipment, excluding school tools, and so on.

The previous sections suggest that the establishing entity is responsible for the supply of power and other utilities. Most establishing entities transfer the responsibility for such costs to the schools. Incentives for the school in the area of use of energy are due to their legal position and the form of management. This topic, however, will be discussed in another chapter of the National Report. There are only monopolistic suppliers within the Czech power, water, heating, and gas market. There is no free-market environment in this area, and therefore it is relatively easy to estimate these expenses.

3.6 Professional Supervision

3.6.1 License and Registration of Schools

As far as registration or licenses of the schools are concerned, a system registering schools, pre-primary facilities, and school facilities in a network plays an important role. This system is subject to Law No. 564/1990 Coll. on State Administration and Self-Administration in the Educational Sector, as amended. The basic principle of this system is that the conditions and scope of the educational process, for example the accredited validity of final documents for pupils and the system of financing of education is effective only in case of schools registered in the network of schools, pre-primary facilities, and school facilities.

The Ministry registers the network of all establishing entities based on data provided yearly by the state administration bodies and it publishes it. The school office includes schools established by municipalities into the network. Ministry includes all other schools. Each school, pre-primary facility or school facility in the network must specify:

- name, address, legal form, and identification number;
- name and address of the establishing entity, first name, last name, and permanent residence of the establishing entity if it is a physical entity;
- all kinds and types of schools that are part of the school;
- list of fields of study and apprenticeship fields, and specialization if applicable;
- list of pre-primary facilities, schools, and school facilities that are part of the school's association;
- date of becoming part of the network;
- subject area of pre-primary facilities and school facilities.

The application to become part of the network includes the following information in addition to basic information and the basic documentation of the school:

- document certifying the establishing entity's right to use the building;
- positive evaluation of a hygiene expert and authorities responsible for the construction sector, certifying the appropriateness of the building for the proposed purpose;
- evaluation of the municipality, on the territory of which the school is located;
- the educational plan of the school including teaching plans and other educational documentation;
- number of pupils, the expected capacity, and so on.

3.6.2 Education of Teachers

University education is a prerequisite for the teaching profession. The basic type of education are Master's studies. The student must choose two majors. Sometimes, Bachelor's studies are also available. In this case, there is only one major. Those who completed their studies of the teaching field, also took classes in basics of pedagogy and completed the required exam to teach as well.

During the university studies, the teacher should acquire a solid knowledge of the field, methodology of teaching of the given subject, and the knowledge of related subjects such as pedagogy, psychology, child psychology, and so on. Internships at schools including observations of classes but also the actual teaching are part of the education. At the end of the studies, the students have to pass state exams and complete and defend their Master's thesis.

There is no relief for a teacher who has just started teaching. However, it is recommended to have the new teacher supervised by an experienced teacher who teaches the same subjects at the school. Such a teacher is referred to as the guiding teacher. Currently, no regular and systematic continuing education is available for teachers. An entire system of career advancement is being prepared. This system should determine the continuing education of teachers and financial benefits for those who have completed it. This way, the current system of flat salaries would be changed. Today, the increase of salaries only depends on the years of experience in the field.

Continuing education of teachers depends on their interest or the pressure of their supervisors. Employees taking classes can be remunerated only within the framework of a limited personal extra pay. Many organizations offer classes, during which it is possible to acquire particular knowledge or skills. Among them are mainly pedagogical centers preparing educational events for school employees. These centers are managed by the Ministry of Education, Youth, and Sports. In addition, new institutions are being established that offer educational courses and training.

The Ministry of Education tries to monitor the situation. It gives accreditation to education institution, which is considered to be a guarantee of quality and a sign of compliance with the Ministry's educational policies. Some colleges also participate in this process to a certain extent. Many of these educational events are not free-of-charge. The tuition can be paid either by the participant (teacher) or the organization that requires the participant to take the class. Due to low salaries of teachers and limited school budgets, it is not possible to take advantage of all available educational activities.

The completion and introduction of the career advancement program for teaching staff could have the desired effect—the life-long systematic education of teachers, which would be also re-munerated based on the results.

Specialized magazines focusing on the topics of the individual subjects are part of the education of teachers.

The Ministry is currently preparing a program aimed at enabling all schools to use the Internet. This way, the teaching staff will get the opportunity to use the knowledge resources available in this new medium.

Since an overall educational plan is missing, the school offices or establishing entities are trying to provide continuing education for teachers. Due to the existing legal norms, the economic situation, and the capacity limitations, colleges cannot play a decisive role in this process.

3.6.3   Inspection and Monitoring

Based on the monitoring body, the monitoring activities towards organizations can be divided into the following groups:

- internal;
- external.

The internal activities are carried out by the school/organization in order to monitor its own activities. Based on these activities, it prepares an evaluation and plans its activities. It looks for deficiencies and tries to correct them by taking appropriate measures.

The external activities are monitoring activities by state bodies, which monitor the school and determine if it fulfils the tasks that were the purpose of the establishment of the school. They determine if it complies with laws, decrees, and regulations. In cooperation with the establishing entity, it tries to determine the appropriate measures to be taken in order to correct the deficiencies. Based on the content, the monitoring activities can be divided into the following group:

- pedagogical;
- operational-economic.

The management of the school is responsible for internal pedagogical monitoring. The management develops a plan of monitoring activities for each school year. During the preparation of such a plan, it takes the evaluation from the previous school year and the result of the previous checks into account. It also sets priorities for the current school year. There are also attempts to gain an overview of all pedagogical activities. On-site checks are the main tool of the monitoring activities. Such on-site checks are carried out mainly by the director of the school and his/her representatives. The on-site checks can be complex and focus on the monitoring or the teacher's and pupils' work in the class. However, it can also focus on a certain area (monitoring, testing and evaluation of pupils, use of tools, methods of refreshing and practicing certain topics, etc.). At the end of the on-site check, there is an interview, during which the results of the check are to be announced and proposals made, which are to be taken to achieve improvement.

The chairman of the curriculum commission can be invited to the on-site check who can monitor the level of the teacher's expertise. At the same time, on-site checks of teachers are also possible. However, they have an informative rather than a monitoring character.

Another part of the monitoring process is the monitoring of teaching documents, including the pupils' assignments. Among them is the monitoring of homework (frequency, volume, correction, and evaluation of homework), written assignments, notebooks, products, pictures, and so on.

The compliance with the internal organizational order is also monitored. This includes the quality of supervision, escorting of pupils, punctual beginning of classes and so on.

The operational-economic monitoring is focused on the compliance with the binding regulations for the operational-economic workings of the school. General legal-economic regulations provide the framework for such rules. The establishing entity specifies the rules in greater detail and they are embodied in the internal order of the organization.

The management of the school monitors the compliance with financal indicators, the use of the budget, the compliance with budgeting guidelines, the effective use of funds, and so on. It monitors the management of property and the related file records.

At basic schools, there is a separate monitoring for funds earmarked from the state budget (wages, deductions, funds for tools and textbooks, education, etc.) and funds for operation earmarked from the municipal budgets (repairs, maintenance, services, power, etc.).

At secondary schools, the individual funds are monitored, which are divided into wages and non-investment expenses. Wages and funds for deductions are monitored separately. Other non-investment expenses must be divided into the priority operational expenses (including power, and necessary repairs) and funds related to classes, in other words tools and textbooks.

There are the following three groups of funds that must be registered and monitored separately:

a)   funds from grants;

b)   investment funds;

c)   funds from commercial activities.

Funds under group a) must be monitored based on the grant documentation, which determines the division and purpose, which must be fulfilled.

Funds under group b) must be monitored with respect to the total amount, use and accounting period.

Activities under group c) are regulated by a general decree determining the basic rules for the operation and the use of funds obtained through such activities. The establishing entity specifies the rules in greater detail based on concrete examples. The monitoring must guarantee the appropriateness of commercial, the compliance with all valid rules and the effective use of the funds.

The results of the monitoring carried out by the school should lead to appropriate measures taken in order to correct the deficiencies.

The external pedagogical monitoring is conducted by an independent body—the Czech School Inspection. It carries out the monitoring in the form of inspection.

Such activities are based on an inspection plan for a certain school year. There are two types of school inspections:

a)   orientation inspections;

b)   deep inspections.

Orientation inspection under type a) should provide an overview of the school's activities, especially with respect to the pedagogical and organizational area as they relate to the main purpose of the school-education. It also monitors operational-economic indicators, especially those having an effect on teaching.

Deep inspection under type b) is carried out over a longer period of time. A higher number of inspectors with necessary specialization participate. Based on this monitoring, an overview of the overall pedagogical activities of the school should be gained.

The monitoring activities make it clear what measures are to be taken in order to correct the deficiencies. If the inspecting bodies decide so, there can be a follow-up inspection, the purpose of which would be the monitoring of the measures to be taken.

In addition to such inspection activities, the inspection addresses proposals from the public, predominantly parents but also pupils, and the establishing entity of the school. The establishing entity does not have qualified employees for the monitoring of the educational process. Therefore, the Czech School Inspection fulfils this task. It also informs the establishing entity about the results of all types of inspections and recommends measures to be taken. Such measures are proposed based on the inspection activities carried out at the school. The establishing entity helps to correct the existing deficiencies by providing organizational, material or personal resources. The external operational-economical monitoring is carried out by the state bodies and the establishing entity. The financial office and the Social Security Administration are state bodies monitoring schools that are legal entities. The monitoring is carried out with respect to the deductions for wages and social security. Possible prescribed additional deductions including penalties are part of the monitoring.

Regular monitoring of management is carried out by the establishing entity in form of quarterly and annual statements. In addition to these regular activities, it carries out monitoring aimed at the overall accounting and management or focusing on a certain fact. Also in these cases, results are formulated and necessary measures determined.

Since the school conducts all activities of an organization, it also has all duties of a organization. These include fire-fighting and security work, and tasks of a contributory organization. The monitoring activities of the establishing entity are aimed at this area, as well. Monitoring activities conducted by state bodies are also possible in these areas.

This also holds true for the technical condition of the buildings if the school is responsible for all technical equipment in the building (elevators, boiler rooms, air-conditioning, monitoring of the electrical system, lightning rods, and so on).

The director of the school is responsible for the operation and the education process of the school. He also has comprehensive rights with respect to decision-making in the organization. He can transfer his competencies to other employees within the framework of the organizational structure. However, he will still remain liable with respect to the monitoring activities. The monitoring body imposes sanctions on the director of the school and takes measures concerning him. The school director can use the same approach towards his employees within the organizational structure of the school.

The Institute for Educational Information conducts monitoring of the Czech school system. It collects all available information from the educational sector, evaluates and compares it. It is difficult to monitor the quality and effectiveness of the educational process, and the quality of the school. One of the reasons is that it has not been agreed upon yet what is the key factor of the quality of education and a school.

3.7 Financing of Schools

Expenses in the educational sector in the Czech Republic can be divided into two basic categories, as discussed in section 3.5.5: *direct education expenses and other expenses of schools.* The previous sections and the section describing the responsibility of institutions suggest that the state is clearly responsible for the financing of direct educational expenses of schools of all establishing entities. The following section describes in greater detail the process of allocation of funds from the ministry and the process of determination of wages at individual schools by school offices.

3.7.1 Direct Educational Expenses: Teachers' Salaries

The budgets of schools and school facilities is prepared according to methodological instructions of the Ministry of Education, Youth, and Sports of the Czech Republic (MEYS CR) and based on principles valid for the preparation of a budget that are determined by the school office (SO) based on experience with previous budgets.

The first level is purely normative and is only based on the total number of units per district (i.e. the number of pupils, persons eating at the school cafeteria, beds). Funds for wages constitute one of the components of the budget. Based on the total number of units and norms determined by the Ministry (i.e. the number of pupils, persons eating in the cafeteria, etc. per employee) the number of employees necessary in a certain group of subjects or schools in the district is calculated. At the same time, the Ministry calculates the average wage of employees in the entire group in the Czech Republic. Based on the total number of employees and their average wages, the total funds for wages allocated for a district are calculated (the average wage determined by the Ministry is 1/12 of the total wages per year.)

On the second level, the funds from the Ministry are redistributed and allocated to schools and school facilities. The school office determined the number of teaching hours at the individual schools and school facilities, their parts (e.g. school, day-care center, youth home, and so on), and the individual professional groups (teaching staff and other staff). The school office allocates funds for wages for these groups (i.e. normative number of employees).

The normative number of teaching staff at all types of schools is calculated based on the number of pupils shown on the statistical statement that schools issue every fall. This is the basic supporting document for the allocation of funds for wages. The determination of the normative number of teaching staff at basic and secondary schools is subject to the Order of the Ministry of Education No. 10/1997 of 11 June 1997 on the Maximum Number of Teaching Hours (referred to as 'yellow book'). The maximum number of teaching hours per week is calculated based on the yellow book. All reduced teaching hours are deducted (director, deputies, educational consultants, first-grade teachers, etc.). The rest is divided by the basic number of teaching hours of teachers. The number of deducted reduced teaching hours is added and the total is the normative number of teaching staff.

Special classes and integrated children raise the number of normative employees at schools—this increase is discussed with individual schools. The number of educators in day-care centers, school clubs, and youth home is determined normatively.

The normative number of employees other than teaching staff is determined according to the normative principle. However, school offices, which are aware of the situation at individual schools, take this situation into account and adjust the number of employees other than teaching staff accordingly (including maids, security guards, administrative employees, employees working in the cafeteria, boiler men).

According to the situation on 12 December, the school office calculates the average regular component of the wage per employee according to certain parts of the school and professional groups (including extra salaries, extra pay for management, work as class teacher, and all other extra pay that is an irregular component of the wage).

Then, the school office determines the percentage of the irregular component of each professional group and employees of the individual types of schools and their parts, which will raise the regular component. This percentage may not exceed 25%. The percentage of the irregular component is determined in a way so that the total funds for wages earmarked for a certain type of school or school facility in the entire district do not exceed the amount that was transferred to the district from the Ministry for this type of the school and facility.

The total funds for wages allocated to the school for teaching staff will be calculated as the regular component of the wage raised by the irregular component percentage. This amount will be multiplied by the number of wages (12) and multiplied by the normative number of teaching staff. The calculation is the same in case of employees other than teaching staff.

Funds for wages calculated this way are allocated to the school no matter if the real number of employees is higher or lower than the normative number of employees. These funds for wages are meant to finance both the internal (full time staff) and the external (part time) employees. The school determines which part of the funds it will keep for the wages of internal employees and how much it will allocate for the wages of external employees (which are referred to as "other payments of the conducted work").

The calculation of the total funds for wages is based on the highest possible division of classes and the highest possible offer of selective subjects. If the director does not take advantage of this, he/she saves a part of the funds for wages, which can be used for the increase of the irregular component. If the highest possible division of classes and the highest possible offer of selective subjects is taken advantage of, a paradoxical situation can occur at basic schools. Teachers teaching at such a school can receive a much lower wage than teacher at schools where the classes are not divided and where only one selective subject is offered. Sometimes, such situation also occurs at basic schools in smaller villages where there is no competition. Directors of secondary schools, which have to compete for pupils, try to take advantage of the available opportunities so that their school has a reputation of a facility offering high-quality education.

Upon the allocation of the funds for wages, the director can either distribute them among the highest possible number of employees, which will decrease the average wage per employee at his school, or he can pay for some hours as over-time work to other employees, which raises the average salary.

The average monthly salary in the Czech Republic is CZK 12 811 this year. The average salary of teaching staff amounts to CZK 12 864, which is 0.4% more than the average salary in the Czech Republic. The average salary of teachers has not changed considerably compared to the previous year. The main reason is that many new employees started working in the educational sector due to the decrease in mandatory teaching hours. This year, the number of teachers increased by 4 200. However, the budget was not raised by an amount corresponding with the wages of the new teachers. And it was up to the directors of the school offices and the directors of schools that are a legal entity to decide how they approach the decrease in mandatory teaching hours. They could pay for over-time work or hire more teachers. The hiring of new teachers resulted in a decrease in the average salary. The labor unions in the educational sector are trying to raise the wage tariff by 15% of the highest income level.

Another source of a teacher's income can be the wage for auxiliary economic activities at the school (e.g. vehicle repairs, developing projects, qualification courses, language courses, machine repairs, catering, social events, etc.). Remuneration is an irregular component of the wage. The director of the school determines the amount based on his consideration and evaluation of work results of the teacher and the remaining funds for wages, which were not used for the regular wages. Teaching staff at schools with higher regular personal extra pay usually receive lower remuneration compared to teaching staff at schools with lower personal extra pay. The directors at such schools can redistribute more funds and use them for remuneration. If the replacement for sick colleagues is paid for as over-time work, funds can be saved, as well, and redistributed as remuneration.

The wages of teachers at all schools regardless of the establishing entity are financed from the state budget.

3.7.2   The Role of Municipal Budgets in the Financing of Education

The municipalities are responsible for other expenses of (state) basic schools and kindergartens. Exact economic definition of other expenses:

1.   *Investment expenses*

- especially expenses and investment subsidies for school that are a legal entity used for the construction of school buildings, reconstruction, modernization or expansion of school buildings are included in this category;

- expenses and investment subsidies for schools that are a legal entity used for long-term property are also part of this category (over CZK 40 000, period of use over 1 year). Kitchen equipment, office machines and equipment, appliances that are not part of the building, etc. can be part of this category;

2.   *Non-investment expenses*

- equipment of schools—small investment (long-term) property=school and office furniture, appliances and equipment up to CZK 40 000);

- material—cleaning and office supplies, textiles, cleaning tools, maintenance material;
- services—phone fees, financial and legal services, technical services, revisions, evaluation, etc.;
- repairs and maintenance of buildings and objects;
- expenses of power, heating, water, gas, fuels or solid fuels;
- amortization of fixed assets (long-term assets); School must establish a fund for the replacement of these assets.

These non-investment expenses created more room for the school to use the funds effectively. Currently, municipalities as legal entities can only establish schools in form of contributory organizations that do not return funds that have not been used and include them into their own funds as improved results. Such approach creates incentives for schools regarding effective management. If the municipality sets correct binding indicators within the framework of the relationship to contributory organization, i.e. the operation contribution, the school can count on being able to keep the funds remaining at the end of the business year. Financial means from the funds can be mainly used for the further development of the organization but also for extra-ordinary remunerations from the remuneration fund.

The normative—performance method based on the number of pupils is not always used for the determination of funds for school allocated from local budgets. The local conditions, the character of the building, the capacity of the school, methods of heating etc. also play an important role. The expenses per pupil will be different at a school located in a small village in a one-story building with three rooms heated by a solid fuel oven than at a four-story palace-type historic building from the 18th century located in the center of Prague with 6.2m high ceilings in classrooms that can be used only for a limited number of pupils, with large halls, and heated by a separate gas boiling room.

Pursuant to legal provisions, municipalities are obligated to cover non-investment expenses for pupils that fulfill their mandatory school attendance in a municipality other than where their permanent residence is.

Subsidies for non-investment expenses covered by municipalities are allocated from the state budget through district authorities to municipalities based on the number of pupils. In 1999, expenses per pupil covered from municipal budgets were about CZK 7 000 and the state provided CZK 1 250 per pupil. That means that the state covered more than one sixth of the expenses of municipalities in the educational sector.

The municipalities have to take care of less than five sixths of expenses in the educational sector. In order to do so, the municipalities use income from tax revenues that belong to them pursuant to valid legal provisions. These revenues include revenues from direct taxes of gainfully employed persons and from the property tax.

Donations from sponsors, both physical and legal entities, to municipalities to be used in the educational sector are another source. Within the framework of taxation of physical entities, it is possible to recognize a donation for educational purposes as a deduction up to 10% of the taxable income. In case of legal entities, such deduction can be up to 2%.

The third source that can be used by municipalities for the financing of the educational sector are revenues from extra activities. These usually include renting out municipality's commercial space or available building.

The last source used by municipalities for the financing of schools are contributions from parents for partial coverage of non-investment costs of kindergartens, day-care centers, and clubs. The municipality determines the amount of such contributions by issuing a generally binding decree. They must not exceed one third of the real total non-investment costs of the operation of the kindergarten, day-care center or school club. Pursuant to legal provisions, the municipality must not demand the contribution from citizens with low income. Low income means that the total income of the household members is lower than 1.25 fold of the life minimum.

3.7.3   The Role of School Revenues

The contributions from parents collected at private schools should guarantee higher standards compared to state schools. They also help to cover other expenses. Direct educational expenses based on the number of pupils are allocated in the form of subsidies earmarked from the state budget. Depending on the type of the school, such subsidies cover a certain percentage of the actual expenses. The situation at private schools is addressed in the following sections.

Figure 4.1
Scheme of Financial Flow Before the Reform

Description:

1.   Funds earmarked from the state budget for the educational sector

2.   Funds earmarked from the state budget for other expenses of schools and school facilities established by the region or municipalities that relate to their operation and investment expenses

3.   Full financing of schools and school facilities established by the Ministry of Education, Youth, and Sports, universities, and other directly administered organizations

4.   Subsidies from the educational funds for wages and deductions, operational expenses (not investment expenses) for private and patrimonial schools

5.   Funds earmarked from the state budget for the direct educational expenses for schools and facilities established by regions and municipalities

6.   Financing for individual patrimonial schools and school facilities distributed by the regional office (wages, deductions, operation)

7.   Financing for individual private schools and school facilities distributed by the regional office (wages, deductions, operation)

8.   Full financing of school and school facilities established by the region (direct educational expenses and other school expenses)

9. Direct educational expenses for schools established by municipalities
10. Financing of other expenses of schools for schools and school facilities established by municipalities
11. Distribution of other expenses among individual municipalities from the district authorities
12. Distribution of direct educational expenses from district authorities to individual schools and school facilities established by the municipality
13. Distribution of other expenses among individual schools and school facilities from the municipality

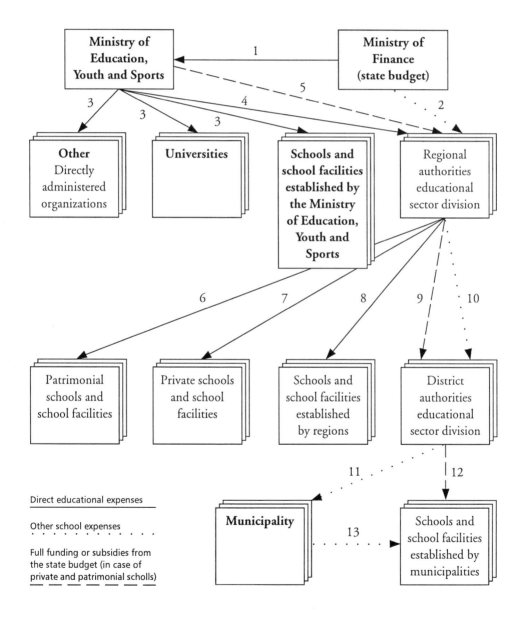

Figure 4.2
Scheme of Financial Flow After the Reform

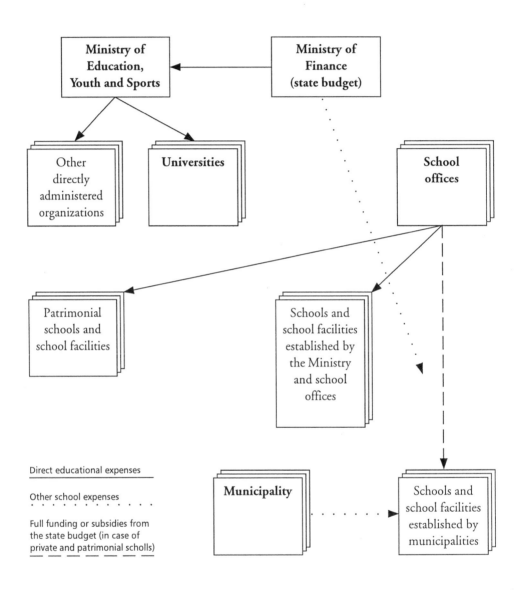

The decision-making of schools regarding the use of revenues from the rental of available commercial space is limited in case of state property. Pursuant to generally binding legal provisions, the revenues from sale and rental of state property must be contributed to the state budget. Thus, schools located in buildings that are state property have no incentive to use these buildings for other purposes. If the school claims that there are justified unplanned investment or non-investment needs, the state can decide about the use of the gained funds for an approved plan. In case of municipal property, the decision-making rules for schools concerning the complementary income from the rental of available space are different. Municipalities usually let schools use the gained funds for repairs and the maintenance of buildings or the partial financing of investment needs or further development of schools, e.g. purchase of teaching tools for pupils that go beyond the normal standards. If the municipality is too generous with respect to the decision-making by schools on the income from rental, it can also be counterproductive. The management of the school could rent out the available room as commercial space to the detriment of hobby activities of pupils in the afternoon, and therefore the hobby activities will be eliminated at the school.

4.   EFFECTIVENESS, FAIRNESS, AND EFFICIENCY OF EDUCATION

As far as the effectiveness is concerned, the two-way financing of basic schools and kindergartens plays a negative role in the current situation with the current responsibility sharing. Direct educational expenses are financed from the state budget and municipalities finance other expenses of these schools.

The two-way financing has negative impact in two basic areas.

The first one is the different approach to the financing and prosperity of schools of institutions administered by the state and local self-governments. It is natural that there is a different approach to a certain school. State officials focus on the effective allocation of funds within the region. The local authorities stress the development and prosperity of the school. This approach has negative impact. If the school saves funds allocated to the municipality and distributes them to the remuneration fund within the framework of the improved economic results and plans on using them as an incentive for extraordinary work of teaching staff, the state body will reduce the contribution from the state budget by a part or the entire amount of funds transferred to the remuneration fund since the state body has a different approach to the priorities of the region. In this case, the local authorities subsidize the school budget in the area of direct educational expenses, which the state if responsible for, without raising the standards of the school. It is logical that the municipality reacts negatively to this and will stop supporting the school in the area of personal expenses and increasing its standards. This fact can have negative effect on the positive cooperation between the school and the establishing entity.

The second case is the problematic classification of school expenses. For example, it is not possible to determine what the item the school plans on buying will serve for example if it will predominantly serve as a teaching tool or part of the school equipment. Thus, the school is unable to decide what sources should be used. Sometimes, the school buys a tape recorder that the director uses in the morning to listen to the radio news or to play music for the school radio, and at the same time the tape recorder is used by a teacher for music classes. What is the school buying? Is it a teaching tool or equipment of the director's office? How to proceed, if the school uses a copy machine purchased from the municipal funds to copy parts of textbooks? What funds did the school use when it bought an antenna system for a television used during classes? There are dozens of similar examples.

Another important problem is the employment of technical-economic employees by state institutions and their work related to areas for which the municipality is responsible, as discussed before.

It would not be useful to describe partial problems occurring as a result of the two-way financing of basic schools and kindergartens in the Czech Republic.

Unfortunately, the new system of the public administration of the educational sector will keep the two-way financing of basic schools and kindergartens despite different opinions of politicians on the state and local level.

Capacities of the municipality as establishing entity are the best prerequisite for meeting the local needs of the municipality. An example would be the opening hours of kindergartens and day-care centers. It would be difficult to determine the opening hours of such institutions centrally. It is not possible not to mention that the responsibility of local self-governments has a political dimension as well. A good and prospering school in a municipality should be one of the basic points on the agenda of a successful mayor of politician in the local self-government. Teachers and parents of pupils are also voters.

The municipality can keep a good teacher in the municipality, for example by providing him/ her with a municipal apartment or accommodation.

Municipalities respond more sensitively to the existing needs in the area of leisure time of children and youth and can ensure that the school and teaching staff are more involved in providing leisure opportunities for children and youth. Questions are raised, for example why should a school playground be empty in the afternoon or why should it not be used by adult athletes?

4.1 Possible Impact of the New System of School Administration

Central school administration was carried out by the Ministry of School, Youth, and Sports through the school offices. They also decided about the allocation of funds and directly supervised the directors of schools and decided about their appointment and dismissal. The school office gave orders and instructions to the individual schools.

The school office prepared statements for the entire region. At the same time, it took the necessary measures according to the report of the school inspection.

If the school is not a legal entity, it distributes wages and takes care of the accounting within the framework of its budget.

The school office is also responsible for the used state funds, and therefore it prepared improvement projects. This measure proved right since the first improvement measures were only based on statistical data collected by the Ministry of Education, Youth, and Sports, and was not effective. The school office could evaluate possible mergers or establishments of schools since it was familiar with the situation in the region.

The new system of school administration due to the new division of the Czech Republic in regions transfers these competencies to the elected regional bodies. These bodies will probably administer schools from the perspective of regional needs. It will probably give preference to schools and apprenticeship schools the completion of which will guarantee marketability of pupils. It is not clear how these bodies will approach schools the graduates of which will not have many work opportunities in the region, which are, however, the only school of their kind in the Czech Republic to which pupils have to commute, need housing, and so on.

Basic funds for the operation of such schools—predominantly wages—will be bound on funds to be allocated for certain purposes. The regional bodies will give preference to those types of schools that they will consider key.

Since they will be the establishing entity of those schools, they will have the right to abolish or establish them. Thus, the regional interests in the school sector are getting stronger to the detriment of the policy interests on the state level.

4.2 The Decrease in Population and the Impact on Schools

The population curve is currently decreasing. Thus, the number of children completing school is falling. There is an advantage for teachers, however. Classes are not as full any more and it is possible to work with pupils individually. The disadvantage is the economic part—financing per number of students. The positive effect of the decrease in the number of pupils is the competition for pupils, which leads to an increase in quality of education the schools offer in order to attract pupils that do not live in the surrounding area. This way, the position of high-quality schools is strengthened. Schools in which the education has lower quality are negatively affected by this development. The establishing entity has to make improvements or abolish the school.

This is the case in larger towns where there are more schools available. Schools in towns and municipalities where there is only one school and where it is not possible to gain more pupils are negatively affected by the decrease in population. It is not possible to abolish the school, for example because the transportation situation does not allow for the merger of two schools.

In the case of secondary schools, there are attempts to keep the capacity of the existing school. Therefore, the ratio of the applying and accepted pupils is changing—the number of accepted students is relatively increasing. This is the case at secondary schools that are not very prestigious. The lack of pupils leads to the introduction of new courses of study at secondary schools (complementary classes, additional classes, executive studies, and so on).

According to the Ministry of Education, Youth, and Sports, the number of pupils has decreased but the number of teaching hours has not been reduced.

4.3 Integration of Handicapped Children and Ethnic Minorities

Handicapped children can be integrated in kindergartens or basic schools only on the basis of an evaluation of a special pedagogical center (SPC) or a pedagogical-psychological consulting center (PPCC). The evaluation includes the type and level of handicap, the validity of the evaluation, the name of a SPC or PPCC employee that the teaching staff will work with during the integration of the pupil. Also an educational program for the child to be integrated is prepared. Individual educational program specifies special methods of work with the pupil, the reduction of the number of pupils in the class, and special material conditions necessary for the pupil. The responsible school office provides a school that includes such a pupil in statistical statements with funds allocated based on the prepared program. The documents to be submitted include the balance sheet regarding funds for wages and the provision of material prerequisites of education of handi-capped pupils integrated into a group of healthy children.

In towns where there are 25 to 30 children in a class classes for integrated pupils are predominantly formed in the first grades. In higher grades children are integrated into the group of children without handicaps. Classes for integrated pupils have approximately half of the usual number of children (about 12 children). This makes it possible to teaching staff to approach the pupils individually. At higher educational levels, these children are no more excluded from the group of children of the same age. The integration of handicapped children among healthy children is of great social importance.

The ethnic Roma group deserves special attention in the Czech Republic. Preparatory classes for children from social-culturally disadvantaged background have been tested. Children who were immature with respect to their social or communicative skills attended these classes. In order to overcome obstacles related to communication and adaptation, the class teacher had an assistant who was familiar with the background of the pupils—an assistant who was part of the Roma community. The Ministry of Education, Youth, and Sports recommends to basic and special schools in regions where the majority of pupils are children from the Roma ethnic group to form an office of the Roma assistant. Pursuant to existing legal provisions, the minority educational system can exist up to the secondary school level. Such schools are established for the Polish and Slovak minority.

4.4 Basic Schools in Villages

Schools administered by the municipality have played an important role in the development of the Czech Republic. The establishment of a school was highly recognized by the public and increased the prestige of the village compared to others. Even today, many believe that a school makes the municipality more visible and this is why schools exits even in municipalities where they are not really needed (for example when there is another school in the surrounding area, which is larger and better equipped, and the transportation system allows for commuting). The existence of these small and expensive schools is possible thanks to two types of financing of these schools in villages. The municipality remains the establishing entity and thus continues the historical tradition of the educational system in our country. It covers operational expenses, investment expenses, and material expenses. This is subject to law. The state provides through the school offices funds for wages of teaching staff (teachers and educators) and employees other than teaching staff (maids, boiler man, maintenance workers, administrative employees, cooks). The municipalities very often establish 'incomplete' schools that are referred to as small-class schools for pupils up to the 5th grade. Pupils attending different grades are part of the same class. Less frequently, municipalities establish incomplete schools in which there is a class for each grade. After 1989, the number of basic schools increased, which was mainly due to the re-establishment of this type of schools. (They accounted for 80% of the total number of new schools). Currently they account for 40% of all basic schools and the number of pupils attending them accounts for 8.5% of the total number of basic school pupils. There are also 'complete' schools attended by pupils from the 1st to the 9th grade where grade 1 to 5 can be combined into one class. This means that the smallest complete schools have 6 classes. The directors of basic schools are responsible for the establishment of grades without any limitations posed by the state administration. Thus, the combination and organization of the individual classes can greatly differ within a smaller self-governing unit (for example class I is attended by pupils from the 1st, 3rd, and 4th grade at one school; at another school class I is attended by pupils from the 1st, 2nd, and 4th grade) The organization of grades (for example the rule that pupils start taking foreign language classes in the 4th grade) is regulated only by pedagogical criteria, not legal regulations. The basic criteria concerns the size of classes, which is ruled by a decree issued by the Ministry of Education, Youth, and Sports determining the minimal number of children per class with respect to the organization of the school (number of pupils per class at different types of schools: incomplete with combined grades—13 pupils, incomplete 15 pupils, complete—17 pupils). At kindergartens and basic schools, the number of children can decrease below the number of children determined by decrees of the Ministry of Education, Youth, and Sports. In this case, two solutions are possible. The municipality can decide to keep the facility and submit a request to the Ministry of Education, Youth, and Sports. It can commit to cover the part of wages and deductions in question. If approved, the school continues to function without any organizational changes. If the school does not make the commitment to cover the wage expenses, the school might be abolished or organizational changes might be carried out that would not increase the expenses to be covered by the Ministry of Education, Youth, and Sports. The total expenses per pupil range between CZK 13 000 and CZK 19 000 per school year. The exact amount is calculated based on the salaries of teaching staff working at the school. In some municipalities, keeping a school currently costs hundreds of thousands of Czech crowns.

Children attending incomplete schools that are referred to as small-class schools are more independent, they are able to concentrate on their work much better, since the class is organized in the form of group teaching. The lower number of children in a class is also positive since the teacher can approach the pupils individually. The fact that the age structure is heterogeneous is also positive. Children from different age groups are part of the same class. Among the negative factors are clearly the higher expenses per pupil. There are different opinions concerning the quality of classes. It depends on the capabilities of the teacher much more than in other schools. The municipality uses the school building for events it organizes (elections, meetings of the municipal council). The teacher in a municipality is usually involved in the municipal boards and is an embodiment of culture and education, much more so than in towns. This is also due to the fact that the school is one of the important items within the budgets of individual municipalities. The council uses the knowledge of teachers with respect to legal issues to solve problems in the educational sector and to set priorities for the financing of operating expenses.

In connection with the new self-governing organization of the Czech Republic, it is increasingly important that a school established by the municipality is a legal entity. All secondary schools in the Czech Republic are legal entities. As far as the basic schools and kindergartens are concerned, some of them are legal entities, others are not. Schools that are legal entities can act under their own name and on their own responsibility in legal matters within the limited determined by the establishing entities. As to schools that are not a legal entity, the state administration fulfills this task through school offices. The establishing entity is partly involved as well. The directors of schools that are legal entities are statutory bodies and are entitled to take legal action under the name of the school. The directors of schools that are not legal entities can only take legal action within the framework determined by law for the execution of state administration in the educational sector. In all other legal relations, the director acts on behalf of the school office or the establishing entity. Upon the introduction of the new administration organization, the capacities of the state administration might be transferred to the municipal councils. As of 1 January 2000, schools established by the state will be administered by higher self-governing units (e.g. secondary schools, special schools). Schools established by municipalities will be administered by the responsible district authorities for a limited period of time.

4.5 Private Schools

The existence of private schools in the Czech Republic is very problematic and it is a subject of many discussions. There is an opinion that there are no private schools. Truly private schools should not receive any subsidies from the state. Therefore, we can only speak about schools that were established by a private establishing entity. Currently, private establishing entities are in a favorable position compared to schools established by the state or municipalities since they can charge tuition, which usually corresponds with the amount per pupil calculated by the state. The same rules should be valid for a private establishing entity as for the state or a municipality in the role of establishing entities. Pursuant to legal provisions, state and municipality as establishing entities must cover the expenses pertaining to the operation of the school.

The new school code will take this fact into account. It plans on introducing a special legal form, the 'school legal entity,' which is unprecedented in the Czech Republic and in other European countries, and is still to be defined in greater detail. The proposed change should bring more order into the existing variety of possible legal forms, and give both equal rights and obligations to all schools regardless of the establishing entity. This is also in response to the request of private schools to receive state subsidies, calling for equal rights. However, the obligations of private schools, e.g. towards their pupils are subject to different legal norms than the obligations of other schools, which are established by the state or municipality. Private schools can be abolished by a decision of the establishing entity. There are no legal provisions that would prevent that as it is the case with respect to schools established by the state of municipality. In such a situation, the pupils can only go to the court and claim their contractual rights. This process might last for a year or two. They can also ask the school administration for help. Even though the school administration has no legal obligations to do so, it would enable the pupils to complete their studies at one of the available state schools and cover the necessary expenses. This should not happen in the new system of equal obligations. Only upon this change, it would be right to speak about the equal access to subsidies from public budgets.

Private schools are members of the Association of Private Schools of Bohemia, Moravia, and Silesia. The chairman of the association represents them when making claims. Two thirds of Czech private schools are members of this association. Unlike the state schools, they can usually assert themselves when making claims. The new law on financing is a good example of this.

However, private schools are under strict control within the educational sector. NKÚ reports on unjustified use of subsidies or monitoring of the uneconomical use of state funds are discussed very frequently. However, the evaluation sometimes concerns only individuals and not the private school as a whole even though the opposite impression is sometimes made. These problems should be solved by the introduction of mandatory audits. Last year, audits were conducted at all private schools requesting higher subsidies. Pursuant to valid regulations, a negative evaluation of the auditor results in the termination or return of state subsidies. Private schools can only survive if they can offer high-quality education. According to recent reports of the Czech School Inspection, 61% of schools were evaluated as excellent or good. Almost 11% of schools had the highest score and were evaluated as excellent. Only 6.5% of state schools were given such a score. On the other hand, 6% of private schools were evaluated as "still satisfactory," which is the second last level of the scale used by the Czech School Inspection. Only 2.8% of state school had such a negative evaluation.

The budget proposal for the educational sector plans on raising the subsidies for private schools by a third in 2001 despite the fact that the total number of pupils at private schools has decreased. This increase would mean a hope of stability for decent private schools. It would mean that schools would not have to raise the tuition, and parents would not have to pay such high contributions for the financing of the operation of the school. The ideal of providing higher standards could finally become reality. Nowadays, some schools offer higher standards to a certain extent, other schools not at all. Some schools even lag behind the standards. The above mentioned approach to the use of raised subsidies is the only way how to stop the decrease in applicants that was evident this year. This also had financial reasons. However, this idea could be changed if the proposal to give establishing entities the same rights and obligations is passed. According to this proposal, a private establishing entity just as any other establishing entity would cover the operational expenses of the school that have been subsidized so far. In the end, it would be the parents who would have to pay more since the tuition would have to be raised by 30% as a result of this amendment.

The regional organization in 2001 should not have any radical consequences for private schools. It will be rather formal. The financing of private schools is subject to a separate law that was amended within the package of laws related to the public administration reform. The contractual relationships will be transferred from school offices to regional bodies.

The existence and workings of private schools as a competition element or an educational alternative to the state schools plays an indispensable role in the educational sector. It is also very important for the country with respect to the integration in the European Union.

The provision of subsidies to private schools is subject to Law No. 306/1999 Coll. on Provision of Subsidies to Private Schools, Pre-Primary and School Facilities. Based on this law, the following rules are valid for private schools that want to be subsidized:

- the school must be registered in the school network of the Ministry of Education, Youth, and Sports;

- subsidies are provided for the financing of non-investment expenses related to education and the usual operation of the school or facility;

- the school must file an application with the school office (in the future the regional office) to conclude a contract on the provision of subsidies;

- in addition to the application, the prerequisite of the conclusion of the contract is the timely submission of accounting documents for the subsidies provided in the previous year, annual report on activities, annual report on management, (records of related discussions in the school board, if applicable) to the school office.

The subsidy amount is determined on the basis of the real number of students taking theoretical classes or attending apprenticeship training. The maximum number of students that can be claimed is, however, the number specified in the official document of the Ministry of Education, Youth, and Sports concerning the registration in the school network. The calculation is also made based on the percentage of the normative costs such as non-investment expenses, funds for wages, and mandatory deduction per pupil completing a course of study in a comparable form at a school established by the state.

The basic subsidy includes:
- Special schools and apprenticeship school: 80% of the normative costs;
- Basic schools: 60% of the normative costs;
- Secondary schools and higher vocational schools: 60% of the normative costs;
- Special facilities: 80% of the normative costs;
- Other schools and facilities: 60% of the normative costs.

Raised subsidies include:
- Special schools and apprenticeship schools: 100% of the normative costs;
- Basic schools: 100% of the normative costs;
- Secondary schools and higher vocational schools: 90% of the normative costs;
- Special facilities: 100% of the normative costs;
- Other schools and facilities: 100% of the normative costs.

Prerequisites for the raised subsidies are:
- The school meets the prerequisites for the provision of the basic subsidy and has been functioning for at least a year;
- The evaluation of the Czech School Inspection is "good" or better;
- The school is a non-profit organization or it has made a contractual commitment to use the entire profits for the calendar year for educational expenses.

4.6 Apprenticeship Schools

One of the characteristics of the financing of apprenticeship schools in the Czech Republic was the maintenance of previous bonds to organizations (former state-owned companies) for which the pupils would work upon the completion of their training.[1] Funds for financing of these schools would originate from three basic sources:

- The budget of the educational sector;

- Other sources of schools and school facilities providing professional training;

- Funds originating from legal and physical entities for which the pupils would work upon the completion of their training.

All schools and other state organizations have the first two sources in common. However, as far as other sources are concerned, there is an important element at apprenticeship schools, "productive work of pupils" existing due to the specific character of these educational programs.

The third source is typical for apprenticeship schools.

In an ideal situation—if all students were trained for a job provided by a concrete physical or legal entity—all three sources would be balanced (of course, wages would differ in the individual fields, and so would the operational expenses and opportunities to gain income from the productive work of pupils).

This means that apprenticeship schools as a whole could cover about 30–40% of total expenses per pupil from each of the sources.

The main problem of the current financing of expenses at apprenticeship school is the fact that the financing by physical and legal entities has been decreasing. This is due to the continuing increase in the percentage of pupils that are referred to as 'state pupils' (these pupils are not trained to work for a concrete physical or legal entity). The number of such pupils has increased by almost 30% in the last five years (from about 66% in 1994 to about 95% in 1999).

As a result, the state has had to cover the educational expenses, accommodation, and catering of pupils instead of the future employers. Thus, expenses covered from the state budget have increased considerably.

The change of the individual types of financing has not been taken into account during the preparation of the state budget. Therefore, there are considerable deficits in the financing of operational expenses in the regional educational sector as a whole. Ministry of Education, Youth, and Sports has been distributing this decrease in financing evenly in the entire regional educational sector, so it has not affected only the vocational or apprenticeship schools.

As opposed to the ideal situation, the percentage of funds from the individual sources used for the financing of the apprenticeship schools is as follows: the budget for the educational sector covers about 60% of expenses, income from the own activities amount to about 30%, future employers cover only about 2%, and the remaining 8% are a deficit that cannot be covered by the educational sector. This leads to debts in the educational sector (affecting especially the area of innovation, maintenance, and replacement of property).

The current situation in the sector of apprenticeship schools is close to the model of full financing of the pupils' professional training from the state budget. Both the apprenticeship sector and the labor market have been negatively affected by many aspects of this model.

The elimination of the category 'pupil trained for work for a concrete physical or legal entity' and the transfer of responsibility for financing of apprenticeship schools to the state and the use of other resources of schools and school facilities is the seemingly easiest solution to the existing problems at the vocational schools. However, there is a danger that the gap between the content and structure of education at apprenticeship schools and the real needs of the labor market will continue to grow, in addition to the necessity to expand the budget for the educational sector. For this reason, this solution is not acceptable as a final solution of the existing problems. It is necessary to look for other sources of financing and more effective ways to use the available funds.

The apprenticeship schools are financed according to the same rules as theoretical courses of study at secondary schools.

The financing of the regional educational sector as a whole has been defined in such a detailed manner that is unprecedented in the history of the financing of the educational sector by the state. The normative method of financing the teaching based on the need for teaching is one of the most transparent forms of financing in the entire budget. The calculation is based on the number of teaching hours per week, the number of pupils in a class (the 'yellow book'), and is valid for the entire regional educational sector including apprenticeship schools. The method of combining the normative method with the financing of operational expenses of state schools (regardless of the type and kind of the school), which has used since 1999, increases the transparency and the effectiveness of financing to an extent that is very close to the maximum. Detailed financial statements on the needs and sources are prepared and consulted up to the level of the individual expense items.

One of the main reasons of the existing problems at vocational schools but mainly at apprenticeship schools is the low number of students due to the lacking interest of pupils and their parents in this type of studies, the lacking interest of employers to motivate the children to complete training in a particular field. This holds true with respect to the actual training, but also the future job opportunities. Furthermore, the situation in the industrial sector is getting worse. Many companies go bankrupt or face considerable financial problems.

In the current situation, which is influenced by the existing legal regulations, the preparation of new legal norms for the educational sector (educational law, new budget regulations, public administration and self-administration etc.), and the current state of financing, the solution to the financing of the vocational school sector (including apprenticeship schools) has to be considered at two basic levels:

- the educational standards guaranteed (and financed) by the state to be maintained even after the establishment of regional self-governments;

- the creation and allocation of complementary sources for the financing of the vocational schools meeting the development and innovation needs of this type of education and guaranteeing the necessary interconnection of the educational programs with the needs of the labor market. Employers should continue to influence this development.

ANNEX 1

Basic Comparative Data from Czech School Office (1990 and 1995)

- The percentage of expenses in the educational sector covered from public budgets increased from about 4% in 1990 to 6% in 1990.

- These were the following changes between school year 1990/1991 and 1995/1996:

    — The number of children in kindergartens fell by 5%.

    — The number of female teachers decreases by 13%

    — The number of schools dropped by 13%.

    — The number of pupils in basic schools decreased by 16%.

    — The number of teachers has not changed noticeably.

    — The number of schools increased by more than 6%.

    — The number of pupils in grammar schools increased by 20%, the number of grammar school teachers increased by 42%, and the number of grammar schools increased by more than 58%.

    — In the school year 1995/96, more than a fifth of all pupils at vocational schools and 11% of pupils in grammar schools did not attend state schools.

ANNEX 2

State Expenses for Kindergartens, Basic and Secondary Schools

Table 4A.1

Expenses in the Educational Sector 1998 [millions of CZK]

	Kindergartens	Basic Schools	Secondary Schools	Secondary Vocational Schools	Secondary Apprentice-ship Schools	Total
Expenses	5 088	17 816	3 279	7 251	7 402	40 836
% of GDP	0.28	0.99	0.18	0.40	0.41	2.27
% of SB	0.95	3.32	0.61	1.35	1.38	7.61
Expenses	2 461	8 023	128	81	11	10 704
% of LB	1.53	5.00	0.08	0.05	0.01	6.68
% of GDP	0.14	0.45	0.01	0.00	0.00	0.60
Total expenses	7 549	25 389	3 407	7 332	7 413	51 540
% of GDP	0.42	1.44	0.19	0.41	0.41	2.87

GDP: Gross Domestic Product
SB: State Budget
LB: Local Budget

ANNEX 3

Educational Expenses

Table 4A.2
Educational Expenses

	1993	1994	1995	1996	1997	1998
Educational expenses in % of GDP	5.3	5.5	5.3	5.3	4.8	4.5
Expenses of the State Budget	356.9	380.1	432.7	484.4	524.7	566.7
Share of educational expenses in % of State Budget	15	16.6	16.6	16.9	15	14.2

ANNEX 4

Average Income of Teachers

Table 4A.3

Average Income of Teachers in % of GDP per Person [in usual prices]

	School Year 1997/98		School Year 1998/99	
	Salary per Employee [CZK]	% of GDP on One Inhabitant 1998	Salary per Employee [CZK]	% of GDP per Person 1999
Kindergartens	97 752.79	55.96	101 690.33	56.94
Basic Schools	127 031.79	72.72	133 128.85	74.55
Grammar Schools	146 747.35	84.01	151 556.15	84.87
Secondary Vocational Schools	143 573.87	82.19	150 004.10	84.00
Secondary Apprenticeship Schools	129 406.44	74.08	136 353.72	76.35
Total	128 902.45	73.79	134 546.63	75.34

ANNEX 5

Number of Pupils and Teachers

Table 4A.4
Number of Pupils and Teachers

Number of Pupils	Number of Teachers	Number of Pupils per Teacher
BASIC SCHOOLS		
1 195 000	63 110	18.94
1 166 000	64 072	18.20
1 115 000	65 186	17.10
1 061 000	63 767	16.64
1 028 000	63 531	16.18
1 005 000	63 019	15.95
1 100 000	69 578	15.81
1 092 000	65 259	16.73
1 082 000	65 370	16.55
1 071 000	67 678	15.82
GRAMMAR SCHOOLS		
111 006	7 135	15.56
113 450	7 050	16.09
117 765	8 402	14.02
122 171	8 965	13.63
127 828	10 057	12.71
133 093	10 903	12.21
126 424	10 987	11.51
126 575	10 419	12.15
126 137	10 284	12.27
127 500	10 749	11.86

Table 4A.4 (continued)
Number of Pupils and Teachers

Number of Pupils	Number of Teachers	Number of Pupils per Teacher
SECONDARY VOCATIONAL SCHOOLS		
190 569	12 889	14.79
191 298	12 798	14.95
201 209	14 537	13.84
219 249	16 854	13.01
247 083	17 310	14.27
259 419	18 458	14.05
205 028	16 563	12.38
200 367	14 989	13.37
191 512	17 584	10.89
180 114	17 296	10.41

ANNEX 6

List of Basic Laws

Educational Sector:

1. Law No. 29/1984 Coll. on System of Basic Schools, Secondary Schools –Higher Vocational Schools, as amended.

2. Law No. 564/1990 Coll. on Public Administration and Self-Administration in the Educational Sector, as amended.

3. Decree No. 35/1991 Coll. on Kindergartens, as amended.

4. Decree No. 291/1991 Coll. on Kindergartens, as amended.

5. Decree No. 354/1991 Coll. on Secondary Schools, as amended.

6. Decree No. 353/1991 Coll. on Private Schools, as amended.

7. Decree No. 452/1991 Coll. on the Establishment and Activities of Patrimonial Schools and Schools of Religious Communities, as amended.

Management of Schools:

1. Law No. 218/2000 Coll. on Budgetary Rules (Organization Established by State Institutions)

2. Law No. 250/2000 Coll. on the Budgetary Rules of Territorial Budgets (Organizations Established by Municipalities and Regions)

NOTE

[1] The current situation with respect to the financing of apprenticeship schools as described in a document of the Ministry of Education, Youth, and Sports—*Current Problems of Apprenticeship Schools.*

CHAPTER 5

Education Management and Finance in Slovakia

Peter Berčik
Ladislav Haas
Anita Lehocká
Peter Zvara

Table of Contents

Introduction 261

1.   Basic Data on Education 263
    1.1 Demographic Trends 266
    1.2 Level of Education 267

2.   Organisation and Management of Education 268
    2.1 Constitutional Guarantees of Education 268
    2.2 School System in the Slovak Republic 269
        2.2.1 Primary Schools 270
        2.2.2 Secondary Schools 271
        2.2.3 Educational Facilities 271
        2.2.4 Special Schools 273
        2.2.5 Current Changes in Primary and Secondary Education 273
    2.3 State Administration in the Area of Education 274
        2.3.1 Organization of State Administration 274
        2.3.2 School Director and Head of Educational Facility 276
        2.3.3 District Office and Regional Office 276
        2.3.4 State School Inspection 278
        2.3.5 Ministry of Education of the Slovak Republic 278
    2.4 School Self-government 279

3.   Quality of Upbringing and Education Process 281

4.   Quantitative Development of Education 283
    4.1 Kindergartens 284
    4.2 Primary Schools 286
    4.3 Grammar Schools 288
    4.4 Secondary Vocational Schools 290
    4.5 Secondary Vocational Apprentice Centres 292
    4.6 Special Schools 295

4.7   Primary Schools of Art 295

4.8   Educational Facilities 296

     4.8.1   Upbringing Prevention and Substitute Upbringing 298

     4.8.2   Services in the Area of Interest Study 299

     4.8.3   Services to Schools and Educational Facilities 300

5.   Personnel 300

     5.1   Age Structure of Teachers 302

     5.2   Teacher's Qualification 302

     5.3   Legal Status and Salary Conditions 304

     5.4   Rate of Educational Duty 306

     5.5   Trade Unions in the Area of Education 306

6.   Public Finances 307

7.   Financing Education 309

     7.1   Current System of Education Financing 309

     7.2   Education Expenditures 312

     7.3   State Budget Expenditures on Education 315

     7.4   Municipal Financing of Education 318

     7.5   Decentralization of Education Management and Financing 321

8.   Conclusion 322

Sources 325

Annex 1:   Structure of School Education in the Slovak Republic
     and its Classification in ISCED Structure According to UNESCO 326

Annex 2:   Excerpt from Draft of the Act on Financing of Primary
     and Secondary Schools and Educational Facilities 332

Annex 3:   Tables 340

Notes 362

INTRODUCTION

The goal of this study is to present the basic introductory information on organization, management and system of financing of regional education[1] in the Slovak Republic serving as a basis for comparative study, which will compare with the situation in Czech Republic, Hungary and Poland.

With regard to this circumstances it may be useful to present the short introductory characteristics of development in the last decade as well as current state of education in the Slovak Republic in a context of overall social, economic and political development.

To meet this goal the selected parts of introduction to comprehensive publication dealing with situation in education area in Slovakia are quoted.

There are many urgent issues and questions in relations between economy, education and upbringing. The most substantial include:

- *relation between economy and education in conditions of transition to market economy as well as in 'pure' market conditions;*

- *economic approaches to labor, human resources development and education questions;*

- *current economic paradigm, state and performance of economy as a real upbringing environment and many others.*

Apart from specifics of modification of the 'Slovak approach,' the transformation of economy has had a severe impact or will have an impact on education, especially in a way that:

- *the decline of economy performance in a transformation process causes a decrease of investments on schooling, upbringing and education;*

- *the school has been left without clear upbringing concept and ideal, which would give framework and overall meaning to the upbringing and education process;*

- *the hierarchy and importance of social and personal dimensions and meanings of education has started to change. The existing services, upbringing institutions and their performance are being reduced, they are shifted to over-standard category (some services in the area of education offered in previous regime without any limitations free of charge or for a very small fee are gradually being reduced or paid in market prices), and so on. The social differentiation in education, so far in modest form, has occurred sooner than the citizens were able to asses their requirements, skills, possibilities and ambitions in the transformation process. The market type components are coming into education, although the education market has not been fully created and stabilised yet. In reality, it has not started to function;*

- *the pressure on performance parameters of education according to momentary needs of the labor market is increasing;*

- *the working force demand is decreasing and the future need of qualified employees is not clearly formulated;*

- *the new mechanism of redistribution of financial means on upbringing and education as well as structure, organization and mechanism of functioning of school administration are activating changes in organization and management of education;*

- *envisaged integration to European and other structures is causing the increasing need for integration tendencies in schooling, upbringing and education.*

The influence of the transformation process in the whole society on regional education was not systematic. The positive changes were implemented gradually, mostly in the content of education and upbringing at all types and kinds of regional schools. The content changes may be found in innovated, or completely new educational plans and curricula as well as in a new or integrated study and vocational specialization or even in a new type of school (grammar schools with 8 year study programs, vocational schools, adjusted system of vocational preparation in secondary vocational apprentice centers, higher vocational schools, and so on). At the beginning, the effort to innovate the content of education was concentrated on removal of ideological and political influences on the content of education coming from the socialist school."

At the other end of the scale serious problems appeared in education management, but mainly in the quality of financial management. Due to objective reasons the economic management of the school and educational facilities was not transferred to self-government in the time of its formation in 1990. This deviation from the standard of most European countries has not yet been solved. The whole education in the Slovak Republic is financed through the system of state administration. The permanent discussions are being held on the pros and cons of this state. It is difficult to make definite conclusion in the situation when the deficit of state budget increases constantly and the municipalities are in a difficult financial situation as well. The decentralization of education management to self-government is the priority task of the program of the current government."

"The quality and effectiveness of upbringing in a school is declining recently, even though, the need for good education, especially moral in the widest sense of this notion was never so topical as nowadays. The conditions for social forming have changed and are being changed in a radical way. The social environment differentiates very fast and brings beside the positive also a lot of negative aspects and influences, most of them not existing before, e.g. moral nihilism, sleight, thefts, cheating, corruption, bribery and delinquency. These and other negative occurrences are manifested in thinking, judgements and attitudes as well as in the behavior of children and young people.

The opening of the borders has brought together positive and negative impacts. The family environment of pupils differentiates from material, cultural and other points of view. In the mid 1990s the number of children attending the kindergartens has been falling, which has had negative impacts on moral education, readiness for school and overall culture.

The number of unemployed secondary school leavers is increasing together with social uncertainty. Unemployment often leads these young people to personal moral decay and criminality. The criminality of youth is increasing; drugs are being spread unexpectedly fast.

After 1989, the gap between the need for development of upbringing and education as an important and irreplaceable development factor and limited possibilities of state to invest to education necessary means for its optimal performance is being widened. The degree of quality of regional education, its increases and declines, differentiates between the regions. The development of regional education as a whole was surely not ascending. In the best case it would be possible to speak about the stagnation with the remarkable signs of decrease. If specific schools or kind of schools succeeded, they are exceptional cases, in which the accomplished result was at the expense of extreme effort of its employees. The key to the revitalization of education development is to ensure the appropriate financial resources, even though there is no direct relation between the allocated financial means for education and the increase of its performance and quality. The permanent growth of quality of education requires much more than financial means, but they are indispensable. The context of economic development is relentless and possibilities for allocation of resources on education are limited. The restrictive financial policy causes different limitations and sometimes also hardly reparable damages.

The quality of financial management is not sufficient, the conceptual work is being replaced by operational solving of indebtedness. To illustrate it with a metaphor, it is possible to say, that the fight for a new, democratic school is being changed to fear and fight a for survival." [2]

The above quotation illustrates the real situation in education in the Slovak Republic at the beginning of a new decade. The legislative activities of the current Ministry of Education allow the assumption that present problematic situation will be partially solved.

Firstly, it is necessary to say that the works on this study started in the second half of the year 2000. In that time, the statistical data on school year 2000/2001 were not available. Due to these reasons the study uses data for school year 1999/2000 and accountancy data for 1999.

1. BASIC DATA ON EDUCATION

The Slovak Republic is a country with an area of 49 035 sq. km and borders with the Czech Republic, Poland, Ukraine, Hungary and Austria. The territory of Slovakia lies at the altitude from 94 m to 2655 m above sea level.

As of 31 December 1999, there were 5 398 657 inhabitants resident in 2 883 municipalities in Slovakia, of which 136 had the status of a town and four were military districts. Over two-thirds of the total number of municipalities have a population less than 1 000. The majority of inhabitants are Slovaks (85.6%), followed by Hungarians (10.5%), Gypsies (1.5%), Czechs (1.1%), Ruthenians and Ukrainians (0.66%), Germans (0.1%) and other nationalities.

The Slovak Republic was established as an independent, sovereign state on 1 January 1993. Since the dissolution of the Czech and Slovak Federal Republic, Slovakia has focused on transforming a centrally controlled economy into a free market economy, reform of public administration, approval of constitutional laws and guarantees of fundamental human rights and freedoms and harmonization of the legal system to be consistent with the norms of the European Union.

The Slovak Republic is a parliamentary republic in which the Parliament plays a key role in relation to the executive and legislative branches.

The government is the supreme executive body. The central and local bodies of state administration are established by law. 15 line ministries and 10 other central bodies of state administration have been established.

The Ministry of Education of the Slovak Republic is the central body of state administration responsible for primary schools, secondary schools and universities, educational facilities, lifelong education, science and technology, area of information technology and state care of youth and sport. The State School Inspection reports to the Ministry of Education.

The first step of local public administration reform took place after the principal constitutional changes in the beginning of 1990. The self-government of municipalities and towns was renewed. Local state administration bodies and local self-government bodies have by virtue of law strictly separated competencies. At the same time co-ordination principles in the solving of particular situations (like territorial planning and emergency situations) are determined.

The territory of the Slovak Republic was from the administrative point of view divided into 8 regions and 79 districts as a result of further steps of public administration reform, which took place in 1996. The system of local state administration bodies consist of 8 regional and 79 district offices. These offices have integrated almost the whole local state administration, including financing of primary and secondary schools. Only tax offices, custom offices, military administration, inspection administration and some other bodies with specific tasks carry out their activities outside of these offices.

The regional office co-ordinates joint activities with other state administration authorities and territorial self-government bodies in providing for economic and social development of the territory, especially in encouraging healthy ways of living and in developing education, culture, tourism and state care of youth and physical education.

The financial deconcentration is substantial. The regional offices have taken over some functions from the level of ministries. Every regional office is an independent budgetary category of state budget and their budgetary means are determined by the Act on state budget. Total budget of the regional offices amounts approximately to 47.6 Billion Slovak Crowns (SKK)—approximately one-fifth of the total state budget. There are around 8 000 budgetary organizations (e.g. schools, hospitals, libraries and social care institutions) in the area of education, health care, social care and culture, which employ 149 000 employees.

Local self-government is constituted in municipalities, which are territorial and administrative units. Within the possibilities given by law municipalities may posses property and have their own budget. Local self-government may issue ordinances, which are binding on all individuals or corporate bodies within their jurisdiction. These ordinances may only be cancelled by the Constitutional Court or the National Council. The local self-governments may be delegated additional powers necessary for local administration, and these have to be financed by state funds. Interference with the powers of local authorities is possible only by law.

The local self-governments ensure mainly technical operation of municipalities, public order and infrastructure development on the territory. Within the limits of their budgetary resources they take care of social matters, local culture, sport and other local needs. Their competencies in the area of education are limited. They usually assist to solve emergency situations of school buildings and purchase the teaching aids and computers.

The bodies of municipality are the municipal assembly and the mayor. They are elected directly by citizens. The municipal assembly consisting of between 5 and 60 members decides on all crucial issues of municipality. The executive body of a municipality is a mayor. The local self-government bodies may freely associate with other local self-government bodies and thus create regional or interest-bound organizations. This option is used rarely by municipalities. In 2000, the Slovak Republic has ratified the European Charter of Local Self-government.

The Government of the Slovak Republic has committed itself to modernize and reform public administration. In April 2000, it has agreed with the decentralization of responsibilities of regional offices and district offices in the area of education, culture, social affairs and health to local self-government and self-government of higher territorial units. Eight regional councils were elected in December 2002 and will assume responsibility for secondary and vocational education during 2002. Municipalities will assume responsibility for basic and pre-school education also during 2002.

1.1 Demographic Trends

The Slovak Republic is undergoing the process of social and economic transformation, which is reflected also by change of several population development indicators that are coming closer to the values in the countries of western Europe. The indicators of those events and processes, which are influenced by individual population behavior (indicators of natality, fertility, marriages, divorces, migration) have shown rather significant changes.

In relative expression it means, that average annual increase went down from 0.96% (in period between 1970 and 1980) to 0.19% in the last decade, while the total increase of inhabitants is constantly falling. Internal migration of inhabitants is characterized by the significant decline of migration flow to cities, which is shown by the reduction in pace of urbanization. Decrease of migration activity in most Slovak cities is partially caused by relative depletion of demographic sources in some areas as well as by slowing down of collective housing development.

The age structure of inhabitants (see Table 5.1) has been changing especially during the last decade. The ratio of inhabitants of productive age increases permanently (at this time it amounts almost to 62% of population), significant changes may be observed in decreasing of population in pre-productive age (in 1970, population in age bracket 0–14 made up 27.3 % of the population in Slovakia, in 1998 (only 20.4%). The natural increase of inhabitants in the last three decades felt from 0.89% in 1980 to 0.08% in 1998.

Table 5.1
Changes in the Age Structure of Inhabitants in Slovakia and Women Representation

	Pre-productive Age [%]	Productive Age [%]	Post-productive Age [%]	Vitality Index [%]	Ageing Index [%]	Share of Women [%]
1970	27.3	56.3	16.4	166.46	60.07	50.65
1980	26.1	57.7	16.2	161.11	62.07	50.78
1991	24.9	57.4	17.6	141.48	70.68	51.22
1993	23.5	59.1	17.4	135.05	74.04	51.28
1994	22.9	59.6	17.5	130.85	76.42	51.29
1995	22.3	60.2	17.5	127.42	78.47	51.31
1996	21.7	60.7	17.6	123.29	81.11	51.32
1997	21.1	61.2	17.7	119.21	83.89	51.33
1998	20.4	61.8	17.8	114.61	87.25	51.35

SOURCE: Population development in the Slovak Republic, Bratislava (Statistical Office of the SR), 1999

The most important demographic trend is the process of aging of the Slovak population, accompanied by a decrease in the children's component (decrease in natality) and increase in number of inhabitants in post productive age (southern and western part of Slovakia has higher representation of post-productive groups of inhabitants). After 1989, Slovakia experienced a remarkable decrease in the number of births accompanied by increased number of single persons. The number of marriages and rate of marriages is decreasing permanently. The most serious problem from the demographic point of view seems to be bad health condition of population, which is reflected in a slow increase in average life expectancy.

1.2 Level of Education

In spite of partial deficiencies in the educational system in post-war decades and lack of resources during the last decade, the level of education of inhabitants of the Slovak Republic is rather high. The Education index according to the Human Development Report (1999) reached the rate 0.91, which is on the level of Greece, Portugal, Slovenia, Hungary and Czech Republic, and ranks in the third decile (ie between the 20th and 30th place) among all the countries in the world.

According to the census in 1991, 24.2% of the total number of inhabitants in age 15 and above finished comprehensive secondary education. The percentages reached in Bratislava (31.3%) and Košice (33.6%) were significantly above the standard; above the standard were also values reached in districts of Banská Bystrica (28.6%), Martin (27.1%) and Žilina (26.2%). Average and slightly above the average levels of secondary education were reached in districts along the development axis between Bratislava and Košice. The lowest levels occurred in geographically marginal and educationally not sufficiently saturated areas (Čadca, Senica, Dunajská Streda, Veľký Krtíš, Rimavská Sobota, Košice–vidiek). The data presented above reflects to a certain extent the fact that part of educated population leaves remote districts and moves to centers with better life opportunities. Because of this development the ratio between the secondary school leavers and citizens with lower education is worsening.

On average, 7.8% of inhabitants at the age of 15 and above had university education in 1991. The portion of inhabitants with the university education is highly above the standard in Bratislava (21.9%). The high level of education was observed also in Košice (13.8%) and Banská Bystrica (10.1%). Some districts with the university centers (Žilina, Martin, Nitra) have shown the values above the standard. On the other hand, strips of the southern districts have shown statistics below the average (Dunajská Streda, Komárno, Galanta, Nové Zámky, Veľký Krtíš, Lučenec, Rimavská Sobota, Rožňava, Košice–vidiek, Trebišov) and the same applies to marginal districts at the North (Čadca, Stará Ľubovňa, Bardejov). The portion of inhabitants with university education was lower than 5% in mentioned regions.

The educational level of inhabitants is remarkably differentiated not only according to location but also ethnic affiliation. The most significant difference is between the educational level of the Roma population and the majority population along with other minorities. For example in 1991, the ratio of inhabitants with secondary education was, in the case of the Roma population 0.5 %; in the Slovak population 18.1%; and in the Hungarian population 14.9%. In the case of the number of the population with university education this difference was also rather distinct (Roma 0.1%; Slovak 6.1%; and Czechs 16.0%).

Taking into account the above stated negative demographic trends on the Slovak territory, it is desirable to direct demographic development through the use of suitable tools by the state. An independent demographic policy in the Slovak Republic actually does not exist, although partial elements may be found in social, health care and regional policy. The present situation reflects continuous unfavorable conditions for demographic development in the Slovak Republic.[3]

2. ORGANIZATION AND MANAGEMENT OF EDUCATION

2.1 Constitutional Guarantees of Education

The provisions of the Constitution of the Slovak Republic guarantee to the citizens of the Slovak Republic the conditions for free education in state pre-school facilities, primary schools, secondary schools and educational facilities, in special schools or special educational facilities. The compulsory school attendance is finished after ten years of attendance or by accomplishing the age limit (16-year). Exemption from compulsory school attendance is not allowed.

Education of national minorities and ethnic groups is provided in the language of national minority or ethic group. The school or school facility could be established beside the state bodies also by church or religious societies, natural or legal persons. The bodies of local self-government (towns and communities) may establish only an educational facility. These schools and school facilities may charge money for the provided education.

Study at universities is enabled according to the abilities of the applicant. The full time study at the state universities is for free. The other forms of education may be charged. Apart from the state, natural or legal persons may also establish a university. In these cases their may be a charge for the education.

The citizens, during their education, and under certain conditions, have the right for state aid in the form of different kinds of scholarships (social and merit), or individual forms of education, and so on.

Every citizen has the right for the free choice of occupation or career, and the preparation involved in obtaining that occupation.[4]

2.2 School System in the Slovak Republic

Basic democratic principles of education in Slovakia are of historical nature with the roots in the 17th century. They originate in the work of the 'Teacher of the Nations' by Ján Amos Komenský (1592–1670). J.A. Komenský has reflected in his work democratic principles (for example, the access to education for all without gender or social discrimination; and compulsory school attendance), and developed in detail progressive methods and forms of upbringing and education. The general compulsory education came into being in the Austro-Hungarian Empire in the 19th century and Komenský's pedagogical ideas attracted at the same increased attention. His methods and forms of education were fully developed and introduced into practice in the 20th century regardless of political establishment in Slovakia and the former Czechoslovakia respectively.

The present school system in the Slovak Republic[5] came into being in 1948 as a so called 'Integrated School.' The latest substantial reform in education was implemented in 1960. Since that time some minor modifications concerning the length of compulsory school attendance and changes in content of education have taken place. Its democratic character, consistency and openness ensure the stability of the system. The democratic character implies that the education is accessible to every citizen irrespective of sex, religion, national or ethnic origin. The integrity means that the upbringing and education are functioning uniformly in harmonic and comprehensive education. The openness is guaranteed by the possibility to pass from one school to the other or pass from one type of school to other, in case of change of educational specialization or orientation the differential exams are required.

The primary and secondary schools provide upbringing and education on the basis of scientific knowledge in compliance with the patriotism, humanity and democratic principles. They provide moral, aesthetic, working, and health, ecological and physical education. At the same time they form the intellectual and moral development of pupils and students, prepare them for further study or the labor market. The religious education is enabled in alternative with ethical education and they both form an inseparable part of education process.

The schools exercise uniformity of upbringing and education, linkage of school with life and ensure comprehensive harmonic development of student personality. The training and education are delivered in a state language; the right for education in the nationality or ethnic language is guaranteed in adequate proportion necessary for their national development. Hearing and visually impaired have the right for education in their language with a use of gesture language or Braille's type.

The upbringing and education since the 5th grade at primary school and at secondary school may be carried out also in a foreign language on the basis of cultural agreement between the relevant state and the Slovak Republic and on the basis of Ministry of Education approval (bilingual grammar schools). The Slovak language and literature has to be included in the curricula of such school.

The education at the state primary and secondary schools is free of charge; anything other than state schools may be fee paying. The textbooks for compulsory subjects are lent to pupils free of charge.

The system of education and upbringing at primary and secondary schools consists of primary school, apprentice center, secondary vocational apprentice center, grammar school, secondary vocational school and special schools.

2.2.1   Primary Schools

The primary schools provide basic education. The primary school is divided into two levels, the first level are grades from 1 to 4 and the second level grades from 5 to 9.

The small class school is a school that does not have, on the first level, a separate class and teacher for each grade. The school that does not have all nine grades may be established in places in which the conditions do not allow the establishment of a school with all grades. The school may be organized so that the first four grades are in one class or that the first and the third grade come under one class and the second and the fourth grade under another one. The small class schools with grades between five and nine exist only in a limited number of cases. A class with one teacher may have at least two grades and at the most four grades in a class. There were 845 small class schools in the 1998/99 school year. There are some districts with 75% small class schools out of all directly managed schools (e.g. Rimavská Sobota, Bardejov districts). The pupils, who finished the last grade at such a school, should complete their compulsory school attendance at the primary school with all grades.

The small class schools appeared since the very beginning of the school system creation in Slovakia. The fully organized primary schools have appeared in urban areas as a result of industrialization. Within the last two decades small class schools have gone through the development and decay phases. These periods were closely related to economic development.

The results of education at the small class schools are similar to those achieved at fully organized schools. The evidence of this is successful continuation of pupils from small class schools in study at fully organized schools, where they achieve equal results (in grading) as the pupils of these schools. The official measurement has not taken place, the statement comes out from evaluations of pedagogic employees acting at the fully organized primary schools. However the conditions for education at these schools are much more difficult.

The role and position of small class schools, particularly in municipalities with small number of inhabitants is indisputable; however they are inefficient from the economic point of view. The costs of their operation and maintenance are comparable to fully organized schools. Their mission is not limited only to the provision of education, but also to the promotion and development of social life in the municipality. The social life has disappeared in municipalities, which closed the small class schools in the past. Therefore municipalities resist closure of these schools, and often subsidize them from their own budget.

2.2 2 Secondary Schools

The secondary schools provide secondary vocational education, complete secondary education, complete secondary vocational education and higher vocational education, and prepare students for occupation and study at universities.

The pupils and other applicants, who have successfully completed primary school according to their skills, knowledge, interests and health condition, have the right to study at the secondary schools. The study may be full-time, part-time or combined. The change of study or educational specialization, passage to other school, repetition of class or study suspension is also allowed.

The secondary schools are divided into the following categories:

- secondary vocational apprentice centers offers general education and vocational preparation. The study lasts between 2 and 4 years and is completed by successful final examination in study or vocational specialization.

- grammar school and secondary vocational school (prepares for study at the universities and provides training in some vocational activities) offers a broader and more in depth general education and professional differentiation according to type of secondary school. The study at grammar school lasts 4 or 8 years (the pupils completing 8 years at grammar school leave basic school after finishing the fourth grade), at secondary school 4 years, and is completed by successful final examination.

- art school (conservatoire) is specific type of secondary school, which prepares for the following specialization: music, canto, dance, dramatic arts and study at the university. The study usually lasts from six to eight years and is finished by 'absolutorium.'

The natural and legal persons for which students are trained at the secondary vocational apprentice centers established by the state should cover the expenditures of training beside the wage of pedagogic employees. The textbooks for compulsory subjects are lent to pupils for free.

2.2.3 Educational Facilities

The educational facilities are equivalent part of school educational system. Their activity is focused on area of upbringing and area of spare-time education.

The educational facilities are as follows:[6]

a) upbringing and educational facilities:

— pre-school facilities (kindergarten and special kindergarten);

— children school clubs, free-time centers;

— boarding houses;

— "schools in nature" (outdoor schools).

b) special upbringing facilities:

i) facilities of educational prevention, which are:

— educational and psychological prevention center;

— therapeutic and educational sanatorium;

— diagnostic center.

ii) facilities of alternative education, which are:

— re-educational children's homes;

— re-educational youth homes.

c) advisory facilities:

— pedagogical and psychological advisory service center;

— special pedagogical advisory service center;

— children's integration center.

d) free-time and education facilities:

— state language school;

— state stenographic institution.

e) specific educational facilities:

— school catering facilities (school kitchen, school canteens);

— school farms;

— practical education center;

— school services center;

— school computer center.

The state, church, religious associations, and municipalities, natural and legal persons may establish the educational facilities. The non-state facilities may be established only after Ministry of Education approval.

If a municipality or the state establishes the educational facility, it may be a budgetary or a subsidized organization, which may perform entrepreneurial activities in a compliance with its mission. The parents or persons responsible for the dependant shall contribute to some of the expenditures on education and services in selected educational facilities specified in legal regulation of Ministry of Education.

2.2.4   Special Schools

The special schools by using specific upbringing and educational methods, means and forms prepare handicapped pupils to join the society and working life. These schools include special primary and secondary schools, practical schools and vocational apprentice centers. The education obtained at these schools is not in all cases equal to education obtained at primary school and other secondary schools. The special primary schools have nine or ten grades.

The study at the special secondary schools may be prolonged by two years. They are divided into the following categories:

*   secondary vocational apprentice centers;
*   grammar schools;
*   secondary vocational schools;
*   practical schools.

The special apprentice centers prepare for occupation relevant to educational specialization. The preparation lasts between one and three years. The study is finished by final exam. The content of training is focused on the simple activity of those students, who are able to work individually, but whose working and social activities have to be guided by other persons.

The practical school provides education and preparation for simple working activities of pupils with mental handicaps, who finished special primary school or who were not admitted to the vocational apprentice center or special apprentice center or who were not able to cope with its content of education.

2.2.5   Current Changes in Primary and Secondary Education

The project of integrated schools and classes has been recently launched at the kindergartens and primary schools in the Slovak Republic. The aim is to place handicapped children between healthy population, which is to diminish or remove the handicap of those children.

At the primary schools the project of so called zero grades is being experimentally tested with the aim to improve the education and upbringing of the Roma population. The financial costs of its implementation are considerably higher than in case of regular schools where each class has two teachers and two tutors, who work with the pupils approximately for 8 hours in a day. This project is implemented at the schools in some districts with higher rate of Roma population (e.g. Košice, Spišská Nová Ves, Kremnica) with financial and methodological assistance of experts from the Netherlands.

In the case of primary and secondary schools the association (integration) of the schools was initiated with the aim of cost savings on school operation. The association is implemented on the basis of the strength of population in a given municipality (basic schools) or on the basis of affinity of study specialization. Thus the associated secondary schools are created which comprise e.g. secondary vocational school and secondary apprentice center of relevant specialization.

The topical problem in relation to present school system is the fulfilment of compulsory school attendance, which was in 1998 set to ten years and passes from primary to secondary school. The article No. 35 of the Constitution on free choice of occupation is violated in the case of pupils of primary school, who passed the entrance examination, but are not admitted to school due to insufficient room at the chosen secondary school. In the case of a higher number of appeals against this decision, the founder of the school has to open additional classes, which has a rather big negative impact on the state budget. This problem has not existed in the past, when the compulsory school attendance was fixed to nine-years.[7]

2.3 State Administration in the Area of Education

The area of education with regard to its specific position within the state administration has undergone various reforms aimed on seeking optimal management meeting the expectation of the general public and professionals.

2.3.1 Organization of State Administration

The Act No. 69/1967 Col. on the National Committees in compliance with later regulations established school departments within the National Committees on local, district and regional levels. The form of management in the area of education in relation to educational policy at that time may be considered as optimal. It may be characterized by rather great scope of responsibilities in economic and personnel area of the head of education department. The political changes in Czechoslovakia after 1989 recalled the need for changes in education management. These changes were implemented by the Act No. 542/1990 Col. on state administration in the area of education and school self-government, which achieved the following changes:

- it has increased the responsibility of the basic units—schools, in a way, that secondary schools became the subjects with legal entity (mainly in financial and personnel area) and gradually also part of primary schools acquired this status. It has led to certain decentralization and democratization of regional education management;

- it has enabled self-government bodies to act in management: at the level of regions— elected regional school boards and at the level of schools—elected school boards;

- it has created a specialized state administration in education by establishing school administrations (4 for secondary schools and 38 for primary schools). They disposed with necessary competencies in the area of school and educational facilities management.

The Central Inspection Center fulfilling the tasks of school inspection—control of quality of upbringing and education process—has been established at the same time. This way of education management (education managed strictly by branch) is even now considered by the professional public as optimal. In comparison with the other countries, the Slovak Republic may be characterized as a country with minimal involvement of territorial self-governments in the education management. Decentralization to municipalities, cities and regions is now in progress, but the extent of their responsibilities for schools is still not settled.

The Act No. 222/1996 Col. on the organization of local state administration moved competence to establish primary and secondary schools and educational facilities as well as responsibility for professional and economic management to regional and district offices. The Departments of Education, Youth and Physical Training have been established within the integrated state administration at district and regional offices. This model of school management is characterized to a great extent by the authority granted to the principals of these offices, and the limited authority of the head of departments. With reference to substantive dissatisfaction of senior officials in the area of education the government has decided by its Resolution No. 548/1999 to shift certain responsibilities (financial, personnel and informative) from principals of these offices to heads of Departments of Education, Youth and Physical Training. In spite this step of the government, there is a pressure for creation of specialized state administration in the area of education within the modernization and decentralization of public administration. In 1999 the State School Inspection was re-established as a specialized state administration in the field of upbringing and education process by the Act No. 301/1999.

At the time of writing the bodies of state administration in education are as follows:

a) school director and director (head) of educational facility;

b) district office;

c) regional office;

d) State School Inspection;

e) Ministry of Education of the Slovak Republic;

f) Other central state administration bodies, if enacted by a special Act.

Parts of the regional and district office responsibilities will pass to regional and municipal self-governments later in 2002.

2.3.2 School Director and Head of Educational Facility

The school is managed by a director, as is the educational facility who are appointed and recalled by founder. The tender for these positions is called by the founder in the case of state schools, and educational facilities by self-governmental body—school board, in the case of private and church schools, and educational facilities to which the self-governmental body gives only its opinion.

The school director has to ensure the following:
- that the generally binding legal regulations, educational plans and curricula are observed;
- professional and pedagogical standards of training and education at the school are met;
- that allocated financial means are effectively used;
- that the property in possession or use of the school (educational facility) is properly managed;
- he/she carries out state administration in the first instance;
- he/she decides on the admission of pupil to school;
- relieves the pupil from duty to commute to school;
- relieves the pupil from study of particular subjects or their parts;
- allows the study according to an individual plan;
- permits the taking part in study abroad in similar institution;
- permits the interruption of schooling, change of study or educational specialization, or the repeating of a year;
- he/she imposes educational measures on the pupil;
- permits corrective exams;
- notifies the respective body of state administration on failure of parents to look after the proper school attendance of the pupil;
- grants scholarships;
- decides on amount of parental contribution, which is to cover part of expenditures occurred in connection with care for the youth in school and educational facility;
- further decides on the postponement of compulsory school attendance and on additional postponement of compulsory school attendance. Exemption of compulsory school attendance is not possible.

2.3.3 District Office and Regional Office

The primary schools, primary schools of art and some educational facilities (kindergartens, children school clubs, free time centers, school canteens, etc.) fell under responsibility of district office

(Department of Education, Youth and Physical Training). Municipalities will take over the position of founders during 2002.

Within the responsibility of Regional Office are (Department of Education, Youth and Physical Training):

- secondary schools and secondary vocational apprentice centers;
- special schools;
- special kindergartens (kindergartens for handicapped children);
- special educational facilities (re-educational children's homes, re-educational boarding houses, diagnostic centers, therapeutic and educational sanatoriums);
- school farms at the secondary vocational schools;
- free time educational facilities besides the language schools at the primary schools;
- boarding houses;
- school canteens and kitchens, kitchens and canteens at the boarding houses, which are part of schools and educational facilities;
- vocational practice centers;
- school computer centers;
- pedagogical and psychological advisory services for secondary schools;
- central catering services for school catering.

Regional self-governments will become the founders of most of these institutions during 2002. The Regional Office and District Office establish and close schools and educational facilities according to the network of schools and educational facilities upon negotiation with local self-government bodies. They decide in the first instance on equality of documents on education issued by foreign schools.

The Regional Office and District Office in order to ensure the upbringing and education create financial, personnel, material and technical conditions for schools and educational facilities. They ensure investment construction of schools and educational facilities, co-operate with other state bodies, municipalities, organizations and bodies of school self-government, control observation of generally binding legal regulations, ensure the catering of pupils in school catering facilities. They carry out state administration in the second instance in matters dealt with in the first instance by the school director or educational facility director. They assign financial means to church and private schools and perform control of management. They issue directives for schools and educational facilities directors in the area of their responsibility and offer legal services. They perform complex control over the management with allocated financial and material means. They ensure data collection and pre-processing and transfer of information through unified information system.

2.3.4 State School Inspection

The State School Inspection is responsible for state control over the quality of pedagogical management, quality of upbringing and education and material and technical conditions including the practical education at the schools and educational facilities.

The State School Inspection is a state administration body in education; part of it are the School Inspection Centers on the level of regions. The Chief School Inspector is responsible for its management. He is appointed and recalled by the Minister of Education. His/her term of office is five years.

2.3.5 Ministry of Education of the Slovak Republic

The Ministry of Education of the Slovak Republic as a central government body governs state administration in the area of education. It establishes and closes State Pedagogical Office and methodological centers for the purposes of research and methodological guidance, training and education of pedagogical employees.

The Ministry of Education

- after negotiation with the relevant central bodies, regional offices and district offices designates network of schools and educational facilities and lists of vocational practice centers;[8]

- sets the rules for selection and appointment of senior positions, functions of inspectors, methodological experts and further positions in area of education;

- sets the policy for the pedagogical management of the school, including the schools established by other founders;

- breaks down the financial means allocated from state budget to methodological centers and further organizations established by ministry and controls the effectiveness of their use;

- elaborates in co-operation with regional offices and district offices the development conception of schools, educational facilities and vocational practice centers;

- proposes the methodology of a breakdown of state budget means (with an exception of salaries) to schools and educational facilities and controls its fulfilment.

It sets by generally binding legal regulations further details for:

- the establishing, closing, and organization of schools, educational facilities and vocational practice centers and for their upkeep and educational activity;

- the professional and pedagogical qualification of pedagogic employees, their further education and complementary pedagogical study;

- the admissions for study in the secondary schools and on completion of the study;

- the organization of the school year at primary and secondary schools;

- the tasks and proceedings of central bodies and organizations during management and planning of youth preparation for work;

- educational advisory services;

- the granting of scholarships, rewarding and material benefits of secondary schools students;

- conditions for the entrepreneurial activities of schools and educational facilities (after agreement with the Ministry of Finance of the SR) and rules for distribution of financial means acquired within this activity;

- the means of education of imprisoned citizens (after agreement with the Ministry of Justice of the SR).

2.4 School Self-government

After the overall changes in Slovakia in 1989, the pressure of the general public and self-government bodies on state administration has been intensified with the aim to create conditions for the active involvement of the local self-government, parents and teachers' community in school management. The NC SR Act No. 542/1990 Col. on state administration in education and school self-government has created conditions for the establishment of school self-government bodies, which are school board and territorial school board. In the first years of its existence, the school self-government underwent rapid development and enjoyed strong support as an advisory and initiative body. The next years were marked only by attempts to influence personnel policy at schools and educational facilities, which raised the negative attitude of the pedagogical public towards those tendencies. The school self-government gradually fell into isolation. The previous government has markedly limited the competencies of school-self-government and assigned it the position of an advisory body without significant competencies. The mentioned reasons caused decrease of interest in work of these bodies. The school self-government reached again its positions after the elections in 1998 namely after the approval of the NC SR Act No. 301/1999 Col. which amended the Act No. 542/1990 Col.

The 'school boards' and the 'educational facility boards' were re-established at schools and educational facilities to pursue democratic principles in education management. The 'district school boards' and 'regional school boards' are established at district and regional offices. Their term of office is set for four years.

They are initiative and advisory self-governmental bodies that express and advocate the interests of local self-government, parents and teachers in the area of upbringing and education. They review the activity of schools and educational facilities with regard to their mission as an educational institution. They perform the function of public control over superior employees of schools, educational facilities, regional offices, district offices and some other institutions, which participate in creating the conditions for upbringing and education on a given territory.

The school board proposes on the basis of competitive tender a candidate for appointment to a position of school director or educational facility director. It has right to propose his recall or give a standpoint to his recall, if the proposal for recall is submitted by the State School Inspection or the founder of school or educational facility in case of finding out the violation of the law or generally binding regulations by the director. What concerns private or church schools and educational facilities the school board gives its opinion on candidates to the position of director of school or educational facility; it gives its opinion when director is recalled as well. The school board express its views on the conceptual plans of school development and on further issues concerning the upbringing and education process.

The district school board and the regional school board give their opinion on work of district and regional office in the area of education, youth and physical culture, issues related to the establishment and closure of schools, upbringing and education, budget draft, results of budgetary economy of district and regional offices and conception of investment development of schools and educational facilities. In the case of newly established schools and educational facilities it performs the tasks of school board.

The members of the school self-governmental bodies are elected representatives of pedagogical and other employees of school or educational facility, elected representatives of parents, delegated representatives of municipal assembly and representatives of some other bodies and organizations, which participate on upbringing and education, including trade unions. At the secondary school the pupils of that school are also members of the school board.

The school board consists of 5 to 11 members, district school board and regional school board have 11 members. The school board may adopt decisions when single majority of members is present. The costs of boards activity are covered from the school budgets, and budgets of regional and district offices.[9]

The decentralization of financial management of education to local and regional self-government will necessitate to specify the status of school self-government bodies in the new system of education management.

The sensitive issue will be definition of the relation of two self-governments—school and territorial (municipalities, cities and regions).

3. QUALITY OF UPBRINGING AND EDUCATION PROCESS

The excellent achievements of secondary school students accomplished abroad (exchanges on the basis of cultural agreements notably with France and Austria) prove the high quality of education at primary and secondary schools in the Slovak Republic. The similar situation is in case of exchanges of university students (especially with the USA). But with regard to economic situation in Slovakia we can observe a decrease in knowledge level of students after 1989.[10] The schools are increasingly limited by lowering the allocation of financial means (Slovakia allocates only 4.2% of GDP to education, in comparison to the U.K. which allocates 5.5% of GDP; the Czech Republic which allocates 6.1% of GDP and Denmark which allocates 8.3% of GDP),[11] to economic operation of schools as well as to modernization of the education process (for educational aid, didactic and computer technique). The problems with recruitment of personnel in the area of upbringing and education are rising (lack of qualified pedagogic employees, nowadays 34.78% of teachers have not required academic qualification, 8% of teachers are pensioners—more details are provided in section 5). The graduates of universities with pedagogic specialization refuse to work in schools due to very low salaries (the initial gross salary of teacher with a university degree is, at the time of writing, 6 750 Sk per month).

In spite of the permanent lack of financial means, the results achieved in Slovakia in the education process are very good. This is based on various grounds:

a) There is a deeply rooted tradition in Slovakia that most parents of the pupils are expecting the best results of their children in schools following the common aim: 'If you finish the school with a good result you will have less problems in finding a good job.' Therefore children in most families are encouraged to be responsible for the preparation of the education process. The parents are generally actively involved in the co-operation with a school. They visit the school and consult the school results of their children. They are voluntarily involved in different activities of the school out of the education process (free time activities of pupils, small scale maintenance and upkeep works).

b) Teachers have, in most cases, very responsible attitudes towards their work. They are systematically educated and trained in new methods and forms of education. The state has created conditions for further education free of charge at the methodological centers. In 1978, the city and district pedagogical centers were established by the NC SR Act No. 78/ 1978 Col. on educational facilities. They were responsible for methodology of education on schools and educational facilities and education of teachers on the level of cities and districts. This function was performed on the level of regions by regional pedagogical institutes. These methodical and educational institutions were cancelled in 1990 by the NC SR Act No. 542/1990 Col. and four new methodical centers were established in the City of Bratislava and three regions (Bratislava, Banská Bystrica, Prešov) performing the same tasks. Their existence at the present time is threatened (economy of state—audit). The closure of these centers would have negative impacts not only on further education and methodical assistance to teachers, but also on the quality of the educational process. The methodologists of educational departments on district and regional offices who are in direct contact with teachers in schools and educational facilities are closely co-operating with methodological centers. In spite of changes under consideration, the Ministry of Education in its concept assumes to maintain these methodological and educational facilities within a so called 'School Services Center' located on the level of regions.

In a direct inquiry addressed to senior employees of Departments of Education of Regional and District Offices, we have found out that the unified system of quality assessment of upbringing and education process (e.g. in the form of comparison of success of school leavers in entrance examination to higher level of school or success in study at this schools) has not been applied since 1991.

All schools, non state included, have to teach according to nationally prescribed educational plans and curricula issued by Ministry of Education. The educational plans in several variants precisely determine the subjects and number of hours to be taught in individual grades. The curricula for individual grades prescribe subjects, their goals and content of thematic units. There is possibility to modify 30% of the content of the curricula in order to support teacher's creativity, humanization of education and special conditions of schools. The quality of fulfilment of tasks and meeting the goals of education in schools is controlled by the school director and State School Inspection through the observations in classes.

A prominent Slovak pedagogic professional Vladislav Rosa[12] gave the following assessment on the issue of content of education at schools:

In the area of content of education in spite of the worsening of material and personnel conditions some positive facts may be observed. In pre-school education the innovation program of education work is widely examined, the number of kindergartens participating in the projects 'School Supporting Health' and 'Open School' is increasing. The examination process of educational standards of all subjects in the first and the second level of primary schools and variants of verbal assessment is carried out. A substantive innovation of basic pedagogic documents educational plans and curricula at secondary schools is implemented, the lists of optional and free subjects are widened, the new study specialization are introduced. The process of examination of educational standards has started as well.

In the area of special education the new up-to-date methodical materials, guidance and directions have been elaborated. They are for example related to individual integration of handicapped into regular classes or to establishing special classes.

The students at bilingual grammar schools have entered their final years and passed school leaving exams. The results may be assessed as very good, and excellent. Germany since 1998 on the basis of decision of the Center for Foreign Education recognizes Slovak school leaving exam reports at German section of these schools which allows students direct access to German universities. The results of TIMSS project—Third International Mathematics and Science

Studies are promising as well. The Slovak Republic within the framework of this project (the projects of similar size have not been undertaken yet) has participated in assessment of knowledge level in mathematics and natural science subjects of population in age between 13 and 14. Our students, meeting all specified criteria among 45 countries of the world have reached the excellent 7th place. The results have attracted attention of international mass media. It would be useful and necessary to use this comparative information for further curricula development.

In spite of mentioned optimistic interpretations concerning the quality of education at Slovak schools the concerns related to quality at primary and secondary schools are rising and to be more specific concerns related to study results assessment. The proper evaluation is not possible in absence of comparable and reliable data on achieved results. Moreover, the need for transparency and comparability of achieved results is increasing not only with regard to the possibility of international comparison and fast development of international exchange and co-operation, but also due to internal reasons. Widened access to university education, existence of non–state educational sector, decrease of interest in apprentice education and other similar development tendencies are opening the question of the impacts of these changes on the quality of education. The coexistence of two concurrent types of schools on the second level of primary schools and lower level of grammar schools is another factor which increases the concerns on quality of education. As the quality is not controlled systematically it is not possible in this way to manage and direct the system according to need. It is generally admitted that there is a necessity of new approach to pupils evaluation, but no concrete proposals are known. In any case it is not possible to omit these problems. Their solution can be decisive in realization of transformation efforts in the Slovak education.

4. QUANTITATIVE DEVELOPMENT OF EDUCATION

The qualitative transformation change after 1989 has affected some types of school to a greater and sometimes to a smaller extent. The increase in number of schools and classes, in spite of reductions in the school age population may be generally explained by the fact that since 1989 the private and church schools and educational facilities have been founded regardless of population development—spontaneously—according to public requirements. The number of state schools is approximately without change; increase is not observed. Nowadays, a rationalization of the network of schools is taking place (cancelling and subsequent merging with so called 'catchment' schools), which will significantly decrease the number of state schools (primary as well as secondary schools). With regard to small class schools it may be said that the number of schools and classes cannot decrease linearly together with the decrease in number of children. This is given by high portion of small schools due to dispersion of settlements (large number of small municipalities) and by the existence of national minority schools on nationally mixed territories, which necessitates to maintain classes with low number of pupils in small municipalities. The aim of rationalization is to cut the costs of state on upbringing and education.

4.1 Kindergartens

At first, the kindergartens as an optional form of upbringing and the education of pre school population, were perceived as something subsidiary which could be replaced by other form of preparation. This led, after two years, to a serious decrease of all indicators in kindergartens. Fortunately, they have recovered and future prognosis are nowadays rather optimistic. On the other hand, primary schools in their indicators did not undergo such a difficult development. The most important influences are decreasing population trend and introduction of the ninth grade at primary schools.

The Program Declaration of the new government in 1998 supported development of pre-school upbringing in Slovakia by stating that the government "will ensure capacity of pre-school facilities that allow children to enter the first grade of primary school well prepared."

From 1989 to 1998 the number of children in the age between 3 and 5 dropped by 62 200, which represents decline by the one entire population year. This indicator was falling by 6 200 in a year. Since 1997, the rate of decrease became steeper. Decline continued until 2000, when it stopped on the level of 184 000. The rate of decrease will regress according to prognosis.[13] The minimum will be reached in 2009 (174 000) and until 2015 it will go up approximately to 180 000.

Three different phases may be recognized in the development of the statistics in number of children in kindergartens within the last ten years. In the years between 1989 and 1991 this indicator dropped by 22%, which reflects the system's collapse in the first years of transformation. During following four years the number went down by another 14%, i.e. the system's regress diminished, and almost stopped. In 1996, a notable change in the attendance of children in kindergartens occurred. The ratio of children in kindergartens to the total population aged between 3 and 5 has increased within three years from 70.8% to 84.2% in a balanced growth of 5% in a year. This third phase (1996–1997) may be denoted as a developing phase, as this indicator was growing in spite of the decrease in the population. Since 1998, the number of children in kindergartens has been decreasing due to population decrease.

The dynamics of development of a number of children in kindergartens in the years 2000–2015 may be characterized as follows. In the first variant it fell to approximately 150 000. In the second variant it followed the development of the last three years; and in the third variant it ranged from 165 to 175 000 children.

Children aged five make up the biggest percentage of the number of children in kindergartens. This share is, on average, 33.9%. It is followed by children aged four–25.8%; aged three– 20%; aged six–15.2%; and aged under 3–5% (1999/2000). The age structure of children in kindergartens is rather stable. The small shift was observed in favor of children in the age range five and six at the expense of children aged under three.

The state kindergartens are attended by 99.1% of children, municipal by 0.4% and both private and church by 0.2% of children (1999/2000). The kindergartens with education in the Slovak language are attended by 93.4 % of children, in the Hungarian language by 6.1% and other by 0.5% of children.

In comparison with changes in a number of children the number of classes and teachers reached a minimum in 1994, and since 1996 grew up and anticipated the third revitalization phase. In 1999, a moderate decrease occurred due to rationalization measures. Between 1989 and 1994 the number of teachers fell down by 4 000 which represents approximately 22%. During the third phase, it has increased by 1 300 teachers.

The highest number of children in kindergartens per 1000 inhabitants is in the Region of Prešov (34) and the lowest ones are in the Regions of Bratislava and Nitra (28). Among districts this number is the highest in Košice I (39) and the lowest in Prievidza (21).

The highest number of children per class was reached in 1989 (25.7). This number was lowered by steep decline to 21.8 in 1991. By 1994, it had been raised to 23.6 and nowadays there are 20.7 children in a class. The prognosis forecasts fluctuation around 22 children per class.

In view of the intention to decentralize the responsibility for management of kindergartens to self-government of municipalities, it is interesting to present the data on number of kindergartens in different settlements (especially in small municipalities). In the case of municipalities with a number of inhabitants up to 199, only 4% of them have kindergartens. In a group size ranging from 200 to 499 inhabitants, 60% of municipalities have kindergartens, in a group size ranging from 500 to 999 inhabitants, 96% of municipalities have kindergartens. The problems with the management of kindergartens may occur only in the case of municipalities with the number of inhabitants up to 500. It concerns 507 kindergartens with 528 classes and 8, 084 children, which makes up 5% of the total number of pupils in kindergartens in Slovakia. Based on the replies of the municipalities on questionnaire (see section 7.5), the difficulties with the financial management in kindergartens may occur only in approximately 150 municipalities.

In 2000, a further wave of kindergartens reduction appeared. The population decrease, the decrease in the number of children in kindergartens (due to unemployment of their parents) as well as rationalization measures of founders, resulted in the cancellation of 36 kindergartens. As there is no legal duty to ensure institutional pre-school upbringing, some district offices are trying to cut the costs by cancelling the kindergartens. At the same time, placement of children into kindergarten is not the duty of the parents. In this context, the problems are observed in the case of children from a socially undeveloped environment, mostly from Roma families.

4.2 Primary Schools

According to a demographic prognosis, the number of children 6 years old has steeply decreased until 2001. The number of newly admitted pupils to the first grades will decrease accordingly. This number after 2001 should fluctuate at the level of 60 000 with a deviation plus (or minus) 1 500 children. On average, 0.25% of primary school pupils leave for special schools. Out of this, a prevalent part comes from the first level of the school (around 80%).

Since 1991, the number of newly admitted students to grammar schools (those with study programs lasting 8 years) has increased steadily. The annual increase was, on average, 800 students. The share of pupils in Grade 4 has also increased. In 1991, it started at the level of 0.5%, and nowadays makes 7.5%. The prognosis assumes that it will come soon to a saturation point, and that the share will fluctuate around 8%.

Before 1995, the number of pupils who finished primary schools fluctuated in the range between 84.3 and 91.9 thousand. The statistical development has not shown a particular trend. The transformation of primary schools (introduction of the ninth grade) was reflected in a dramatic decrease of this number to 73.4 thousand in 1997, to 67.6 thousand in 1998 and in 1999 even to 41.3 thousand. The indicator has been coming back to its original level since 2000. It is assumed that it will show a decreasing trend in the future as a result of the decrease in the number of newly admitted in the 1990s. From 2000 to 2010 the number of school leavers will fall from 81.2 thousand to 53.4 thousand. The number of pupils who leave the school in lower grades makes up approximately 7% of school leavers.

The decreasing trend in population is also gradually reflected in the decreased number of pupils at primary schools. By 1996, it fell by 80 thousand which represents 11%. In the last two years, a moderate increase has been observed due to introduction of the 9th grades. In 1999/2000 school year it was markedly raised to 671 600 pupils. It is expected that the indicator will decline in the future. In 2005, it should reach 547 000, in 2010 501 000 and in 2015 approximately 492 000 pupils.[14]

The number of pupils at the first level (grades from 1 to 4) will be falling in the same current pace until 2003. In the course of five years, it should decline from 300 thousand (1999) to around 250 thousand. In the next few years it should decline at a more moderate pace. In 2010 it will reach 238 thousand and in 2015 237 thousand.

The number of pupils at the second level (grades from 5 to 9) has been growing since 1997. It has reached maximum in school year 1999/2000, when the number of pupils was raised from 341 thousand to 371.7 thousand. Until 2005, it will drop approximately to 255 thousand.

The 89.6% of pupils at primary school have the Slovak language as their teaching language. On average, 7% of pupils are being taught in Hungarian. The remaining 3.4% of pupils have their education in the Ukrainian, German or Bulgarian language. This division of pupils according to teaching language is stabilized and is not assumed to change in the near future.

The number of classes has been evolving independently from the number of pupils. Internal changes of the content and way of education has been probably reflected in the way in which the classes were established. In the last ten years, a development of the indicator has not shown clear signs of any trend. It has fluctuated around the level of 28.5 thousand of the classes. It has slightly increased in the last two years. In the school year 1999/2000 it raised to 29 773 classes. As long as the ratio to number of pupils is maintained, the indicator should continue to fall. In 2005, it should be 25 000 in 2015; 23 000; and in 2015 approximately 22 000 of classes.

The number of pupils per class has been falling down in total as well as at individual levels. The average number of pupils per class has decreased from 26.3 in 1989 to 22.6 in 1999. At the first level it dropped from 25.2 to 21.4 and at the second level from 27.5 to 23.6. At the same time difference between the first and the second level has been maintained. The prognosis predicts at the first level 21 pupils per class and at the second level 23 pupils per class.

The development of number of teachers at the primary schools shows some irregularities, but in total has increasing tendency. There were 36 000 teachers at primary schools in 1989 and at present there are 40 500. The transformation of primary schools has contributed to this growth in the last two years. As of 1 September 2000, in connection with the increase of teachers' educational duty, their number has decreased. In the following years, with regard to the number of pupils, this should also be decreasing, in 2005 to 35 000, in 2010 to 32 000 and in 2015 to approximately 31 000 teachers.

The number of pupils per teacher dropped from 20 in 1989 to 16.4 in 1999. A decrease at the first level was from 25 to 20 and at the second level from 16.7 to 13.7. The prognosis mentions 19.4 as average number at the first level and 13.5 at the second level.

The number of classrooms at the primary schools has increased from 29 500 to 34 600, whilst out of this figure, 4 100 are vocational classrooms. The need for the classrooms will be decreased in 2005 to 29 000 and in 2015 approximately to 26 000.

With regard to the envisaged decentralization of education management, the analysis of placement of primary schools within the settlement structure may be interesting. There are only 12 small class schools with 283 pupils in category of municipalities with number of inhabitants up to 200. Only 240 municipalities out of 815 in category with number of inhabitants from 201 to 499 have small class schools with 593 classes and 9, 220 pupils. In Slovakia there are 953 municipalities in total with number of inhabitants up to 500 without primary school.

4.3 Grammar Schools

The upbringing and education at the grammar school underwent substantial changes after 1989. The most important function of this kind of school is the preparation of students for further study. The conceptual changes, which created the basis of grammar school renewal after 1989 included:

- restoration of continuous 8 years study at grammar school (1991);

- cancelling of duty to attend the professional preparation;

- addition of economic and technical subjects to optional subjects;

- reduction of total number of classes in a week in each grade;

- increase in number of lessons of social subjects and foreign languages;

- introduction of new subjects like ethics with alternation of religious subject;

- strengthening of physical education;

- change in proportion between compulsory and optional education.

The new conception of grammar school has been formulated with stress on:
- development of comprehension abilities and learning activities of students;

- preparation for individual/collective creative work;

- development of communication skills;

- development of computer and foreign languages skills;

- development of skills to look for, sort, process and effectively use information, formulate and solve problems, express and justify own opinions and standpoints;

- strengthening of ecology, health and environmental education;

- creation of a new system of values and attitudes, including emotional development of students.

The wide scale of possibilities for differentiation of education according to study interests, needs and abilities of students has been created. This is ensured in curricula through the system of so called 'extra' lessons (on average 4 hours in a week), which may be used to expand time available for compulsory subjects, introduction of further compulsory subjects specific for study specialization or for optional subjects.

The teaching aid and didactic technique is missing in most grammar schools, in the most cases in newly created ones. Also, the existing aid has not been sufficiently renewed due to financial reasons. The need for practical working experience with communication and information technologies is being solved through a program called 'Infovek.'

Bilingual study exists at 14 Slovak grammar schools. The foreign partners are Belgium, France, Austria, Germany, Spain, Italy and the U.K. Different subjects are taught in individual sections in bilingual form, but mathematics and natural science are taught in this way in all sections. Within the whole period of study of bilingual sections in Slovakia the 1 475 school leavers have been admitted to universities. Out of them, 417 (28%) have been admitted to faculties with technical orientation or orientation to natural sciences (in Slovakia or abroad) and 343 (23%) to foreign faculties with a different orientation, mostly of economic and social science character.[15]

The development of grammar schools has been very dynamic. The number of students since 1945 has multiplied 7 times; the number of classes 10 times; the number of teachers 6 times; and the number of schools 3 times. The average number of students in class has fallen by 10. The average number of students per teacher is 12.

In the school year 1999/2000, 76 662 students (21.3% of the population aged between 15 and 18) studied at 209 grammar schools with 2 609 classes. The education was ensured by 6 165 of teachers in fulltime occupation.

The number of newly admitted students culminated in 1996. This was due to an increase in the number of students admitted to an eight year study period. The percentage for 4 or 5 year study has been declining since 1993.

In 2000, the total number of newly admitted students came back to its previous level i.e. to 20 thousand students. With regards to demographic decline it will drop by 5 thousand until 2010. The future prognosis does not assume that trend will maintain its previous increasing tendency for newly admitted students at 8 years study. In years between 2000 and 2005, this number should drop from 6 000 to 4 800. Beyond 2010, half the number of students of 4 or 5 year study programs should be admitted to 8 year study programs.[16]

The number of students at grammar schools has been increasing remarkably since 1990. The increasing trend temporarily stopped in 1998 due to the transformation of primary schools. This development was a result of two contradictory trends. After 1995, the decrease in the number of students in 4 or 5 years study programs has been compensated by accelerated increase in case of grammar schools with 8 years study programs. The share of students at the 8 years study programs from the total number of students has increased from 2.8% to 33.8%.

The transformation of primary schools appeared to decrease the number of students only in 1999, when 76 600 students studied at grammar schools. The growing trend from the first half of 1990s will continue in the following years. The culmination is expected approximately in 2003, when the number of 100 000 students will be reached. In the following ten years it will be declining approximately to the present figure of 80 000 students.

In the first half of 1990s, the number of school leavers has been growing in a fairly balanced way. In the second half of the decade, the increasing trend has changed to an oscillating trend. In these years, the total number of grammar schools leavers oscillated between 15–16 000. Almost 100% of them were students from 4 or 5 years study programs. Transformation of primary schools will influence the number of grammar school leavers in years between 2001 and 2003. The rapid decrease of school leavers from 4 or 5 years study programs will be partially compensated by leavers from grammar schools with 8 years study programs.

In years between 1990 and 1998 the number of classes increased almost by 1 000 and the number of teachers by 3 000. During this period, the number of schools increased by 81. The number of classes and classrooms has reached transformation minimum in 1999. The trend occurred before transformation will continue after 2000 by an increase of both figures. The maximum will be reached in 2003. It is assumed that at that time there will be 3 000 classes and 4 500 classrooms. In the next years it will be constant or moderately decreasing. The maximum number of teachers at grammar schools will be reached in 2003. The need of teachers at that time will be 1 500 higher than it is now. Later it will gradually decline to 7 200 (2010) and then stagnate around the level of 6 700 teachers.[17]

4.4 Secondary Vocational Schools

The secondary vocational schools are responsible for the upbringing, education and preparation at the secondary level for the labor market and practical life, with a possibility to continue in education at university.

The secondary vocational schools follow the development and trends of a dynamically changing labor market and react to its needs and requirements. In the last decade the teaching of foreign languages and social sciences has been strengthened, whilst the scope of interlinking subjects— IT, environmental education—has been widened. New subjects like management, marketing, gastronomy, banking, ethics, or legal education have been introduced. The content of already existing subjects has been innovated in connection with the introduction of new technologies and work organization. The creation of an integrated, wide-profile study specialization resulted in a decrease in the number of narrowly oriented specialization. The new specialization and professional orientation have been gradually introduced in relation to structural changes in economy and transformation of society.

The upbringing and education process consist of a general component of education, which represents approximately 42–45% of teaching time and professional component representing around 55–58% of teaching time. The professional component consists of a theoretical and practical part, which represents 25–30% of teaching time of professional component.

The specialization of education has been shifted to higher grades, follow up study has been widened and higher professional education has been introduced (follow up specialization study). The optional subjects and professional specialization have been introduced. The integration of education of handicapped children in common classes with healthy children is carried out. The retraining forms of study are offered in co-operation with labor offices.

The positive achievements of secondary vocational schools are accompanied also by several problems:

- lack of information on labor market requirements and its future needs;

- high number of school leavers, who are not able to find a job;

- low interest of entrepreneurial and employment sector in education and preparation of youth, which results in situation, when only schools or parents of students are participating in the creation of new educational and training programs;

- weak linkage between theoretical education and practical application of knowledge and skills due to lack of training facilities for practical education;

- high number of professionals (teachers, technicians, economists and foreign languages teachers), who leave their positions due to other more lucrative offers;

- rapid and insufficiently co-ordinated growth of schools, study specialization and professional orientations;

- outdated legislation, which does not allow for the integration of secondary schools. openness and flexibility in introducing new forms and ways of study and adequate adjustment of certification.

The amendment to the School Act, which is under preparation should solve part of these problems.[18]

The number of students at secondary vocational schools since 1945 increased seven fold; the number of classes were 9 times higher; and the number of schools almost by 4 times. The average number of students in a class has dropped from 35 to 27. The number of teachers was raised from 2.7 thousand in 1960 to the current 13.3 thousand.

There are 99 070 students at 379 secondary vocational schools in 3 632 classes. The most prevailing types are industrial schools (with 37.2% of students) and business colleges (32.6% of students). The state school provides education to 94.1% of students. The dominant type of study is 4–5 year lasting comprehensive secondary study finished by school leaving exam. This type of study is attended by 90.6% of students.

The number of newly admitted students has been growing since 1990. The growth strongly accelerated especially in the beginning of 1990s. This number increased by a third up until 1993. Later, this development became more stable. The number of newly admitted students raised from 25 500 to 33 300 in the years between 1990 and 1996.

291

Moreover, in comparison with the relevant population, the updating coefficient was raised from 23.5 % to 37.3%.[19] The decrease in the following years was due to primary schools transformation. The figure will therefore be back at its original level (the level before transformation) in 2001. It will be in decline (until 2010) due to the population decrease to a level of 20.2 thousand newly admitted students, and then it will stagnate on the level of 20.3 thousand of students until 2015.

The growth of number of students at secondary vocational schools had been balanced until 1996 when it reached 122 thousand. During these years the igure increased by 40%. Decrease, which occurred in 1997 was caused by primary school transformation. The number of students should be growing until the year 2003, to 108.2 thousand and it will start to decline in following years.

In the 1990s, the number of school leavers raised from 18 thousand to 30 thousand. The transformation effect will be more influential in the next three years. The lowest number of school leavers will be reached in 2003—approximately 19 thousand. In 2004, it will be back on level of 28 thousand and due to population trends it will decline.[20] In 1999 (as of 30 September 1999), 47.9% of 32, 594 secondary vocational school leavers became unemployed. The biggest percentage of unemployed school leavers was reached in the Prešov Region–57.3%.

From 1990 to 1996 the number of classes grew. It then moderately declined to 3 300 classes (2001). In 2003 it will again raise to 3 600 classes. Later, it will decrease to 2 700 in 2010, and then to 2 400 in 2015.

The number of classrooms during the last decade, up until 1998 has been increasing. The pace of growth was quite fast, especially in the years from 1992 to 1995. The premises for classrooms were obtained also from state enterprises after their bankruptcy.

The number of classrooms will reach its maximum in 2003 when it will be 6, 900. Later, it will gradually decrease to 5 200 in 2010 and to 4 600 in 2015. The number of schools increased during last decade by 195. In the next period within the process of school association it will be moderately declining.

The number of teachers has been growing together with the number of classes. In relation to the development in a number of classes, the number of teachers will be gradually falling. It will reach approximately 13 000 in 2003. Later, it will decline to 8 500, which was the level of the year 1989.[21]

4.5 Secondary Vocational Apprentice Centres

Their mission is an education and preparation for practical skilled occupations. The centers run vocational and study specialization. Preparation in vocational specialization allows the student to acquire the qualifications necessary for carrying out the set of working activities including a good command of work methods and relevant working means.

Preparation in study specialization allows the student to obtain qualifications necessary for activities, which require more extensive and higher level of theoretical vocational education. It allows the independent performance of large scales of working activities in different situations, requiring a higher level of intellectual skill. It concerns often the tasks in production preparation, planning and the co-ordination of work.

The general component of education provides knowledge of social, mathematical and natural science disciplines. The vocational component of preparation and education focuses the foundation of student's profile.

The educational process is carried out in secondary vocational apprentice centers in:

- vocational specialization and its professional orientations (fulltime study lasts two or three years). The school leaver will obtain secondary vocational education. The study is accomplished by the final exam and student receives a 'vocational certificate' in a given specialization;

- study specialization and its professional orientations for students who finished vocational specialization at secondary vocational apprentice centers (fulltime study lasting two years). The school leaver will receive comprehensive secondary vocational education. The study is finished by school leaving exam and student obtains a 'graduation certificate';

- study specialization and its professional orientations in which fulltime study lasts four years. The school leaver will receive comprehensive secondary vocational education. The study is finished by school leaving exam and student obtains a 'graduation certificate' and a 'vocational certificate' in a given specialization.

The social and economic changes have created strong pressure on innovation of individual educational programs.

The problems occurred in the years between 1989–2000 may be summarized as follows:

- low interest of social partners in education and preparation in secondary vocational apprentice centers. The innovations of educational programs are prepared mostly by the schools. The entrepreneurial sphere is rather passive;

- twofold management of secondary vocational apprentice centers (regional offices and individual line ministries);

- difficulty to ensure the quality of professional preparation of pupils in individual industrial branches due to outdated equipment at workplaces of practical training;

- exit of pedagogic employees from education sector to other sectors;

- insufficiently co-ordinated development of schools, study and vocational specialization;

- obsolete legislation, which prevents integration of secondary schools into associated secondary schools.[22]

The number of students at secondary vocational apprentice centers raised since 1945 by 5 times, the number of classes by 5 times as well and the number of schools almost by 4 times. The average number of students per class fluctuated around 25. The number of teachers has risen from 877 in 1945, to a current 7 900.

The secondary vocational apprentice centers were most heavily affected by system changes in society after 1990. While the other two kinds of schools recorded the qualitative growth, figures pertaining to the vocational centers were either decreasing or stagnating.

The development in the area of vocational education has been quite complicated. The extensive growth of previous decades was replaced by overall decline of its figures. The number of students has dropped by 52.7%, the number of classes by 2 300 and the number of teachers almost by 1 000.

The most remarkable decrease in the number of newly admitted students to the secondary vocational apprentice centers occurred in 1990 and 1991. In following years the development has levelled out to an average level of 45 700. The decline in 1997 and 1998 was due to the transformation of primary schools. In 2000, the number of newly admitted students went back to the level above 40 000. In the next years it will be declining: in 2005 to 35 800 and in 2010 to 28 400. There will be no significant changes until 2015.

The remarkable decrease of students at secondary vocational apprentice centers occurred in the years between 1990 and 1992. The number of students dropped from 150 000 to 139 000. In the following years it fluctuated around the level of 139 000 students. In 1999, due to the transformation of primary schools it declined to 102 500. The original level will be restored in 2003. There will be 118 000 students at secondary vocational apprentice centers. Subsequently it will decrease to 102 000 in 2005, to 80 000 in 2010 and to 70 000 in 2015.

In the 1990s, the number of school leavers fluctuated at a level of 44 000. The exemption appeared in 1993, when 57 000 students finished the schools. The number of school leavers will now be decreasing until 2002. This number will reach 28 000 in 2002. Later, the original trend will be restored. There will be 40, 000 school leavers in 2003. In following years, this number will declining to 38 000 in 2005, to 33 000 in 2010 and up to 27 000 in 2015. In 1999 (as of 30 September 1999), 42% of the 45 918 leavers from secondary vocational apprentice centers became unemployed. The biggest percentage of unemployed school leavers was reached in the Presov Region which peaked at 51.4%.

The number of classes dropped from 6 000 to 4 400 in 1999. Until 2002 it will grow to 4 700 and later it will decline. It will reach 4 100 in 2005; 3 100 in 2010; and 2 800 in 2015. The number of classrooms will be decreasing in proportion to the number of classes.[23]

The number of teachers ranged from 8 000 (1993) to 8 800 (1999) and after 2000 it will have the tendency to decline. It is expected that there will be 7 300 of teachers at secondary vocational apprentice centers in 2001; 6 500 in 2005; 5 000 in 2010; and 4 400 in 2015.[24]

4.6 Special Schools

There is currently quite a well developed network of special schools in Slovakia. In these schools, the handicapped children and youth are educated in different ways according to type of their handicap. The aim is to reach maximal working and social integration of handicapped individuals with regard to type and degree of handicap. The personal education is provided by qualified professionals with university education. Generally, very good results are achieved in the upbringing and education.

At present there are two basic ways in which this kind of education is provided:

1. at special schools;
2. at regular schools:

    a) in a form of individual integration (i.e. in a class together with the other pupils)

    b) in a special classes

The system is currently undergoing radical change. The practical result of giving the stress on the humanization of education, is an increased respect of the specifics of personal development of each individual. This has led to transition from almost exclusively segregated education of handicapped pupils to a system of alternative choices between the optimal integration at regular schools or special schools. The specific modification of conditions for the upbringing and education will enable a greater majority of the handicapped population to attend mainstream primary and secondary schools. This should support the process of smooth social inclusion and overall personal development.[25]

In total, 30 736 students attended 381 special schools of all kinds in school year 1999/2000.[26] 274 of them were special and individual schools attended by 10 265 pupils in grades ranging from preparatory grade to grade 4 and 11 971 in grades from 5 to 9. The number of pupils in lower grades is declining due to gradual integration of pupils into regular classes at primary schools.

4.7 Primary Schools of Art

Art education offers the younger generation the possibility to develop their natural talent in creative disciplines. The components of its system and their outputs are arranged in a way that allows pupils to continue in art preparation at a higher level or qualify for professional performance of art career.

The education at primary schools of art is part of system of art education in Slovakia which is also highly appraised abroad. It offers basics of art education in individual art specialization. It has a character of spare time education of gifted children.

The primary schools of art prepare for the study of practical and study specialization at secondary schools oriented on arts, conservatoires or eventually at universities with art orientation. They also widen the general educational level of pupils of primary and secondary schools, and eventually universities, by giving the possibility to master certain component of art.

The primary schools of art represent with their musical, scenic, dance and dramatic specialization a poly-aesthetic character.

They are attended by pupils in the age between 7 and 15. The preparatory study has at the most two grades. The basic study is divided into two levels: Level I which consists of 8 grades and Level II which has 4 grades. The extended study is assigned for pupils who will show during the basic study exceptional talent and extraordinary study results. Study for adults has at the most four grades, and the parents contribute financially to this study.

The primary schools of art considerably contribute to cultural and social activities in individual cities and municipalities. They create conditions for the artistic activities of primary and secondary schools students in their free time.

Presently, approximately 14% of primary school students are attending the primary schools of arts. The number of primary schools of arts was increased during the last decade by 50. There are 194 primary schools of art, 17 of them are private and 3 are church-owned. These schools have 118 branches. The number of students increased from 778 000 (1990) to 95 600 in 1999 (24.3%).[27] The increase was observed in creative art by 31.2%; in music specialization by 15.2%; and in dance specialization by 63.1%. Dramatic specialization recorded a moderate decline. The number of school leavers in a year ranged from 5 700 to 6 500. The number of full time teachers increased from 2 769 to 3 498, and in case of part-time teachers from 562 to 856 in the years between 1990 and 1999.[28]

4.8 Educational Facilities

The educational facilities are an important part of the educational and upbringing system. They are focussed mostly on upbringing area and free time education area. This category includes also facilities responsible for institutional upbringing, protective upbringing and preventive care as well as advisory services for children and youth.

The educational facilities are in charge of different functions including the following:

* pre-school education (kindergarten and special kindergarten);

* care for children and youth in their free time (children's school club, school center for free time activities, free time center);

* boarding and lodging (youth boarding houses);

* substitutive upbringing in families, protective and preventive care (facilities of upbringing prevention and facilities of substitutive upbringing);

* professional assistance in the area of psychological advisory services, special and pedagogic advisory centers, diagnostic integration centers);

* professional services in the area of interest study (language schools) and services for schools and educational facilities (school economy centers, practical education center, school computer center).

The children's school clubs ensure upbringing and education during the holiday and after school-time for pupils in the age of mandatory school attendance. Nowadays, they have lost their original function—to provide upbringing and education in order to satisfy interests of students in their free time and to prepare them for classes. Due to lack of financial resources, they are mostly educational facilities with a social function serving to children from lower grades of primary school as preparation to classes. The rest and free time activities for upper grades are organized in a smaller scale. In 1999, the school clubs were attended by 142 362 pupils, 137 435 of them were pupils of primary schools; 4 832 of special schools; and 95 students of grammar schools with 8 year study programs. In comparison with the situation in 1990, it represented a decrease by 30%.

The free time centers are one of the most important places implementing the state program of care for children and youth in free time area. They create conditions for the development of the skills in practical activities and the effective use of free time on the basis of interest and free choice during school year and in time of holidays. The spectrum of activities covers wide range of interests, spontaneous one as well as recreational. Different regular and occasional activities are organized, including summer activities and camps, competitions, displays, methodological and publishing activities.

The number of free time centers—130—has been levelling out with some small deviations during the last decade. The number of units of free time activities decreased from 5 598 in 1989, to 4 871 in 1999. The number of members declined from 89 575 to 68 031 and 86.3% of them are pupils under 15 years of age. The number of full time employees decreased from 1 473 to 962.

The youth boarding houses provide boarding and lodging to secondary school students. They combine the family upbringing along with the upbringing and education activities in a school. The youth boarding houses are in the most cases of a regional character. Their number remained steady between 1989 and 1991 (115); the biggest increase appeared in 1992 (when there were 127), and then a dramatic downturn can be observed in years 1996–1999 (the number dropped to 99). The number of accommodated students has been permanently falling since 1989 from 25 366 to 13 761 (1999). The prevailing number of accommodated students comes from secondary vocational schools and secondary health schools, their share fluctuated between 70% and 85%.

School catering ensures meals for pupils at all kind of schools in the form of lunch, whilst in the case of pupils accommodated in youth boarding houses there is full board. In 1999, there were 4 588 school canteens in operation, and they offered services to 518 800 children and pupils.

The real situation in school catering may be characterized by articles from daily newspaper:

> *The parents simply do not have means to ensure appropriate meals for their children in a form of catering in school canteens, which meet the standards of healthy nutrition. This state is getting worse each time the food or energy price is increased. That is reflected in a further decrease of efforts to enrich and improve the variety and nutritious quality of school catering. The situation is further deteriorated by poor and outdated technical state of school canteens with equipment older than 20 or 30 years. It is inevitable to invest in this area within the whole Slovakia, at least 3 billion Slovak Crowns.* [29]

The outdoor schools are upbringing facilities, which allow children and youth in areas with a poor quality environment to be educated in a better environment without interruption to their upbringing and education process. The number of students staying in outdoor schools has been declining since 1989 from 111 329 to 72 329 (1995). A certain increase was observed afterwards and the statistic has stabilized in last years (to 80 156). The primary school pupils have the biggest share amongst the outdoor school participants (between 83% and 89%).

4.8.1   Upbringing Prevention and Substitute Upbringing

These are a system of institutions which provide children and youth between the ages of 3 and 18 protection against unfavorable impacts of dysfunctional family or social environment. The children may be placed in these facilities on the basis of a court ruling on the order of institutional upbringing or on the basis of parents' request or request of an expert consultant. The special upbringing facilities are in charge of children protection against social and pathologic phenomenon, prevention of problematic development of children, prevention of offender (misbehavior) development and in carrying out the institutional and protective upbringing.

This category includes facilities of upbringing prevention (upbringing and psychological prevention center, therapeutic and upbringing sanatorium, diagnostic center) and facilities of substitute upbringing (re-educational children's homes, re-educational youth homes). In compliance with the 'Measures for fighting against drugs' 29 upbringing and psychological prevention centers have been established at the level of districts and regions in the course of years 1995–2000.

The diagnostic centers provide upbringing, psychological, psychotherapeutic and health care to children placed to facility on the basis of decision of relevant state administration body or request of child legal representative. They are boarding upbringing facilities, which ensure a complex examination of children and youth from psychological and special pedagogic point of view. On the basis of complex examination, the children and youth are placed in upbringing facilities. The number of children in these facilities was stabilized during the years 1989–1999.

The facilities of substitute upbringing includes re-educational children's homes and re-educational youth home. The children are placed to these facilities on the basis of a court ruling on the order of institutional or protective upbringing, on the basis of preliminary measure or on the request of legal representative. There are seven re-educational children's homes with 343 beds. The number of re-educational youth homes is stable (at nine), but their bed capacity moderately decreased since 1999. The number of placed persons has been decreasing since 1990.

Therapeutic and upbringing sanatorium provides psychological, psychotherapeutic and upbringing care to children with disrupted psychosocial development (learning and behavioral disorders). The number of these facilities has increased from 3 to 5 since 1989. The number of children placed to these facilities has remarkably increased since 1990 (by 61.5%). There were 174 children in these facilities; 88.5% of them were under 15.

Pedagogical and psychological advisory service facilities fulfil the tasks in the professional pedagogic and psychological diagnostics and care for children and advisory tasks in the upbringing, education, personal and professional development issues. Nowadays there are 85 such facilities, 8 of them regional and 77 district ones. Their activity is oriented on advisory services concerning personal development, educational development, from diagnostics of the causes to processing of the proposal for placement/displacement of client to another type of school.

4.8.2   Services in the Area of Interest Study

The language schools have their importance and justification in the system of educational facilities, especially with regard to the provision of language training for all groups of inhabitants within the long-life education. The number of state language schools has been stabilized, the same relates to language schools. In 1999 there were fourteen state language schools, four language schools and eight private language schools (accredited by the Ministry of Education) in the network of language schools. The number of courses has been permanently increasing from 798 (1989) to 1 223 (1999), similarly the number of participants has been growing in all forms of courses i.e. from 17 950 in 1989 to 21 497 in 1999. The English language has a dominant position in the education.

4.8.3 Services to Schools and Educational Facilities

The school computing centers belong to this category. Currently there are five school computing centers, which are regional processing nodes of information system for the Ministry of Education. They participate in the solutions, creation and processing of information. At the same time they are internet providers for secondary schools and universities and they train employees of ministry in individual regions.[30]

5. PERSONNEL

There are almost 100 000 pedagogic employees,[31] who work at the schools and educational facilities functioning under the direct responsibility of district and regional offices in the Slovak Republic.

The pedagogic employees are an important professional group, which has a decisive influence not only on individual development of pupils and students and their education, but also on the implementation of educational policy and indirectly on social and economic development of the society. The sufficient number, optimal structure and qualification level of pedagogic employees is an important indicator of the Concept of State Policy in Education, which outlines short-term and medium-term perspective of the quality of educational process in Slovakia.[32]

The new long-term concept of upbringing and education, which would reflect changes in social, political and economic conditions has not been elaborated yet. Unfavorable consequences of this situation have appeared also in a network of schools, including the schools preparing the teachers which have to foresee the expected social needs of particular categories of pedagogic employees for 10–15 years in advance.

The changes in the concept and content of education gave rise to changes in the professional qualification of teachers. On the one hand they have caused a lack of teachers of ethics, foreign languages, some professional subjects and on the other hand a surplus of kindergartens teachers, teachers of Russian language and apprentice centers teachers.

The changes in the organization of schools in the system of their management and administration, decentralization of responsibilities to lower levels of management, accompanied by a weakening of the regulatory function of the state (center), led to an unbalanced development of some attractive kinds and types of schools (study specialization), mostly of economic, art and language orientation, which brought up an acute need of professionally qualified teachers as well as a diversification of school network, increase in operational costs and number of teachers. On the contrary the students are not interested in preparation at vocational apprentice centers, and a decline in the number of students and a surplus of teachers and other pedagogic employees can be observed in these schools as a result of privatization and a high rate of unemployment among the leavers from vocational apprentice centers (and some vocational schools).

The system of university preparation of teachers has dropped from uniform conception of content of education. The sufficient co-ordination and co-operation of respective faculties preparing the teachers has been ensured through the Teachers' Faculty Union, which started its activities in 1994.

The unbalanced demographic development, especially rapid decline of birth-rate in comparison to 1990 by 28.4% has caused a decrease in the number of pupils in schools, a decrease of the average number of pupils in classes and decrease in the number of classes. The stability of the school network and the organization of education has been corrupted, which raises feelings of social insecurity.

In April 1998,[33] there were 99 880 pedagogic employees in total, 84.58% of which were teachers; 7.36% were tutors; 6.69% were the foremen of vocational training; and 1.3% were other pedagogic employees.

The highest percentage of pedagogic employees have worked in primary schools: 44.82%; 15.69% in kindergartens; 12.65% in secondary vocational apprentice centers; and 11.26% in secondary vocational schools.

The highest percentage of teachers (46.14%) have worked in primary schools; whereas in kindergartens 18.32%); in secondary vocational schools (12.77%); and in secondary vocational apprentice centers 7.49%.

With regard to the above mentioned insufficient social and economic security of pedagogic employees, there are temporary difficulties in fulfilling the systemic functional positions of teachers and tutors in some territorial areas, especially in remote municipalities, small class schools and schools with the Slovak teaching language on nationally mixed territories.

All this has caused an acceptance of under-experienced, substandard or older teachers—including pensioners and unqualified employees, which has produced negative impacts on the continuous organization of education, its professional delivery and quality.

In May 1999, the government decided to decrease the number of employees in the offices of state administration as well as in public sector by 10%. This decision also affected the education sphere, where during the years from 1999 to 2000, the number of teachers fell by 3 068—2 466 of whom were internal teachers. This represents total decrease by 3.26%.

Further data indicates that the gender structure of teaching staff on individual levels and types of schools is considerably unbalanced. The highest representation of women teachers is in kindergartens (99.92%) and in grades between 1 and 4 at primary schools (91.16%). The relatively lowest representation is at secondary vocational apprentice centers (59.50%) and in secondary vocational schools (65.57%). The overall Slovak average of women's representation in teaching staff is 80.97%.

5.1 Age Structure of Teachers

The adequate age structure of teachers is a prerequisite of the continuous functioning and development of education. The balanced age structure allows to replace aged leaving teachers by young qualified teachers.

The results of statistical ascertaining have shown that the age structure is unbalanced. The following age groups have the biggest representation: group between 41–45: 14 092 teachers i.e. 16.68 %; the age group between 46 and 50: 13 564 teachers, i.e. 16.06%; and the age group between 51–55: 11 581 teachers i.e. 13.71%.

The differences have also been observed at individual levels and types of schools. The situation is unfavorable in primary schools (particularly in grades 1–4) with a high percentage of women and high rate of pensioners among the teachers.

The age structure of teachers at secondary schools is different. The situation is rather balanced and favorable at the grammar schools, where the younger categories (under 40) are fairly represented. The high number of younger age groups is mostly given by extensive development of this kind of schools after 1989 and resultant increase in newly hired graduates with specialization on general subjects, who preferred to be employed at the secondary school. The number of newly hired teachers is relatively lower in primary schools; however the latest information shows us that the number of hired teachers exceeds the average number of teachers in one class.

Total number of newly hired teachers (9 626 i.e. 11.39%) proves that it would correspond to increased needs providing that the age structure is more balanced.

A typical unfavorable phenomenon in education is the high number (7 149 i.e. 8.46%)[34] of teachers who are pensioners. This is mostly caused by the high number of qualified teachers who leave the profession to other more lucrative and better paid occupations and by the reduced interest of young university graduates in teaching. In 1998, there were 2 439 teachers i.e. 14.47% in retirement age in grades 1–4; and 1 813, i.e. 8.19% in grades 5–9. These numbers are relatively lower in the case of kindergartens (2.6% of teachers there are pensioners).

5.2 Teacher's Qualifications

According to the Education Act a general criterion for qualification is professional and pedagogic qualification, civic respectability and moral qualities.

The professional qualification is characterized as a pool of professional knowledge, skills and habits acquired by study at university or secondary school and professional experience. The pedagogic qualification means possession of knowledge related to upbringing and education, abilities and skills necessary to perform pedagogic activity, which are acquired by study at university with teacher's specialization or by complementary pedagogic study.

The university degree is in principle required in order to be qualified to teach in schools. In the case of primary schools of art and kindergartens, the completion of secondary school or higher secondary school (conservatoire) is accepted. The professional and pedagogic qualification of school directors is conditioned also by the completion of a relevant form of further education.

Only 65.22% of the total number of teachers (84 483) meet this requirement in all regional schools (beside the kindergartens and primary schools of arts); this percentage is rather high in case of grammar schools (94.29%) and in grades from 5 to 9 at primary schools (89.06%), the lowest percentage is observed at special schools (55.81%) and in grades 1–4 of primary schools (65%). The rather high number of teachers at schools without pedagogic qualification (at special schools 15.48%; at secondary vocational schools 8.39% and at secondary vocational apprentice centers 7.66%) proves that sufficient attention is not paid to pedagogic qualification of teachers, which is a precondition for quality and effectiveness of training.[35]

The unqualified teachers or teachers with an unsuitable qualification are striving to reach the necessary qualification in part time study. The 4, 016 teachers in total are involved in different forms of education in order to widen or increase their qualification.

The term "professionality of education" is understood as a rate of classes taught by teachers with specified professional qualification (approbation). Thus the professionality of education expresses the rate of utilization of professional qualification potential of teachers in teaching the individual subjects.

The Notice of Ministry of Education on professional and pedagogic qualification of pedagogic employees classifies them into 15 groups, 7 of which are teacher's groups.

Data presented in the Annex shows the professionality of education of compulsory and optional subjects at all primary schools regardless of teaching language. The highest professionality of education is reached in the French language (95.28%); the Slovak language (92.58%); and in Mathematics (92.19%). The lowest is observed in teaching the Civic Education (44.57%); Musical Education (49.85%); and the English language (52.86%).

In the case of grammar schools (all types) the highest professionality of education is achieved in the teaching of the Ukrainian language (100%); Slovak language and literature (99.5%); Physics (99.21%); Chemistry (99.16%); Biology (98.88%); and Hungarian language and literature (98.18%). A high rate of proffesionality is also reached in other subjects, which corresponds to the high level of teacher's qualification and meaningful organization of education.

The summary data for all kind of secondary vocational schools regardless of their professional specialization and teaching language, shows that the highest rate of professionality is reached in the teaching of the Ukrainian language and Geography (100%); Chemistry (98.94%); the Russian language (98.84%); the Slovak language and literature (98.17%) and in Mathematics (98.14%). The relatively high level is reported also in case of other subjects. The lowest professionality of teaching is in Civic Education (75.81%) and Ethics (80.18%).

The issue of professionality of education at special schools is specified by its close linkage to relevant special pedagogy. It is not possible to provide professional education without special pedagogy. As this issue relates to education at primary schools as well as secondary schools, which are often mutually interconnected, the data on professionality of teaching of general subjects are shown together for both primary and secondary schools.

The mutual comparison of data on professionality of teaching of general subjects according to type of schools shows that:

- the highest professionality is reached at grammar schools and secondary vocational schools (13 subjects with professionality of education higher than 90%), followed by the secondary vocational apprentice centers (10 subjects). There are only 5 such subjects in grades between 5 and 9. The special schools have only 1 teaching subject with this rate;

- the lowest level of professionality is observed at special schools (nineteen subjects with a rate under 70%), and even nine subjects are below 60%. There are ten subjects with a rate below 70% at the primary schools, in grades between five and nine. The secondary vocational apprentice centers have two subjects with this rate. The professionality of education of all teaching subjects is above 70% at grammar schools and secondary vocational schools.

The level of professionality of education is unbalanced in individual subjects at schools. The positive sign is that the professionality of education is the highest in case of subjects, which could be regarded as key ones, like the Slovak language, natural sciences and Mathematics. The lowest level of professionality is in teaching of subjects less represented in educational plans (Civic Education, Ethics, Musical Education, Arts) or subjects of differentiated education at schools with a small number of classes.

5.3 Legal Status and Salary Conditions

The teachers and the other pedagogic employees are decisive factors in upbringing and education at schools and educational facilities. The school in close co-operation with the family strives for unity of education and upbringing and looks after health development of pupils through improvement of their physical and psychical abilities.

The recruitment of pedagogic employees is exercised according to the Labor Code. The labor contract is concluded with a school (schools and educational facilities with legal entity) or with the respective founder (schools and educational facilities without legal entity).

At the beginning, the new pedagogic employee without relevant experience has to undergo the 'initial practice' organized by a school during the one year under guidance of senior, professionally experienced pedagogic employees. At this time he/she is ranked to the eighth salary category in the first grade. After finishing this 'initial practice' he/she has to absolve the final interview with a school director and senior pedagogic employee. After positive appraisal he/she is promoted to the ninth salary category and grade corresponding to the duration of his/her practice. When not achieving required results within a trial period of three moths he/she is dismissed in most cases. The pedagogic employees with a university degree have the possibility to take part in further education and pass 'the first qualification exam' after five years of experience. The education and exams are organized by methodical centers, State Pedagogic Institute and universities. The aim is to verify a teacher's ability to apply creative pedagogic experiences in solving professional and methodical problems of education. The final exam includes thesis presentation and oral exam in front of an examining body consisting of five members. After successful examination, the pedagogical employee is promoted to the tenth salary category and relevant salary grade. There is no deadline for passing the 'first qualification exam.' The pedagogic employee may continue in further education and pass the 'second qualification exam,' which may be reflected in a personal bonus.

The salary categories and grades are regulated by the NC SR Act No. 143/1992 and Government Regulation No. 249/1992 on salary conditions of employees in budgetary and some other organizations and bodies as amended. The tariff salary may be increased by personal bonus, extra pay for work in class (also in a form of decrease of rate of educational duty by 1 hour in a week), for advisory services (also in a form of decrease of rate of educational duty according to number of classes in a school). The special bonus may be granted to pedagogic employees in connection with a notably difficult working environment (special education). The rate of teaching duty of pedagogic employees in senior positions is reduced and they receive extra pay for managerial work.

The Ministry of Education considers further education of pedagogic employees as an important tool for increasing the quality of educational process.[36]

The model for the 'Working Order' of pedagogic and non-pedagogic employees of schools and educational facilities was issued by the Ministry of Education after an agreement concluded with the Trade Union in 1999. It contains the rights and duties of employees. The Annex (under preparation) shall specify individual working activities with job descriptions. The founders of schools and educational facilities have elaborated this model according to their local conditions.

5.4 Rate of Educational Duty

The education and upbringing work of pedagogic employees is of a special character. It has its own specifics that other occupations do not possess. According to the Labor Code there are 42.5 working hours in a week, and 8.5 working hours in a day. The Government Regulation sets the rate of educational duty in a week (direct working activity with pupils). The teachers within the 8.5 working hours in a day have to perform some other activities related to education and upbringing process.

The rate of educational duty (basic duty) is set as follows: The teachers in pre-school facilities –28 hours; teachers at primary schools in the first grade–22 hours; in grades from two to nine–23 hours; teachers at a secondary schools–22 hours; the foremen of vocational education–from 21 to 35 hours according to type of school; tutors at school clubs 27 hours; tutors at youth boarding houses–30 hours; tutors in social care facilities–from 27 to 29 hours.

The rate of educational duty may be decreased to form masters for work in a class by one hour in a week. Similarly, it can be shortened for advisory services at primary and secondary schools by one-three hours. Directors and Deputy Directors may have their rate of teaching duty reduced according to the number of classes in a school directly managed by them. For example the Director of a school with all grades and number of classes up to nine, has a teaching duty eight hours in a week and his deputy for twelve hours in a week.

With regards to the economic situation in the Slovak Republic in 1999 as well as in 2000, and in effort to save some costs the Government has approved regulation on increase of rate of educational duty of pedagogic employees at primary and secondary schools (with an exemption of teachers in gradeone) by one hour in a week. It has resulted in dismissal of approximately 3 000 pedagogic employees. The Departments of Education, Youth and Physical Education of District Offices have solved this situation mainly by dismissal of teachers of retirement age and unqualified pedagogic employees.

5.5 Trade Unions in the Area of Education

As of 1 January 2000, the trade union had 86 710 active members (pedagogic employees, non-pedagogic employees and operational employees) who were full time employees. Out of them:

- 53 522 were employees of primary schools;

- 21 831 were employees of secondary schools;

- 11 357 were employees of universities.

The members of trade union are beside the above mentioned also former employees—pensioners in a number of approximately 9 500.

After 1989, the trade union of employees in the area of education and science in Slovakia underwent complicated development, which was reflected in significant decline of membership. This decline was due to the trade union's passivity in relation to dismissals of pedagogic employees in the period between 1989–1991, and efforts to create a new trade union through so called Teachers' Forum. Nowadays the trade union is very active in pursuing the interest of employees in the area of education. It is a competent and professional partner when negotiating with the Ministry of Education of the SR. Due to this, the number of members has an increasing tendency in spite of rather high membership fees. Nowadays, the teachers' forum practically does not exist. The reasons for its gradual downfall are personal attitudes of its representatives, lower level of professionality, inadequate approach to negotiation and extreme, often non-acceptable views (not supported by pedagogic public) on complex development in the education sphere.

6. PUBLIC FINANCES

Nowadays the system of public finances in the Slovak Republic includes aggregate of national budgetary organizations (state budget), budgets of state funds, budgets of social insurance fund, health insurance fund, National Labor Office, National Property Fund, Slovak Land Fund and budgets of self-government of municipalities.

The final consumption of households (real) amounted to 395.4 billion Sk in 1999 and was raised annually by 0.5%. The final consumption of state administration was 157.1 billion Sk and went up annually by 0.3%. The formation of gross fixed capital to the amount of 257.3 billion Sk registered an annual decline by 12.1%.

The public administration deficit of 29.2 billion Sk was predetermined by deficit economy of all its components. In comparison to 1998 the better results have been achieved (lower deficits) in state budget, state funds and municipalities. The worsening (increase of deficit) occurred in Social Insurance Company, National Labor Office and health insurance companies. There are relations of various intensity among individual public budgets. The state budget as a dominant subsystem of public finances is in intensive relation with all other parts of public budgets.

A decisive part of state budget revenues are tax revenues. In 1999, they represented 74% of total state budget revenues. In comparison to 1998, the volume of tax revenues increased by 7 459.3 million Sk (relatively by 4.9%). All types of taxes brought about this growth apart from corporate income tax. It is important to asses the tax power of a territory with regard to envisaged changes in the organization of public administration, and above all the decentralization of financial flows. Taking into account the complex economic development in the last years, the situation in the territory is varies considerably. The region of Bratislava has a dominant position, for example; it is ten times more powerful (tax power calculated per capita) than the region of Prešov.

An overview of state budget expenditures according to branches which is provided in the following table shows the substantive growth of expenditures in group three—monetary and technical services—157.7% due to the fulfillment of debt service (18 988.4 million Sk) and capital deposits to capital stock of commercial banks to the amount of 20 900 million Sk. On the other hand, expenditures for defense and security fell by 16%.

A substantive part of expenditures on public services is allocated through regional offices (which number eight) which are an independent budgetary category. They are founders of budgetary and contributory organizations in the areas of education, social affairs and culture. A considerable part of these competencies will be the subject of the decentralization process.[37]

The present responsibilities of regional offices for secondary vocational schools, grammar schools, special schools and educational facilities, selected social care facilities of over municipal importance and cultural facilities will be transferred to self-government of higher territorial units. The responsibility of district offices for primary schools and their facilities and some social care facilities will be transferred to self-government of municipalities.

Expenditures of regional and district offices (1999) are mainly directed to education–53.8%; further on social care facilities operation and social benefits–30%; transfers to cultural facilities and their operation–2%; support to capital expenditures in health care–0.7%; transfers to local public transport–2.1%; operation of offices and their facilities (civil defense and fire corps including)–11.3%. The regional and district offices employ approximately 17 000 administrative staff.

A serious problem of financial economy of regional and district offices in last years as well as in 2000 is their indebtedness in a form of uncovered expenditures. As of 31 December 1999, they amounted to 611.78 million Sk, the highest debt was at the Regional Office in Prešov (186.333 million Sk) and Regional Office in Košice (134.902 million Sk). The share of education in total amount of debts is 352.739 million Sk and debt in operation of internal administration is 127.826 million. This financial indebtedness and so called 'hidden' debt in the form of postponed maintenance of buildings and equipment will complicate the process of transfer of these premises to self-government bodies.

The budgets of municipalities and cities are autonomous parts of the public budgets. They are connected to state budget and state funds budgets by revenue from shared taxes (personal and corporate income tax, road tax) which produce 26.9% of total municipal revenues (1999). The earmarked and non-earmarked grants and transfers of current and capital character make up 12.3% of total municipal revenues. Other incomes result from their own activities (including real estate tax–12.3%) and accepted loans–11.6%.

In 1999, the revenues of municipal budgets represented 27.3 billion Sk and expenditures of 26.1 billion Sk. The expenditures were directed mostly to services to inhabitants (39.8% of total expenditures) and to administration (25.6%). The capital expenditures made up 26.9% of total expenditures of municipalities and towns.

7. FINANCING EDUCATION

7.1 Current System of Education Financing

The framework for financial management of schools and educational facilities which are established by state administration body is given by the Law on Budgetary Rules. The secondary schools and part of bigger primary schools are established as budgetary and contributory organizations. It means they are legal subjects in the personnel, financial and property management areas. The smaller primary schools, all kindergartens and facilities are financed through individual district offices, which are responsible for the budgeting, accountancy, personnel and wage agenda, bigger repair works and eventually also investment construction works and machine purchases. They provide schools with advance payments for small current expenditures. The regional and district offices grant also transfers to church and private schools and facilities.

The individual budgetary categories ensure financing of education from state budget in the following structure since 1996:

A)   the budgetary category of the *Ministry of Education* covers the financing of:

- universities and organizations under direct responsibility of Ministry of Education;

B)   *regional offices* (which number eight in total), which are independent budgetary categories of state budget cover the financing of:

- secondary schools and educational facilities, which are established by regional office;

- schools and educational facilities managed by district offices (kindergartens, primary schools and facilities);

C)   the budgetary category of the *Ministry of Health* covers the financing of:

- secondary health schools;

D)   the budgetary category of the *Ministry of Interior* covers the financing of:

- police schools and school of fire protection;

E)   the budgetary category of the *Ministry of Defense* covers the financing of:

- military schools;

F)   and budgetary categories of *the Ministry of Economy, the Ministry of Agriculture, the Ministry of Transport, Posts and Telecommunications, the Ministry of Construction and Regional Development* cover the financing of:

- vocational apprentice centers, which are also established by them.

The state budget, which is approved annually by the National Council of the SR, defines limits of revenues and limits of expenditures for:

- the Ministry of Education for the financing of universities, including science, school canteens, boarding houses as well as other activities at the universities, school inspection, methodological centers and other organizations under its direct responsibility like the State Pedagogic Institute, the Institute of Professional Preparation, the Institute for Information and Prognosis in Education and Iuventa—institution ensuring the free time activities of children and youth;

- regional offices for the financing of pre-school education, primary, secondary and special education (including 'post secondary' education) and activities of educational facilities;

- and other above mentioned ministries, which within their responsibility allocate in their budgetary category financial means for professional schools under their managerial responsibility.

In addition to the purpose bound limits for financing of education (and especially education in apprentice centers) are defined in the budgets allocated to regional offices for overall activity. The binding limits in division between current and capital expenditures are defined within a limit on expenditures, and furthermore out of them limits on wage resources and current expenditures without wages.

The parents also contribute to the financing of education expenditures. In the case of kindergartens, parents contribute to the upbringing, food and educational aid. At the level of primary schools parents pay for meals; the school fees in primary schools specializing in art; the board of children in outdoor pursuit schools; accommodation in boarding houses; they also contribute towards the extra-curricular children's clubs and personal teaching aid. The textbooks for a school year are lent to pupils (with the exception of pupils in the first grade). The parents also pay the school fees in private schools and educational facilities at all levels.

Along with the state budget, non-budgetary sources are also used for the financing of education. They may include sponsor's gifts, national or foreign grants, financing from different foundations, and so on. The part-time students themselves also pay for the study at some schools.

The level of financial means from the state budget necessary for education is partly determined in normative way.

The number of students visiting the individual school or educational facility is the basis for the budgeting of wage costs. The District Office Department of Education decides on the number of employees on the basis of the number of pupils and the amount of financial means allocated for given calendar year by the Regional Office in the budget break-down. The office usually discusses the budget break-down with every school and assists also in filling the planned staffing posts. This basic performance unit is modified by uniform indicators in order to establish equal qualitative level of staffing and its remuneration according to an overall Slovak average. This is achieved by using the statistics of an average class size, number of employees per performance unit index, and indicator of the average salary. The areas with national minorities are treated in a special way, in that the indexes are set to a higher level. A similar approach is used in areas with a higher occurrence of small class schools.

The school also receives within the break-down of wage means a certain volume for bonuses and allowances, the award of which is decided by the school director. The bonuses and allowances to directors are approved by the Department of Education at the District or Regional Office. The small schools which do not posses the legal entity are in the area of remuneration as well as financing of school operation under the responsibility of the Department of Education of District Office.

The finances for operation are supposed to be allocated also on the basis of a normative approach. The real situation in the financing of education at this time does not allow this. The part of financial means determined for fixed expenditures (mainly energy costs and rental) is budgeted according to the needs of the previous year. Often it is not possible to consider an increase in prices of primary energy. The use of calculation according to average temperature in a year in individual regions remains only in theory. A part of further means (current expenditures) is allocated in a form of variable expenditures usually by calculation per pupil. The finances for maintenance are generally provided only in the case of emergency situations.

The sources for investment construction are allocated individually, namely on particular building constructions within a limit set in the state budget for every category. The scope of the new school building construction is limited.

In 1994, the modernization deficit in regional education reached 3.5 billion Sk, of which 2.7 billion Sk was allocated to the primary school.[38] If we take into account the further increase during years 1995–2000, it is clear that in order to remove this defict it will be necessary to increase the expenditures in the next 4–5 years. This deficit undermines the transfer of schools to regional and municipal government.

The financial flows of primary schools will be affected to a great extent by a modification of prices of input energies and services. It is necessary to take into account the gradual increase of prices of electrical energy, gas, telecommunication and other services. For example as of 1 August 1999, within the framework of government recovery, the price of electric energy increased for the big consumers by 5%; telecommunication fees by 21%; and railway fees by 15%.

It is supposed also to gradually increase the prices of heat (as of 1 August 1999, the prices had already increased by 40%) and following removal of heat prices regulation by cap price. The shift to economic price of heat supplied will represent a rather significant increase of expenditures.

311

Above mentioned changes of prices will be reflected in the prices of construction products, materials and services. Therefore, it is necessary to take into account the growth of the modernization deficit, not only because of unsettled investment activities, but also due to the increase of price of construction and repair works. In this connection, the real scope of the modernization deficit in the course of the next few years could be raised considerably, and this may not be only due to increase in volume of reconstruction works.

It has been known for a long time, that the current system of financing of education is outdated. It is not sufficiently fair in the distribution of financial means to individual kinds of schools and facilities, but mainly in distribution of means to territorial units. The school management is not sufficiently motivated to spend public financial resources in the most rational way. This is proved by remarkable differences in average expenditures per pupil or class between individual regions and districts, which is shown in next part of the study.

Therefore, the Ministry of Education has elaborated the Draft of the Act on the financing of primary schools, secondary schools and educational facilities,[39] which solves in a systematic way the principles of expenditures budgeting on individual schools and facilities in present organizational structure of regional education. The Act may serve as a good basis for the creation of a system of financing of regional education after decentralization of responsibilities in education from regional and district offices to self-government of municipalities and higher territorial units.

7.2 Education Expenditures

In the phase of data gathering for the purposes of this study, we have been confronted with the problem of compatibility of different sources of data in an aggregated and partial form.

The development of expenditures on education as a branch of the public sector in the years between 1990 and 1999 is documented with the usage of data from the sources of the Ministry of Education.[40] The data is ascertained from the results of budgetary management of the budgetary category of the Ministry of Education (including the expenditures on administration and other tasks), data on regional education and registered expenditures covered from non-budgetary revenues.

To analyze the structure of school and educational facilities expenditures in financial and territorial division we have used the database from the accounts of regional and district offices between 1997 and 1999 and data from the state closing account statement in years 1998 and 1999. Those data are analyzed in the next sub-section. This situation in the basic structure of financial databases on education shows the need for the innovation and synchronization of current system of accountancy and statistical records and adaptation to new organizational conditions, as well as the need for their compatibility with the EU standards.

It is necessary to say that in the 1980s, the Ministry of Education had a well established and consistent information system. Unfortunately the organizational changes in the last decade were not accompanied by the co-ordinated adaptation of information flows.

The total increase of revenues and expenditures on education in the last decade expressed in absolute numbers in the next table was influenced by the development of the state related to transformation of economic, social and political system.

The amount of expenditures has been partially influenced by organizational and methodical changes in the management of budgetary resources (for example the new budgetary classification was introduced in 1996). Inflation has been strongly influential as well. Table 5.2 shows its impacts on education financing.

Table 5.2

Total Expenditures on Education in the SR in Current and Constant Prices [Bill. SKK]

	1990	1991	1992	1993	1994	1995	1996	1997	1998	1999
Expenditures in current prices	14.2	17.6	19.6	19.2	19.3	26.1	26.2	30.8	32.0	34.2
Expenditures in constant prices	14.2	10.9	11.1	8.8	7.8	9.6	9.1	10.1	9.8	9.5
Expenditures in constant prices*	38.6	29.7	30.1	23.9	21.2	26.1	24.8	27.4	26.7	25.8

SOURCE: 2

* in relation to 1995 to rate of inflation measured by index of consumer prices in average

Table 5.3 presents growth of expenditures on regional education and education in the SR in total in different inter-annual increases as a result of changes in the organization and methodology of financing. There is an increase in expenditures in spite of a decreasing population. The significant growth of current expenditures since 1995 reflects the introduction of mandatory payroll tax as an insurance to health and social insurance company and to employment fund in the amount of 38% of salaries paid in total. This increase of the volume of salary sources has ensured gradual valorization of salaries. The growth of current transfers (from 1.3% of current expenditures in 1995, to 18.6% in 1999)—more remarkable since 1995 reflects gradual shift of some, mostly professional schools and facilities to a subsidized system of management. The small and at the same time stagnant volume of expenditures on capital assets in education (4.6% out of total volume of expenditures) proves that the construction of new capacities and the modernization of equipment in education is continuously insufficient.

There is always a large number of unfinished buildings which are not possible to complete, so they became run down, or were sold, and eventually rented. In connection with the lack of investment resources, the proposals for the isolation of buildings were not accepted in spite of submitted calculations proving profitability and fast return of investment.

Table 5.3

Development of Total Expenditures on Education According to Type of Expenditures [Bill. SKK]

Indicator	1990	1991	1992	1993	1994	1995	1996	1997	1998	1999
REGIONAL EDUCATION										
Current expenditures of which:	10.87	13.16	14.83	14.65	14.77	20.09	19.85	23.09	24.15	25.79
• means for wages and salaries	5.37	6.46	8.04	8.49	8.97	9.34	10.25	11.39	12.22	12.79
• current transfers	0.08	0.55	0.72	0.85	0.94	3.66	2.01	4.47	4.65	4.65
Acquisition of capital assets in education	0.19	0.46	0.55	0.60	0.56	0.76	0.54	1.09	0.75	0.74
Expenditures in total	11.07	13.78	15.55	15.37	15.50	20.95	20.52	24.19	24.97	26.57
EDUCATION IN SR IN TOTAL										
Current expenditures of which:	13.44	16.18	18.06	17.67	17.85	23.63	24.65	28.56	30.20	31.05
• means for wages and salaries	6.38	7.59	9.50	10.70	11.43	11.26	12.39	13.77	14.85	15.56
current transfers	0.18	0.80	0.98	1.12	1.17	4.00	2.59	5.14	5.41	5.78
Acquisition of capital assets in education	0.68	1.02	1.14	1.18	1.09	1.54	1.38	2.23	1.68	1.59
Expenditures in total	14.15	17.61	19.60	19.17	19.25	26.06	26.18	30.82	32.01	34.19

SOURCE: 2

The development of expenditures on education according to kind of schools and facilities according to the timescale is presented in Table 5A.16 in the Annex 3. The next table in Annex 3 (Table 5A.17) describes the development of expenditures on education in comparison with the total expenditures of state budget and % share on GDP according to level of schools. The GDP share of expenditures on education, which dropped from 5.9% in 1992, to 4.19% in 1999 is alarming. The main purpose of this subsection was to present trends in the financing of education in the last decade. The deeper insights into the financing of individual kinds of schools are provided in the next chapters.

7.3 State Budget Expenditures on Education

This section presents an analysis of expenditures on education on the basis of accountancy reports of regional and district offices and results of state closing account statement in period between 1997 and 1999.

In 1999, the expenditures of the state budget on education in the amount of 32 515.2 million Sk represented 14.05% of the total state budget expenditures, 10.07% of aggregate of public budgets expenditures and 4.19% of the gross domestic product in current prices. The annual increases of expenditures on education in 1998/1997 and in 1999/1998 are approximately only in half of inflation increase.

The development of expenditures on education within last three years was as follows:

Table 5.4
State Budget Expenditures on Education [Million SKK]

Indicator	1997	1998	1998/1997	1999	1999/1998
Expenditures in total	29 524.6	30 632.5	103.8	32 515.2	106.1
of which					
• regional and district offices	23 954.5	24 757.1	103.4	26 166.2	105.7
of which					
• current expenditures in total	27 164.8	28 800.4	106.0	30 819.6	107.0
• of which regional and district offices	22 887.5	23 969.9	104.7	25 429.6	106.1
• capital expenditures in total	2 359.8	1 832.1	77.6	1 695.6	92.5
• of which regional and district offices	1 067.0	787.2	73.8	736.6	93.6

SOURCE: 1 and 8

315

The conflict between the resources and expenditures in the state budget has been reflected mainly in a decrease of capital expenditures.

The division of expenditures according to the kind of school and educational facility was in previous two years as follows:

Table 5.5

State Budget Expenditures on Individual Kinds of Schools and Facilities [Bill. SKK]

Code	Schools and Educational Facilities	1998	1999		
		Expenses in Total	Expenses in Total	of which	
				Current Expenses	Capital Expenses
4001	Kindergartens	3 049.7	3 323.9	3 302.3	21.6
4002	Primary schools	9 319.0	10 136.4	9 762.3	374.1
4003	Grammar schools	1 224.2	1 233.4	1 164.4	69.0
4004	Secondary vocational schools	2 314.0	2 439.6	2 286.7	152.9
4005	Secondary vocational apprentice training centers of the education department	867.1	798.5	754.9	43.6
4006– 4007	Sports schools and special schools	1 107.8	1 152.0	1 122.9	29.1
4008	Providing meals at schools	1 352.8	1 412.3	1 397.5	14.8
4009	Establishments of substitutive education	465.5	498.1	486.8	11.3
4010	Youth hostels	351.0	353.1	344.5	8.6
4011	Schools and establishments offering education in areas of interest	612.4	637.5	634.3	3.2
4012	Leisure time centers	243.3	254.6	243.7	10.9
4013	Outdoor schooling	46.9	46.3	46.2	0.1
4014	School servicing centers	212.0	231.0	229.5	1.5
4015	Educational advisory facilities	124.2	130.8	129.5	1.3
4016	Adult education establishments	246.6	505.7	466.9	38.8
4017	Secondary professional art schools	130.8	157.3	134.6	22.7
4018	Institutions of higher education	4 223.0	4 390.2	3 828.6	561.6

Table 5.5 (continued)
State Budget Expenditures on Individual Kinds of Schools and Facilities [Bill. SKK]

Code	Schools and Educational Facilities	1998	1999		
		Expenses in Total	Expenses in Total	of which	
				Current Expenses	Capital Expenses
4019	Theological faculties, seminars and boarding schools	64.6	65.6	65.6	—
4021	Secondary vocational apprentice training centers of other departments	3 184.9	3 209.3	2 890.1	319.2
4025– 4026	Church schools and private schools	704.4	738.0	738.0	—
4039	Other activities in the field of education	788.3	801.6	790.3	11.3
Total			30 632.5	32 515.2	30 819.6	1 695.6

SOURCE: 1 and 8

The biggest volume of expenditures is allocated to primary schools–31.17% out of the total amount; to universities 13.5%; to secondary vocational apprentice centers 12.32%; to kindergartens 10.22%; to secondary vocational schools 7.50%; and to grammar schools 3.79%. The share of schools and educational facilities within the managerial responsibility of regional and district offices (hereinafter 'regional education') on total expenditures is 80.47%.

The presented data are, to certain extent, distorted by the indebtedness of schools and educational facilities due to the fact that the volume of financial means in state budgets in the period between 1997 and 1999 did not cover the basic needs of schools and facilities. A partial decrease in indebtedness in 1999 was reflected by a more expressive inter-annual increase of expenditures (5.67%) between 1998 and 1999; in comparison to the previous period (3.35%).

The more significant increase of salaries in 1998 (by 7.32%) was due to the salary valorization in that year. This was reflected in growth of current transfers to subsidized organizations by 5.2%. At the other end of the scale, the inter-annual expenditures on goods and further services moved down (9.15%) as a result of the lack of resources in the overall budget. This was reflected by the growth of debts and decrease of expenditures on maintenance by 27.93%, which made the physical state of the buildings worse, and further enhanced hidden debt.

Table 5A.18 in the Annex 3 presents the issue of primary schools financing in a view of territorial location. The data from 19 districts (out of 79) mainly from upper and lower size group (according to number of inhabitants) and from all 8 regions were selected. Only current expenditures in

317

total and sub-items: "personal expenditures" (expenditures on salaries—contributions to funds); expenditures on energy and water; and routine and standard maintenance are compared.

The recalculation of data per inhabitant and mainly per class and per pupil shows 50–70% differences between individual district offices. Basically, they result from the former budgetary practice, when the financial means to individual districts were allocated according to the principle: "actual expenditures of last year plus increase/decrease due to considerable changes in performance indicators and changes in salary tariffs determined by law." The differences between districts, which have been from one year to the other maintained or even deepened, are result of subjective planning used during the past years.

The elements of normative budgeting introduced in recent years are used only in the break-down of salary means, and they could not rectify in full scope the deficiencies accumulated many years ago.

The normative budgeting of material expenditures and services will have to be used from 2002. Its introduction is complicated by considerably limited volume of financial means for education, which causes the permanent indebtedness of educational facilities.

The relation between differences in funding and educational performance may be only subsidiary, namely in relation to the modernization of technical equipment and teaching aid (for example didactic technique or IT).

7.4 Municipal Financing of Education

As already mentioned in section 2, municipalities may establish only educational facilities. The municipalities are more or less in the position of sponsors in relation to primary and secondary schools. Municipalities assist them mainly to solve emergency situations in the operation of buildings and the purchase of didactic aid.

The municipalities operate only 11 kindergartens with 28 classes and 605 pupils.

As it is presented in the following table, municipalities have from one year to another less free resources to assist education. Expenditures on education in comparison of years 1991/1996 went down to 40.6% of starting year and represent only 2.05% of the total expenditures of municipalities in a year. This situation will change with the devolution of responsibility for pre-school and primary education during 2002.

Table 5.6

Revenues and Expenditures of Municipalities Budgets on Education [Million SKK]

Section	Paragraph	Title	Year	Revenues in Total	Expenditures in Total	Current Expenditures	Wages, Salaries, etc.	Goods & Other Services	of this Routine & Standard Maintenance	Current Transfers	Capital Expenditures	Credits and Loans, etc.
40	01	Kindergartens	1996	4.8	46.0	38.1	3.8	0.7	20.8	7.3	12.8	7.9
			1997	3.5	46.5	32.8	4.0	0.7	16.9	4.1	11.2	13.7
			1998	3.2	32.7	24.4	4.2	0.7	12.5	4.1	7.0	8.3
			1999	3.8	31.1	24.3	4.9	1.0	11.5	2.5	6.9	6.8
40	02	Basic schools	1996	2.2	66.0	25.4	0.4	0.1	14.3	6.1	10.6	3.0
			1997	6.1	47.8	22.1	0.3	0.0	10.1	3.6	11.7	25.7
			1998	0.3	16.6	10.1	0.2	0.0	3.8	1.5	6.1	6.5
	31	Municipal educational facilities	1999	0.2	13.6	3.1	0.1	0.0	1.1	0.4	1.9	10.5
			1996	0.6	2.9	2.9	0.2	0.0	1.1	0.1	1.5	0.0
40	08	School cafeteria meals	1997	0.4	2,2	2.2	0.1	0.0	1.0	0.1	1.1	0.0
			1998	0.1	0.6	0.6	0.1	—	0.3	0.0	0.2	0.0
			1999	0.1	0.7	0.7	0.0	—	0.4	0.0	0.3	—
			1996	—	6.6	6.6	—	0.0	6.6	0.0	0.0	—

Table 5.6 (continued)

Revenues and Expenditures of Municipalities Budgets on Education [Million SKK]

Section	Paragraph	Title	Year	Revenues in Total	Expenditures in Total	Current Expenditures	Wages, Salaries, etc.	Goods & Other Services	of this — Routine & Standard Maintenance	Current Transfers	Capital Expenditures	Credits and Loans, etc.
40	22	Employee training	1997	0.0	6.7	6.7	—	—	6.7	—	0.0	0.0
			1998	0.0	6.4	6.4	—	—	6.4	—	0.0	—
			1999	—	8.0	8.0	—	—	8.0	—	0.0	—
40		Education	1996	7.7	131.4	80.5	4.5	0.8	45.2	13.8	30.0	50.9
			1997	10.8	118.4	78.3	5.0	0.7	39.8	8.9	32.8	40.1
			1998	5.1	66.7	49.7	4.6	0.7	26.8	6.1	17.6	17.0
			1999	4.1	53.4	36.1	5.0	1.0	21.0	2.9	9.1	17.3

SOURCE: 9

7.5 Decentralization of Education Management and Financing

Taking into account the constitutional right to unpaid upbringing and education at primary and secondary schools, the state has a duty to ensure the balanced financing of the whole network of schools and facilities. In fact it will be delegated implementation of state administration.

This leads to some open issues which have to be solved in the process of creation of new decentralized system. They are as follows:

- the allocation of school network in relation to size structure of settlements with existing schools;

- impacts of changing demographic development on individual types of schools;

- the distribution of modernization deficit on types of schools and their placement within a territory;

- the problem of the different financial power of individual municipalities in regions;

- the assurance of state supervision over the observation of standards of accessibility and quality of education to individual groups of population;

- the extent to which primary schools should reach the status of legal entity;

- the applicability of state guarantees in the area of remuneration of pedagogic employees;

- the creation of acceptable labor legal guarantees concerning the conditions of transfer of schools under the management of self-governments;

- the creation of a financial mechanism, which will increase in a differentiated way (according to requirements resulting from real data on schools) financial revenues of municipalities in order to cover the expenditures on operation, maintenance and development of schools and educational facilities;

- the financing of service facilities in accordance with the commercial principle (with a possibility of privatization) while respecting the social solidarity principle for students from weaker income categories.

The data of breakdown of the state budget in 2000 have been used for the specification of the scope of the financial resources, which will have to be the subject of decentralization process.

The expenditures for primary schools and facilities to the amount of 15.618 billion SKK should be decentralized from the district level.

The resources for grammar schools financing in the amount of 1 237.5 billion SKK may be decentralized to towns or regions. The resources for financing of further secondary schools and facilities in the amount of 8 628.9 billion SKK should be decentralized to self-government of higher territorial units.

68% out of the total volume of finances to decentralized education to the amount of 25 484.4 billion SKK belongs to wages and contributions to funds. This part of expenditures will have to be guaranteed by purpose bound transfers from state budget.

In connection with the aim to decentralize the financial management of kindergartens and primary schools to towns and municipalities, the Ministry of Interior of the Slovakian Republic has conducted a survey in the municipalities with 5 000 or less inhabitants. The municipalities were requested to answer the question as to whether they will be able, in the case of transfer of responsibilities, to ensure the financial management of kindergartens and primary schools (grades 1–4, grades 1–9) by their own administrative apparatus, or if they will need assistance through inter-municipal co-operation. The replies to the questionnaire were received from 370 municipalities and 262 of them have had on its territory at least one of the mentioned schools and educational facilities. The majority of municipalities have expressed the opinion that they will ensure the financial management of those facilities by their own resources and capacities (in the case of kindergartens—84% of municipalities; 77% of municipalities in the case of primary schools with grades 1–4 and 75% of municipalities in the case of primary schools with grades 1–9). Only the municipalities with number of inhabitants up to 199 (61%), and municipalities with a number of inhabitants between 200 and 499 (30%) have proposed to establish a certain form of inter-communal co-operation in order to ensure these new tasks. This situation will have to be solved, but the scope of this problem (it concerns 22 municipalities out of 262 questioned) cannot complicate, in principle, the process of decentralization by a generalized need to establish common administrative offices of municipalities.

8.   CONCLUSION

Taking into account the current knowledge of the state of work on preparation of public administration reform, it is possible to state that there is a certain political agreement on the necessity to decentralize in the near future management of schools and educational facilities from regional and district offices to territorial self-government bodies. The only exception, will probably be the bilingual grammar schools and some secondary vocational schools of national importance.

The whole range of issues connected to the actual decentralization steps in the area of the legal status of schools, labor-legal status of directors and teachers, property transfer and its management as well as financing system still remain open. In spite of the fact that these problems are being solved, the solutions are not documented in one compact study. With regards to the priority area of our interest—financing—we will quote in the next paragraphs the conclusions from one comprehensive expert study, which presents the complexity and openness of the issue.

There is the whole range of conditional factors, which may postpone or undermine the practical implementation of the proposed solution of the financing of regional education in conditions of transfer of competencies of state administration in education to self-government. These relates to the following possible risks and problem areas:

1. *If the transfer of competencies will be realized according to assumed schedule (1 January 2002) and the new legal regulation on financing of primary and secondary schools and educational facilities will be in force at the same time, the financial problems will occur on the side of local and regional budgets (differences between revenues and expenditures in amounts of billions of SKK approximately). This will lead to the necessity to apply restrictive policy also at the level of those budgets and consequently to reduce the sources for financing of education to the competence of local and regional self-governments. This opinion arises from the fact, that municipalities are financially exhausted to certain extent (they have sold their property) and they will not be able to increase the resources allocated up to now by the state. It will result in lower resources for material expenditures, deepening of problems of educational system and increase of its modernization debt.*

2. *The considerable disproportion may occur between the duty to overtake some activities in the area of education by self-governments and real transfer of property rights to self-government bodies. It will result in pressure to transfer the property rights or refusal to take over the competencies.*

3. *It is a matter of fact, that during the next few years it will be necessary to maintain at least in part the subsidies for local and regional bodies. The transfer of competencies will lead to pressure to decrease the budgetary category oriented on education and this will be reflected in the necessity to cut the subsidies for school operators (self-governments and private owners), which will threaten the material conditions of schools. Moreover, it is clear that a lot of disputes will appear in connection with allocation of subsidies to individual activities of schools and educational facilities.*

4. *The solution of problems concerning the implementation of variant of establishing the school associations (the municipalities and cities within a catchment area of a school) and guaranteed payments for study of pupils in other cities or municipalities give rise to certain concerns. This relates also to open issue of territorial restructuring of school system (small class schools, complex schools, schools on nationally mixed territories, etc.) and this also in relation to standard and non-standard equipment of schools. The maintaining of basic standard will be considerably more difficult, especially in problem regions with low tax power, which do not have sufficient resources neither for education nor for their own development in general.[41] The clarification of principle of equalization of economic differences between the territorial units as well as between individual municipalities and cities is missing. The government within the state regional policy should look for the tools to solve the disparities, which are arising after the transformation of economy. The created system of mutual linkages of individual regions should solve the lack of resources.*

5. *The system of compound financing might be a solution of future financing of educational system (it corresponds to transfer of responsibility to citizen, region), however it may be confronted with an overall capital insolvency of individual resources (state, self-governments, enterprises,*

citizens), which may result in too small volume of resources to handle the new tasks altogether and specially in the education area. In this context the development in the bank sphere may be indirectly influential (loan policy).

6. *The legal, but especially financial status of secondary vocational apprentice centers is seen as a serious problem. As a matter of fact, this kind of school should fall under the regional, eventually local bodies (self-government) and state bodies (Ministry of Education and respective line ministries). The preparation of qualified working force should be an important development impulse.*

7. *In a state of overall lack of resources for education the pressures against the private schools may occur (development in the Czech Republic) and against solution of situation in mixed regions (under headline "to ensure at least the one kind of school.")*

8. *One of the key issues is the actual transfer of competencies to local bodies. At the one side the formal delegation of powers is taking place and at the other side the financing of material costs is creating the big financial burden on local budgets. Therefore it is desirable to define precisely the agreements on property management and its transfer. The open question is also debts settlement. The state will not be able with the highest probability to settle the hidden debt on transferred property.*

9. *It is necessary to take into account that in the initial stage, the local and regional self-governments will be overwhelmed by the transfer of competencies as a whole and the problems of education will be solved later on. But in the meantime, the financial situation in education may become worse. Therefore it is necessary to look for internal reserves in education itself, in order to overcome this initial period. In this situation it will be possible to make use of foreign assistance through some development and restructuring funds within pre-accession co-operation with the EU. In this context it is necessary to create an atmosphere of co-operation between the local and regional bodies themselves and also in relation to state.*

10. *The risk lies also in certain reluctance of internal state administration as a whole and specially in the area of education to support and accept the project of public administration reform. It means the whole range of competence disputes in preparatory stage of reform and also during the initial stage of its implementation. However, the proposed changes in system of financing of education may be accomplished after the systemic re-evaluation of decentralization projects. In this context the non-readiness for this new situation on both levels (state administration, self-governments) may be regarded as one of the key barriers. This will require a great amount of work. But the fact is, that the education system without the internal restructuring will not be able to further exist (not only from material point of view but also systemic one).* [42]

The presented quotation documents the current state of knowledge of the issue at the Ministry of Education in the second half of 2000. As the decisive legislative and organizational steps should take place in order to implement at least the first wave of decentralization by 1 January 2002, the scope of documented open issues is exceptionally large and does not allow to be optimistic about timely solution of strategic aims.

SOURCES

1. Data for the State Closing Accounts, Ministry of Finance of the SR, 1997, 1998, 1999.

1a. Special Statistical Ascertaining, Ministry of Finance, DATACENTRUM 1999.

2. The Education in the SR on the Crossroad of Millenniums, Ministry of Education of the SR, Bratislava, 2001.

3. Hospodárske noviny, 2001 (Slovakia's daily newspaper).

4. Data from Special Statistical Ascertaining as of 24.4.1998, Institute of Information and Prognosis in Education, 2000.

5. Statistical Yearbook of the SR, SO SR, 2000.

6. Special Statistical Ascertaining, Institute of Information and Prognosis in Education, 2000

7. Annex No. 6 to the Government Regulation No. 193/2000 Col.

8. Regional offices budgets expenditures, Ministry of Interior, 2001.

9. Input data from the Record Úc10. RO 2-04—Balance of Revenues and Expenditures of Municipalities' budgets in 1996, 1997 and 1998, Ministry of Finance of the SR—Department of local self-government finances, 1997–1999.

11. Herich Ján : Quantitative development of kindergartens and primary schools by 2015, Institution for Information and prognosis in Education, Bratislava, 1999.

12. Herich Ján: Quantitative development prognosis of secondary schools and universities by 2015, Institution for Information and prognosis in Education, Bratislava, 2000.

ANNEX 1

Structure of School Education in the Slovak Republic and Its Classification in ISCED Structure According to UNESCO

Level 0

The pre-school education is voluntary. Pre-school facilities are defined as a basic level of organized upbringing and education. A minimal age of child to attend this facility is set in range from two to three years of age. These facilities are attended by approximately 75% of children in pre-school age. The remaining 25% children do not attend any facility or stay in family care. This category includes also special kindergartens—for handicapped children (with mental, sensual, physical or communication disorders).

Teachers' qualification requirements: pedagogic qualification on the level of secondary professional school for teachers in kindergartens.

Level 1

The age limit for compulsory education is set for 6 years. The grades from 1 to 4 create the first level of elementary school. The educational programs are oriented on provision of basic knowledge in reading, writing, calculating, and basics from other disciplines like geography, natural science, social science, arts, music, physical education, ethics or religion, in some cases also basics of foreign languages.

Teachers' qualification requirements: university degree (4 years "magister study") with specialization on pedagogy at the first level of elementary school, eventually with specialization on music, physical or art education or foreign languages. In case of teachers at the special elementary schools a university degree with specialization on special pedagogy-psychopedy is required.

Level 2

2A

The age limit is set for ten years; upper limit is fourteen years of age. The second level encompasses the grades from 5 to 9. The education on this level is inseparable continuation of education at the first level of elementary school. The aim of education is to lay down the foundations for further education, long life education and personal development of individual. The educational programs are subject oriented, classes are taught by teachers—specialists on individual subjects. The education provides basic knowledge of mother tongue and literature, mathematics, history, geography, ethics or religion, biology, zoology, health education, polytechnics, environmental education, physical education, music and art education and foreign languages.

The law sets the compulsory school attendance for ten years. It means that compulsory school attendance is not finished at the second level of elementary school.

The first four years of education at the grammar schools (those with 8 grades) belong to this level of education (the students are admitted to study at this type of school on the basis of entrance examination and study results at the first level of elementary school).

2C

The group 2C includes programs at the second level of elementary school for the children requiring special care (similar alternative as in Level 0,1). In this case the age limit is not binding. The educational programs for children who due to poor results (grade repetition) finish the second level of elementary school in lower grade are oriented on achievement of simple basic skills necessary for direct involvement in a labor market (2C)—apprentice centers. In this cases the second level of elementary school encompasses also the tenth year of education i. e. education up to 16 years of age (experiment).

Teachers' qualification requirements: university degree (5 years "magister study") with specialization on pedagogy at the second level of elementary school—specialist in one, two or three subjects. For practical training—foremen, employees with vocational certificate, school leaving exam certificate and additional pedagogic qualification.

The educational programs in group 2A are assigned for direct access to the third level of education (a further education) i.e. 3A, 3C.

The educational programs in group 2C are aimed directly for employment (practice); the pupils at this level are not admitted to the programs of the third level.

Level 3

The educational programs at the third level require completion of previous 9-year education at the first and second levels of elementary school (since the beginning of education beside pupils at the 8-year grammar school). To be admitted to this level it is necessary to meet the requirements of individual educational programs (study specialization on different kinds and types of schools). The education at this level prepares students for a study on universities or professional preparation directly for labor market.

The compulsory education is set for ten years and is extended to the third level in a length of one year. The entry age is 14, 15 and upper age limit is 16, 17, 18 or 19 respectively according to type of educational program.

Teachers' qualification requirements: pedagogic qualification, university degree (5 years "magister study") with specialization on pedagogy

3A

Grammar school (gymnasium)—the goal of educational programs is to prepare for study at universities. School leaving exam finishes the study. The school leavers may be employed in administration (state administration, local government), culture and so.

Age: entry—15; finish—up to 19, 20 years old students.

8 years grammar school (8 years of study) the educational goal is the same as in previous case. The educational programs in Grades 5–8 are the same as programs in elementary school and the further grades have the same programs as "classical" grammar school, but the study at 8 years grammar school is finished one year earlier. School leaving exam accomplishes the study.

Age: entry—10, 11; finish—up to 18, 19 years old students.

Secondary vocational school—the aim of educational programs is preparation of employees who will be able to succeed directly on labor market. School leaving exam finishes the study. They have an option to continue in study in groups 5A, 5B or 4A (at university, follow up study etc.). The individual schools are oriented on following professional specialization: engineering, hotel and catering services, food industry, electrical engineering, building industry, economy, education, health service, art, culture and so.

Age: entry—15; finish—up to 19 year old students.

Conservatoire—represents special type of secondary school, which prepares the students in following specialization: singing, music and dance. The education is finished by school leaving exam (at the level 3) with an option to continue in study at the level 5A, 5B.

Age: entry—15 years old; finish—up to 21/22/23 year old students according to study specialization.

3C

*Secondary vocational apprentice centers—study specialization—*study programs last 4–5 years. This education is not oriented particularly on preparation for study at the university but 1–3% of students continues in study at university. The study is oriented on engineering, electrical engineering, building industry, etc. In the first three years the educational programs include 25–40% classes of practical training. The study is finished by school leaving exam, which enables to enter programs 5A and 5B. The students receive in Grade 3 before school leaving exam a "training certificate".

Age: entry—14/15 years old; finish—up to 18/19 year old students.

Secondary vocational apprentice centers—practical training specialization—educational programs last 2–3 years. They are oriented on preparation of employees for direct access to labor market. The students are trained in specialization like mason, car mechanic, carpenter, butcher, shop assistant, turner, etc. The study is finished by theoretical and practical examination in given specialization and student receives "training certificate."

With regard to their theoretical knowledge the school leavers are not able to access study programs 5A and 5B directly. They may continue in follow-up full time study (level 3A) that lasts 2 years and is finished by school leaving exam or at the level 4B respectively.

Age: entry—15 years old; finish—up to 17/18 year old students.

Apprentice centers—educational programs provide vocational preparation in practical training specialization with adjusted curricula. These educational programs are designed for pupils who successfully finished grade 9 of special elementary school. The study lasts from one up to three years and is finished by final exam. The school leavers have no access to educational programs 3A, 5A and 5B.

Age: entry—15; finish—up to 16/17/18 year old students.

Level 4

4A

Follow up education—this type of education includes programs that increase professional qualification in individual specialization like finances, economy, IT, tourism, etc. The study lasts less than two years. The school leavers have direct access to programs 5A, 5B.

Age: entry—18–19 years old; the upper limit is not set.

4B

The educational programs increasing the qualification level within the further education for school leavers who finished programs at level 3C. The study is shorter than one year.

The age limit is not set.

The educational programs do not allow access to programs at level 5.

Level 5

Non-university education (5B)

Higher follow-up education

a) professional education (suitable for direct access to labor market) in the range up to three years in the area of economy, IT, administration, etc. There is possibility to access level 5A. Age: entry 18–19 and above, the upper limit is not set.

b) higher vocational education—the length of study 3 years

c) specialization study in the length 2 up to 4 years, e.g. for health service personnel, higher grades of "Conservatoire"

Possibility to access level 5A. Age: entry 18–19 and above, the upper limit is not set.

University education (5A)

This study is performed at the universities.
Regular education (full time study or part time study)

a) bachelor's study (lasts for 3–4 years)

b) master's study—"magister," "engineer" study (may last in minimum 2 years if it is follow up to bachelor's study)

- "magister" study (4–5 years)

- "engineer" study (in minimum 5 years)

- medicine study (6 years)

The state final exam and elaboration of thesis finish the study. The documents proving graduation are diplomas specifying the field of study, type of education, title, and report on examination.

Level 6

Ph.D. study

Ph.D. study for successful university graduates leads to scientific-academic degree. The length of study is from 3 to 5 years. The age limit is not set.

Figure 5A.1
Structure of School Education in the Slovak Republic

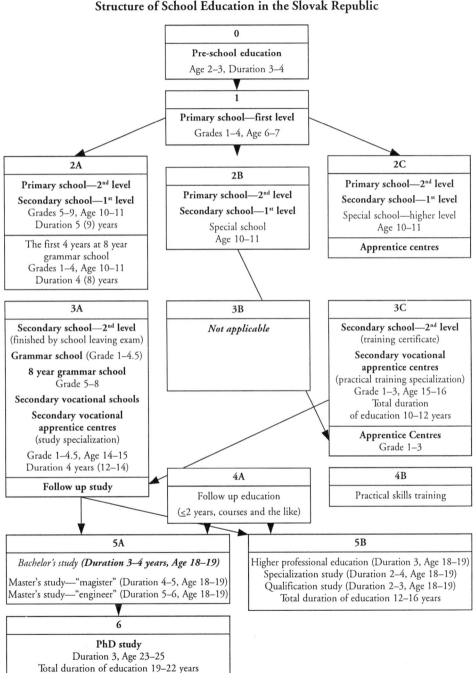

ANNEX 2

Excerpt from Draft of the Act on financing of Primary and Secondary Schools and Educational Facilities
(approved by the Government of the Slovak Republic in February 2001)

The submitted draft of the act regulates the financing of the schools, which constitute a system of primary and secondary schools and educational facilities included in the network of schools and educational facilities.

1.   General Principles of Draft of the Act

The parents or other persons who have obligation to pay child alimentary contribute to partial reimbursement of costs related to material care in state educational facilities which provide also material care of children and youth. The partial reimbursement of the costs is in a form of contribution on accommodation catering as well as part of the costs related to spare time study in educational facilities like free time centers, language schools, school clubs, etc.

The sources of state school and state educational facilities financing are sources of state budget, sources from entrepreneurial activity, parents' contributions, or contributions of other persons who have obligation to pay child alimentary, contributions from entrepreneurs including support programs, contributions and gifts from national and foreign legal persons, natural persons and other sources according to special regulations. Other sources may be, for example, sources from major school and educational facilities' activities, sources from productive works of pupils and students, sources from sale and services, from charges for educational services carried out of regular curriculum, sources gained according to provisions on income tax and other.

The sources of non-state schools and non state educational facilities financing are beside the sources used for financing of state schools and educational facilities also contributions from founders and parents' or other persons' contributions which are to cover costs of study. At the same time, the non state school or educational facility is obliged to publish the amount of required contribution. The non state schools and non state educational facility receive from state budget contribution.

The normative setting of the number of pedagogic employees comes out from the number of pupils, number of classes or groups, number of classes taught per week in a class or group, including number of split up classes and rate of educational duty or duty of tutor's work. This setting in state educational facilities comes out from number of pupils (children, wards, boarders) and tutor's work duty. *The normative setting of the number of other employees* in state schools and state educational facilities comes out mostly from kind, type and technical equipment of state school or state educational facility.

The financial resources for wages, salaries, service incomes and other personal settlements of employees of state schools and educational facilities are determined on the basis of number of employees, which is set in normative way and employees' salary bracket regulated by a special legislation.

The state offers to state schools and state educational facilities *financial means on goods and further services*, which cover expenditures on energy and water (fixed costs), rents and expenditures according special regulations. *The volume of financial means on other expenditures on goods and further services (variable costs) will depend on resources of state budget.*

Within capital expenditures the financial means for acquisition and appreciation of tangible and intangible property are provided to state schools and educational facilities.

Within current transfers the financial means to state schools and state educational facilities, which are subsidized organizations are provided to cover at least wages of employees who ensure upbringing and educational process and other employees who are in charge of services related to operation and development of school and educational facility. These means are provided also to cover insurance and contribution of employer to insurance companies and the National Labor Office.

The basic amount of contribution per pupil in non state school or non state educational facility is 100% of current expenditures per pupil in comparable kind and type of state school or state educational facility, if respective body of state administration don't decide on decrease of the contribution.

The basic amount of contribution is lowered by 30% if non state school or non state educational facility collects the contributions to cover expenditures on education and upbringing or if non state educational facility collects contribution to cover partially the costs related to material care in educational facilities, which is higher than in comparable kind of state educational facility.

The basic amount of contribution is lowered by 10% if non state school or non state educational facility doesn't follow the curricula or programs of upbringing work which are applied in comparable kind and type of state school or state educational facility.

The basic amount of contribution is lowered by 10% if the non state school doesn't provide upbringing and education in study specialization or vocational specialization which are necessary to meet the tasks of regional development or preparation for occupation in public interest or if provides preparation for occupation, which in long-term does not meet labor market needs (expression long-term means at least 3 years).

The municipal educational facilities are financed from the budget of municipality. The contribution from state budget per pupil is in the amount of 100 % of current expenditures per pupil in comparable state educational facility.

The Ministry of Education on the basis of this Act will issue generally binding regulation, which will determine in normative way the number of pedagogic employees and other employees, the way how to allocate financial means for wages, salaries, service incomes and other personal settlements, financial normative on energies and water, other expenditures on goods and further services and on further expenditures within current transfers in schools and educational facilities.

The aim of this directive is to tie the number of pedagogic employees to number of classes, groups and furthermore to number of pupils. In this way it will be possible to effectively regulate number of employees by setting the parameters.

The directive in connection with the number of employees set in this manner will determine also the volume of financial means for their wages according to currently valid salary regulations.

Furthermore, the directive by means of financial normative will enable more equitable allocation of expenditures on energies and water, expenditures on goods and further services free from expenditures on energies and water and rents and other expenditures resulting from special regulations. This will result in more equitable allocation of financial means provided through current transfers.

2. Normative Way of Determining the Number of Employees at the State Schools
(Draft of the Ministry of Education Directive)

2.1 *Normative Way of Determining the Number of Teachers at the State Schools*

The recalculated number of teachers (PPU) in state school is set as sum of need of recalculated number of teachers in individual classes taking into account basic duty of teacher—the rate of educational duty (PPUt) according to the Government Regulation,[43] need of recalculated number of teachers resulting from duties, which are according to Government Regulation lower than basic duty of teacher (PPUu).

$$PPU = \sum PPUt + PPUu$$

The recalculated number of teachers in class (PPUt) is given by recalculated number of pupils in class (PPZt) divided by normative number of pupils in class (NPŽt) and multiplied by number of teachers per class (PUt), both (NPŽt) and (PUt) are specified in this Directive.

$$PPUt = (PP\check{Z}t : NP\check{Z}t) \times PUt.$$

The recalculated number of pupils in class (PPŽt) is given by actual number of pupils in class increased by two pupils per each integrated pupil with health disorder (not applicable for secondary vocational apprentice centers, apprentice centers and special schools). The students, who are at part-time study (along with regular occupation) are included with coefficient 0.2 and students studying in evening classes with coefficient 0.45.

The number of teachers (PUt) per class is determined with accuracy of two decimal numbers and is given by number of lessons in week per class (PVH) divided by basic duty of teacher (ZÚ) according to the Government Regulation No. 229/94. The number of lessons in class is specified by curricula.

$$PUt = PVH : Z\acute{U}$$

The recalculated number of teachers resulting from duties, which are lower than basic duty of teacher (PPUu) in state school is given so that sum of differences between basic duties of teacher (ZÚ) and duties lower than basic duty of teacher (ZNÚ) is divided by basic duty of teacher (ZÚ).

$$PPUu = \sum (Z\acute{U} - ZN\acute{U}) : Z\acute{U}$$

Table 5A.1

Normative Number of Pupils in a Class at Primary Schools

Grade	Fully Organized in Municipality with Over 1000 of Pupils at Primary School	Fully organized in Municipality with Less than 1000 of Pupils at Primary School	Small School with Grades 1–4.	Small Class School
between 1 and 4	24 pupils	21 pupils	16 pupils	16 pupils
between 5 and 9	25 pupils	22 pupils		

Table 5A.2
Requirements of T Primary Schools

Grade	Basic Variant	Extended Variant	Nationality Variant	Sport Variant	Gifted and Talented
1	1.00	1.00	1.15	1.05	1.05
2	1.00	1.00	1.15	1.05	1.09
3	1.12	1.12	1.25	1.21	1.23
4	1.14	1.24	1.27	1.23	1.25
5	1.25	1.28	1.31	1.26	1.29
6	1.31	1.31	1.42	1.32	1.36
7	1.35	1.44	1.51	1.42	1.45
8	1.37	1.46	1.55	1.44	1.49
9	1.39	1.48	1.59	1.46	1.55

3. Financial Normative on Energy and Water and Other Expenditures within Goods and Further Services and on Further Expenditures within Current Transfers in State Schools and State Educational Facilities

3.1 *Financial Normative on Energy and Water*

The financial normative (FN) on individual kind of energy or water set according § 9 par. 4 is given by normative consumption of energy or water in financial expression (NS) multiplied by coefficient of increase in price of energy or water (KN).

$$FN = NS \times KN$$

The normative consumption of energy or water (NS) is an average of expenditures on energy or water during previous three finished calendar years with consideration of price increases

$$NS = \frac{S_1 \times k_1 + S_2 \times k_2 + S_3}{3}$$

whilst: S_1, S_2, S_3 is actual consumption of respective kind of energy or water in financial expression in individual years in previous three finished calendar years,

k_1 coefficient of price increase of respective kind of energy or water reflecting the price increase between the first and the third year within the considered time period

k_2 coefficient of price increase of respective kind of energy or water reflecting the price increase between the second and the third year within the considered time period.

The coefficient of price increase of energy or water (KN) represents energy or water price increase between the last finished calendar year and current year.

Example of financial normative calculation for 2002:

Input data

- *the amount of disbursed invoices for electric energy in 1998 in a school: 2 888 SKK—S_1*
- *the amount of disbursed invoices for electric energy in 1999 in a school: 4 185 SKK—S_2*
- *the amount of disbursed invoices for electric energy in 2000 in a school: 7 560 SKK—S_3*

- k_1 *(price increase index in 2000 in relation to 1998)* = 1.75
- k_2 *(price increase index in 2000 in relation to 1999)* = 1.29

Calculation of normative consumption of electric energy (NS)

$$NS = \frac{S_1 \times k_1 + k_2 + S_3}{3}$$

$$NS = \frac{(2880 \times 1.75) + (4\,185 \times 1.29) + 7\,560}{3}$$

$$NS = \frac{17999}{3} = 6\,000$$

Example of calculation of financial normative FN for 2002

Coefficient of increase in price of energy **KN** for 2001 in relation to 2000 is **1.05**.

$$FN = NS \times KN = 6000 \times 1.05 = 6\,300 \text{ Sk}$$

3. 2   *Financial Normative on Other Expenditures on Goods and Further Services*

The financial normative on other expenditures on goods and further services (FNV) per one pupil in particular kind and type of state school or state educational facility is given by the product of total volume of financial means on other expenditures on goods and further services (COFP), which is set by the Act on state budget in relevant year and coefficient of variable expenditures in particular kind and type of state school (KVV), divided by number of pupils in particular kind and type of state school (PŽ)

$$FNV = (COFP \times KVV) : PŽ$$

The coefficient of variable expenditures in particular kind and type of state school or state educational facility (KVV) is share of given kind and type of school or educational facility on financial means assigned to variable costs of all state schools and state educational facilities. The coefficients of variable expenditures will be set by this Directive in a form of table, which is being prepared.

Furthermore in selected kinds of schools, for example state secondary vocational schools the financial normative per pupil according to studyspecialization is determined.

The financial normative per pupil according to study specialization (FNO) is set so that financial normative per pupil (FNV) determined in above presented way is multiplied by coefficient of economic demandingness of particular study specialization (KEN)

$$FNO = FNV \times KEN$$

3. 3   *Financial Normative on Further Expenditures within Current Transfers*

The financial normative on further expenditures within current transfers per pupil in particular kind and type of state school or state educational facility (FNVT) are set so, that product of total volume of financial means on further expenditures within current transfers set by the Act on state budget in relevant year (COFT) and transfer coefficient of individual kind and type of state school and state educational facility (TK) is divided by number of pupils in particular kind and type of state school or state educational facility (PŽ)

$$FNVT = (COFT \times TK) : PŽ$$

The transfer coefficient of particular kind and type of state school or state educational facility (TK) is share of given kind and type of school or educational facility on financial means assigned to further expenditures within current transfers of all state schools and state educational facilities. The transfer coefficients will be determined by the Directive of the Ministry of Education.

Furthermore in selected kinds of schools e.g. state secondary vocational apprentice centers the financial normative per pupil according to study or professional specialization is determined. The financial normative per pupil according to study or professional specialization (FNOT) is set so that financial normative per pupil (FNVT) determined in above presented way is multiplied by coefficient of economic demandingness of particular study or professional specialization (KENT)

$$FNOT = FNVT \times KENT$$

The economic demand of the study and professional specialization will be determined by the Directive of the Ministry of Education.

ANNEX 3

Tables

Table 5A.3
Kindergartens—Basic Indicators

Indicator	Type of School	1994	1995	1996	1997	1998	1999
Schools	church	—	2	5	5	6	9
	private	—	11	16	15	14	11
	municipal	—	20	17	12	10	11
	state	—	3 224	3 238	3 255	3 261	3 243
	other	—	65	56	43	36	36
	total	3 343	3 322	3 332	3 330	3 327	3 310
Classes	church	—	3	7	7	9	16
	private	16	17	23	23	21	17
	municipal	—	39	34	29	25	28
	state	—	7 210	7 436	7 592	7 717	7 647
	other	—	176	164	130	113	113
	total	7 387	7 445	7 664	7 781	7 885	7 821
Children	church	—	68	166	164	205	354
	private	392	361	523	482	447	336
	municipal	—	816	673	620	558	605
	state	—	156 458	163 111	165 163	163 833	158 296
	other	—	3 994	3 681	2 871	2 461	2 227
	total	174 436	161 697	168 154	169 300	167 504	161 818
Teachers*	total	14 639	14 933	15 382	15 780	15 935	15 807

SOURCE: 5

*   teachers and school directors (full-time occupation)

—   no data

Table 5A.4
Primary Schools—Basic Indicators

Indicator	Type of School	1989	1990	1991	1992	1993	1994	1995	1996	1997	1998	1999	2000
Schools	church	n.a.	2	28	75	81	86	87	87	87	89	92	94
	private		0	0	0	1	1	4	5	4	6	4	3
	state		2 354	2 387	2 397	2 401	2 394	2 394	2 401	2 391	2 389	2 375	2 350
	total	2 302	2 358	2 415	2 472	2 483	2 481	2 485	2 493	2 482	2 484	2 471	2 447
Classes	church	n.a.	26	362	918	1 015	1 045	1 067	1 058	1 087	1 111	1 160	1 152
	private		0	0	0	3	6	29	30	13	17	17	16
	state	27 559	28 313	28 580	28 289	27 500	27 173	27 189	26 971	27 332	27 790	28 596	27 925
	total	29 539	28 339	28 942	29 207	28 518	28 224	28 285	28 059	28 432	28 918	29 773	29 093
Class rooms	total		30 669	31 826	32 943	33 053	33 228	33 327	33 303	33 532	33 781	34 579	34 691
Pupils	church	n.a.	767	9 384	22 749	25 256	25 673	25 420	24 717	24 732	25 015	26 148	25 521
	private		0	0	0	49	96	527	544	144	197	174	180
	state	724 919	719 559	707 032	681 370	664 884	650 044	635 135	619 641	621 065	622 665	645 384	625 265
	total	720 326	716 416	704 119	690 189	675 813	661 082	644 902	645 941	647 877	671 706	650 966	
School-leavers[1]	total	89 387	90 619	86 400	93 128	93 869	91 771	87 905	85 672	73 416	67 596	41 274	81 934
Teachers[2]	total	36 242	37 244	37 812	39 867	38 874	38 813	39 224	39 213	39 535	40 482	40 950	42 174
of which: Women	total	29 715	30 397	31 026	32 643	31 916	31 996	32 561	32 597	32 864	33 660	34 155	34 348

SOURCE: 5

[1] In the last school-year

[2] teachers and school directors (full-time occupation)

n.a.   not applicable

341

Table 5A.5

Grammar Schools—Basic Indicators

FULL-TIME STUDY

Indicator	Type of School	1989	1990	1991	1992	1993	1994	1995	1996	1997	1998	1999	2000
Schools	church	n.a.	2	9	17	19	23	27	31	31	33	36	38
	private		0	3	5	7	10	13	14	15	17	17	17
	state	128	130	135	143	149	150	150	151	152	155	156	157
	total		132	147	165	175	183	190	196	198	205	209	212
Classes	church	n.a.	6	41	90	135	190	235	269	287	313	327	351
	private		0	5	14	26	42	58	70	89	106	111	115
	state	1 638	1 714	1 815	1 910	2 008	2 074	2 152	2 199	2 207	2 227	2 171	2 275
	total		1 720	1 861	2 014	2 169	2 306	2 445	2 538	2 583	2 646	2 609	2 741
Class rooms	total	2 362	2 536	2 647	2 873	3 105	3 385	3 519	3 774	3 772	3 931	4 005	4 071
Students	church	n.a.	162	1 192	2 726	4 232	5 942	7 395	8 371	8 950	9 694	9 822	10 513
	private		0	133	359	656	1 018	1 337	1 599	2 116	2 481	2 616	2 615
	state	51 531	55 174	57 847	60 437	63 116	65 112	67 648	69 406	69 050	68 494	64 224	67 487
	total		55 336	59 172	63 522	68 004	72 072	76 380	79 376	80 116	80 669	76 662	80 615
School-leavers[1]	total	10 463	11 422	12 419	12 996	13 720	15 279	15 051	16 216	16 098	15 775	15 421	15 754
Teachers[2]	total	3 886	3 909	4 199	4 659	4 815	5 073	5 457	5 695	5 849	6 142	6 165	6 259
of which: Women	total	2 503	2 607	2 797	3 111	3 281	3 508	3 812	4 056	4 253	4 457	4 526	4 526

PART-TIME STUDY

Indicator	Type of School	1989	1990	1991	1992	1993	1994	1995	1996	1997	1998	1999	2000
Students	total	427	305	175	160	98	160	320	647	809	1 369	1 698	1 532

SOURCE: 5   [1] In the last school-year   [2] teachers and school directors (full-time occupation)   n.a.   not applicable

Table 5A.6
School-leavers, Unemployed School-leavers (Grammar Schools) and Rate of Unemployment as of 30.9.1999

Region	School-leavers (Grammar Schools)	Unemployed School-leavers (Grammar Schools)	Rate of Unemployment (Grammar Schools)
Bratislava	2 878	372	12,9%
Trnava	1 389	338	24,3%
Trenčín	1 395	361	25,9%
Nitra	1 753	514	29,3%
Žilina	1 845	536	29,1%
Banská Bystrica	1 879	471	25,1%
Prešov	2 122	624	29,4%
Košice	2 375	710	29,9%
Slovak Republic	15 636	3 927	25,1%

SOURCE: 2 and 11

Table 5A.7

Secondary Vocational Schools—Basic Indicators

FULL-TIME STUDY

Indicator	Type of School	1989	1990	1991	1992	1993	1994	1995	1996	1997	1998	1999	2000
Schools	church	n.a.	0	5	10	10	11	11	11	11	11	11	11
	private		0	1	5	9	16	21	22	22	24	27	28
	state		184	268	300	321	334	332	334	332	341	341	335
	total	179	184	274	315	340	361	364	367	365	376	379	374
Classes	church	n.a.	0	27	45	61	83	80	81	79	81	77	82
	private		0	1	14	32	74	109	145	167	182	158	154
	state	2 677	2 820	3 048	3 323	3 549	3 667	3 716	3 753	3 633	3 576	3 397	3 463
	total	2 677	2 820	3 076	3 382	3 642	3 824	3 905	3 979	3 879	3 839	3 632	3 699
Class rooms	total	3 873	4 088	4 338	4 993	5 442	5 866	6 237	6 456	6 468	6 536	6 612	6 682
Students	church	n.a.	0	641	1 295	1 780	2 412	2 394	2 331	2 209	2 207	2 050	2 198
	private		0	20	350	821	1 915	2 753	3 630	4 131	4 351	3 572	3 361
	state	80 545	87 149	94 534	102 148	109 063	112 818	114 706	115 972	110 341	104 633	93 448	93 520
	total	80 545	87 149	95 195	103 793	111 664	117 145	119 853	121 933	116 681	111 191	99 070	99 079
School-leavers[1]	total	18 747	18 250	19 888	20 726	21 662	24 461	27 014	28 928	29 615	30 081	30 242	31 120
Teachers[2]	total	6 322	6 558	6 844	7 812	8 494	8 827	9 558	9 934	10 104	10 416	10 184	10 092
of which: Women	total	3 580	3 690	3 985	4 667	5 226	5 598	6 276	6 554	6 803	7 083	6 982	6 903

SOURCE: 5   [1] In the last school-year   [2] Teachers and school directors (full-time occupation)   n.a.   not applicable

Table 5A.8

Secondary Vocational schools—School-leavers, Unemployed School-leavers and Rate of Unemployment as of 30.9.1999

Region	School-leavers (SOŠ)[1]	Unemployed School-leavers[2]	Rate of Unemployment (SOŠ)
Bratislava	4 785	1 163	24,3%
Trnava	2 856	1 474	51,6%
Trenčín	3 255	1 521	46,7%
Nitra	3 948	2 086	52,8%
Žilina	4 286	2 090	48,8%
Banská Bystrica	4 262	1 955	45,9%
Prešov	4 457	2 556	57,3%
Košice	4 745	2 462	51,9%
Slovak Republic	32 594	15 307	47,0%

SOURCE: 2 and 11

[1]   SOŠ—secondary vocational schools

[2]   Full-time study school-leavers and part-time study school leavers in total

Table 5A.9

Secondary Vocational Apprentice Training Centers—Basic Indicators

FULL-TIME STUDY

Indicator	Type of School	1989	1990	1991	1992	1993	1994	1995	1996	1997	1998	1999	2000
Schools	church	n.a.	0	1	4	4	5	5	5	5	5	5	5
	private		0	6	11	12	12	11	14	13	9	10	10
	state	311	311	310	333	328	342	341	336	328	335	346	353
	total	311	311	317	348	344	359	357	355	346	349	361	368
Classes	church	n.a.	0	2	11	18	26	35	37	37	37	36	39
	private		0	31	61	78	76	93	138	140	84	80	71
	state		5 960	5 818	5 632	5 354	5 236	5 247	5 093	4 821	4 655	4 258	4 381
	total	5 953	5 960	5 851	5 704	5 450	5 338	5 375	5 268	4 998	4 776	4 374	4 491
Class rooms	total	5 010	5 202	5 228	5 236	5 223	5 207	5 242	5 223	5 294	5 304	5 360	5 337
Students	church	n.a.	0	49	269	500	702	888	926	964	923	894	909
	private		0	609	1 486	2 083	1 909	1 709	2 878	2 867	1 637	1 549	1 294
	state		149 981	142 624	137 653	135 882	135 562	137 091	131 892	122 967	114 947	100 079	103 665
	total	155 240	149 981	143 282	139 408	138 465	138 173	139 688	135 696	126 798	117 507	102 522	105 868
School-leavers[1]	total	42 898	45 105	50 338	44 567	57 538	41 729	42 043	44 290	44 173	42 289	40 588	36 073

Table 5A.9 (continued)

Secondary Vocational Apprentice Training Centers—Basic Indicators

Indicator	Type of School	1989	1990	1991	1992	1993	1994	1995	1996	1997	1998	1999	2000
Teachers[2]	total	6 441	6 334	6 076	6 112	5 929	6 019	6 056	6 062	6 097	6 038	5 882	5 805
of which: Women	total	3 891	3 756	3 783	3 703	3 591	3 721	3 754	3 838	3 913	3 880	3 832	3 857
Foremen of skilled training	total	8 030	7 794	7 163	7 207	6 754	6 600	6 502	6 472	6 232	5 965	5 609	5 450

SOURCE: 5

[1]   in the last school year

[2]   teachers and school directors (full-time occupation)

n.a.   not applicable

347

Table 5A.10

Secondary Vocational Apprentice Training Centers—School-leavers, Unemployed School-leavers and Rate of Unemployment as of 30.9.1999

Region	School-leavers (SOU)[1]	Unemployed School-leavers[2]	Rate of Unemployment (SOU)
Bratislava	4 867	1 049	21,6%
Trnava	4 905	2 101	42,8%
Trenčín	5 974	2 183	36,5%
Nitra	6 161	2 683	43,5%
Žilina	6 579	2 985	45,4%
Banská Bystrica	5 148	2 069	40,2%
Prešov	6 901	3 544	51,4%
Košice	5 383	2 688	49,9%
Slovak Republic	45 918	19 302	42,0%

SOURCE: 2 and 11

[1]   (SOU—secondary vocational apprentice training centres)

[2]   full-time study school-leavers and part-time study school leavers in total

Table 5A.11

Special Schools—Basic Indicators

Indicator	1989	1990	1991	1992	1993	1994	1995	1996	1997	1998	1999	2000
Schools	417	417	420	420	419	412	400	406	392	385	381	377
Classes	2 658	2 718	2 890	2 991	2 979	3 093	3 167	3 232	3 229	3 340	3 437	3 412
Children	31 348	30 415	29 612	29 205	29 292	29 947	29 914	29 720	29 222	29 816	30 736	30 867
of which: at special schools for handicapped children	22 893	22 199	21 655	21 035	21 048	20 999	20 976	20 480	22 268	22 469	17 822	17 961
Teachers	3 573	3 630	3 745	4 086	4 048	3 706	3 862	3 925	3 933	4 169	4 371	4 241
of which: Women	2 762	2 785	2 886	3 120	3 157	3 048	3 187	3 266	3 283	3 485	3 650	3 587
Foremen of skilled training	34	34	30	49	34	546	561	557	542	558	552	552
Workshop teachers	399	409	424	476	485	n.a.	n.a.	n.a.	n.a.	n.a.	n.a.	n.a.

SOURCE: 5

n.a.   not applicable

349

Table 5A.12
Primary Schools of Arts—Basic Indicators

Indicator	1994	1995	1996	1997	1998	1999
Schools	177	181	182	173	192	194
Students of which: field	84 860	88 506	88 877	88 654	94 451	95 561
Dancing	11 321	12 057	11 906	11 751	13 152	13 250
Fine arts	23 050	24 845	25 607	26 291	28 343	29 302
Literature and drama	3 595	3 595	3 560	3 556	3 692	3 739
Music	46 894	48 009	47 804	47 056	49 264	49 270

SOURCE: 5

Table 5A.13
Age Structure of Teachers

Type of school	Teachers	Up to 25	26-30	31-35	36-40	41-45	46-50	51-55	56-60	61 & More
Kindergartens	15 480	1 143	1 413	2 346	3 270	2 338	2 823	1 885	207	55
Primary schools 1–4.	16 844	1 747	2 327	2 198	1 632	2 444	2 194	1 979	1 836	487
Primary schools 5–9.	22 135	1 563	1 555	1 967	2 388	4 131	4 072	4 300	1 595	564
Grammar schools	5 976	652	675	650	841	1 056	1 010	526	369	197
Secondary vocational schools and conservatoires	10 791	731	1 010	1 296	1 711	1 860	1 586	1 343	828	426
Secondary vocational apprentice training centers	6 334	316	468	678	1 256	1 216	897	787	489	227
Special schools	3 424	237	324	397	515	604	559	414	268	106
Primary schools of arts	3 499	587	382	485	452	443	423	347	242	138
Total	84 483	6 976	8 154	10 017	12 065	14 092	13 564	11 581	5 834	2 200
[%]	100.0	8.26	9.65	11.86	14.28	16.68	16.06	13.71	6.91	2.60

Source: 4

Table 5A.14

Qualification of Teachers in the SR by Type of School and Level of Education

Type of school	Teachers	Required University Education	[%]	Other University Education	[%]	Required Complete Secondary Education	[%]	Other Education	[%]
Kindergartens	15 480	302	1.95	17	0.11	14 648	94.63	513	3.31
Primary schools 1–4.	16 844	10 949	65.00	431	2.56	n.a.	n.a.	5 464	32,44
Primary schools 5–9.	22 135	19 714	89.06	593	2.68	n.a.	n.a.	1 828	8.26
Grammar schools	5 976	5 635	94.29	140	2.34	n.a.	n.a.	201	3.36
Secondary vocational schools and conservatoires	10 791	8 681	80.45	905	8.39	n.a.	n.a.	1 205	11.17
Secondary vocational apprentice training centers	6 334	5 343	84.35	485	7.66	n.a.	n.a.	506	7.99
Special schools	3 424	1 911	55.81	530	15.48	n.a.	n.a.	983	28.71
Primary schools of arts	3 499	2 561	73.19	112	3.20	282	8.06	544	15.55
Total	84 483	55 096	65.22	3 213	3.80	14 930	17.67	11 244	13.31

SOURCE: 4

n.a.   not applicable

Table 5A.15

Comparison of Salaries of Pedagogical Employees in Budgetary Area and Average Salary in National Economy

Average Salary in	1995	1996	1997	1998	1999
National economy	7 195	8 154	9 226	10 003	10 728
Kindergartens	5 929	6 033	7 292	7 839	8 091
Primary schools	7 711	7 967	7 967	9 340	9 800
Grammar schools	7 983	9 402	10 606	11 141	11 464
Secondary vocational schools	7 959	8 722	10 106	10 696	11 054
Sports schools	8 257	9 042	10 446	12 407	11 203
Special schools	7 925	8 312	9 812	10 490	10 672
Institutions of higher education	10 646	11 768	12 614	13 510	13 920

SOURCE: 3

353

Table 5A.16

Expenditures on Education in the SR According to Kind of School Recalculated per Pupil/Student

Type of School	1995 Expenditures in Total [Thous. SKK]	1995 Per Student [SKK]	1996 Expenditures in Total [Thous. SKK]	1996 Per Student [SKK]	1997 Expenditures in Total [Thous. SKK]	1997 Per Student [SKK]	1998 Expenditures in Total [Thous. SKK]	1998 Per Student [SKK]	1999 Expenditures in Total [Thous. SKK]	1999 Per Student [SKK]	Index % 1999/1995	Index % 1999/1995
Kindergartens	2 370 016	14 689	2 684 127	15 978	2 904 249	17 182	3 049 729	18 293	3 383 227	20 998	142.80	143.00
Primary schools	7 812 875	12 296	8 385 130	13 470	9 054 910	14 516	9 318 741	14 862	10 298 520	15 808	131.80	128.60
Grammar schools	862 859	12 755	992 997	14 689	1 209 131	17 984	1 224 194	18 402	1 235 859	19 543	143.20	153.20
Secondary vocational schools1	597 767	15 146	1 766 103	16 749	2 067 575	20 661	1 995 935	21 244	2 071 880	24 954	129.70	164.80
Secondary vocational apprentice training centers of the education department	3 025 350	21 976	302 283	9 643	816 497	28 635	857 509	34 168	798 203	35 869	26.40	163.20
Sports schools	49 381	28 445	62 816	36 184	63 263	34 836	68 459	34 768	72 187	36 330	146.20	127.70
Special schools	776 094	26 114	837 542	32 038	982 944	37 516	1 039 333	38 362	1 071 501	39 205	138.10	150.10
Secondary professional art schools	106 499	80 559	99 065	47 309	123 867	58 017	130 776	59 255	142 901	64 573	134.20	80.20
Secondary vocational apprentice training centers of other departments	0	0	1 172 445	11 661	2 746 674	29 080	2 865 441	31 891	2 899 042	37 250	n.a.	n.a.
State schools without m.r.z.*	16 600 841	14 558	16 303 508	14 486	19 969 110	17 938	20 550 117	18 674	21 973 320	20 151	132.40	138.40
Church schools	464 060	13 280	413 227	11 702	566 269	15 771	590 855	16 034	594 050	15 236	132.40	114.70

Table 5A.16 (continued)

Expenditures on Education in the SR According to Kind of School Recalculated per Pupil/Student

Type of School	1995		1996		1997		1998		1999		Index % 1999/1995	
	Expenditures in Total [Thous. SKK]	Per Student [SKK]	Expenditures in Total [Thous. SKK]	Per Student [SKK]	Expenditures in Total [Thous. SKK]	Per Student [SKK]	Expenditures in Total [Thous. SKK]	Per Student [SKK]	Expenditures in Total [Thous. SKK]	Per Student [SKK]		
Private schools	57 443	7 249	46 442	5 046	81 121	8 303	85 453	9 351	79 109	8 498	137.70	117.20
Schools in total without m.r.z.*	17 122 344	14 471	16 763 177	14 328	20 616 500	17 789	21 226 425	18 515	22 646 479	19 887	132.30	137.40
Ostatná cin. region. skolstva	3 764 752	3 182	3 674 252	3 140	3 505 561	3 025	3 647 540	3 182	3 878 352	3 406	103.00	107.00
Total without m.r.z.*	20 887 096	17 653	20 437 429	17 468	24 122 061	20 814	24 873 965	21 697	2 654 831	23 293	127.00	131.90
m.r.z.* total (regional education)	58 545	n.a.	86 107	n.a.	66 201	n.a.	97 845	n.a.	49 809	n.a.	85.10	n.a.
Regional education expenditures in total	20 945 641	17 702	2 052 536	17 542	24 188 262	20 871	24 971 810	21 782	26 574 640	23 337	126.90	131.80
Institutions of higher education without m.r.z.*	4 009 760	52 158	4 270 931	46 603	5 045 730	52 347	5 431 570	52 424	5 448 807	50 639	135.90	98.80
Institutions of higher education in total	4 286 540	54 797	4 642 646	50 659	5 422 538	56 256	5 797 351	55 955	5 918 017	55 000	138.10	100.40
Other activities in the field of education	826 275	n.a.	1 065 279	n.a.	1 212 219	n.a.	1 240 663	n.a.	1 702 069	n.a.	206.00	n.a.
Education in total	26 058 456	n.a.	26 231 461	n.a.	30 823 019	n.a.	32 009 824	n.a.	34 194 726	n.a.	131.20	n.a.

SOURCE: 2

* m.r.z. = non-budgetary resources   n.a.   not applicable

355

Table 5A.17

Total Expenditures on Education According to Kind of School —In Comparison to Total Expenditures of State Budget and GDP

Indicator	1990	1991	1992	1993	1994	1995	1996	1997	1998	1999
Total expenditures on education in current prices [Bill.SKK]	14.20	17.60	19.60	19.20	19.30	26.10	26.20	30.80	32.00	34.20
of which: non-budgetary resources [Bill. SKK]	—	—	—	—	0.28	0.35	0.53	0.52	0.57	0.58
State budget expenditures on education [%]	100.00	100.00	100.00	100.00	98.60	98.65	98.00	98.20	98.23	98.30
State budget expenditures in the SR (total)	129.50	133.50	141.10	191.10	180.00	189.10	213.80	244.50	197.00*	231.50
Public expenditures on education in ratio to total expenditures of state budget in %	10.96	13.18	13.89	10.04	10.50	13.60	12.00	12.30	16.25	14.70
Gross domestic product [Bill. SKK] in current prices	278.00	319.70	332.30	390.60	466.20	546.00	606.10	686.10	750.80	815.30
Total expenditures on education per GDP [%]	n.a.	5.51	5.90	n.a.	n.a.	4.77	4.33	4.49	4.26	4.19
ISCED 0—pre-schools per GDP [%]	n.a.	0.54	0.60	n.a.	n.a.	0.43	0.44	0.42	0.41	0.41
ISCED 1—2 primary schools per GDP [%]	n.a.	1.61	1.78	n.a.	n.a.	1.43	1.38	1.32	1.24	1.26
ISCED 3—grammar schools per GDP [%]	n.a.	0.18	0.19	n.a.	n.a.	0.16	0.16	0.18	0.16	0.15
ISCED 3—secondary vocational schools*** per GDP [%]	n.a.	0.73	0.92	n.a.	n.a.	0.87	0.56	0.84	0.79	0.73
ISCED 5—institutions of higher education	n.a.	0.95	0.97	n.a.	n.a.	0.73	0.70	0.83	0.72	0.67
Special schools per GDP [%]	n.a.	0.13	0.15	n.a.	n.a.	0.14	0.14	0.16	0.14	0.13
Other activities in the field of education	n.a.	1.37	1.29	n.a.	n.a.	1.01	0.95	0.74	0.80	0.84

SOURCE: 2

*   Revenues of state budget since 1998 do not include revenues from repayment of foreign credits and accepted credits. Expenditures do not include repayment of principal from accepted credits.
Data concerning calculation of share on GDP are used from table fsk 4.

**   ISCED 3—Secondary vocational schools include (for calculation) secondary vocational schools, secondary vocational apprentice centres (under responsibility of Ministry of Education), secondary vocational schools of art and secondary vocational apprentice centers of other ministries.

n.a.   not applicable

Table 5A.18
Primary Schools—Analysis of Current Expenditures from State Budget in 1999 in Selected Districts

Region	Number of Inhabitants	Number of Municipalities	Classes	Pupils	Pupils/Classes	600 Current Expenditures	of which [Thous. SKK]		
							Personnel Expenditures (610+620)[1]	632-Energy, Water and[2] etc.	635-Routine and Standard[3] etc.
Bratislava I	46 080	1	188	4 482	24	74 059	60 694	8 193	1 919
Bratislava V	128 658	1	490	11 253	23	209 789	171 114	27 704	2 446
Skalica	47 265	21	244	5 763	24	112 963	96 951	11 471	1 099
Trnava	126 500	45	632	14 105	22	231 389	199 935	20 441	2 432
Myjava	29 468	17	137	3 212	23	51 037	44 056	4 240	1 542
Povazská Bystrica	65 862	28	356	9 143	26	116 785	101 072	12 474	1 212
Prievidza	141 242	52	762	17 654	23	260 801	223 921	28 283	3 779
Nitra	163 418	59	908	19 009	21	322 949	271 831	40 808	2 683
Sala	54 475	13	298	6 598	22	98 603	83 493	11 771	658
Bytca	30 489	12	169	4 085	24	49 421	42 546	4 282	513
Námestovo	55 366	24	406	9 549	24	112 321	92 958	14 192	1 202
Zilina	156 921	53	804	19 206	24	255 711	211 485	29 305	5 635
Banská Bystrica	112 736	42	545	13 038	24	195 391	166 896	23 070	1 436
Zarnovica	27 633	18	150	3 140	21	47 113	40 521	5 380	204

Table 5A.18 (continued)

Primary Schools—Analysis of Current Expenditures from State Budget in 1999 in Selected Districts

Region	Number of Inhabitants	Number of Municipalities	Classes	Pupils	Pupils/Classes	600 Current Expenditures	of which [Thous. SKK]		
							Personnel Expenditures (610+620)[1]	632-Energy, Water and[2] etc.	635-Routine and Standard[3] etc.
Levoca	31 331	33	191	4 361	23	61 310	46 779	1 980	777
Poprad	103 074	29	611	13 470	22	194 048	165 144	23 958	1 820
Kosice II	82 480	1	427	10 683	25	129 623	120 077	6 802	530
Roznava	61 764	62	334	7 232	22	124 299	101 706	19 723	1 000
Sobrance	23 263	47	144	3 013	21	48 266	40 233	6 241	294
SR	5 398 657	2 883	28 596	645 384	23	9 762 339	8 161 512	1 233 189	111 218

Table 5A.18 (continued)
Primary Schools—Analysis of Current Expenditures from State Budget in 1999 in Selected Districts [SKK]

Region	600/ Inhabitant	600/Class	600/Pupil⁴	Personnel Expenditures per Inhabitant	Personnel Expenditures per Class	Personnel Expenditures per Pupil	632/Class	632/Pupil	635/Class	635/Pupil
Bratislava I	1 607	393 931	16 524	1 317	322 840	13 542	43 580	1 828	10 207	428
Bratislava V	1 631	428 141	18 643	1 330	349 212	15 206	56 539	2 462	4 992	217
Skalica	2 390	462 963	19 601	2 051	397 340	16 823	47 012	1 990	4 504	191
Trnava	1 829	366 122	16 405	1 581	316 353	14 175	32 343	1 449	3 848	172
Myjava	1 732	372 533	15 889	1 495	321 577	13 716	30 949	1 320	11 255	480
Povazská Bystrica	1 773	328 048	12 773	1 535	283 910	11 055	35 039	1 364	3 404	133
Prievidza	1 846	342 259	14 773	1 585	293 860	12 684	37 117	1 602	4 959	214
Nitra	1 976	355 671	16 989	1 663	299 373	14 300	44 943	2 147	2 955	141
Sala	1 810	330 883	14 944	1 533	280 178	12 654	39 500	1 784	2 208	100
Bytca	1 621	292 432	12 098	1 395	251 751	10 415	25 337	1 048	3 036	126
Námestovo	2 029	276 653	11 763	1 679	228 961	9 735	34 956	1 486	2 961	126
Zilina	1 630	318 049	13 314	1 348	263 041	11 011	36 449	1 526	7 009	293
Banská Bystrica	1 733	358 516	14 986	1 480	306 231	12 801	42 330	1 769	2 635	110
Zarnovica	1 705	314 087	15 004	1 466	270 140	12 905	35 867	1 713	1 360	65
Levoca	1 957	320 995	14 059	1 493	244 916	10 727	62 723	2 747	4 068	178

Table 5A.18 (continued)

**Primary Schools—Analysis of Current Expenditures from State Budget
in 1999 in Selected Districts [SKK]**

Region	600/Inhabitant	600/Class	600/Pupil[4]	Personnel Expenditures per Inhabitant	Personnel Expenditures per Class	Personnel Expenditures per Pupil	632/Class	632/Pupil	635/Class	635/Pupil
Poprad	1 883	317 591	14 406	1 602	270 285	12 260	39 211	1 779	2 979	135
Kosice II	1 572	303 567	12 134	1 456	281 211	11 240	15 930	637	1 241	50
Roznava	2 012	372 153	17 187	1 647	304 509	14 063	59 051	2 727	2 994	138
Sobrance	2 075	335 181	16 019	1 729	279 396	13 353	43 340	2 071	2 042	98
SR	1 808	341 388	15 126	1 512	285 407	12 646	43 125	1 911	3 889	172

SOURCE: 1 and 8

1   610—Wages, salaries and other personnel defrayments

    620—Insurance premiums and contributions payable by employers to insurance agencies and to the National Labour Office

    600—Personnel expenditures = 610+620

2   632—Energy, water and telecommunications

3   635—Routine and standard maintenance

4   Pupil as of 15.9.1999

NOTES

[1] "Regional education" includes all schools and educational facilities with the exception of universities.

[2] The Education in the SR on the Crossroad of Millenniums, Ministry of Education of the SR, Bratislava 2001.

[3] Elaborated according "National strategy of sustainable development in the Slovak Republic," The Ministry of Environment of the SR, 2000.

[4] Text source: Constitutional articles No. 34, para 2, No. 35, para 1, No. 42, paras 1, 2, 3, 4. and NC SR Acts: No. 29/1984 Col. on system of primary and secondary schools (Education Act) in wording of later regulations. No. 542/1990 Col. on state administration in education and on school self-government in wording of later regulations. No. 279/1993 Col. on educational facilities in wording of later regulations. No. 172/1990 Col. on universities in wording of later regulations.

[5] Detailed description of the school system in the SR is attached in Annex 1.

[6] Detailed description of specialisation of particular educational facilities may be found in Annex 2.

[7] According to wording of the Act No. 29/1984 on system of primary and secondary schools (Education Act) in compliance with later regulations.

[8] Inclusion into the network of schools and educational facilities is precondition for establishment of the school or educational facility.

[9] According to wording of the NC SR Act No. 542/1990 on state administration in education and school self-government in compliance with later regulations.

[10] These facts are mentioned in document "Millennium," elaborated by the Ministry of Education as an conceptual material, which sets the priority objectives in upbringing and education in Slovakia for the next 15 years. This statement appears also in presentations of university representatives (e.g. statement of professor Devinsky, rector of the Commenius University in Bratislava). They have observed decrease in knowledge levels of students who have been applying for study at the university.

[11] Data: Statistical Yearbook. Paris: UNESCO,1997, Academia, Vol. 9, 1998, No. 2.

[12] Rosa Vladislav, Education and Science, pp. 588, 589 In: Bútora, Ivantyšin: Slovakia 1997, Bratislava 1998, Institute for Public Issues. Unofficial translation used.

[13] Herich Ján: Qualitative development of kindergartens and primary schools until 2015 Institution for Information and prognosis in Education, Bratislava 1999, pp. 6–11.

[14] Details are presented in Table 5A.4 in Annex 3.

[15] The Education in the SR on the Crossroad of Millenniums, Ministry of Education of the SR, Bratislava 2001.

[16]   Herich Ján: Quantitative development prognosis of secondary schools and universities until 2015, Institution for Information and prognosis in Education, Bratislava 2000, pp. 3–14.

[17]   Details are presented in Tables 5A.4 and 5A.5 in the Annex 3.

[18]   The Education in the SR on the Crossroad of Millenniums, Ministry of Education of the SR, Bratislava 2001.

[19]   The updating coefficient is ratio of indicator to relevant population. It expresses the rate according to which a given potential (population) is updated in relevant indicator (newly admitted).

[20]   Herich Ján: Quantitative development prognosis of secondary schools and universities until 2015, Institution for Information and prognosis in Education, Bratislava 2000, pp. 15–25.

[21]   Details on secondary vocational schools are presented in Tables 5A.5 and 5A.6 in Annex 3.

[22]   The Education in the SR on the Crossroad of Millenniums, Ministry of Education of the SR, Bratislava 2001.

[23]   Herich Ján: Quantitative development prognosis of secondary schools and universities until 2015, Institution for Information and prognosis in Education, Bratislava 2000, pp. 26–35.

[24]   More detailed statistical information on secondary vocational apprentice centres are presented in Tables 5A.9 and 5A.10 in Annex 3.

[25]   The Education in the SR on the Crossroad of Millenniums, Ministry of Education of the SR, Bratislava 2001.

[26]   Details are presented in Table 5A.11 in Annex 3.

[27]   Details are presented in Table 5A.12 in Annex 3.

[28]   The Education in the SR on the Crossroad of Millenniums, Ministry of Education of the SR, Bratislava 2001.

[29]   Dropa Martin: The economic nightfall of school canteens, in Hospodárske noviny, March 9, 2001, page 4, quotation of the opinion of school methodologist for school boarding in District Office Liptovský Mikuláš, unofficial translation used.

[30]   The Education in the Slovakian Republic on the Crossroad of Millenniums,' Ministry of Education of the Slovakian Republic, Bratislava: 2001.

[31]   According to article No. 50 of the Act No. 29/1984 on system of primary and secondary schools (the Education Act), the pedagogic employees are all teachers, including deputy directors and directors of pre-school facilities, primary, secondary and special schools, educational facilities, secondary vocational apprentice centres, apprentice centres (including vocational practice centres), foremen of vocational training, head foremen, tutors and other pedagogic employees (instructors and trainers) of educational facilities.

[32] The analysis of these facts comes out of special statistical ascertaining carried out in April 1998. Some absolute data are not corresponding to standard statistical data acquired every year as of 15 September.

[33] Data provided in this chapter and in Annex 3. in Tables 5A.13 and 5A.14 are result of special statistical ascertaining carried out in April 1998.

[34] Within an overall reduction of number of employees in education this number decreased significantly as of 1 September 2000.

[35] Details are provided in Table 5A.14 in Annex 3.

[36] Further education of pedagogic employees is regulated by:

— MoE SR Regulation No. 41/1996 on professional and pedagogic qualification of pedagogic employees in compliance with later regulations,

— MoE SR Regulation No. 42/1996 on further education of pedagogic employees.

[37] The Government of the Slovak Republic approved by its Resolution No. 230/2000 of April 11, 2000 on Concept of Decentralization and Modernization of Public Administration in point A.2 decentralization of responsibility of regional and district offices mentioned in Concept concerning founding, economy and management of organisations in the area of education, culture, social affairs and health care to local self-government of higher territorial units.

[38] 'Small passportisation in the Slovak Republic—an overview of necessary repairs and financial requirements according to school administrations,' Bratislava: Institute of Information and Prognosis in Education. 1995.

[39] Draft of the Act was submitted to legislative process. More details are presented in Annex 2.

[40] The Education in the SR on the Crossroad of Millennium, Ministry of Education of the SR, Bratislava 2001.

[41] Buchta, S.: The economic power of regions in Slovakia is declining with the exception of Bratislava. In the last year the regional polarity increased and the volume of financial means for redistribution from economically stronger regions to weaker ones, which depend on territorially social solidarity is continuously falling. In: Hospodarsky dennik,, 30/8/2000.

[42] Straka Pavel: Financing of regional education in conditions of transfer of competencies of state administration in education to self-government. Institute of Information and Prognosis in Education, Bratislava 2000, pp. 61–63.

[43] Government Regulation No. 299/1994 Col. on Rate of educational duty of teachers and duty of tutors' work of other pedagogic employees.